THE SOVIET UNION TODAY

THE SOVIET UNION TODAY

An Interpretive Guide

SECOND EDITION

Edited by James Cracraft

THE UNIVERSITY OF CHICAGO PRESS

Chicago and London

The University of Chicago Press, Chicago 60637
The University of Chicago Press, Ltd., London
First edition © 1983 by the *Bulletin of Atomic Scientists*
Second edition © 1988 by The University of Chicago
Printed in the United States of America
97 96 95 94 93 92 91 90 89 88   54321

LIBRARY OF CONGRESS CATALOGING-IN-PUBLICATION DATA

The Soviet Union today.

Bibliography: p.
Includes index.
1. Soviet Union.   I. Cracraft, James.
DK4.S56   1988   947.085   87–10904
ISBN 0–226–11661–1
ISBN 0–226–11663–8 (pbk.)

JAMES CRACRAFT is a research fellow at the Russian
Research Center, Harvard University, and professor
of history at the University of Illinois at Chicago.

Contents

Preface to the Second Edition   ix

Preface to the First Edition   xi

H I S T O R Y

1. From the Russian Past to the Soviet Present   3
   James Cracraft

2. Lenin and His Cult   13
   Nina Tumarkin

3. The Stalin Question   21
   Stephen F. Cohen

P O L I T I C S

4. The Leadership and the Political Elite   37
   Mark R. Beissinger

5. Policy-making in Foreign Affairs   53
   Alexander Dallin

6. Dissent   64
   Joshua Rubenstein

7. The KGB   77
   John E. Carlson

T H E   A R M E D   F O R C E S

8. Organization and Deployment   89
   David R. Jones

9. The Conscripts   105
    Mikhail Tsypkin

10. Military Strategy in the Nuclear Age   114
    Eugenia V. Osgood

11. Arms Control   126
    David Holloway

THE PHYSICAL CONTEXT

12. Basic Geography   137
    Chauncy D. Harris

13. Environmental Problems   154
    John M. Kramer

14. Architecture and Urban Planning   164
    William C. Brumfield

THE ECONOMY

15. An Overview   177
    James R. Millar

16. The Consumer   191
    Marshall I. Goldman

17. Agriculture   198
    D. Gale Johnson

18. Foreign Trade   210
    Perry L. Patterson

SCIENCE AND TECHNOLOGY

19. Science Policy and Organization   223
    Loren R. Graham

20. Soviet Science in Practice: An Inside View   234
    Vladimir Z. Kresin

21. Education, Science, and Technology   245
    Harley D. Balzer

CULTURE

22. A Survey of the Cultural Scene   261
    Irwin Weil

23. The Politics of Literature   272
        Geoffrey Hosking

24. The Cinema   284
        Ian Christie

25. The Mass Media   293
        Ellen Mickiewicz

SOCIETY

26. Ethnicity   303
        Ralph S. Clem

27. Religion   315
        Paul A. Lucey

28. Women   327
        Mary Ellen Fischer

29. Law   339
        Peter B. Maggs

30. A Troubled Society   349
        David E. Powell

Further Reading Suggestions   365

A Note for Travelers   373

Authors   375

Index   379

Preface to the Second Edition

The very positive reception accorded the first edition of this book encouraged us to undertake a second. The original chapters have been updated and in part revised, and several new chapters have been added, keeping in mind the book's overall purpose of providing expert answers to the questions most frequently asked about the Soviet Union. Our thanks to the many students, teachers, reviewers, colleagues, and friends whose comments have guided us in this endeavor. I must also thank personally each of the contributing authors, old and new, for his or her courteous collaboration in seeing this new edition into print.

J.C.
Chicago
June 1987

Preface to the First Edition

Workers in the field of Russian and Soviet studies have long seen the need for a book on the Soviet Union written by experts but addressed to the general reader. This book aims to fill that need. Twenty-five experts in their respective branches of the field have contributed chapters on major aspects of Soviet life combining fact and interpretation in ways designed to attract both students and the wider lay public. This is a book for anyone wanting to understand the Soviet Union today.

Perhaps I should stress what the book is not. It is not a textbook— not in the comprehensive and mainly factual sense of the term. It is more personal than that—more interpretive, more varied in approach, concerned less with "covering" the subject than with responding to the questions most commonly asked of experts. Nor is this book a scholarly monograph, written by specialists for other specialists. The notes appended to the chapters are there only to identify certain sources of information, to indicate where dedicated investigators might look further in the matter at hand, or to provide supplementary details. Most readers, therefore, will quickly pass over the notes.

Although the chapters were written by different authors and can be read as self-contained essays, they are arranged in chronological and then thematic order, and so are better read in succession, as presented. A selection of both textbooks and more specialized works in the field of Soviet studies will be found at the book's end. These "Further Reading Suggestions," carefully prepared with the advice of the authors, are meant to assist students and others determined to know more. We hope that this may be everybody. Understanding the Union of Soviet Socialist Republics, the biggest country in the world and one of its two most powerful, is no easy task.

A note on one or two technical matters. Readers of Russian will notice inconsistencies in transliteration, and wonder what is going on. With regard to the notes to the chapters, Russian words have been transliterated in accordance with the modified Library of Congress system used by the *Slavic Review,* the journal of the American Association for the Advancement of Slavic Studies. With regard to the text of the chapters, the same system has been followed, except that soft signs have been omitted and double-"i" endings of proper names have been rendered by the letter "y." Similarly, the maps in chapter 12 follow established geographical usage except that soft signs have been dropped and Lake Baikal is spelled thus and not "Baykal." But the case of Baykal/Baikal reminds us that many Russian names are known in the West, in the United States particularly, in some other spelling; and when that is so, the more familiar spelling has been retained. But then "Yuri" Andropov, favored by such publications as the New York Times, is, like "Gorki," an intolerable solecism; and "Yury" is employed here.

In money matters, unless otherwise noted sums given in rubles can be converted at the rate of $1.50 per ruble, which is roughly the current official rate of exchange. But this is a poor guide to the ruble's real worth, for two reasons: the official rate is far too high (on the free market one dollar will fetch three, four, even five rubles); and the operation of money within the Soviet and Western economies is quite different, with barter in goods or services and payment in kind or with coupons redeemable at special stores playing a much greater role on the Soviet side. In the Soviet Union, indeed, many if not most of the good things in life cannot be bought for cash.

The authors of this book have lived and worked in the Soviet Union for varying periods of time. Moreover, as both the chapter notes and "Further Reading Suggestions" will indicate, they have published numerous works on Russian and Soviet subjects while holding responsible positions in teaching and research. I must record my gratitude to each of them for the efficient and amicable way in which our business here was conducted despite the pressing demands on their time. Many of the authors have also been associated at one time or another with the Russian Research Center at Harvard, where much of this book was planned—indeed, written. And I must acknowledge my manifold debt to that distinguished house of higher Russian and Soviet studies, in particular to Professors Abram Bergson, Marshall I. Goldman, Edward L. Keenan and Adam B. Ulam.

This book originated in a series of articles on the Soviet Union published in the *Bulletin of the Atomic Scientists* between January 1982 and the fall of 1983. Reaction to the series was such that the *Bulletin*'s editor, Ruth Adams, and her colleagues decided to expand it into a book. As the editor of the series I was asked to assume editorial responsibility for the book, which I did gladly, thinking that apart from the project's importance working with the *Bulletin*'s staff had been a most satisfying experience. I want to thank especially, for their support in seeing the book into print, Lisa Grayson, Ruth M. Grodzins, Thomas Hazinski, Steven McGuire, and, above all, Ruth Young.

J.C.
Chicago
July 1983

HISTORY

This first section of the book does not provide a systematic history of the Soviet Union, much less of the Russian Empire that preceded it. For that, readers are encouraged to consult one or more of the textbooks listed in the corresponding section of the "Further Reading Suggestions." Rather, the following three chapters deal with major historical questions that frequently arise when discussing the Soviet Union today.

The first of these concerns the links between the Russian past and the Soviet present, a question given renewed urgency by Aleksandr Solzhenitsyn and his critics. Nina Tumarkin then takes up the cult of Lenin, the founder of both the Communist (originally Bolshevik) Party and the Soviet state. And Stephen F. Cohen raises the "accursed question" of Stalin, whose shadow, even more than Lenin's, looms over so much of contemporary Soviet life.

All three essays make the basic point that free historical inquiry has been suppressed in the Soviet Union with varying, largely negative results, especially for the country's political development. At the same time, polemical or ill-informed treatments of Russian and Soviet history published in the West have contributed their share to a distorted picture of that history, a point brought out in chapter 1. It is also suggested there, and in chapter 3, that free, disinterested historical study could do much both to liberate the Soviet people from the burdens of their past and to ease East-West tensions.

1

From the Russian Past to the Soviet Present

JAMES CRACRAFT

What links the Soviet present with the Russian past? In one form or another this question is frequently put to historians—by their students in class, by colleagues and friends, by representatives of the media, and even by government officials.

One can point, in reply, to obvious linguistic and closely related cultural continuities: the Russian language, its roots reaching deep into the Middle Ages, is overwhelmingly the language of the Soviet Union, just as it was of the empire that preceded it; and language is never—cannot be—entirely value free.

There are fundamental geopolitical constants as well: the Russian state has been the largest territorial entity in the world since the seventeenth century, its borders have been the longest and most difficult to defend, and its principal neighbors—China and Europe—have been generally hostile to its pretensions, if not to its very existence. Plainly, these factors have always influenced the policies of Russia's rulers; and with the arrival of such powerful rivals as Japan and the United States, they will continue to do so indefinitely.

The natural environment in which the history of the Russian people has unfolded since the beginning of the present millennium—its northerly location and frequently poor soils, its erratic rainfall and extreme continental climate, its short growing season—has of course also helped to determine the course of that history. It will continue to do so, we can be sure, technological advances notwithstanding.

Moreover, these and other environmental, geopolitical, and cultural factors continuously at work in Russian historical development have helped to produce a tradition of centralized, authoritarian gov-

3

ernment supported by extensive armed forces. It is a tradition that is rooted in history—as was discovered by the revolutionary elite in Russia after 1917.

Or one could point to a persistent element of Russian national chauvinism—obviously pre-Soviet in origin (Lenin vigorously condemned it)—in Soviet domestic and foreign policies.

But the apprehensive and often strongly negative views of the Soviet Union generally held in the West ensure that the basic question before us readily assumes an urgent political and even moral aspect, an aspect that these professionally chaste replies fail to address. So historians are asked, in addition, to explain and even to judge contemporary Soviet political behavior in light of the Russian past, to predict its future course, to recommend—or justify—policy. It is a trap into which many of us, amateur and professional alike, have fallen.

Aleksandr Solzhenitsyn, for one, insists that "there is no continuity in the transition from pre-revolutionary Russia to the USSR. There is instead a *fatal fracture of the spine* [italics his], a break which nearly ended in complete national destruction." He could not be more emphatic: "Soviet development is not an extension of Russia's but rather its diversion in a completely new and unnatural direction." The terms "Russian and "Soviet," "Russia" and "USSR," not only are "not interchangeable, not equivalent, and not unilinear—they are irreconcilable polar opposites and completely exclude each other."[1]

Solzhenitsyn's motive here is to explode the "distorted and biased picture of several centuries of Russian history" that he finds to be prevalent in the West and to be manifest, for example, in that "persistent and tendentious generalization about the 'perennial Russian slave mentality,' seen almost as a inherited characteristic, and about the 'Asiatic tradition.'" For Solzhenitsyn, understandably, national honor as well as the cause of historical truth is at stake. But for our purposes now, it is worthwhile to emphasize his more general point—namely, that the evil, Marxist-inspired Soviet system is an utterly alien imposition on a far older and different Russia, a Russia that still yearns to reassert itself.

Solzhenitsyn's pronouncements, with their sweeping denunciations of Western scholarship on Russia and the Soviet Union, naturally have provoked rebuttal.[2] Specialists have condemned various factual errors, methodological shortcomings, and his alleged biases. Contrary to his assertions, many profound and often determinative continuities have been discovered, or rediscovered, by historians. Indeed, an aggressive, hard-line historiography, one seeking to explain the allegedly ugly Soviet present by reference to a more or less distant Russian past, has reemerged—part of the more general "neoconservative" revival in the United States that was abetted by the sharp downward turn in U.S.-Soviet relations that began in the late 1970s.

Reflections of this largely deterministic and negative view of Russian and Soviet history are to be found everywhere—and sometimes take an extravagant turn.

Edward L. Rowny, for instance, has declared that his experience of negotiating arms-control agreements with the Soviet Union "convinced me that the Soviets have not changed their inherited traits— they are still Russians." What are these "inherited traits"? An obsession with "seemingly picayune details" and with "their security," an "extreme penchant for secrecy" and an unwillingness to compromise, both a "serious inferiority complex" and a habit of bullying, duplicitous behavior in the ruthless pursuit of objectives laid down by their Kremlin masters. And General Rowny's authority for describing such traits as "inherited"? An old textbook on Russian history is mentioned, as are two similarly outdated as well as highly idiosyncratic treatises on Russian culture and the dubious memoirs of a French aristocratic visitor to the Russia of about 150 years ago.[3] Rowny refers here to his experience of the uncertain Soviet diplomacy of the later 1970s; presumably, in any future account of his continuing work in this field, he will have to find other sources of other "inherited traits" to explain the much more sophisticated Soviet diplomacy of the later 1980s.

A popular biography of Peter the Great, the famous "tsar-reformer" of eighteenth-century Russia, offers another fine example of what is at issue. "In *The Gulag Archipelago*," its author states, "Solzhenitsyn is bewildered by the 'rabbits,' the millions who submitted to Stalin's terror and went to the camps quietly. Blind submission to arbitrary authority is part of the Russian tradition—there were rabbits enough in Peter's time, too." These lines could only have been written in willful disregard of the widespread and violent opposition in Russia to Peter's program of forced Westernization— and only after a careless reading of *The Gulag Archipelago* itself, whose "rabbits" have much in common with the millionfold victims of the Nazi camps. Yet in the United States this book was selected for sale to its members by the editors of the History Book Club, guaranteeing it additional thousands of readers.[4]

The foremost exponent of the hard-line historiography is Professor Richard Pipes of Harvard University. Owing to his prominence as a contributor to journals of opinion and as an advisor to statesmen, it is perhaps not generally appreciated that Pipes is also one of our leading historians of Russia and the Soviet Union. Nor is it generally known that his *Russia under the Old Regime* offers one of the most original (and best-written) interpretations of virtually the whole of Russian history currently available in English.[5]

Pipe's grand theme is the rise in the later Middle Ages of a "patrimonial state" in Russia, its "partial dismantling," under Western influence, from the time of Peter the Great, and its sudden transformation, during 1878–81, into the first modern "police state." His narrative largely ends in the 1880s because by then, he avers, the old regime in Russia had yielded to a "bureaucratic-police regime which in effect has been in power there ever since." It was there, and then, that the "germs of twentieth-century totalitarianism" were sown.

A "patrimonial state" is one in which "political authority is conceived and exercised as an extension of the rights of ownership, the ruler (or rulers) being both sovereigns of the realm and its proprietors." It is an ancient type of government—and one alien to the West, where authority over people and objects has come to be split into authority exercised as sovereignty and authority exercised as ownership. "One may say that the existence of private property as a realm over which public authority normally exercises no jurisdiction is the thing which distinguishes Western political experience from all the rest." Everywhere else, "the lines separating ownership from sovereignty either do not exist, or are so vague as to be meaningless."

This is one cardinal point of Pipes's interpretation: in Russia the separation referred to occurred "very late and very imperfectly" (by comparison with Western states); thus the "essential quality of Russian politics derives from the identification of sovereignty and ownership, that is, from a 'proprietary' way of looking at political authority on the part of those who happen to be in power."

Pipes's second cardinal point is that in the later nineteenth century, owing to the survival of the "patrimonial principle" in public life, the corresponding "impotence or apathy" of the social classes with respect to state authority, and the "notorious underdevelopment in Russia of legality and personal freedom," the government was able to impose, in the midst of an apparent crisis, a quick succession of emergency measures that completed the subjection of society to the arbitrary power of the bureaucracy and police. After 1881, in Russia "the 'state' meant the tsar and his officialdom; internal politics meant protecting both from the encroachments of society." Alexander III's decree of August 14, 1881, codifying and systematizing the repressive legislation dating back at least to 1845, "has been the real constitution under which—brief interludes apart— Russia has been ruled ever since."

Even more, if "all the elements of the police state" were thus present in the Russian Empire of the early 1880s, certain measures carried out experimentally by the Imperial government in the first years of the twentieth century "moved into the even more sinister realm of totalitarianism."

So the emergence of the Soviet state forms only a brief epilogue— less than two pages of a total of more than 300—to *Russia under the Old Regime.* Here it is "not in the least surprising that almost the instant they took power, the Bolsheviks began to put together the pieces of the Imperial proto-police apparatus." Again the sim- ilarity of provisions against antistate crimes in Soviet and Imperial legal codes is remarked on. "Then, with each passing year, the mechanism of repression was perfected until under Stalin's dicta- torship it attained a level of wanton destructiveness never before experienced in human history."

And not just Stalinism: "This type of legislation, and the public institutions created to enforce it, spread after the revolution of 1917 by way of Fascist Italy and Nazi Germany to other authoritarian states in Europe and overseas. One is justified in saying, therefore, that Chapters Three and Four of the Russian Criminal code of 1845 are to totalitarianism what the Magna Carta is to liberty."

Russia under the Old Regime is not in the ordinary sense a text- book. It is not, more plainly still, a narrative history of the sort beloved by book clubs and the popular press, one calculated to leave the reader aglow from an access of wonder, pity, terror, and nostalgia. Equally, although it sometimes quotes from documents and frequently cites its secondary sources, the book is not a work of scientific or academic history. It does not proceed—nor does it pretend to proceed—from an exhaustive accumulation of primary data via rigorous inference to hypothesis and tentative conclusion. It rests both on a body of accepted historical facts and on a corpus of values. It is a work of synthesis rather than analysis; its style is more rhetorical than logical. And it proposes, in sum, a theory of history of enormous explanatory potential. No one who reads the book, expert or layman, can fail to be challenged by it.

Challenged—but perhaps not wholly persuaded. The values on which *Russia under the Old Regime* rests plainly are those once called liberal, laissez-faire, or individualist but now "conservative" or "neoconservative." Central to the book's argument (see, especially, chapter 8) is the myth of the "Western middle class" as the historical bearer and protector of liberty, the rule of law, personal rights, and "liberal ideas"; much of its remaining force derives from Pipes's broad and highly questionable use of the term "totalitarianism." [6] At the same time, the attitude regarding nearly everything Russian is pitiless, hostile, even xenophobic. In short, the degree to which the reader is convinced by this brilliant book hinges on the degree to which he shares its author's own outlook and values. And the same may be said about the hard-line historiography generally— about any history written in the venerable rhetorical tradition and committed to purposes, usually unstated, beyond itself.

Where does that leave us? Solzhenitsyn's negative response to our basic question is scarcely plausible. The proposition that there are no important links between the Russia that was and the Soviet Union that is, owing to the Bolshevik Revolution and its aftermath, does not persuade. The debate is not over whether there are such links, but over their nature and extent.

Moreover, since much of the material needed by historians remains under Soviet lock and key, leaving much of the Soviet and, to some extent, earlier Russian past in need of clarification, any very emphatic or precise generalizations emanating from this field must be viewed with appropriate skepticism. This is to stress the difficulties—technical, logistical, but especially political—to be encountered in pursuing Russian history by comparison with American or British or, say, Indian history.

If anything, we in the West suffer from a surfeit of history, from a swelling babble of competing and even mutually exclusive claims to historical truth that are based on ever more esoteric sets of data. But in the Soviet Union, as in Soviet Eastern Europe, history has been suppressed. History in the sense of free, disinterested inquiry into the records of the past, and the associated right of open publication, do not exist in the Soviet Union (an important *discontinuity* between it and the late Empire). The resulting amnesia, duplicity, and manipulation of the past for immediate political ends, and the painful doubts and confusion that this in turn brings, have been noted by Western observers—just as a restoration of their history has been one of the principal demands of Eastern dissidents and reformers. Yet we in the West, awash in history, cannot seem to grasp their sense of loss.

In 1986 the Polish philosopher-historian Leszek Kolakowski remarked, in his Jefferson Lecture in Washington, D.C., that "we learn history not to know how to behave or how to succeed, but to know who we are." Kolakowski had been forced to leave his homeland for publicly criticizing the communist regime, and his remark prompted a leading British authority on Poland to observe that "this viewpoint lies close to the heart of the present generation of intellectuals in Poland, where national self-discovery was one of the foremost goals of the Solidarity movement [of 1980–81], and uncensored history one of its great passions."[7] The same general point was made in Moscow, also in 1986, by the poet Yevgeny Yevtushenko, speaking to a congress of Russian writers. There he declared that when reading the great pre-Revolutionary Russian historians,

> you see Russia's real history, complete and unconcealed. But when you read the periodically retouched pages of our modern history, you see with bitterness that the pages are interspersed with white spots of silence and concealment, darkspots of obsequious truth-stretching, and smudges of distortion.
>
> The fear of a creative analysis of our Revolution has led to the flagrant, unacceptable fact that in the [popular biographical] series "Lives of Famous People" we still have no book on Lenin. In many textbooks, important names and events are arbitrarily excluded. They not only fail to list the reasons for the disappearance of leading people in the Party, but sometimes even the date of their death, as if they were peacefully living on pension.
>
> A nation that allows itself to analyze its own mistakes and tragedies bravely knocks the ideological weapon out of its enemies' hands, for it is then spiritually invincible. Only fearlessness in the face of the past can help to produce a fearless solution to the problems of the present.[8]

Indeed, the loss of his history explains in large part both the course of Solzhenitsyn's literary career and the passion of his attack on Western "distortions" of the Russian past. It is as if Western historians were failing not only in their duty to their own public but, so long as history cannot be freely practiced in the Soviet Union, in their duty to the Russian people as well. The charge is, all things considered, a just one. Indeed, too much of the Russian history that is written in the West invites the reflective Russian to find little or no hope in the story of his country's past. It requires him, in effect, to renounce his own history and to try to emulate the West's as a condition for building a better world. And this is not the way to break down walls of misunderstanding, allay suspicion between peoples, or further the cause of knowledge itself.

Policymakers and others who would be informed by history should not look for simple, all-encompassing truths. The state of the discipline, certainly in the Russian and Soviet field, simply does not provide for that. Yet this is not a counsel of despair. Carefully circumscribed, thoroughly researched, detailed monographic studies can yield, for a wider audience, liberating results.

Take the case of Afghanistan. The Soviet invasion of that country in December 1979 set off a wave of anti-Sovietism in the United States that engulfed the Russian past in bitter condemnation. The invasion was seen as but the latest aggression in a long history of ruthless Russian expansionism—not just "expansion," a matter of fact, but "expansionism," a matter of alleged ideological imperatives. Thus viewed, the invasion was not only a concrete diplomatic and perhaps military problem to be dealt with here and now but a problem of immense historic dimensions requiring a proportionate response ("historic," the adjective favored by those who use history—not "historical," favored by those who study it).

Patient investigation of the relevant sources, however, leads to somewhat different—and perhaps unsettling—conclusions. Here is what one careful historian has to say:

> Russian expansion in this part of Asia, for all its momentous consequences, was more a matter of accident than of a carefully considered master plan. A series of decisions of limited scope designed to meet specific circumstances achieved a cumulative power that was greater than the sum of its parts. . . . [Yes,] there was an attitude toward expansion that affected the overall climate in which these decisions were made. [But] this had nothing to do with some legendary Russian drive to obtain warm-water ports or some grand design for the conquest of Asia. Instead, Russia, after a century of Westernization, developed a colonialist outlook that was consciously imitative of Western overseas expansion. Exotic alien lands made attractive targets for colonialization because it was believed that they could make their colonial master rich and because the colonial master could in turn benefit the subject peoples by introducing them to civilization. Furthermore, all of this would prove that Russia, too, was as great and civilized an empire as those of Western Europe.[9]

Similarly, a detailed study of U.S.-Soviet conflict in the same area after World War II makes this basic point:

> The process by which American interests in the region are gradually defined grows out of the traditional rivalry between Britain and Russia; this rivalry, however, takes on a different character as new players—the United States and a powerful Soviet Union— are involved. The ideological baggage which accompanies them

both tends to confuse the conflict by portraying their rival national interests as a clash between two world views. . . .
[Moreover] there is an almost insurmountable difficulty in differentiating between the Soviets' aggressive and defensive actions, just as there is in distinguishing between the nationalistic and ideological elements of their policies. This problem is somewhat analogous to that of distinguishing between ideals and self-interest in American foreign policy.[10]

History at its best can indeed widen our perspectives. It can help to expose, and perhaps to eliminate, the elements of hypocrisy and self-righteousness that still afflict the Western (perhaps especially the American) worldview. More positively, the patient, disinterested study of Soviet and Russian history reveals unmistakably that the Soviet Union of today is the product of a long yet complex, ever-changing, sometimes edifying, and often tragic past—a past that is no more amenable to simple explanation than is life itself.

NOTES

1. Aleksandr Solzhenitsyn, "Remarks at the Hoover Institution," *The Russian Review* (April 1977), p. 188. A sharp discontinuity between pre- and post-Revolutionary Russia is similarly posited by two Soviet historians who were also, like Solzhenitsyn, exiled from their homeland: see Mikhail Heller and Aleksandr Nekrich, *Utopia in Power: The History of the Soviet Union from 1917 to the Present,* trans. Phyllis B. Carlos (New York: Summit Books, 1986).
2. See, for example, Aleksandr I. Solzhenitsyn, *The Mortal Danger: How Misconceptions about Russia Imperil America* (New York: Harper & Row, 1981; 2d ed., 1983), which includes commentaries by six critics.
3. Edward L. Rowny, "The Soviets Are Still Russians," *Survey: A Journal of East and West Studies* (Spring 1980), pp. 2–9.
4. Alex de Jonge, *Fire and Water: a Life of Peter the Great* (New York: Coward, McCann & Geoghegan, 1980); History Book Club *Review* (May 1980), pp. 1–7.
5. Richard Pipes, *Russia under the Old Regime* (New York: Scribner's, 1974; new ed. forthcoming).
6. For a history and critique of the term, see Abbott Gleason, " 'Totalitarianism' in 1984," *The Russian Review* (April 1984), pp. 145–59; for the same with regard more specifically to Soviet history, see Stephen F. Cohen, *Rethinking the Soviet Experience; Politics and History Since 1917* (New York: Oxford University Press, 1985), chap. 1. Cohen argues here that in the 1950s the "totalitarianism school" came to dominate Soviet studies in

the United States " on the basis of generalizations that claimed to explain the Soviet past, present, and future. It turned out to be wrong, or seriously misleading, on all counts"—a view that is now shared by most specialists.

7. Norman Davies, *The New York Times Book Review* (October 5, 1986), p. 11.

8. Excerpts from Yevtushenko's speech were published in *Literaturnaia gazeta* (December 18, 1986); complete version in English trans. in the *New York Times* (December 19, 1986), p. 6.

9. Muriel Atkin, *Russia and Iran, 1780–1828* (Minneapolis: University of Minnesota Press, 1980), pp. 162–63.

10. Bruce R. Kuniholm, *The Origins of the Cold War in the Near East: Great Power Conflict and Diplomacy in Iran, Turkey, and Greece* (Princeton, NJ: Princeton University Press, 1980), pp. xviii, 428.

2

Lenin and His Cult

NINA TUMARKIN

An anecdote currently circulating in Moscow tells of an old man who looked high and low for an apartment, with no success. He wrote to his local Party committee and even to the Central Committee but got no reply. Finally, in desperation, he marched off to the Central Committee and asked to see Lenin. "Lenin?" exclaimed the astonished receptionist, "but Lenin died in 1924!" "How come," muttered the old man, "when *you* need him, he's alive, but when *I* need him, he's dead?"

This story shows the paradox of Lenin's historical legacy in the Soviet Union. Dead for some 65 years, he retains a reputation as the one ruler whose office door was open to his people, who cared about them enough to provide them with housing. At the same time, the Party upholds the myth of Lenin's perpetual accessibility by proclaiming his immortality. "Lenin lives!" is the watchword of an organized cult that resembles a religion. Lenin's ubiquitous portraits and busts are its icons, his writings its scripture, his idealized biography its gospel. And its central shrine is the Lenin Mausoleum in Red Square, displaying his preserved remains.[1]

The ironic twist to the story about the homeless old man turns on another widespread slogan of the Lenin cult: "Lenin is more alive than all the living." Its real meaning is that the immortal Lenin lives to provide the Party with legitimacy—not the needy with apartments. Indeed, the glorified leader is meant to symbolize a higher reality in which day-to-day popular needs give way to the generalized vision of a socialist utopia whose future realization was made certain through the heroic life, death and afterlife of Vladimir Ilyich Ulianov, also known as Lenin.

13

Lenin himself never intended to become the object of a cult, but the Party and government that created the cult bore the profound imprint of his personality and life experiences. And then the symbolic Lenin himself went through many shapes and guises: the standard cult figure of the 1920s—the martyred hero of genius— was quite distinct from the benign dimpled gentleman in soft focus who was peddled by the managers of the Lenin cult during the Khrushchev era (1956–64). The real Lenin was neither hero nor gentleman, but he was a genius in revolutionary politics.

"Lenin in October": since his death countless Soviet books, articles, poems, paintings, and films have celebrated this dramatic confrontation between the man and the moment, in October of 1917, of the Bolshevik Revolution. All of Lenin's talents were uniquely suited to the crisis: his extraordinary sense of timing; his uncanny ability to gauge correctly the weakness of his opponents; and something else that was a combination of rage, courage, and hysteria. He did indeed play a central role in the Bolshevik seizure of power, although that event could not have happened without both the escalating surge of anarchy that engulfed Russia in the summer and fall of 1917 and the political bankruptcy of the Provisional Government established in February, after the abdication of the tsar.

But when it came to creating the Bolshevik system of government and directing it through the incredible trials of its first years, Lenin's contribution was extraordinary. For almost five years, until illness forced him out of the Kremlin in 1922, Lenin ruled Russia as chairman of the Council of People's Commissars, providing the country with its most dynamic leadership since the death, in 1725, of Peter I ("the Great"). He was the primary architect of the new government and the author of its policies.

Once in power, time and again Lenin found himself in direct conflict not only with the armed enemies of Russia and the Revolution, but also with opponents from within his own Party. The first of these battles was the hardest—that of ending the futile war with Germany, begun under the tsar. Early in 1918 Lenin forced the humiliating Treaty of Brest-Litovsk on a resistant Party, summoning all his authorty and talent to attain its ratification. In the end, of course, the outcome of World War I—Germany's surrender to the western Allies—nullified the treaty and Lenin's decision was vindicated. This was often the case with his policy shifts. Lenin's remarkably acute sense of timing, his feel for what at any given moment was necessary for political survival, did not fail to impress itself on his lieutenants, who helped to create his cult.

Lenin held no office that invested him with formal Party leadership; technically, he was simply another member of the ruling Central Committee and Politburo. In practice, however, he was unquestionably the Party's most authoritative voice, a role he had assumed in the years of exile before 1917 and that he retained with energy and skill. Yet as leader of both Party and government Lenin had his blind spot; he was unable to separate himself from either, and thus was unable to provide for the transition that would follow his death. It was precisely this loss of the indispensable leader in 1922 that prompted the creation of an immortalized Lenin to replace the living one, and in the process paved the way for the establishment of the basic institutions of the cult.

The only immortality Lenin had envisioned for himself was through his writings and his revolutionary transformation of Russia. Difficult as it is to speculate on any individual's sense of self, few aspects of Lenin's personality are more apparent than his confidence in his own ideas and his determination to communicate them to others with the full force of their power and clarity. He, and only he, would forge the true path to socialism by means of his teachings, his directives, his constant supervision, and his personal example.

This last characteristic of Lenin was to be transformed into the most enduring aspect of the cult. Even today, he remains the ideal model of behavior for all Soviet citizens. The image of Grandpa Lenin is imprinted on the minds of schoolchildren, who are inundated with stories and poems about the leader, especially about his exemplary childhood. Emphasis is placed on his outstanding schoolwork and, even more to the point, his excellent study habits. Lenin's institutionalized persona as an embodiment of the highest socialist virtues is rooted in Lenin himself; his self-conscious and developed role as exemplar provides the strongest link between Ulianov the man and Lenin the cult figure.

Would the real Lenin have admitted into his office a petitioner looking for an apartment? Probably, yes. He liked to keep foreign dignitaries waiting as he welcomed humble workers and peasants who came with complaints, requests, and often with gifts of food, which he donated to orphanages and day-care centers. Visitors frequently marveled at the simplicity of Lenin's style of life—another characteristic that immediately entered cult literature. He was also later praised for the personal modesty that prevented him from fostering or even tolerating any manifestations of a cult during his lifetime.

In fact, Lenin *was* a man of modest tastes. His apartment was small, his salary low. He preferred to avoid photographers, sculptors, portraitists, flatterers. But his disinclination to become a cult figure is explained not by his modesty alone. Lenin's concept of the rewards of power was simply different from that offered by the frequently empty conventions of ceremonial praise. He was supremely self-confident and had no need of such vanities. As both revolutionary and statesman, he demanded from his followers submission in the form of obedience, dedication, and hard work. For Lenin, ritualized praise was not an acceptable alternative expression of submission.

Yet the foundations of the Lenin cult were laid during the years of Lenin's active rule. Its builders were diverse: workers, peasants, Party agitators, and the highest Party dignitaries came to laud him as a leader of genius. This development was evoked in part by Lenin's forceful leadership, but to an even greater extent by the political imperatives that called for dramatic images and symbols to legitimize the Bolshevik regime. Whatever Lenin's personal inclinations, in the end he allowed the portraits to be hung and the odes to be published. As the first Commissar of Education, Anatoly Lunacharsky, once observed: "I think that Lenin, who could not abide the personality cult, who rejected it in every possible way, in later years understood and forgave us."[2]

As an organized system of rituals and symbols, the cult of Lenin developed gradually during the five years that he ruled Russia. It acquired an institutional base in 1923, when he was incapacitated by progressive cerebral arteriosclerosis, and exploded nationwide immediately after his death—from a stroke—in January 1924. A massive campaign to mobilize the population was mounted by his heirs. The first stage was "mourning week." Every factory, every school, every conceivable organization held meetings packed with mourners, and half a million people attended a three-day lying-in-state in Moscow, which culminated in a grand funeral in Red Square.

A regime that derives its legitimacy from a single ruler risks instability after his death. But if that ruler becomes the object of a cult predicated on his continuing power, the cult can serve as a stabilizing force. This is precisely what happened with Lenin. In order to retain his power and the popular emotions of solidarity his death had unleashed, Party and government propagandists followed "mourning week" with a campaign to establish the Lenin cult throughout the Soviet Union.

At this, its earliest and most vigorous period, the nationwide Lenin cult was still only partially regulated, reflecting the widest possible range of motivations and moods. From the desperate need of his successors to establish a base for their legitimacy to kindergarten teachers' assignments of poems on his death; from genuine outpourings of grief by the faithful to attempts to sell such products as cigarette packets, cups, even cookies by imprinting them with his portrait—the growing obsession with Lenin provided the emotional underpinning of the cult, and tapped the real concerns of a vast and diverse group of people.

For the Party and government leaders who were its architects, the ritualized veneration of Lenin was to serve several functions. It was to evoke in both Party and people a mood of loyalty to the system and its values. At best it would mobilize genuine popular sentiments in a surge of political enthusiasm at a time—seven years after the Revolution—when such enthusiasm had long since waned. At the very least, the organized cult was plainly a display of power by those who wielded it, a demonstration of their ability to direct political activity by fiat. From the day of his death until the end of the 1920s, Lenin was celebrated as an immortal who was accessible to his people through his writings ("Leninism"), his portraits, and his embalmed flesh, which was put on display in a hastily-built wooden mausoleum (replaced in November 1930 by the stone edifice that still stands).

The cult of Lenin did not survive the tenth anniversary of his death. By 1934, the idealized Lenin was relegated to the supporting role of Sacred Ancestor as the cult of Stalin took center stage in Soviet political ritual. For the next two decades Lenin remained an object of organized reverence, but only within the context of his "worthy continuer," who on Revolutionary holidays stood atop the Lenin Mausoleum expressing their symbolic relationship. The dead Lenin was a pedestal for the living Stalin—until 1953, when Stalin joined his predecessor inside the mausoleum.

In 1956, in his "secret speech" delivered to the Twentieth Congress of the Communist Party, Nikita Khrushchev fulminated against the "cult of the personality," a reference, of course, to Stalin. "It is impermissible and foreign to the spirit of Marxism-Leninism to elevate one person, to transform him into a superman possessing supernatural characteristics akin to those of a god." In the same breath, Khrushchev introduced a new cult of Lenin. All legitimate Party doctrine was poured back into its original Leninist vessel, a vessel that, according to Khrushchev, had been broken by Stalin in an extraordinary drive for power matched only by his overweening vanity.

The revived cult of Lenin took shape speedily and with careful orchestration. Handbooks and bibliographies told Party propagandists what to read about Lenin. Thousands of other publications— biographies, reminiscences, laudatory essays—quickly crowded the shelves of Soviet bookstores. Paintings, statues, busts, posters, and little badges were produced in enormous quantities, even as the once ubiquitous Staliniana were fast disappearing from the Soviet political landscape.

Grand, sentimental, and rosy-red, Khrushchev's cult of Lenin was cleansed of the funerary qualities that had characterized the cult rituals of the 1920s. The annual commemoration of Lenin was moved from his deathday to his birthday, April 22, a date which, Khrushchev explained, "better corresponds to the spirit of Leninism as an eternally alive, life-affirming teaching." Pure optimism characterized all cult rituals, speeches, and articles—all of which linked Lenin's immortal spirit to every achievement of the Party and Soviet government. Annual Lenin celebrations included poems, songs (usually written in a sprightly major key, even the one called "At the Mausoleum"), and declamations that observed the appropriateness of the fact that Lenin's birthday comes in the spring. The cult of the 1960s was entirely standardized and regulated from above, providing the Party with a legitimacy that was unassailable. It did not skip a beat when, in 1964, Khrushchev fell from power.

Lenin of course figured prominently in the lavish celebrations of the fiftieth anniversary of the Bolshevik Revolution in 1967. His gargantuan face looked down on the multitudes from buildings and even from the Moscow heavens, for an illuminated portrait was suspended from a balloon. As the decade progressed the cult built to a crescendo with the Party and government preparations for observing Lenin's hundredth birthday on April 22, 1970.

The Lenin jubilee was a meticulously orchestrated extravaganza. Its main slogan was "Lenin is always with us," and indeed Lenin's spatial pervasiveness was its most striking aspect. Factories, publishing houses, looms, kilns, bakeries—everything that could produce artifacts—contributed some manner of memento for the occasion. The Soviet Union became a giant display case for busts, statues, posters, poems, banners, bric-a-brac, and commemorative volumes.

The centennial had been intended to saturate political, civic, and cultural life with the image and words of Lenin. But the celebration was a disaster for the credibility of communist propaganda and

political ritual. The barrage of Leniniana was so vast and unre-
lenting that the jubilee took on the aspect of a burlesque performance. It is likely that, with the exception of a tiny group of dissidents, the population at large and Party members in particular
retained their respect for Lenin's talents and a measure of admi-
ration for his achievements. But too many slogans and busts, too
many speeches, too many articles in every periodical for months
and months beforehand, and too many rhapsodic declamations turned
an event designed to evoke enthusiasm into one that provoked
disdain and even ridicule.

An awareness of the centennial's excesses is clear from the speed
with which the authorities moved to diminish the frequency and
pitch of the rituals. Obviously, they must have intended to ease up
on the Lenin theme after April 1970, but the reduction was particularly marked and sharp. During the 1970s, even the yearly celebrations of Lenin's birthday were far more modest than those of the
previous decade. The author of a 1977 Soviet book on communist
ritual suggested that the modesty of the Lenin holiday is meant to
reflect Vladimir Ilyich's own simplicity.[3] But it seems clear that
Soviet propagandists had learned the virtues of moderation only
after the 1970 fiasco. That event seems to have made it impossible
to rekindle popular interest in most aspects of the Lenin cult.

Today, cult museums in the Soviet Union attract few individual
visitors, and there are few buyers for Lenin's writings, phonograph
records of his speeches, or the busts that come in all sizes. College
students proudly boast to foreigners that they make it a point to
forget promptly everything they must learn about Lenin and Leninism in their required courses. The iconographic representations
of Lenin, the sacred writings, the commemorative meetings, and
the grand Lenin museums appear to evoke little more than
indifference.

Nonetheless, in some ways the cult still works. For example,
children doubtless are impressed by the curly-haired little Vladimir
Ulianov who was such a fine student and grew up to emancipate
Russia. And certain Lenin shrines still attract crowds of visitors.
One of these is his boyhood home in Ulianovsk (formerly Simbirsk),
on the Volga; another is the villa, not far from Moscow, in which
he died. In both of these houses, Soviet tourists appear genuinely
animated as they shuffle past the cordoned-off rooms in outsized
canvas slippers tied over their shoes to protect the floors.

Surely the most successful locus of the cult is the stately Lenin
Mausoleum in Moscow's Red Square. Party and government leaders
gather on its tribunal on major holidays. Contemporary Soviet writ-

ings refer to it as a "sacred" place that "provides an inexhaustible supply of revolutionary energy." It is to the Mausoleum that Soviet cosmonauts come both before their space flights (to gather courage) and after their return (to give thanks). And it is customary for newlyweds to lay flowers outside the Mausoleum right after their wedding.

The demeanor of Soviet visitors to the Lenin Mausoleum is serious and respectful. Even during the long wait in line most stand silently or chat in low tones, and admonish restless children who skip and jump to relieve the tedium. Once inside, all eyes are riveted on the body that rests, awash in light, on an ornate bier in the center of a dark gray chamber. In the decades since Lenin's entombment, tens of millions of ordinary Soviet people have patiently waited in long queues for their permitted 80 seconds with the founder of both the Communist Party and the Soviet state.

NOTES

1. This chapter is adapted from portions of Nina Tumarkin, *Lenin Lives! The Lenin Cult in Soviet Russia* (Cambridge, MA: Harvard University Press, 1983).

2. A. V. Lunacharsky, "Shtriki," in *Lenin—tovarishch, chelovek,* 2d ed. (Moscow: Politizdat, 1963), p. 179. See also the same author's "Vladimir Ilyich Lenin," in *Revolutionary Silhouettes,* trans. Michael Glenny (New York: Hill & Wang, 1968), pp. 35–56.

3. *Nashi prazdniki* (Moscow: Molodaia Gvardiia, 1977), pp. 28–30.

3

The Stalin Question

STEPHEN F. COHEN

It has been called the "accursed question," like serfdom in pre-Revolutionary Russia. Stalin ruled the Soviet Union for a quarter of a century, from 1929 to his death at the age of 73 in 1953. For most of these years, he ruled as an unconstrained autocrat, making the era his own—*Stalinshchina,* the time of Stalin. The nature of his rule and the enduring legacy of Stalinism have been debated in the Soviet Union for more than another quarter of a century, first in the official press and, since the mid-1960s, in *samizdat*—or "self-published"—writings. And yet it remains the most tenacious and divisive issue in Soviet political life—a "dreadful and bloody wound," as even the government newspaper once admitted.[1] "Tell me your opinion about our Stalinist past," goes a Moscow saying, "and I'll know who you are."

The Stalin question is intensely historical, social, political, and moral. It encompasses the whole of Soviet, and even Russian, history. It cuts across and exacerbates contemporary political issues. It calls into question the careers of a whole ruling elite and the personal conduct of several generations of citizens. The Stalin question burns high and low, dividing leaders and influencing policy, while generating bitter quarrels in families, among friends, at social gatherings. The conflict takes various forms, from philosophical polemics to fistfights. One occurs each year on March 5, when glasses are raised in households across the Soviet Union on the anniversary of Stalin's death. Some are loving toasts to the memory of "our great leader who made the Motherland strong." Others curse "the greatest criminal our country has known."

These antithetical toasts reflect the history that inflames and perpetuates the Stalin question. Historical Stalinism was, to use a So-

21

viet metaphor, two towering and inseparable mountains: a mountain of national accomplishments alongside a mountain of crimes. The accomplishments cannot be lightly dismissed. During the first decade of Stalin's leadership, memorialized officially as the period of the First and Second Five-Year Plans for collectivization and industrialization, a mostly backward, agrarian, illiterate society was transformed into a predominantly industrial, urban, literate one. For millions of people, the 1930s were a time of willingly heroic sacrifice, educational opportunity, and upward mobility. In the second decade of Stalin's rule, the Soviet Union destroyed the mighty German invader, contributing more than any other nation to the defeat of fascism; it also acquired an empire in eastern Europe and became a superpower in world affairs. All this still inspires tributes to the majesty of Stalin's rule.

But the crimes were no less mountainous. Stalin's policies caused a Soviet holocaust, from his forcible collectivization of the peasantry in 1929–33 to the relentless system of mass terror by the NKVD or MGB (as the political police were variously known) that continued until his death. Millions of innocent men, women, and children were arbitrarily arrested, tortured, executed, brutally deported, or imprisoned in the murderous prisons and forced-labor camps of the Gulag Archipelago. No one has yet managed to calculate the exact number of deaths under Stalin. Among those who have tried, 20 million is a conservative estimate.[2] Nor does this figure include the millions of unnecessary casualties that can be blamed on Stalin's negligent leadership at the beginning of World War II or the eight million souls (another conservative estimate) who languished in his concentration camps every year between 1939 and 1953. Judged only by the number of victims, and leaving aside important differences between the two regimes, Stalinism created a holocaust greater than Hitler's.

Most of the Stalin controversy pivots on this dual history. The pro-Stalin argument, of which there are both primitive and erudite versions among Russians, builds upon the proverb, "When the forest is cut, the chips fly." It insists that "Stalin was necessary." The sacrifices—they are usually termed "mistakes" or "excesses" and are said to be exaggerated—were unavoidable, it is argued. The economic advantages of collectivized agriculture made rapid industrialization possible. Repression eliminated unreliable, alien, or hostile elements and united the country under Stalin's strong leadership. These events prepared the nation for the great victory over Germany and its achievement of great-power status. In this version of the past, which has again become standard in Soviet textbooks and novels, Stalin is exalted as a great builder, statesman, and generalissimo.

Anti-Stalin opinion says just the opposite: "Yes, there were victories, not thanks to the cult [of Stalin], but in spite of it." The brutality of collectivization did more harm than good; there were other and better ways to industrialize. Mass repressions were both criminal and dysfunctional. They decimated the labor pool and elites essential for national defense, including the officer corps. The atmosphere of terror and corrupt Stalinist leadership caused the terrible disasters of 1941 and made the whole war effort more difficult. Soviet prestige in the world, then and now, would be far greater without the stigma of Stalin's crimes.

These arguments seem historically symmetrical, but they do not explain fully why so many, probably the great majority, of Soviet officials and ordinary citizens alike still speak mostly, or even only, good of Stalin and thus justify crimes of this magnitude.[3] It is true that official censorship has deprived many citizens of a full, systematic account of what happened. But much of the story did appear, however elliptically, in Soviet publications by the mid-1960s. Moreover, most adult survivors must have known or sensed the magnitude of the holocaust, since virtually every family lost a relative, friend, or acquaintance. Why, then, do not most people share the unequivocal judgment once pronounced, even in a censored Soviet publication, on these "black and bitter days of the Stalin cult"— that "there is no longer any place in our soul for a justification of his evil deeds"?[4]

Two categories of Soviet citizens had an intensely personal interest in the Stalin question after 1953: victims of the terror and those who had victimized them. Most of the victims were dead, but many remained to exert pressure on high politics. Millions of people had survived—some for 20 or more years—in the camps and in remote exile. Most of these survivors, perhaps 7 or 8 million, were eventually freed after Stalin's death. They began to return to society, first in a trickle in 1953 and then in a mass exodus in 1956. To salvage what remained of their shattered lives, the returnees required, and demanded, many forms of rehabilitation: legal exoneration, family reunification, housing, jobs, medical care, pensions.

Their demands were shared by a kindred group of millions of relatives of people who had perished in the terror. The criminal stigma "enemy of the people" on these families, many of whom had also been persecuted, kept them from living and working as they wanted. Posthumous legal exoneration or "rehabilitation" and restitution were therefore both a practical necessity and a deeply felt duty to the dead. These demands of so many surviving victims had enormous political implications, if only because exoneration and restitution were official admissions of colossal official crimes. Still more, some victims demanded a full public exposure of the crimes and even punishment of those responsible.

In addition to its size and passion for justice, the community of victims had direct and indirect access to the high leadership. Returnees from the camps became members and even heads of various Party commissions set up after 1953 to investigate the Gulag system, the question of rehabilitations, and specific crimes of the Stalin years. (One such commission contributed to Nikita Khrushchev's anti-Stalin speeches to the Party congresses of 1956 and 1961.) Quite a few returnees resumed prominent positions in military, economic, scientific, and cultural life. (Unlike those in Czechoslovakia, however, none rose to the high Party leadership.) Some returnees had personal access to repentant Stalinists in the leadership, such as Khrushchev and Anastas Mikoyan, whom they lobbied and influenced. And other returnees, such as Aleksandr Solzhenitsyn, made their impact in different ways. As a result, by the mid-1950s victims of the terror had become a formidable source of anti-Stalinist opinion and politics.

Their adversaries were no less self-interested and far more powerful. The systematic victimization of so many people had implicated millions of other people during the 20-year terror. There were different degrees of responsibility. But criminal complicity had spread like a cancer through the system, from Politburo members who had directed the terror alongside Stalin, to Party and state officials who had participated in the repressions, to the hundreds of thousands of NKVD personnel who arrested, tortured, executed, and guarded prisoners, and to the plethora of petty informers and slanderers who fed on the crimson madness. Millions of others were implicated by having profited, often inadvertently, from the misfortune of victims. They inherited the positions, apartments, possessions, and sometimes even the wives of the vanished. Generations built lives upon a holocaust. The terror killed, but it also, said one returnee, "corrupted the living."[5]

The question of criminal responsibility and punishment, either by Nuremberg-style trials or by expulsion from public life, was widely discussed in the 1950s and 1960s, though public commentary usually was muted or oblique. The official and popular defense—that only Stalin and a handful of accomplices had known the number and innocence of the victims—was rudely shattered on several occasions. When the venerable writer Ilya Ehrenburg later spoke of having had "to live with clenched teeth" because he knew his arrested friends were innocent, he implied that the whole officialdom above him had also known. It may be true, as even anti-Stalinists report, that ordinary people believed the Stalinist mania about "enemies of the people." But when the poet Yevgeny Yevtushenko wrote that the masses "had worked in a furious desperation, drowning with the thunder of machines, tractors, and bulldozers the cries that might have reached them across the barbed wire of Siberian concentration camps," he acknowledged that the whole nation had "sensed that something was wrong."[6]

Of those who were incontrovertibly guilty, a few committed suicide, a few were ousted from their posts, a handful of high policemen were tried and executed, and some became politically repentant. But the great majority remained untouched. The remote specter of retribution was enough to unite millions who had committed crimes, and also many of those who felt some unease about their lives, against any revelations about the past and the whole process of de-Stalinization. "Many people," a young researcher discovered in 1956, "will defend [the past], defending themselves." A great poet who had suffered commented, "Now they are trembling for their names, positions, apartments, dachas. The whole calculation was that no one would return."[7]

A second large dimension of the Stalin question was even more ramifying. Proposals for change throughout the rigidified Soviet system and stubborn resistance to change became the central features of official political life after Stalin's death. The conflict between reformers and conservatives was inseparable from the Stalin question because the status quo and its history were Stalinist. In advocating change, Soviet reformers had to criticize the legacy of Stalinism in virtually every area of policy, whether it was the priority of heavy industry in economic investment; the exploitation of collectivized agriculture; overcentralization in management; heavy-handed censorship and a galaxy of taboos in intellectual, cultural, and scientific life; retrograde policies in family affairs; repressive practices and theories in law; or Cold War thinking in foreign policy. And in order to defend these institutions, practices, and orthodoxies, Soviet conservatives had to defend the Stalinist past.

Unavoidably, Stalin and what he represented became political symbols for both the friends and foes of change. Soviet reformers developed anti-Stalinism as an ideology in the 1950s and 1960s (as did their counterparts in Eastern Europe), while Soviet conservatives embraced, no doubt reluctantly in some cases, varieties of neo-Stalinism. Khrushchev and his allies established the link in the mid-1950s, when they fused a decade of reform from above with repeated campaigns against Stalin's historical reputation. The Stalin question, they said, pitted the "new and progressive against the old and reactionary"; Stalin's defenders were "conservatives and dog-matists." Not all Soviet conservatives actually were Stalinists. But the relationship between attitudes toward Stalin and change was authentic, and it spread quickly to every policy area where reform-ers and conservatives were in conflict.

Popular attitudes were, and remain, an even larger dimension of the Stalin question. The expression "cult of Stalin's personality" became, after 1953, an official euphemism for Stalinism, but it had a powerful and deep-rooted historical resonance. For more than 20 years, Stalin had been officially glorified in extraordinary ways. All of the country's achievements were attributed to his singular in-spiration. Virtually every idea of nation, people, patriotism, and communism was made synonymous with his name, as in the war-time battle cry "For Stalin! For the Motherland!" His name, words, and alleged deeds were trumpeted incessantly to every corner of the land. His photographed, painted, bronzed, and sculpted like-ness was everywhere. Stalin's original designation, "The Lenin of Today," gave way in the 1930s to titles of omnipotence and infal-libility: Father of the Peoples, Genius of Mankind, Drive of the Locomotive of History, Greatest Man of All Times and Peoples. The word "man" seemed inappropriate as the cult swelled into deifi-cation: "O Great Stalin, O Leader of the Peoples, Thou who didst give birth to man, Thou who didst make fertile the earth."[8]

The cult was manipulated from above, but there is no doubt that it had deep popular roots, as did the whole Stalinist system. Many Soviet writers, though they disagree about other aspects of Stalin-ism, tell us that the Stalin cult was widely accepted and deeply believed by millions of Soviet people of all classes, ages, and oc-cupations, especially in the cities. Of course, many people did not believe, or they believed in more limited ways. But most of the urban populace, it seems clear, were captives of the cult. It became a religious phenomenon. And in this deeply personal, psycholog-ical, and passionate sense, the nation was Stalinist.

Stalin's death, on March 5, 1953, dealt an irreparable blow to the divinity of the cult; gods do not suffer brain hemorrhages, enlarge-ment of the heart, and high blood pressure, as described graphically in the published medical bulletin and autopsy. The state funeral it-self was a bizarre blend of old and new. Scores of mourners were trampled to death by a hysterical crowd gathered to view the body, adding to the death toll of Stalin's reign. But new chords were sounded in the eulogies by his successors, the "collective leadership." They praised Stalin's "immortal name"—but significantly less than while he lived. And they ascribed to the Communist Party a role it had not played, except in myth, since Stalin's great terror of the 1930s—the "great directing and guiding force of the Soviet people."[9]

Official de-Stalinization, or partial de-Stalinization, soon followed, as manifested in Khrushchev's speeches to the Party congresses of 1956 and 1961. But when the leadership assaulted the Stalin cult, first obliquely and then with revelations that portrayed the "Father of the Peoples" as a genocidal murderer, it caused a traumatic crisis of faith. In the words of contemporary Soviet writers, de-Stalinization "destroyed our faith, tearing out the heart of our worldview, and that heart was Stalin." Revelations about the past meant "not only the truth about Stalin, but the truth about ourselves and our illusions." Many people underwent a "spiritual revolution" and became anti-Stalinists. But because it forced a person "to reevaluate his own life," it was "hard to part with our belief in Stalin." So hard that many other people could not break with the past. They remained—and remain even today—self-professed Stalinists.

For a decade after Stalin's death, popular and official anti-Stalinism seemed to be an irresistible force in Soviet politics. But the powerful resurgence of pro-Stalinist sentiments on both levels after 1964 seemed no less inexorable. The turnabout was reflected in the career of Aleksandr Solzhenitsyn. In 1964, he was nominated for a Lenin Prize, the Soviet Union's highest literary honor, for his prison camp story *One Day in the Life of Ivan Denisovich;* ten years later he was arrested and deported.

Khrushchev's downfall in 1964 at first encouraged both anti-Stalinists and neo-Stalinists in official circles. The former hoped that the new Brezhnev-Kosygin government would chart a more orderly course of reform and de-Stalinization, while neo-Stalinists sought a mandate to stamp out the "poison of Khrushchevism." Their struggle raged both openly and covertly in 1965 and 1966. New anti-Stalinist publications appeared, rehabilitations of Stalin's victims continued, and in October 1965 the leadership legislated a major (and ill-fated) program of economic reform. At the same time, however, influential figures, including Leonid Brezhnev, began to issue authoritative statements refurbishing Stalin's reputation as a wartime leader, eulogizing the 1930s while obscuring the terror, and suggesting that Khrushchev's revelations had "calumniated" the Soviet Union. Behind the scenes, an assertive pro-Stalin lobby,

proud to call itself "Stalinist," took the offensive for the first time
in several years, apparently with Brezhnev's support. Anti-Stalinists
were demoted, censorship was tightened, new ideological strictures
were drafted, already processed rehabilitations were challenged,
and subscriptions to anti-Stalinist journals were prohibited in the
armed forces.

The decisive battle in officialdom was over by early 1966. Within
18 months of Khrushchev's overthrow, official de-Stalinization was
at an end; a pronounced reverse pattern had developed and anti-
Stalinism was becoming the rallying cry of a small dissident movement. Two events dramatized the outcome. In February 1966, two
prominent writers, Andrei Sinyavsky and Yuli Daniel, were tried and
sentenced to labor camps for publishing their "slanderous" (anti-
Stalinist) writings abroad. The public trial, with its self-conscious
evocation of the purge trials of the 1930s, was a neo-Stalinist blast
against critical-minded members of the intelligentsia. Meanwhile,
a campaign began against anti-Stalinist historians. The first victim
was a Party historian in good standing, Aleksandr Nekrich. He was
traduced and later expelled from the Party for little more than res-
tating the anti-Stalinist historiography, developed during the
Khrushchev years, of the German invasion of 1941.[10]

These events and the fear that Stalin would be officially rehabilitated at the Twenty-third Party Congress in March 1966 gave
birth to the dissident movement and *samizdat*—"self-published"
or underground—literature as a widespread phenomenon. A flood
of petitions protesting the Sinyavsky-Daniel trial and neo-Stalinism
generally circulated among the intelligentsia; they gathered
hundreds and then thousands of signatures, including the names
of prominent representatives of official anti-Stalinism under
Khrushchev. The growing conservative and neo-Stalinist overtones
of the Brezhnev regime drove anti-Stalinists from official to dissident ranks and gave the movement many of its best-known spokesmen, such as Andrei Sakharov, Lydiia Chukovskaia, Roy and Zhores
Medvedev, Solzhenitsyn, Pyotr Yakir, and Lev Kopelev. These people later went separate political ways, but the fallen banner of anti-
Stalinism first turned them into dissidents. And this development
transformed the Stalin question from a conflict inside the Establishment into a struggle between the Soviet government and open
dissidents.

Some dissidents believed that their protests prevented a full
rehabilitation of Stalin at the Twenty-third Congress, where his
name was hardly mentioned. If so, it was a small victory amid a
rout. The policies of the Brezhnev government grew steadily into

a wide-ranging conservative reaction to Khrushchev's reforms. The defense of the status quo required a usable Stalinist past. Increasingly, only the mountain of accomplishments was remembered in rewritten history books and in the press.

By the end of the 1960s Stalin had been restored as an admirable leader. Serious criticism of his wartime leadership and of collectivization was banned; rehabilitations were ended and some even undone; and intimations that there ever had been a great terror grew scant. Indeed, people who criticized the Stalinist past (as Khrushchev had done at Party congresses) could now be prosecuted for having "slandered the Soviet social and state system." Dozens of honored anti-Stalinist writers and historian suffered persecution or were simply unable to publish. Arrests of dissidents grew apace.

If anti-Stalinist reformers in the Establishment still had any hope, it was crushed, along with the "Prague Spring," in August 1968. The Prague Spring had epitomized the anti-Stalinist cause for Soviet anti-Stalinists and neo-Stalinists alike. The language used to justify the Soviet invasion of Czechoslovakia evoked the terroristic ideology of the Stalin years. It soon crept back into domestic publications as well, along with the charge that de-Stalinization was nothing but "an anti-Communist slogan" invented by enemies of the Soviet Union.

Stalinist sentiment in Soviet officialdom grew steadily more fulsome through the 1970s and into the 1980s. With few exceptions, critical analysis of the Stalinist experience was banished from the official press to small circles of *samizdat* writers and readers. References to Stalin's "negative" side, to "harm" caused by his personal "mistakes," appeared in two prominent articles officially commemorating the one hundredth anniversary of his birth in December 1979. In the broader context, they seemed to be little more than carping asides. In a welter of official mass-circulation publications, Stalin's personal reputation soared. He was no longer the subject of religious worship, but he was, once again, the great national leader and benefactor who had guided the country's fortunes for 20 years. His "devotion to the working class and the selfless struggle for socialism" was unquestioned. Above all, the entire Stalinist era, the historical centerpiece of the conservative Brezhnev leadership, was wholly rehabilitated as the necessary and heroic "creation of a new order."

A coarser, more ominous form of pro-Stalinism also emerged in official circles. A variety of publications—including a spate of historical novels, some of them made into prize-winning and popular films—justified Stalin's terror of the 1930s as a "struggle against

destructive and nihilistic elements." Epithets of the terror years—
"enemies of the Party and of the people," "fifth column," and "root-
less cosmopolitans"—reappeared in print. And they were popular-
ized still more widely by Party lecturers, whose daily oral propaganda
throughout the country does much to set the tone of Soviet political
life. Indeed, by the mid-1970s, odious proconsuls of Stalin's terror
had been resurrected as examplars of official values. And in time
for the 1979 centenary of Stalin's birth, neo-Stalinist officials seem
even to have achieved, despite rulings under Khrushchev, the rehabilitation of the notorious show trials of the 1930s, which served
as the juridical linchpin of Stalin's terror against the Communist
Party.

Yet if this resurgence of Stalinist sentiments represented a potential base for a more despotic leadership in the Soviet Union, it
did not signify a rebirth of Stalinism. As a system of personal dictatorship and mass terror, Stalinism was the product of specific historical circumstances and a special kind of autocratic personality;
these factors have passed from the scene. Today, the Soviet political
system is very different, however authoritarian it remains. Neo-
Stalinists may press for and even achieve more hard-line policies
at home and abroad. But actual "re-Stalinization" would be a radical
change opposed by the great majority of Soviet officials and citizens,
whose pro-Stalinist sentiments reflect something different—their
own deep-rooted political and social conservatism. Indeed, the appeals of neo-Stalinism today are diverse and often contradictory.

Pro-Stalin opinion among high officials is easy to explain. For
them, the generalissimo on his pedestal continues to symbolize
their own power and privilege and to guard against change. Not
surprisingly, the main patrons of neo-Stalinist literature are those
authorities responsible for the political attitudes of young people
and the armed forces. These officials know the truth about the past
and thus deserve the harshest judgment of anti-Stalinists; in the
words of one of the latter, "Knowingly to restore respect for Stalin
would be to establish something new—to establish respect for de-
nunciation, torture, execution."

But as a broad popular phenomenon, today's pro-Stalin sentiment is something different, even an expression of discontent. On
one level, it is part of the widespread resurgence of Russian nationalism, to which Stalin linked the fortunes of the Soviet state
in the 1930s and 1940s and which has reemerged, in various forms,
as the most potent ideological factor in Soviet political life. Echoing
older ideas of Russia's special destiny, most of these nationalist
currents are statist and thus identify with the real or imagined

grandeur of the Soviet Russian state, as opposed to the Communist Party, under Stalin. They perpetuate assorted legacies of that era, from pride in the accomplishments of the 1930s and the war years to anti-Semitism and quasi-fascist cults. In this haze of nationalist sentiment, Stalin joins a long line of great Russian rulers stretching back to the early tsars.

Such ideas are also the product of contemporary social problems. Varieties of neo-Stalinist opinion cut across classes, from workers to the petty intelligentsia, reflecting their specific discontents in Soviet society. More generally, though, liberalizing trends and other changes in the 1950s and 1960s unsettled many lives and minds; the open discussion of long-standing social problems made them seem new. By the mid-1960s, many officials and citizens saw a reformed, partially de-Stalinized Soviet Union as a country in crisis. Economic shortages, inflation, public drunkenness, escalating divorce rates, unruly children, cultural diversity, complicated international negotiations—all seemed to be evidence of a state that could no longer manage, much less control, its own society. And all cast a rosy glow on the Stalinist past as an age of efficiency, low prices, law and order, discipline, unity, stability, obedient children, and international respect.

Contemporary discontents, the feeling that "we have been going downhill ever since his death," could only enhance Stalin's popular reputation. By the end of the 1970s, official portraits of a largely benevolent chief of state were reinforced by memories of Stalin as a "strong boss" under whose rule "we did not have such troubles." Little remained to counter this folk nostalgia. While anti-Stalinists have been silenced by censorship, new generations, perhaps 40 percent of the population, have grown up in the post-Stalin era. Raised on parental remnants of the cult, many think that Stalin arrested "20 or 30 people" or "maybe 2,000." When a famous anti-Stalinist told a group of young people that the arrests were "reckoned not in thousands but in millions, they did not believe me."

By the time Leonid Brezhnev died, in 1982, anti-Stalinism—and thus the Stalin question itself—no longer seemed to be potent factors in official Soviet politics. And yet, there are two reasons why this was probably a temporary condition—or even an illusion created by censorship. One is that the reformist movement in Soviet officialdom, which revived strongly after Brezhnev's death, always carries with it a renewal of the Stalin question. This is so mainly because Stalin's institutional legacy—particularly the hypercentralized economic system—is still the source of many serious problems and thus a constant reproach to the Stalinist past; but it is also because a program of serious economic reform requires a compelling reformist ideology to overcome widespread conservative opposition to change. Anti-Stalinism remains the only viable ideology of communist reform from above, as it was under Khrushchev and as it has been in other communist capitals, from Belgrade and Prague to Peking. Not surprisingly, soon after the reform-minded Mikhail Gorbachev became Soviet leader in 1985, anti-Stalin themes began appearing in the Soviet press more loudly and persistently than they had in many years.

The other enduring source of anti-Stalinism is emphasized by the neo-Stalinist complaint against people who *"elevate ethical-moral problems above those of the state and patriotism"* [emphasis in original]. Enthralled by the apparent mountain of achievements, many Soviet citizens (and Westerners, too, it seems) will always admire Stalin as a great leader or "modernizer." But too much has become known for the mountain of crimes to vanish from view, even after all the victims of Stalinism have passed from the scene.

Historical justice is a powerful moral idea that knows no statute of limitations, especially when reinforced by a sense that the whole nation bears some responsibility for what happened. This truth is confirmed by other historical examples. But Russians need look only to the large body of *samizdat* literature, where exposés of Stalinism and the idea of a national reckoning "in the name of the present and the future" have been kept alive. The timelessness of the Stalin question and the prospect of new generations of anti-Stalinists are explained by a *samizdat* historian: "It is the duty of every honest person to write the truth about Stalin. A duty to those who died at his hands, to those who survived that dark night, to those who will come after us."[11] Enough anti-Stalinist themes have forced their way even into the censored Soviet press in recent years to tell us that this outlook still has many adherents in the Soviet Establishment as well.

Official censorship can mute the controversy, postpone the historical reckoning, and allow another generation to come of age only dimly aware (though not fully ignorant) of what happened during the Stalin years. But it is also true, as events since Stalin's death have shown, that making the past forbidden serves only to make it more alluring—and that imposing a ban on historical controversy causes that controversy to fester, intensify, and grow politically explosive.

NOTES

1. Konstantin Simonov, "O proshlom vo imia budushchego," *Izvestiia* (November 18, 1962).

2. See Robert Conquest, *The Great Terror: Stalin's Purge of the Thirties* (New York: MacMillan, 1968), pp. 525–35, and "The Great Terror Revised," *Survey* 17, no. 1 (1971), p. 93. Several unofficial Soviet historians and demographers give considerably higher figures: Anton Antonov-Ovseyenko, *The Time of Stalin: Portrait of a Tyranny* (New York: Harper & Row, 1981), pt. 2, chap. 15; M. Maksudov, "Losses Suffered by the Population of the USSR 1918–1958," in Roy Medvedev, ed., *The Samizdat Register II* (New York: Norton, 1981), pp. 220–76; and the findings of Iosif Dyadkin, reported in James Ring Adams, "Revising Stalin's Legacy," *Wall Street Journal* (July 23, 1980), and in I. Kurganov, "Tri tsifry," *Novoe russkoe slovo* (April 12, 1964).

3. Though Soviet opinion on this subject cannot be polled and quantified, all firsthand accounts suggest a majority of pro-Stalin sentiment.

4. Simonov, "O proshlom."

5. The cancer of responsibility is a central theme of Solzhenitsyn's two great novels of the terror years, *The First Circle* and *Cancer Ward*.

6. Yevgeny Yevtushenko, *A Precocious Autobiography* (New York: Doubleday, 1963), p. 17.

7. Anna Akhmatova, in *Pamiati A. Akhmatovoi* (Paris: YMCA, 1975), p. 167.

8. Quoted in Suzanne Labin, *Stalin's Russia* (London: Gollanz, 1949), p. 65; see also Antonov-Ovseyenko, *The Time of Stalin*, pt. 3, chap. 1.

9. *Pravda* (March 4–10, 1953). For the funeral, see Yevtushenko, *Autobiography*, pp. 84–87; on the death of the cult, see Antonov-Ovseyenko, *The Time of Stalin*, p. 305.

10. See A. M. Nekrich, *June 22, 1941* (Columbia, SC: University of South Caroline Press, 1968). Nekrich later emigrated to the West.

11. Antonov-Ovseyenko, *The Time of Stalin*, p. xviii.

POLITICS

In the first chapter of this section Mark Beissinger directly confronts the question, Who rules the Soviet Union? He suggests, in reply, that a leadership of some 19 senior Communist Party men—full and candidate members of the Party's Politburo—exercises ultimate authority over a vast bureaucracy whose elite is concentrated in the Party's Central Committee, at present composed of about 300 full and 170 candidate members. The Soviet political system, in essence, is both Party-dominated and essentially bureaucratic, at once highly centralized and highly authoritarian. Beissinger discusses the evolution of this system since Stalin's time as well as its internal dynamics, a subject that Alexander Dallin takes up, in the succeeding chapter, with regard to the making of Soviet foreign policy.

The third chapter of this section deals with the question of dissent in the Soviet Union over the last 20 years and more. Some experts consider that the internal political significance of Soviet dissent has been exaggerated by the Western media. But as Soviet society matures the views of leading dissidents are likely to influence both Soviet policy and Soviet public opinion, and thus become a factor in shaping the Soviet future. There is no doubt, moreover, that the plight of Soviet dissidents at home has had negative repercussions on communist parties abroad, in the Third World, and on East-West relations—that it is, in sum, a question of major international significance and one, therefore, that the makers of Soviet foreign policy have had to take into account. And from a chapter on dissent it is one short step to a consideration of the KGB.

But that is not the end of it. Politics pervades Soviet life to a degree unknown in the West, a fact that is reflected repeatedly in the later sections of this book, just as it was in the preceding section on history.

4

The Leadership and the Political Elite

MARK R. BEISSINGER

Who rules the Soviet Union? Under Stalin there was little doubt: no one—including Stalin's most intimate associates—was immune from the terror. Between 1934 and 1939 alone Stalin had 77 percent of the full members of the Party's Central Committee murdered; and of the 25 men who were unlucky enough to have been members of the Party's Politburo from 1924 to 1952, 11 (44 percent) were shot outright, while another three (11 percent) were driven to suicide or died under suspicious circumstances. And there is ample evidence that, had Stalin not fallen victim to a stroke in March 1953, the 10 who had survived until then through the caprice of the dictator would nearly all have been liquidated in the major purge that was being planned. Thus, while particular factions in Stalin's entourage were often influential in shaping policy, none of them was able to exercise a consistent influence independent of Stalin's will.

Under Nikita Khrushchev, those who lost in the political intrigues of the Kremlin no longer paid for their mistakes with their lives— only with their positions. Yet, despite Khrushchev's efforts at de-Stalinization, he continued to rule by means of massive, though bloodless, replacement of personnel. From 1956 to 1961 he replaced over two-thirds of the members of the Party presidium (Politburo), the Council of Ministers, and the regional Party apparatus, as well as half of the members of the Central Committee.[1]

Similarly, in the realm of policy Khrushchev acted as if he were unconstrained by the elite or even by the rest of the leadership. With little consultation he went about shifting investment priorities, dissolving the central ministries and sending their officials off to the provinces, dividing the Party apparatus into industrial and agricultural branches, ordering the planting of corn in regions where it could not grow, and risking nuclear confrontation with the United States by placing Soviet missiles in Cuba. Not only did these policies alienate an elite yearning for stability, but they also largely failed. By the early 1960s the growth rate of the Soviet economy was beginning to slow; the Soviet Union was forced to import grain for the first time in its history; and the embarrassing Soviet retreat from Cuba encouraged further splits within the Soviet camp. Khrushchev's removal in October 1964 was both a response to his "hare-brained" policies and a backlash against the insecurity from which the Soviet elite suffered. It was as if Khrushchev had mistakenly thought that he could enjoy Stalin's dictatorial power without employing Stalin's instruments of control.

In contrast to its predecessors, the regime of Leonid Brezhnev (1964–82) was characterized above all by stability in both policy and personnel. Unlike the situation under Khrushchev, collective rule and policy-making through consensus dominated politics. There were few administrative shuffles. At the same time, there were few significant reforms, since many of the basic features of the Soviet system as it had been fathered by Stalin—for example, the clumsy mechanism of central planning, the grossly inefficient collective-farm program, the priority of military investment, the country's shackled intellectual and cultural life—remained intact. Particularly in Brezhnev's later years, this stability gave way to a cautious, stagnant style of governance that left his heirs with a long list of serious social and economic problems.

Underpinning the political conservatism of the Brezhnev period was a new political contract between the leadership and the elite: the so-called trust-in-cadres policy. This amounted to an informal promise by the leadership to forswear the massive replacements of personnel that were so characteristic of previous Soviet leaderships. The increasing ages of the highest officials of every major Soviet institution were but one indicator of the existence of this contract. From 1966 to 1982 the average age of Politburo members rose from 55 to 68, of members of the Council of Ministers from 58 to 65, and of members of the Central Committee from 56 to 63.[2] Throughout this period, members of the leadership and of the elite continued to be replaced as before. Nevertheless, the degree of stability was striking. Of both the voting and nonvoting members of the 1966 Central Committee elected after Khrushchev's downfall, 44 percent were still in the Central Committee 15 years later, on the eve of Brezhnev's death. By 1982 the average voting member of the Central Committee had been in office approximately 13 years. By contrast, in 1981 the average tenure in office of members of the U.S. Senate—a body also known for its longevity—was eight years.

Brezhnev's formula for rule presented the Soviet leadership with dangers that his successors have been less willing to ignore. The stability of personnel led to the flourishing of materialistic values, careerism, and corruption within the Soviet elite. Moreover, since officials were rarely removed, they were scarcely held responsible for their actions. Under Brezhnev, violations of the economic plan came to be looked on as the norm rather than the exception, and a pervasive complacency took hold throughout the upper levels of the bureaucracy. At a time of robust economic growth, this slack might have been tolerated. But in recent years, as will be seen in chapters to come, the Soviet system has experienced a series of difficult economic dilemmas that have undermined faith in its vitality both at home and abroad.

In response to this situation, Brezhnev's heirs—in particular, Yury Andropov and Mikhail Gorbachev—sought to inject greater "demandingness" and "discipline" into Soviet politics. To a large extent, the evolution of the Soviet system in the post-Brezhnev era can be understood as an attempt to redefine Brezhnev's political contract in reaction to the dangers that both excessive stability and extensive decentralization pose to central authority in a hierarchical bureaucratic system.

The key elements in any discussion of the Soviet political system are the groups that I have referred to as the elite and the leadership. Institutionally, the elite is roughly equivalent to the Party Central Committee. With its current full membership of 307 and candidate membership of 170, it is the one institution of the Soviet political system that broadly includes representatives from the most influential institutions of society. If an analogous body were to be convened in the United States, it would consist of the most powerful corporate executives, politicians, and civil servants in the country. Consideration of the Soviet leadership, however, can be thought of as largely confined to the Party Politburo, whose 19 full and candidate members are responsible for establishing policy in all areas of activity in the Soviet Union.

As do political elites elsewhere, the Soviet elite imperfectly reflects the society that it governs. The Soviet political elite is also unrepresentative of the Party from which it is drawn. Whereas workers make up 62 percent of Soviet society and 44 percent of the Party, they have a 7 percent representation in the Party Central Committee. Only 8 percent of Soviet society and 30 percent of the Communist Party have a higher education, as against 90 percent of Central Committee members. Women constitute approximately 56 percent of the adult population and 27 percent of the Party membership but

Mark R. Beissinger

only 3 percent of the Central Committee.[3] Moreover, certain ethnic groups, particularly the Russians, are represented in the Central Committee in far greater proportion than their numbers in the total population would warrant, whereas 10 major nationalities are underrepresented. If the Central Committee represents anyone in the Soviet Union, it is the educated, white-collar, Russian, male Party member (tables 1, 2).

The fact that the Soviet elite is recruited from a rather narrow stratum in society is hardly surprising, since elites in most political systems tend to overrepresent politically dominant social groups. More significant for understanding Soviet politics is the relationship of the elite to the political leadership. Because the Soviet

TABLE 1. NATIONAL COMPOSITION OF THE SOVIET UNION, THE COMMUNIST PARTY
AND THE CENTRAL COMMITTEE

Nationality	1979[a] Soviet Population (percent)	1983[b] Communist Party (percent)	1986[c] Central Committee (percent)
Slavic:			
Russians	52.4	59.7	68.9
Ukrainians	16.1	16.0	14.7
Belorussians	3.1	3.8	5.2
Muslim:			
Uzbeks	4.7	2.4	0.8
Kazakhs	2.5	2.0	1.6
Azeris	2.0	1.7	0.8
Tadzhiks	1.1	0.4	0.4
Turkmens	0.8	0.4	0.4
Kirgiz	0.7	0.4	0.4
Baltic:			
Lithuanians	1.1	0.7	0.4
Estonians	0.4	0.3	0.4
Latvians	0.5	0.4	0.8
Other:			
Armenians	1.6	1.5	0.4
Georgians	1.4	1.7	0.8
Moldavians	1.1	0.5	0.4
Others	10.5	8.1	3.6

a. Figures drawn from the last (1979) Soviet census, published in *Vestnik statistiki*, no. 2, 1980, pp. 24–26.

b. Figures for total Party membership (full and candidate) according to nationality, from *Partiinaia zhizn'*, no. 15 (August 1983), p. 23. Since the age distributions of various nationalities of the Soviet Union differ substantially, figures for Party membership according to nationality can be compared with the population levels of the nationalities only with caution. In 1983 Party membership totaled 18,117,903, or approximately 10 percent of the total adult population.

c. Percentages computed from the officially listed national backgrounds for 251 of the 307 full members of the 1986 Central Committee.

TABLE 2. SELECTED CHARACTERISTICS OF THE SOVIET LEADERSHIP
AND ELITE[a]

Status	1986 Central Committee (percent)	1986 Politburo (percent)
Nationality:[a]		
Russian	69	74
Slavic	89	84
Family Origin:[b]		
Peasant	35	25
Worker	38	50
White-Collar	27	25
Age Over 60[c]	47	68
Higher Education[d]	90	100
Party Membership before 1950[e]	46	63
Experience in the Military or in Defense-related Industry[f]	45	42
Member of a Regional Party or Governmental Organization	38	32
Current Occupation:		
Party	44	53
Government	27	32
Military	8	5
Diplomatic	5	5
Police	2	5

Note: Unless otherwise noted, the samples included all 307 full members of the 1986 Central Committee and all 19 members of the 1986 Politburo.
a. Information available for 251 full members of the Central Committee.
b. Information available for 60 full members of the Central Committee and 12 members of the Politburo.
c. Information available for 285 full members of the Central Committee.
d. Information available for 279 full members of the Central Committee.
e. Information available for 274 full members of the Central Committee.
f. Information available for 260 full members of the Central Committee.

elite occupies the top positions (outside of the leadership itself) in the most powerful institutions in society, in theory it always has been possible that the elite might act in unison to restrain the actions of political leaders. The role that the elite can play in this regard, however, ultimately depends on the extent to which its members are able to achieve a collective self-consciousness and to combine the power resources that they possess as individuals, rewarding and punishing the behavior of leaders in defense of joint privileges.

Western studies have shown that the degree to which an elite can act cohesively depends in part on the establishment of "sufficient mutual trust, so that its members will, if necessary, forgo short-run personal or partisan advantage in order to ensure stable rule."[4] The fact that the Soviet elite is overwhelmingly drawn from a rather narrow stratum of society and enjoys common backgrounds and experiences creates a potential for developing such trust. Moreover, members of the elite do share common privileges—for example, access to special stores, vacation resorts, country houses and town apartments, chauffeured limousines, special medical clinics, trips abroad, and foreign and restricted literature—that they could jointly defend. Such privileges are guaranteed by one's position in the bureaucratic hierarchy; therefore, personnel stability is an essential precondition if the elite is to enjoy these privileges uninterruptedly.

Indeed, Brezhnev based his legitimacy largely on this yearning for stability and its associated benefits within an elite that had been racked by political upheavals over the previous 50 years. Both the extensive political controls exercised by the regime and the enormous privileges that the system grants to those who serve it conscientiously are major reasons why the considerable differences of opinion that naturally arise rarely overflow the bounds of conventional Soviet politics, thus avoiding the explosions that so often tear apart other political systems. The stakes in Soviet politics—in terms of both the rewards for cooperation and the penalties for deviance—are high.

The Soviet elite is not, however, a ruling class in the usual sense of the term—that is, a relatively closed social group that consciously defends its collective right to transfer its property and privileges from one generation to another. Relatives of top leaders, such as Brezhnev's son Yury or Andropov's son Igor, have at times occupied positions of influence. Some members of the elite and leadership are related to each other by marriage: for example, the late Arvid Pelshe, a Politburo member and chairman of the Party Control Commission, was married to a sister of the Party's chief ideologist, Mikhail Suslov, whereas the former first deputy chairman of the KGB, Semyon Tsvigun, was married to Brezhnev's sister-in-law. But such nepotism has never been publicly condoned by the regime and recently has come under attack. Moreover, information available on the class background of the fathers of the present Soviet elite shows that only 27 percent come from white-collar families. Nor is the Soviet elite primarily composed of the descendants of the workers who carried out the Bolshevik Revolution. Only 38 percent of the 1986 Central Committee grew up in blue-collar families, whereas an approximately equal proportion (35 percent) comes from a peasant background.

In recent years, it is true, the Soviet elite has become more urban than rural in origin. Yet, as the figures above suggest, it would be difficult to maintain that the elite now constitutes a socially closed class. Upward mobility into the halls of power is still the norm rather than the exception. As self-made men who have risen to power in the name of an ideology that preaches social equality, the Soviet elite tends to feel less secure in its social status and to be less assertive about its privileges than the elites who have inherited their social positions from their parents. The Soviet elite has always tried to hide its privileges from public view, leaving its special stores unmarked, building its vacation homes in secluded places, and riding in its limousines with the curtains drawn. This phenomenon of "inconspicuous consumption" contrasts sharply with the openly self-confident behavior of elites elsewhere in the world.

The Soviet political elite corresponds more closely to what Ralf Dahrendorf has called a "cartel of anxiety" than to a self-conscious and assertive new class.[5] It is more a category than a center of authority, and it governs (in the sense of administering, as individuals) more than it rules. Only on the rarest of occasions has the Central Committee, as an institution embodying the will of the elite, played a significant role in Soviet politics. Such was the case during the so-called Anti-Party Crisis of 1957, when some members of the leadership unsuccessfully attempted to overthrow Khrushchev. Outnumbered in the Politburo, Khrushchev nevertheless managed to alert his supporters in the Central Committee, who, with the help of army planes, gathered in Moscow from all parts of the country to aid the beleaguered leader. But rather than demonstrating the independent role of the Central Committee, this crisis illustrated instead how much and how precariously its power depended on the military— and on the decision of the political leadership to mobilize it.

Normally, the Central Committee meets for a few days several times a year. So long as this is the case, it will have an independent say over policy only when the political leadership is sharply polarized, as might be expected in a succession crisis. Yet even Khrushchev's ouster in October 1964 was presented as an accomplished fact by a unified political leadership to a passive Central Committee, although this act was no doubt popular within the elite. All signs indicate that the more recent successions in the Kremlin, including that of Mikhail Gorbachev in 1985, were similarly decided by a small group of leaders and subsequently presented to the Central Committee for ratification.

One indication of its passivity in recent years has been the Soviet elite's failure to defend even the most fundamental precondition for the maintenance of its collective privileges: namely, personnel stability. From 1966 to 1981, at least four-fifths of the previously elected Central Committee were reelected at every Party congress. (Consisting, most recently, of about 5,000 delegates, a congress meets once every five years.) By contrast, of the 319 full members elected in 1981, only 145 (45 percent) were still in office in 1986, whereas 28 (9 percent) had died and 146 (46 percent) had retired or been removed from their posts over the previous 5 years—a rate of removal that rivals that under Khrushchev. At the 27th Party Congress (1986), Brezhnev's policy of personnel stability was openly condemned for leading to excessive leniency and rampant indiscipline. In the words of Yegor Ligachev, a member of the Politburo and of its executive Secretariat, "it is well known that a certain trust in cadres often was replaced by us with unchecked trustfulness and, frankly speaking, lack of control."[6] Indeed, one could argue that, given the bureaucratic nature of the Soviet political system, the rise of a stable ruling class is practically impossible, since the lack of administrative accountability that inevitably accompanies the uninterrupted continuity of the same officials in power would eventually undermine the bureaucracy's effective operation.

If the Soviet political elite lacks the cohesiveness, confidence, and sense of purpose needed for ruling society collectively, has power drifted instead into the hands of competing bureaucratic interest groups, none of which has been able to dominate? To be sure, the Soviet elite is drawn from a wide variety of organizations, each having different institutional goals and missions, and most members of the elite have spent large portions of their careers working within the confines of a single organization. The most numerous occupational group within the Central Committee—about 44 percent of its membership—is drawn from the Party apparatus, and slightly less than one-fourth of these work for the central, as opposed to the regional, apparatus. Officials from the state bureaucracy comprise another 27 percent. The rest of the Central Committee is drawn from the military (8 percent), the diplomatic service (5 percent), the cultural and scientific community (4 percent), the KGB (2 percent), the trade unions (1 percent), and other organizations (9 percent). Representatives of the Party apparatus similarly predominate within the political leadership. In 1986, 10 (53 percent) of the 19 Politburo members were working in the apparatus and another four had done so before taking up other posts; in other words, 74 percent of the Politburo in 1986 had spent a significant portion of their careers working within the Party apparatus.

Yet it would be misleading to speak of the Soviet system as a simple balance of power among equally powerful bureaucracies, if only because some bureaucracies are clearly more equal than others. Undermining the claim that the Soviet Union is ruled by a military-industrial complex, for example, is the fact that military officials are poorly represented in the highest echelons of the political system. As just noted, at present only 8 percent of the membership of the Central Committee consists of military officers, and only one professional soldier, the defense minister, sits on the Politburo—as a candidate rather than as a full member. Even if the notion of a military-industrial complex were to be loosely defined to include members of the elite with any experience of working either in the military or in defense-related industry, less than one-half of the Central Committee (45 percent) and of the Politburo (42 percent) would qualify. Though this is by no means an insignificant figure, it hardly speaks for the dominance of the military in Soviet politics. In fact, since Brezhnev's death the visibility of the military has been reduced, and its influence in the policymaking process has come under challenge. The demotion in September 1984 of Marshal N. V. Ogarkov from his posts as chief of the General Staff and first deputy defense minister, reportedly because of policy disagreements with the political leadership, vividly demonstrated how tenuous is the hold on power of even the highest Soviet military officers.

As the permanent administrative arm of the Party, the Party apparatus is self-avowedly the "leading" institution of the Soviet political system. Through its right of inspection and its control over the *nomenklatura* (a list of sensitive positions that can be filled only with its approval), the apparatus oversees the work of all institutions in Soviet society. It is the most highly represented group within the Politburo and the Central Committee, as we have seen. Time and again, control over the Party apparatus has proven to be the single most important political resource in Soviet politics.

Still, despite its central role in the political process and its relatively superior position compared to other institutions, it is difficult to speak of the Party apparatus as the ruling group of society. For one thing, the variety of activities that it supervises is as diverse as society itself; and, as in any bureaucratic organization, the resulting specialization of tasks within it has tended to dilute its coherence as an institution. For example, provincial Party leaders (first secretaries), the most numerous category of officials within the Central Committee, are well known to be advocates of investment in their regions and frequently lock horns over the distribution of scarce

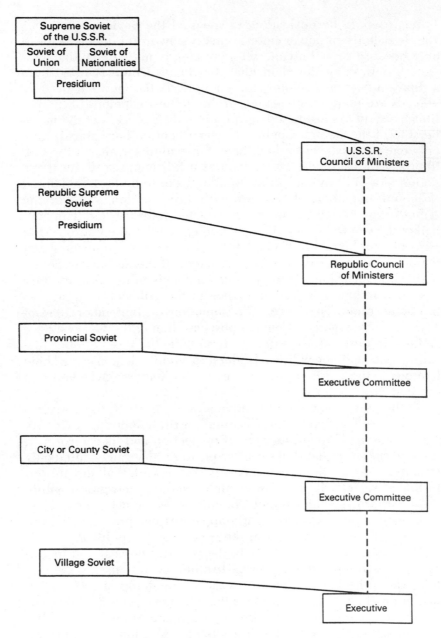

Fig. 1. Structure of the Communist Party of the Soviet Union. (Source for Figs. 1 and 2: John T. Hazard, *The Soviet System of Government*, 5th ed., Univ. of Chicago Press, 1980, pp. 244–45.)

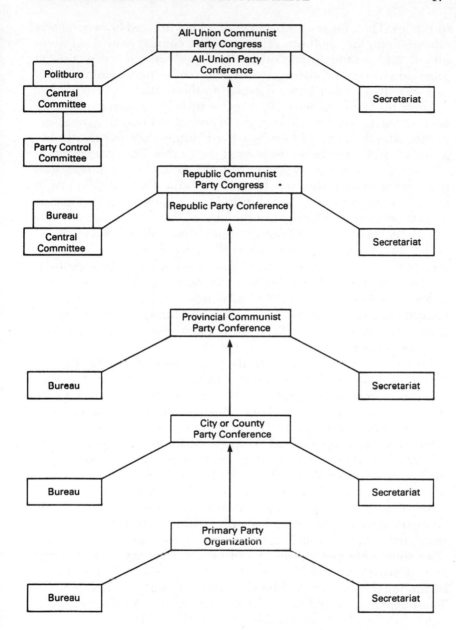

Fig. 2. Structure of the Soviet governmental apparatus.

resources. Thus, for years a major conflict has brewed between Party officials from the southern regions of the country and those from Siberia and central Russia over plans to reverse the direction of Siberian rivers, now flowing north into the Arctic Ocean, in order to deal with a vexing water shortage in the south.

Since the performance of Party officials is judged, in part, on the basis of the success of the regions or industries that they oversee, in the natural course of fulfilling their duties they frequently become advocates for these interests at the center. The specialization of tasks within the Party apparatus and in all Soviet institutions tends to fragment institutional loyalties. Typically, individual Party officials ally themselves with individual planners and ministers against other such clusters of officials. At the same time, officials within the same occupational grouping (the military, for instance, or the Party apparatus) often find that the logic of bureaucratic politics impels them to take stands against one another despite their common backgrounds, professions, or points of hierarchical subordination. As a result, political alliances usually cut across large institutions rather than follow institutional lines, and the Party apparatus becomes an arena for conflict rather than simply an instrument of control.

Moreover, the Party apparatus itself is a hierarchical organization whose members differ enormously in their powers and prestige. The lowly Party secretary of a factory can hardly be compared with the head of a department of the Party's central Secretariat, who might bear responsibility for all heavy industry in the country. Nor is the power of a Party official always superior to that of government officials. The powers of a minister or of the director of a large factory, for instance, dwarf those of the Party secretary of a small rural district. And even the highest Party officials are not immune to removal from office. In just one year (March 1985 to March 1986) approximately one-quarter of all provincial Party first secretaries were removed from office as part of a major purge.

In short, although the sources of power in Soviet politics reside in control over institutions, the distribution of power does not follow institutional lines but is rather hierarchical, fluid, and situational. These features are reflections of the concentration of power in the hands of officials at the top. The core of the leadership's authority derives from the system of the *nomenklatura*, mentioned above. Its existence guarantees to the Politburo and to the members of its executive Secretariat (often the same officials) the power to assign whomever they want to the senior posts in the most important institutions of Soviet society, just as their appointees have the power in turn either to make or to veto appointments to the remaining

important positions. The *nomenklatura* system prevents Soviet politics from giving birth to self-conscious and assertive classes even
while it inhibits the growth of pluralism outside of narrow bureaucratic limits. It provides that hierarchical discipline that is an essential element of any bureaucratic organization.

There is no "new class" in the Soviet Union, no ruling or power
elite, no one amalgam of interests that dominates the political system. Collective action by the elite in pursuit of its common interests
has been weak, and the discipline of hierarchy is such as to rein in
the power of both the elite and institutional groups. But this does
not mean that individual members of the elite and high-ranking
bureaucrats cannot be influential figures in their own right. As far
as we know, the Soviet Union is routinely governed by numerous
state commissions and committees dealing with specific policy areas.
There is the Defense Council, for instance, which is usually chaired
by the Party's general secretary and includes the most powerful
Party officials working in the defense area together with a number
of high-ranking military officers. Similar commissions exist for agricultural, energy, educational, and industrial policy-making as well
as in other areas. Through their participation in such commissions,
members of the elite can have an important impact on decision
making.

Nevertheless, the Soviet policymaking process is sufficiently
fragmented to ensure that all major decisions are ultimately dependent on the will of the political leadership. The power of individual members of the elite, as opposed to the power of individual
members of the leadership, is largely confined to their narrow spheres
of occupational specialization. Soviet experts on Soviet-American
relations would not attempt to influence agricultural policies, for
example, just as officials from the Ministry of Health would have
little influence over nuclear weapons policies. In either case, the
key to the influence of members of the elite lies in their access to—
and persuasiveness with—the political leadership.

The post-Stalin period has witnessed two major transformations
in the character of Soviet leadership positions: the first was from a
personal dictatorship (Stalin's) to a competitive oligarchy; the second was from this competitive oligarchy to a self-sustaining one.
Despite Khrushchev's efforts to rule single-handedly, Soviet leadership in his time resembled more a Hobbesian war of all against
all than a personal dictatorship. As part of this incessant struggle,
24 members of the Politburo were removed for political reasons
during the 11 years when Khrushchev was head of the Party, while

only one died in office. By contrast, during the 18 years in which
Brezhnev headed the Party only nine Politburo members were removed for political reasons and five died in office. The Politburo
increasingly resembled a closed club of lifelong members, a self-
contained social group with a sense of cohesian. The goals of group
maintenance and survival gradually replaced individual ambitions
for dictatorial power.

This stability within the ruling group has been upset, however,
as a new generation of leaders has risen to power. The removal of
three Politburo members closely associated with Brezhnev, following Mikhail Gorbachev's accession in 1985, raised the possibility
that the stability and cohesion that had characterized Soviet leadership politics over the previous 20 years was beginning to break
down. Leadership politics in the Soviet Union, it may be, will come
to resemble the patterns of the Khrushchev era more than those of
Brezhnev's time.

Yet, oligarchical as it has become, the Soviet leadership is not—
and never has been—a mere collection of political equals. At this
writing, the Politburo is divided into 12 full and seven candidate
members (a difference in status connected with voting rights but
whose full import is not entirely known). As in all small groups,
some members of the Politburo are undoubtedly more influential
than others. But since its meetings are held in strict secrecy, we
know little about the actual dynamics of power within the leadership beyond the glimpses that Kremlinologists are occasionally able
to provide through meticulous—and often speculative—analysis.
The Politburo is a self-selecting group that coopts new members
when it sees fit. Thus, not only has the size of the body varied
considerably over time, but the values and outlook of the Soviet
leadership are likely to be self-perpetuating.

The dominance of the Politburo in the policymaking process has
occasionally been questioned by Western observers for the simple
reason that the Soviet leadership is not able to shape its society
entirely on command. But such a mechanistic notion of power would
distort the reality of any political system, since it implies that dominant relationships cannot exist unless domination is total. In fact,
the power of the Soviet leadership, while confined by no legal
limits, and considerable though it is, is subject to informal constraints. For one thing, bureaucracies are often inefficient, and bureaucratic inertia is one of the most outstanding characteristics of
the system through which the Soviet leadership must work. For
another, Soviet leaders, as do political leaders elsewhere, rely on
the information at their disposal in making decisions, and bureau-

crats worldwide have been known to utilize this dependency to their advantage. Finally, Soviet society is often less malleable than Soviet leaders would like it to be, a point that is borne out in nearly every chapter of this book.

Almost all students of the Soviet Union agree that Soviet politics is essentially bureaucratic politics. The Soviet system has frequently been compared to a General Motors writ large or to a single, enormous state bureaucracy. But there is a great variety of arrangements that fall under the heading of bureaucracy. Just as both prisons and libraries qualify as bureaucratic organizations, so too was Stalin's political system no less bureaucratic than Khrushchev's, and Khrushchev's no less than Brezhnev's or Gorbachev's. The nature of Soviet leadership and the relationship of that leadership to the elite and to society have changed considerably over time; however, the hierarchical framework within which the Soviet political system has evolved has remained largely the same since the days of Stalin. This has been so for good reason. Bureaucracies need political leaders to set organizational goals, define organizational missions, and resolve the numerous conflicts that naturally arise within them. Such leadership can be exercised in a more or a less stringent and demanding fashion. Yet, without the strict subordination of bureaucrats to politicians, not only would political authority begin to disintegrate but the vitality of the bureaucracy itself would deteriorate as well, since administrators would be responsible to no external, higher authority for their actions. This is precisely what began to take place under Brezhnev, who chose to exercise his leadership over bureaucratic institutions in a lenient and complacent manner.

It is also in this context that one must assess the actions of post-Brezhnev Soviet leaders—and the dangers that both reform and stagnation pose for them. True reform, in the sense of far-reaching decentralization of authority, would inevitably erode the discipline on which political domination in the Soviet system rests. But in the absence of such reform, bureaucratic governance in the Soviet Union will remain too rigid to adapt to the significant challenges facing the country, a situation conducive to continued political and economic stagnation and to a crisis of effectiveness. The paradox of Soviet politics is that any significant reform would have to be initiated, approved, and implemented by the people who stand to lose the most from it—namely, the Soviet leadership and elite. In such a system, change is likely to be a difficult and protracted process.

NOTES

1. Jerry F. Hough, *The Soviet Union and Social Science Theory* (Cambridge, MA: Harvard University Press, 1977), p. 29.

2. All statistical information, unless otherwise noted, has been computed on the basis of biographies gathered from the following sources, among others: Alexander G. Rahr, *A Biographic Directory of 100 Leading Soviet Officials* (Munich: Radio Free Europe-Radio Liberty 1981); *Deputaty Verkhovnogo Soveta SSSR* (Moscow: 1959, 1962, 1966, 1970, 1974, 1979, 1984); and *Ezhegodnik Bol'shoi Sovetskoi Entsiklopedii* (Moscow: Nauka, 1966–81).

3. *Narodnoe khoziaistvo SSSR v 1984 g.* (Moscow: Statistika, 1985), pp. 7, 29; *Vestnik statistiki,* nos. 1–12, 1980; and *Partiinaia zhizn',* no. 15, August 1983, pp. 14–33.

4. Robert D. Putnam, *The Comparative Study of Political Elites* (Englewood Cliffs, NJ: Prentice-Hall, 1976), p. 122.

5. Ralf Dahrendorf, *Society and Democracy in Germany* (New York: Norton, 1967), pp. 264–65.

6. *Pravda,* February 28, 1986, p. 4.

5

Policy-making in Foreign Affairs

ALEXANDER DALLIN

The record of Soviet foreign policy in the years since the Bolshevik Revolution is replete with remarkable successes and stupendous failures—both of which are due in part to Soviet perceptions and behavior, in part to factors beyond Soviet control. For the Bolshevik leaders in 1917, foreign affairs was an acquired taste; they had not come to power expecting to engage in more or less conventional diplomacy. By the same token, the course of world affairs since 1917 has often challenged and belied the beliefs and expectations of Soviet analysts and decision makers.

There have been numerous areas of ambiguity and tension in the Soviet approach to public policy, foreign policy included. In the past, Soviet secrecy and ritual reiteration of orthodox formulas often made Soviet policy appear far more single-minded, unambiguous, and relentless than either closer inspection of the record warranted or later revelations confirmed. The very survival of the Soviet state between the two world wars in the midst of "capitalist encircle- ment," as well as the failure of revolutions abroad supported by Moscow, heightened the tension between conventional (state) and transformational (revolutionary) perspectives and impulses. Con- flicting pressures have also stemmed from the simultaneous attrac- tions of "expansion and coexistence" (to quote the title of a well- known history of Soviet foreign policy).[1] Whether Moscow stands to benefit more from supporting a stable international order or from challenging it is another issue on which Soviet experts divide. In less public fashion, moreover, they bitterly disagree among them- selves over the question of whether a unique Marxist-Leninist per- spective helps them to understand and act on the international stage or whether, in the nuclear age, a realistic foreign policy must in effect start from insights and assumptions shared with their opposite numbers in the outside world.

Over much of this century one can observe the remarkable growth not of Soviet communism but of the Soviet state. From an impoverished, inexperienced, and underdeveloped outcast in the family of nations in the 1920s it has grown to the status of a formidable superpower, one capable of projecting its power globally, of exercising effective control over a number of other polities, and of wielding considerable influence in many other areas.

Yet, the years particularly since Stalin's death in 1953 have seen contradictory trends. While there has been a fundamental shift in Soviet policy-making from a regional to a global outlook and a major increase of Soviet power, most obviously in strategic weapons, the Soviet Union has also experienced a series of strains and failures in the foreign field. These include the profound rift with China; crises in Hungary, Czechoslovakia, and Poland; the loss of potential client states, from Egypt to Indonesia, in which the Soviet Union had invested heavily; and Soviet miscalculations regarding detente with the United States. Considerably heightened professionalism and competence as well as an increasing use of experts have marked the Soviet conduct of foreign affairs since 1953; but there have also been seriously dysfunctional rigidities, inertia, bureaucratic foot-dragging, and widespread corruption throughout the political system. Soviet assertiveness and extensive involvement in the international scene have been matched by a measure of restraint. Indeed, with some glaring exceptions, the record confirms a rather pervasive Soviet proclivity to avoid high risks in foreign affairs as well as a tendency, even when apparently committed to "adventurous" behavior, ultimately to back down or shy away in crisis situations.

Similarly, the leadership has wavered between optimism and pessimism concerning the Soviet Union's prospects in world affairs. The once mandatory expectation of the inevitable collapse of capitalism has been rather consistently rejected (or at least ignored) since 1956. On the other hand, despite the difficulties and costs involved, no suggestion that Soviet control over Eastern Europe ought to be relinquished has been brought forth. The main sources of optimism have been the notion that the collapse of the colonial empires would mean the rise of new Soviet clients and the belief that the attainment of rough strategic parity with the United States would lead to political parity. But in reality the first yielded to a more modest (and more expensive) expectation that Soviet military, economic, and technical aid could win important Third World clients, a policy that was followed in turn by a considerable downgrading

of Soviet interest in and willingness to help such potential clients—
while policy toward Western Europe vacillated between unsuccessful efforts to mobilize anti-American sentiment there and a re-
lieved recognition that the Soviet bloc's most stable boundaries
were precisely those in Europe. At the same time, Soviet approaches to U.S.-Soviet relations varied from an ill-concealed desire
for global condominium to an expressed conviction that the Americans could not be dealt with.

The extension during the 1970s of Soviet influence into Angola,
Ethiopia, and South Yemen—an extension that was due, at least in
part, to American unwillingness to act forcefully after Vietnam and
Watergate—was followed by several years of stagnation both at home
and abroad. The crises in Afghanistan and Poland beginning late
in 1979, a serious slowdown of the Soviet economy, inertia in the
face of rapid technological advancement elsewhere, a spreading
malaise in Soviet society, and a senescent leadership were only a
few of the problems that faced the Kremlin. But the accession of
Mikhail Gorbachev in 1985 heralded a period of extensive change.
In the areas of foreign affairs, sophisticated new personnel and a
new dynamism were indicative of a broad effort to recapture the
initiative. The change was marked by calls for a reassessment of
previous approaches to foreign relations; by a change of rhetoric
that amounted to an effort at positive engagement with a wide array
of states and parties and international organizations, including, notably, the United States; and, first and foremost, by a number of
forthcoming and flexible proposals on nuclear weapons and arms
control. The new policy also saw Soviet efforts to improve relations
with China and Japan as well as with Western Europe, whereas
expectations in the Third World were, in effect, further reduced.

It all amounted to a remarkable change in image, to greater dynamism and more effective public relations, a combination that by
1986 had given Moscow a new edge in world affairs. Yet this success
was partly offset by a recognition that the Soviet Union was in fact
weaker than either its friends or its enemies had earlier averred and
that its economy in particular was beset by serious and long-lasting
problems. It was also vitiated by a sense that the Gorbachev leadership was facing substantial resistance at home; by a series of
accidents and incidents, such as the catastrophe at the Chernobyl
nuclear power station in 1986, which highlighted the vulnerabilities
of the Soviet system; and by doubts as to whether the new Soviet
posture and proposals were "genuine" and "sincere." Indeed, there
were obvious limits to the changes that Gorbachev was introducing.
And whatever one thought of his reforms, they were of course not

aimed at weakening the Soviet system but at making it more effective and powerful.

In retrospect, Soviet foreign policy may be seen as the pursuit
of a number of interrelated objectives in the face of complex restraints and pressures of both internal and external origin. In more
recent years, these objectives have ranged from self-preservation
and security to others whose relative priority may depend on the
expected price to be paid for their attainment. They have included,
more precisely, avoiding military conflict with the United States;
promoting the integration of Eastern Europe under Soviet auspices;
deriving benefits from stepped-up interaction with the West in science, technology, and trade; attempting to stem or forestall a rap-
prochement among China, Japan, and the West that would leave
the Soviet Union "encircled"; improving relations with the European members of NATO; pursuing arms control while continuing to
build up the Soviet armed forces; and exploiting political crises and
power vacuums in the Third World insofar as this can be done
without incurring undue costs or risks.[2] Not surprisingly, the simultaneous pursuit of these and other objectives has given rise at
times to tensions and incongruities among the component policies,
difficulties that have been heightened still further by the inconsistencies and ambiguities perceived in the behavior of other powers, especially the United States.

The record of Soviet foreign policy is rather mixed, in other
words, as are the considerations that go into making it; and it is
well to guard against oversimplification. The Soviet Union is neither a conventional imperialist state nor an old-fashioned, satiated
status-quo power. It is neither simply traditional Russia in new garb
nor a variant of the Nazi system. And while its role abroad has often
been troublesome and quarrelsome, even foolish and provocative,
whenever it comes to fundamental choices in preferences, orientations, and values, the dominant decision makers in the Soviet
Union have typically remained wedded to the primacy of domestic
over foreign affairs. Never was this more true than under Gorbachev.[3]

Time and again domestic-policy decisions in Moscow have had
foreign-policy components and implications. In fact, the course of
Soviet history suggests an inner logic in the pattern of internal and
external policy choices. Although no single formula will suffice to
explain all such instances of linkage, until recently the single most
persistent and pervasive pattern has been the dichotomy between
"left" and "right" within the communist sector of the political
spectrum.

In essence, the left in this context describes a syndrome centered on transformation, whereas the right opts for stabilization; mobilization of society and resources is found on the left, normalcy on the right; tension management on the left, consensus building on the right. Equally, a willingness to resort to militancy and, if need be, to violence is characteristic of the Soviet left, whereas a preference for incrementalism is typical of the right. The priority of politics belongs on the left, that of economics on the right. Voluntarism tends to be identified with the left, determinism with the right. Going it alone, autarky, and self-isolation are correlates of the left, alliances and interdependence correlates of the right. These are some of the components of two distinct communist tempers and outlooks, at least in their extreme, polarized manifestations.

Such a perspective helps us to understand the logic that has linked divergent Soviet views of U.S. intentions, for example, with bitter arguments over resource allocation, economic reform, military posture, and arms control. But today such a left-right yardstick—one that would connect détente abroad with greater welfare at home, or internal repression with a forward foreign policy—has become an inadequate tool. As the Soviet economy has expanded and choices are no longer so stark as they once were, Soviet policy often manages to combine left and right elements. Nor do all sources of divergence fit neatly into the left-right dichotomy outlined above, as is witnessed in the obvious center-periphery tensions in Soviet politics, regional rivalries, generational alignments, and competing patronage networks and cliques.

Indeed, there would appear to be three kinds of linkage among the seemingly discrete areas of Soviet policy: those rooted in the structural base of the Soviet polity and economy, in Soviet elite politics, and in the leaders' mind-set. The first of these is a function of the central command system and, in particular, of the centrality of decision making regarding resource allocation. Given a pool of limited resources, options respecting the procurement of weapons are bound to affect the availability of assets for agriculture, light industry, and capital construction—and vice versa. Priority given to the acquisition of foreign grain or chemical fertilizer or computer technology implies the adoption of appropriate measures to promote these objectives, along with restraint of others that might imperil them. This is not to argue that foreign-policy decisions are made strictly in terms of financial cost-benefit analyses or of economic needs. But the alternative uses of always scarce resources clearly militate for a rational coordination of domestic and foreign options consistent with an ordering of priorities.

A second source of linkage may be found in the periodic emergence of tacit, informal, or incipient coalitions among policymakers and their advisors. In this case, the pursuit of a given foreign policy may be seen to involve something in the nature of side payments in return for a consensus or deal on domestic policy, or vice versa. Here the linkage is not so much substantive or structural as political and temporary.

A third obvious source of linkage can be sought in the minds of the actors—in the Soviet case, in a psycho-ideological compulsion, rooted in the Leninist tradition, to provide a totalist, homogeneous, analytical framework for the entire domain of public policy.

All three of these sources of linkage between domestic and foreign policy may be present in Soviet decision making at any one time. Yet the evidence increasingly suggests that the specifically Leninist elements are fading in importance and that the other two complexes—the structural and the political—must be given more weight in explaining Soviet behavior in the 1980s.

More specifically, it might be said that over the past generation Soviet foreign policy has come home. The relevant changes include an increase in pragmatic learning by decision makers and those who advise them, the net effect of which, as just mentioned, has been to lessen the role of conventional Marxist-Leninist ideology; an increase in the relative weight of economic and technological pressures and constraints; a return of politics, Soviet-style, within the Soviet elite; a series of choices by policymakers that reaffirm and heighten the primacy of domestic over foreign concerns; and a better informed public that may serve as a further source of constraints on Soviet policy choices.

In other words, over the past few decades Soviet foreign policy increasingly has experienced a spillover effect from discrete decisions in other sectors—those of human rights, for example, or energy, research and development, and price changes. It has also experienced the growing technical, administrative, and intellectual complexity of foreign policy-making in the later twentieth century. And Soviet foreign policymakers have increasingly been conscious of the political, economic, and public-opinion aspects of the domestic arena in which they function.

The notion of the Soviet elite learning from experience—from both their successes and their failures—is one that deserves to be developed. Indeed, although the process often has been slow and reluctant, in the field of foreign affairs the evidence of learning is solid. With some possible exceptions, Soviet decision makers today do not take for granted the successes of communist revolutions abroad in the foreseeable future. Nor do they still assume that all communist-ruled regimes are bound to adopt similar policies or to see the world the same way. The collapse of capitalism is no longer considered inevitable. The inclusion of a "mutual hostage" posture in the SALT I treaty of 1972 marked, for the Soviet side, a recognition of interdependence that previously had been resisted. The notion that in an all-out nuclear conflict there can be no victors has made headway in Moscow—against the same sort of opposition that we have witnessed in the West. As David Holloway makes clear (chapter 11), negotiators who have dealt with their Soviet opposite numbers in arms-control talks testify to the gradual absorption by the Soviet side of "American" concepts and assumptions in the field of international security.[4]

True, such pragmatic learning has been imperfect; there have been instances of backsliding; and, in any event, the official style still requires selective adherence to conventional formulas and jargon. In fact, it might well be asked what role remains for Marxist-Leninist ideology in Soviet foreign policy-making. In a system such as the Soviet one, in which the entire society has been systematically and repeatedly subjected to the same stream of political stereotypes, many people are bound to accept their terms and underlying assumptions unthinkingly and uncritically. However, experience frequently has a way of contradicting doctrinal tenets, creating precisely the sort of ambiguities and tensions that have been alluded to above. Foreign-policy personnel are particularly prone to such pragmatic tests; by the same token, relatively few Soviet citizens have opportunities so to test their beliefs. Thus, more or less orthodox ideology can be described as at most a partial guide to perception—shaping categories and expectations and often limiting the range of the permissible. Yet the extent to which it actually functions in guiding Soviet decision making varies not only from time to time and from place to place but also from individual to individual. In short, the relevance of Marxism-Leninism in Soviet policy-making in any particular instance cannot be deduced, in the way of some Western analysts, from a generalized, aggregated, abstract discussion of either ideology or political culture.

As for the economic problems that have faced the Soviet leadership over the years, one way to try to solve them was to pursue a policy of detente with the West, which meant, in particular, departing from the Stalinist commitment to economic self-sufficiency in favor of greater interaction with the outside world, especially in trade and technology transfer. In essence, it was an attempt to remedy the chronic deficiencies of Soviet development without embarking on economic and administrative reforms that might have provoked more serious political and economic fallout, disruption, and destabilization. The policy, identified with the Brezhnev regime of the 1970s, was at best a mixed and modest success. Its alternative, which has been pursued under Gorbachev during the 1980s, is to provide some relief for the domestic scene by avoiding new commitments abroad and, where possible, new crises. Under Gorbachev, the view came to prevail that there was neither any alternative to radical reforms nor any excuse for delaying them. A program of "acceleration" and modernization of the economy was portrayed as vital both for domestic reasons and for the maintenance, if not improvement, of the Soviet Union's position in the increasingly strenuous international competition of the postindustrial era.

Politics, too, plays a special and often decisive part in Soviet policy-making. The Soviet political system, as the preceding chapter makes clear, remains highly authoritarian, with a political life marked by the tradition and mystique of unity, hierarchy, discipline, and centralization. Yet it would be a serious error to accept claims and pretense as reality and to neglect the evidence of a multitude of tensions and conflicts generated in the Soviet Union by special interest groups and lobbies; power struggles; ethnic, generational, or regional rivalries; and other antagonisms.

Even a cursory survey of Soviet history suggests that there have been significant differences, overt or otherwise, on a wide range of issues in Moscow; and differing perceptions of the international scene have remained a major source of divergent views. Differing judgments concerning the prospects for war and peace, for instance, have affected differing views over the size and composition of the Soviet armed forces. From differing assessments of opportunities abroad—and, with these, differing images of self, of the United States, and of China—flow the central set of problems often described as "strategy and tactics" in relation to the adversary. Indeed, recent internal Soviet differences over detente are but one manifestation of a persistent cleavage that reflects, at least in part, diverse Soviet tempers and temperaments, outlooks, and mind-sets.

We can accept it as fact that the Soviet Union has been firmly and lastingly committed to maximizing its power. Under Stalin this was the clear and overriding objective of state policy, pursued at enormous cost to other sectors of public (let alone private) life and economy. The methods and the mix of objectives have changed since his day, but the strong impulse toward the acquisition of power remains. Yet, the quest has at all times been constrained both by the international environment (including the lethality of contemporary weapons systems) and by the Soviet domestic scene. It was precisely this combination of the greater recalcitrance of the external world and the exceptionally heavy agenda of unresolved and seemingly intractable difficulties at home that presented the new generation of Soviet leaders with fresh challenges during the 1980s.

At the same time, it is essential not to misread the situation. Contrary to the view of some American analysts, the Soviet Union is not on the verge of either internal revolt or collapse. No more justified have been two incompatible extrapolations: on the one hand, that the Kremlin needs successes abroad (perhaps victorious little wars) to take its people's minds off their problems and to legitimize the system or, on the other hand, that Soviet domestic difficulties are so severe as to compel the Kremlin to pursue a conciliatory foreign policy and accept American terms. Historically, with regard to the first charge, it simply is not true that greater domestic weakness has stimulated greater Soviet aggressiveness; nor has Soviet domestic coverage of, say, the Afghanistan conflict portrayed it as anything like a Soviet victory. Meanwhile, the course of Gorbachev's summit meetings with President Reagan should have dispelled any notion that problems at home will compel Soviet submission to the views of a foreign adversary.

Finally, some caution is advised before accepting the tempting and well-argued formula, advanced by a leading analyst, that what we see in the Soviet Union today is the paradoxical simultaneity of internal decay and foreign expansion.[5] The alleged decay is a relative matter (and vastly overstated here), whereas foreign expansion need not be either a systemic attribute or organically linked to the difficulties at home.

Decision making in foreign affairs is a subject on which Soviet sources have been generally unhelpful. But we can be sure that, on this as on other matters of broad policy, the Politburo of the ruling Communist Party has typically had the last word. Moreover, foreign-policy items have come to occupy a growing share of the Politburo's agenda. It is here that politics at the highest level finds reflection in foreign-policy discussions and decisions: the degree of differences within the Politburo has varied considerably over the years.

In practice, the Soviet Foreign Ministry and its sizable staff have managed to maintain a considerable measure of autonomy in translating general policy guidance into specific moves and decisions. Until 1973 the foreign minister was not normally a member of the

Politburo. But in the last years of Leonid Brezhnev as well as under his first successors, Andrei Gromyko, as both foreign minister and a full member of the Politburo, had far-reaching authority to shape policy. He could also protect and promote the foreign-policy establishment in spite of its repeated failures and miscalculations.

Two significant changes took place after Mikhail Gorbachev came to power in 1985. For one thing, the Foreign Ministry saw both an extensive replacement of personnel and a departure from the increasingly rigid, unimaginative, and bureaucratic procedures and approaches of earlier years. At the same time, the appointment of Anatoly Dobrynin, the longtime Soviet ambassador to the United States, to head the International Department of the Party's Secretariat suggested that Gorbachev wished to see this agency become the main source of foreign-policy planning and expertise, something that had been lacking in the Soviet system. Some such role had been played, increasingly, by personnel in the institutes of the Soviet Academy of Sciences and by special "groups of consultants" (including academics, officials, and journalists) advising key officials.

Moscow continues to lack the equivalent of a National Security Council, however. The top-level Defense Council appears not to have a permanent staff of its own. Undoubtedly, military commanders and specialists are consulted on relevant policy matters, but it seems clear that under Gorbachev the Soviet military establishment was once again definitely subordinated to the civilian leadership. This applies to foreign policy as well.

In the years since Gorbachev's accession, the quality of Soviet diplomacy has made a quantum leap. While it is hard to assess the staff work and internal reporting, it can be said that the dynamism and flexibility of top decision makers, the imagination and daring of new initiatives, and the more successful projection of a favorable Soviet image abroad have all been striking—not least by contrast with earlier Soviet behavior in these respects. These elements create the potential for significant changes in Soviet foreign policy—provided, of course, that the constellation of internal resistance and international constraints permits them to come to fruition.

If this much is true, it suggests the need for greater sensitivity to the Soviet domestic scene on the part of foreign observers and policymakers. It suggests the need, first, for greater awareness of the likely effects of U.S. behavior and pronouncements on internal Soviet dialogues and debates and, second, for a closer study of the Soviet leadership's pronouncements and initiatives. Its proposals require testing and exploring: they cannot be written off as familiar and old; nor can they be accepted at face value. The difficulty of interpreting Soviet foreign behavior is exceeded only by the importance of getting it right.

NOTES

1. Adam B. Ulam, *Expansion and Coexistence: The History of Soviet Foreign Policy, 1917–1973* (New York: Praeger, 1974).

2. See further Joseph L. Nogee and Robert Donaldson, *Soviet Foreign Policy since World War II* (New York: Pergamon, 1984); Erik Hoffmann and Robbin Laird, eds., *The Soviet Polity in the Modern Era* (New York: Aldine, 1984); and Franklyn Griffiths, "The Sources of American Conduct: Soviet Perspectives and Their Policy Implications," *International Security* 9, no. 2 (Fall 1984), pp. 3–50.

3. See relevant essays in Seweryn Bialer, ed., *The Domestic Context of Soviet Foreign Policy* (Boulder, CO: Westview, 1981); Erik Hoffmann and Frederic J. Fleron, eds., *The Conduct of Soviet Foreign Policy* (New York: Aldine, 1980). See also Alexander Dallin and Condoleezza Rice, eds., *The Gorbachev Era* (Stanford, CA: Stanford Alumni Association, 1986); and Timothy J. Colton, *The Dilemma of Reform in the Soviet Union* (New York: Council on Foreign Relations, 1986).

4. See also Wolfgang Panofsky, "The Mutual-Hostage Relationship between America and Russia," *Foreign Affairs* 52, no. 1 (October 1978), pp. 109–18; and Raymond L. Garthoff, "SALT I: An Evaluation," *World Politics* 31, no. 1 (October 1978), pp. 1–25.

5. Seweryn Bialer, *The Soviet Paradox: External Expansion, Internal Decline* (New York: Knopf, 1986).

6

Dissent

JOSHUA RUBENSTEIN

Dissent in the Soviet Union had unexpected beginnings. Following Stalin's death in 1953 Nikita Khrushchev initiated significant reforms, as Stephen F. Cohen explains (chapter 3). But Khrushchev was removed from power in October 1964, and within a year his successors, led by Leonid Brezhnev and Aleksei Kosygin, began to reverse the process of de-Stalinization. Among other ominous developments, the writers Andrei Sinyavsky and Yuli Daniel were arrested in Moscow in September 1965 for challenging the regime's censorship controls by sending their stories to the West.

These arrests initiated a crucial series of events. Friends and supporters of Sinyavsky and Daniel organized a petition campaign on their behalf and even held a demonstration in Moscow's Pushkin Square on December 5, 1965, Soviet Constitution Day, demanding an open trial for the two writers. This was the first demonstration in defense of individual rights since Stalin's death. Sinyavsky and Daniel were convicted of "anti-Soviet agitation and propaganda" in February 1966 and sentenced to long terms of confinement in the labor camps of Mordovia, east of Moscow. Their stories, which had been published abroad under pseudonyms, were the principal evidence against them.

The trial, however, did not intimidate their supporters. Aleksandr Ginzburg assembled a history of the case, including an account of the trial, and sent it to the West; he was arrested in January 1967 and brought to trial a year later. Then Vladimir Bukovsky was arrested and tried for demonstrating against other arrests. Pavel Litvinov, a physics teacher and the grandson of Maxim Litvinov, the Soviet foreign minister from 1930 to 1939, was warned by the KGB not to distribute the transcript of Bukovsky's trial, but he did so anyway; and in August 1968 he was arrested in Red Square with six of his friends for demonstrating against the invasion of Czechoslovakia by units of the Soviet army and other Warsaw Pact forces.

Meanwhile, between 1966 and 1968 more than 1,000 Soviet citizens had signed appeals protesting the various trials, and the Soviet human-rights movement had developed its fundamental strategy: to embarrass the regime by exposing how it violated its own laws and constitutional guarantees. The regime responded cynically. During psychiatric examinations, Bukovsky insisted that organizing a demonstration or expressing criticism of the government was perfectly legal. But the psychiatrists replied: "You keep talking about the Constitution and the laws, but what normal man takes Soviet law seriously? You are living in an unreal world of your own invention; you react inadequately to the world around you." Yet the demand for legality became a principal theme of the movement. And more and more petitions and letters were sent to international agencies and to newspapers in the West, where they were often picked up by Russian-language radio stations broadcasting to the Soviet Union, making it possible for other Soviet citizens to contact their authors.[1]

The dissidents also had to devise means for circulating information internally. An unofficial journal, *A Chronicle of Current Events*, was founded in 1968 by poet and translator Natalia Gorbanevskaya. It provided a vehicle for publicizing arrests, court proceedings, and the conditions that prisoners faced in labor camps. Using the chain-letter method, Gorbanevskaya collected reports and sent issues of the journal to readers across the country. Although its editors were variously harassed, imprisoned, or forced to emigrate, more than 60 issues of the *Chronicle* managed to appear before it was suppressed altogether in the mid-1980s.[2]

For nearly two decades the human-rights movement maintained a visible presence in the Soviet Union. Its high point came in May 1976 when Yury Orlov, a specialist in high-energy physics and the design of particle accelerators, founded the Moscow Helsinki Watch Group. Orlov was responding to the fact that in August 1975, 35 countries, including the Soviet Union and the United States, had successfully concluded a Conference on Security and Cooperation in Europe. The various governments, meeting in Helsinki, Finland, signed a Final Act that included humanitarian provisions concerning the reunification of families; greater freedom of communication and contact; and a commitment, in the words of the Final Act, to respect "freedom of thought, conscience, religion or belief," to "promote and encourage the effective exercise of civil, political . . .

cultural and other rights," to accord ethnic minorities "equality before the law," and to "act in conformity" with international commitments on human rights.

Orlov understood that the agreements made in Helsinki gave dissidents a useful opportunity to test the Soviet government's sincerity. He hoped that Western governments would monitor Soviet compliance with the Final Act's human-rights provisions. In the meantime, he organized a group of Soviet citizens who would, on their own initiative, collect information about the government's behavior in this connection and send it to the other governments that had signed the Helsinki Final Act. With Orlov's help, allied groups were also established in Kiev, Vilnius, Erevan, and Tbilisi—the capitals, respectively, of the Ukrainian, Lithuanian, Armenian, and Georgian Soviet Republics. Dissident nationalists in the different republics, religious believers, Zionists, and Moscow human-rights activists were now adopting a common, coordinated approach.

It was the Moscow activists, however, who played the crucial role. They issued 200 documents[3] and sent representatives to the Baltic republics and to the Far East to collect firsthand evidence of political harassment and persecution. The most audacious of such projects was implemented by Alexander Podrabinek, a young paramedic who, in 1976, helped organize the Working Commission against the Use of Psychiatry for Political Purposes. Fourteen people involved in the 22 cases of political incarceration reported by the Working Commission during its first year were released within two months. Using the Helsinki Final Act, Podrabinek and his friends were able to marshal grass-roots resistance to the "cops in white coats."

Soviet Jews, too, were able to organize an effective movement. For decades they had experienced severe anti-Semitic discrimination. As did all religions in the Soviet Union, Judaism suffered official restrictions. By the 1960s, there were fewer than 100 synagogues, barely a handful of trained rabbis, and no operating institutions of Jewish learning. Jews in the Soviet Union are also recognized as one of the country's nationalities and so, like the Russians or the Ukrainians, are "guaranteed" under Soviet law the right to cultural and national expression. Yet while Yiddish is the official language of the Soviet Union's Jewish minority, only one magazine and very few books are published in Yiddish. The teaching of Hebrew, except to highly specialized university scholars, is not officially permitted. Also, Jews have faced discrimination at work and in school. The best universities enforce quotas against Jewish applicants, the foreign and security services are closed to them, and scientific institutions limit how far they can advance in their professions (see chapter 20 below).

Inspired by the example of the human-rights activists, who had begun to campaign openly for liberalizing Soviet society, large numbers of Jews petitioned the Soviet authorities for permission to emigrate to Israel. And when this approach produced little result, several activists adopted more direct and provocative methods. Determined to leave—or at least to create a scandal that neither Soviet officials nor the West could ignore—a group of Jewish activists based primarily in Riga, capital of the Latvian Republic, planned to hijack an airplane to Sweden.

The KGB learned of the plot and arrested 12 people at Leningrad's Smolny Airport on June 15, 1970. At the same time, the security policemen carried out scores of searches in Riga, Kharkiv, and Leningrad, confiscating material on Israel and Jewish history. Using the hijacking plot as a pretext, the authorities tried to crush the emigration movement before it gained momentum, but the strategy failed. The hijacking trial took place in December 1970, generating international publicity. When the two principal conspirators, Edward Kuznetsov and Mark Dymshits, were sentenced to death on December 24, there were immediate protests around the world. Jews began to demonstrate in the Soviet Union, and by the end of 1971 more than 14,000 had been allowed to leave the country. In 1972 and again in 1973, more than 30,000 would emigrate.[4]

The Jewish emigration movement constituted the most visible and, in Western eyes, perhaps the most easily understood expression of Soviet dissent; it also had a large and vocal constituency of supporters among Jewish communities in the West. And it achieved the most tangible results: the emigration of more than one-quarter million Soviet Jews since 1970 marks the most significant humanitarian concession that the regime has made since the release of millions of prisoners after Stalin's death.

The large-scale emigration of Soviet Jews inspired other Soviet groups. Citizens of German origin—those who had been stranded on Soviet territory after World War II, who lived in the Baltic states when they were annexed in 1940, or were descendants of the eighteenth-century Volga German settlers—began a movement to leave. In 1972, the West German government secured an agreement with the Soviet authorities that permitted between 6,000 and 8,000 people to reach West Germany every year for the rest of the decade; and by the mid-1980s, almost 70,000 ethnic Germans had left the Soviet Union. Similarly, Armenians achieved a small emigration, particularly among those from Western countries who had joined their families in Soviet Armenia after World War II. By the mid-1980s, over 15,000 Armenians had also emigrated.

The Soviet invasion of Afghanistan in December 1979 poisoned relations with the West to such an extent that the Kremlin had little to lose by handling dissent more harshly. Andrei Sakharov, the prominent scientist and dissident, was arrested just weeks after Soviet troops arrived in Kabul. The 1980 Moscow Olympics provided another occasion to purge the capital of people who might disrupt the image of a united and orderly society. By the spring of 1980, the KGB was arresting some 5–10 dissidents a week, the total including nearly 100 Christians, 100 representatives of national minorities, and scores of activists who had campaigned on behalf of workers' rights and political prisoners. In addition, several dissidents who were known abroad were compelled to emigrate, among them the worker-activist Vladimir Borisov, Yury Yarim-Agaev of the Moscow Helsinki Watch Group, author Vasily Aksyonov, and three feminists from Leningrad who had founded a feminist journal and had also called for Soviet withdrawal from Afghanistan.

The rise of Solidarity in Poland no doubt was a lesson to the Kremlin in how far dissent could go in the Soviet Union itself if it were not thoroughly suppressed. Thus on August 20, 1980, the jamming of broadcasts from the three principal Western stations—the Voice of America, the British Broadcasting Corporation, and Deutsche Welle—was resumed. (Radio Liberty has always been jammed.) These stations had not been electronically jammed since September 1973; but the success of Solidarity evidently moved the Soviet authorities to restrict the flow of news and commentary from the West.*

Thereafter, the situation of the Soviet human-rights movement grew steadily worse. Sakharov's arrest and subsequent removal to Gorky confirmed the regime's determination to prevent the flow of uncensored information to the West, since Sakharov had been a principal link between Western journalists and a broad variety of active dissidents. All members of the Working Commission against the Use of Psychiatry for Political Purposes were arrested or forced to emigrate; one of its leaders, Dr. Anatoly Koryagin, a psychiatrist who had documented the internment of healthy dissidents in mental hospitals, was sentenced in 1981 to 12 years of imprisonment and Siberian exile. The Moscow Helsinki Watch Group was also disbanded, and in 1986 its founder, Yury Orlov, having spent more than seven years in prison and exile, was expelled to the United

---

*Editor's Note: In 1987 jamming of the three stations stopped.

States in a prisoner exchange. At the same time, the Jewish emigration movement was slowed to a trickle and active "refuseniks" (applicants refused a visa to leave the country), including several Hebrew teachers, were imprisoned.

Despite such adverse developments, the Soviet human-rights movement continues to collect information and to alert the world to the Kremlin's abuses of power. The movement's network of informants continues to exist, as evidenced by the remarkably detailed *USSR News Brief*, edited in Munich by Cronid Lubarsky, an astrophysicist and former prisoner of conscience.[5] Lubarsky bases his reports on information gathered by activists inside the Soviet Union, demonstrating the dissidents' determination to maintain channels to the West. If, in the face of heavy official intimidation, they decline to expose their identities publicly, particularly to Western correspondents in Moscow, it is clear that thousands of dissidents and their sympathizers continue to type and circulate uncensored writings, to collect money for political prisoners and their families, and quietly to document the regime's abuses. Their names remain unknown—either to Western correspondents or to the KGB.

Indeed, just as public expression of dissent does not constitute the only activity of the human-rights movement, neither is the movement the only manifestation of dissent. A dissident in the Soviet context is someone who has openly expressed disagreement with the country's official ideology or with a certain policy adopted by the authorities. As Ludmilla Alexeyeva, an early Moscow dissident and later a member of the Helsinki group, has noted, "It is important to distinguish between the *expression of disagreement* and simply *being in disagreement*." [6]

Since the 1960s, in short, many groups have emerged in the Soviet Union who oppose by nonviolent, legal means some aspect of the regime's policies. These groups have often involved far greater numbers of people than has the human-rights movement. In particular, movements for the preservation of national culture have arisen among Ukrainians, Lithuanians, Georgians, Armenians, and Estonians. As we have seen ethnic Germans in the tens and even' hundreds of thousands have applied for permission to emigrate. Religious believers, especially Baptists, Pentecostals, Seventh-Day Adventists, and Roman or Uniate Catholics have stubbornly resisted suppression of organized religious activity. Let us look at a few instances:

• Ukrainians make up the second largest nationality in the Soviet Union, numbering over 42 million people. Possessing a proud and

distinctive culture, the Ukraine has been under the political control
of Russia for more than three centuries, with only brief periods of
independence. One such period was in 1918, but it was terminated
by the Bolsheviks and followed by a prolonged interval of resistance. Another such time of internal resistance was occasioned by
events of World War II. In retaliation, the Ukraine has suffered sharp
cultural and linguistic repression.

Under the Soviet Constitution the Ukrainians—like the other
Soviet nations—have the right to a wide measure of sovereignty,
including cultural autonomy and even the right to secede from the
Union. Yet in practice they have been subjected to increasingly
militant Russification. This includes reduction in the use of Ukrainian in schools and colleges, neglect or destruction of monuments
of Ukrainian culture, and the arrest of hundreds of intellectuals
simply for their devotion to Ukrainian literature. These arrests have
often come in organized crackdowns, as in 1965 and 1972, when
the KGB rounded up scores of writers, poets, historians, and literary
critics in order to halt their efforts to preserve their people's heritage.

Ukrainian cultural figures appear to have been murdered under
mysterious circumstances. Volodymyr Ivasyuk, for example, was a
25-year-old poet and composer whose arrangements of Ukrainian
folk songs were performed at international festivals and competitions; he was even allowed to perform abroad. But he also had
conflicts with the authorities. According to issue 53 of *A Chronicle
of Current Events,* Ivasyuk refused to compose an oratorio in 1979
to commemorate the fortieth anniversary of the "reunification of
the Ukraine." (In 1939, following the Hitler-Stalin pact, the Soviet
Union occupied and annexed western Ukraine, hitherto part of Poland.) In April 1979, Ivasyuk disappeared. His body was found
hanging from a tree about three weeks later. The authorities claimed
it was a suicide.

At Ivasyuk's funeral on May 22 more than 10,000 people formed
a procession behind his casket. In June, there was a pilgrimage to
his grave. Two members of the Ukrainian Helsinki Watch Group,
Petro Sichko and his son Vasyl, spoke to the crowd, mentioning
other well-known Ukrainians, the painters Alla Horska and Rotislav
Paletsky, who had also died under mysterious circumstances. At
Vasyl Sichko's suggestion, the crowd honored the memory of these
people with a moment of silence. A month later, Petro and Vasyl
Sichko were arrested, convicted of "anti-Soviet slander," and sentenced to three years in a labor camp.

• The struggle of the Crimean Tatars to regain their homeland
has also involved large-scale dissent. In World War II, the whole
nation was accused of betraying the Soviet Union, and in a single

day more than 200,000 Tatars were taken from their homes in the Crimea and resettled in Central Asia. Most able-bodied men were actually at the front, so the deportees were mainly women, children, and the elderly. They were transported in closed trucks and cattle cars, with little food or water, for almost three weeks. Tens of thousands failed to survive the journey.[7]

To this day the Crimean Tatars are trying to return to their ancestral lands. For years they maintained an unofficial delegation in Moscow, attempting to obtain hearings with government and Party leaders. They collected more than three million signatures to various petitions, meaning that each adult Tatar has affixed his name at least ten times. But to little avail. In 1967 the Crimean Tatars were officially cleared of the charge of treason, but a large-scale return to their homeland was not permitted; the matter is still "under discussion."

• The situation in the Baltic republics, particularly Lithuania and Estonia, also deserves attention. A majority of their populations harbor strong nationalist feelings and hostility against the Russians for annexing, in 1940, their once independent states. In Lithuania, nationalist expression is linked with the Roman Catholic Church. Still ethnically homogeneous, its population of over three million is 80 percent Lithuanian and overwhelmingly Catholic. People remember how convents and monasteries were closed at the time of annexation, and several bishops died in labor camps. In the same period thousands of ordinary citizens were imprisoned, executed, or deported to Siberia for resisting the Soviet occupation. In 1980 and 1981, three Catholic priests were killed in questionable circumstances—in all three cases after articles denouncing them had appeared in the official press.

The Soviet government's concern over developments in Lithuania is understandable. Since the early 1970s over a dozen *samizdat*—"self-published" or underground—journals have circulated inside the republic. Catholic priests have been especially active, and *The Chronicle of the Lithuanian Catholic Church*, begun in 1972, has appeared over 50 times. Inspired by the Moscow, *A Chronicle of Current Events*, the Lithuanian *Chronicle* provides reliable information on religious and nationalist dissent.[8] The Lithuanian Helsinki Watch Group established personal contact with its Moscow counterpart, which helped to distribute reports of enforced Russification in Lithuania and attacks on the Catholic Church.

• Dissent in Lithuania has inspired ferment in Estonia. The Estonian Soviet Republic, with a population of about 1.5 million, has witnessed some of the largest and most spontaneous incidents of protest in the whole country, a development that has gone largely unnoticed in the West. In September 1980, the authorities banned a performance by the pop-group "Propeller" because "nationalist themes" were detected in its lyrics. In response, more than 1,000 youngsters demonstrated in a soccer stadium in Tallinn, the Estonian capital. This was followed by the expulsion of several high school seniors from their schools.

The expulsions triggered new protests. On October 1 and 3, 1980, an estimated 5,000 young people held demonstrations in four parts of the city. They carried the forbidden blue, black, and white flag of independent Estonia and shouted "More meat, fewer Russians" and "Freedom for Estonia!" More demonstrations soon followed in the coastal town of Parnu and in the university city of Tartu, where students demanded the removal of Elsa Grechkina, the first Russian ever to be appointed to the sensitive post of Estonian Minister of Education. Estonian national discontent continued to manifest itself in the 1980s.

• Numerous cases of religious dissent have also been reported from the Soviet Union. As Paul A. Lucey makes clear (chapter 27), believers continue to face severe harassment. In fact, believers constitute the largest group of Soviet prisoners of conscience known in the West. They have been harassed and arrested for printing and distributing copies of the Psalms, organizing congregations without government permission, or providing religious instruction to children. Many are imprisoned conscientious objectors who refuse to serve in the armed forces.

The Soviet human-rights movement came to the assistance of religious believers. Fundamentalist Christian groups such as the Pentecostals or Seventh-Day Adventists abhor political activity; but as their misery deepened, they realized the need to publicize their situation, to appeal to the West, and even to seek emigration. At the request of the Moscow Helsinki Watch Group, a young philosophy student spent two weeks with Pentecostal communities in the North Caucasus and in the Far East in December 1976. People stood in line to speak with her, anxious to relate their individual stories of persecution. It was evident that they regularly listened to Western radio broadcasts, a sure sign of social resistance. By the late 1970s, numerous Pentecostals had applied for exit visas, hoping to practice their religion elsewhere without harassment. Only a handful have, in fact, been permitted to leave, but their willingness to insist on their rights indicates how far the lessons of the human-rights movement had reached.

The double issue of peace and nuclear war has been revived in recent years as a prominent aspect of Soviet foreign policy. The official campaign is designed, it would seem, to improve the Soviet Union's image abroad, particularly in Western Europe. The authorities have organized rallies and set up a nationwide peace organization, using them as vehicles to oppose Western deployment of nuclear weapons and to applaud the peaceful intentions of the Kremlin.

No doubt the great majority of the Soviet population abhors the threat of war, nuclear or conventional, but the government has not permitted genuine public debate on the matter. Even Andrei Sakharov, who helped develop the Soviet hydrogen bomb and who made a significant contribution to the negotiations over the 1963 Nuclear Test Ban Treaty, has not been allowed to engage in public discussion of Soviet nuclear policy.

It therefore must have been something of an embarrassment to the government when a dozen Soviet citizens announced the founding of the Group for Establishing Trust Between the U.S.S.R. and the U.S.A. on June 4, 1982. Led by Sergei Batovrin, a young artist, the group's aim was to begin a "four-sided dialogue" in which not only the governments but the general public of the two superpowers would participate. Batovrin and his group advocated an end to nuclear testing and more contact between citizens of the two countries. They suggested that Moscow be declared a nuclear-free zone. Members of the group, including several refuseniks, stated that they were not dissidents, that their aims were identical to those professed by the Soviet government, and that any persecution of them "would only be the result of a misunderstanding."

The government reacted quickly, nonetheless. Within a week almost all of the group's members were threatened with arrest; several had their telephones disconnected; and visitors to their homes were barred entry by police and plainclothes agents. Despite this harassment, the group managed to gather support for its proposals. Within a month over 170 persons had signed their declaration, and still another support list of 70 Moscow students was confiscated.

Batovrin was arrested in August 1982 and placed in a Moscow psychiatric hospital. Under threat of electric shock treatment, he was forced to take aminazin, a strong antipsychotic drug, which made him feel weak and lethargic. But news of his incarceration reached the West, and, in the face of protests from Western peace groups, the government released him in September. In May 1983, Batovrin was permitted to leave the Soviet Union with his wife and baby daughter.

For much of the 1980s, the Group for Establishing Trust was the only organized expression of independent activity whose members were publicly identified. They circulated petitions openly and met with Western peace activists. Several members of the group who wanted to emigrate were permitted to leave. Numerous others have been severely harassed, arrested, or placed in psychiatric hospitals for observation. The KGB has even tried to deprive one member of her parental rights by placing her child in the care of the state. In spite of this kind of pressure, the group has maintained its non-partisan approach and not confronted the regime over its arms-control policies.

The Soviet government's reaction to an unofficial peace group is one example among many that it is not ready to tolerate independent political activity by its citizens. Even a group formed to defend the rights of invalids—to publicize their situation and to improve the education, training, and public-welfare assistance that they receive—has not been allowed to operate freely. Its members, too, have seen their homes ransacked and have faced the threat of arrest. The fate of the Solzehenitsyn Fund, which has aided thousands of Soviet political prisoners and their families for nearly 10 years, is another case in point.

Since the outset of the Soviet human-rights movement, when people began learning more about the labor camps, dissidents have quietly raised money to help support families and provide packages of food and clothing to political prisoners—when the latter were permitted to receive them. In 1974, following publication of *The Gulag Archipelago*, Aleksandr Solzhenitsyn pledged to the fund the worldwide royalties from his three-volume account of Stalin's labor camps. His donation soon accounted for about 70 percent of the fund's income; the remainder was donated by Soviet citizens. Expenditures exceeded $120,000 a year.

Not surprisingly, the authorities have tried to suppress this activity. Managers of the fund have been compelled to emigrate or sent to the labor camps. The KGB used the journalist Valery Repin to try to discredit the fund. Repin had managed the fund in Leningrad, but he broke down after his arrest in 1981 and confessed in court that his work for the fund made him a "thoughtless pawn" of the CIA and its efforts to obtain "military-political" secrets. He was given the minimum prison sentence of two years and three years of internal exile. Meanwhile, KGB efforts to put an end to the fund continue. Any successful effort to help political prisoners and their families reduces, however slightly, the cost of exercising one's political conscience.

Although the human-rights movement has influenced broad sectors of Soviet society, it has not been able to foster significant cooperation with ordinary workers, as Solidarity accomplished in Poland. Neither has the regime accepted as yet a dialogue with the dissidents, which was a principle hope of the activists when they began to petition the leadership in the 1960s. The dissidents offered serious proposals for addressing the country's severe economic and social problems, emphasizing the need for a more open and more democratic political system. That hope remains.

Meanwhile, responding to pressure from the West, the Soviet authorities have been willing to make significant gestures. Sakharov's wife, Elena Bonner, confined to Gorky since May 1984, was permitted to spend six months in the West in 1986 visiting relatives and receiving medical treatment. She also wrote a book during this time about their life in Gorky.[9] Even more heartening was the release in 1986 of Yury Orlov, mentioned above, and of Anatoly Shcharansky, again as part of a prisoner exchange. Shcharansky had been active in the human-rights movement; but as a Jewish refusenik he came to symbolize the desire of thousands of Jews to escape Soviet anti-Semitism.[10] Finally, at the end of 1986, Sakharov himself was allowed to return to Moscow.

Dissent is now part of the fabric of Soviet life. It was perhaps inevitable that in such a large country, with its strong literary and cultural traditions, sustained violations of human rights would generate protest. In any event, since their emergence during the mid-1960s, the dissidents have compelled the regime to remember that the Soviet Union is not as isolated as it was under Stalin. They have provided a consistent and reliable means for both the West and their fellow citizens to see and understand the reality of Soviet life.

If the Soviet authorities, even today, would like to impose the kind of silence and secrecy that Stalin so successfully achieved, the dissidents have made it impossible. They have made human rights in the Soviet Union an international issue and added such words as *samizdat* and *gulag* to the world's vocabulary. Most of all, they provide an example of courage in the struggle against fear.

NOTES

1. See, e.g., Abraham Brumberg, ed., *In Quest of Justice* (New York: Praeger, 1970), pp. 105–6. For the trial of Sinyavsky and Daniel, see Max Hayward, ed., *On Trial* (New York: Harper & Row, 1966); for that of Ginzburg, see Peter Reddaway, ed., *The Trial of the Four* (New York: Viking, 1972). See also Pavel Litvinov, ed., *The Demonstration in Pushkin Square* (New York: Gambit, 1969); Natalia Gorbanevskaya, *Red Square at Noon* (New York: Penguin, 1973); and Vladimir Bukovsky, *To Build a Castle—*

My Life as a Dissenter (New York: Viking, 1979), the last of which provides a vivid account of the beginnings of the Soviet human-rights movement.

2. A compilation of the *Chronicle*'s first 11 issues was published in *Uncensored Russia: Protest and Dissent in the Soviet Union* (New York: American Heritage Press, 1972); individual issues, translated into English by Amnesty International, are available from Routledge Journals, 9 Park Street, Boston MA 02108; from 1974 the *Chronicle* has been published in English by Khronika Press, 508 Eighth Avenue, New York, NY 10018.

3. Many are available, in English, from the Helsinki Commission on Security and Cooperation in Europe, U.S. House of Representatives, House Annex #2/Room 237, Washington, DC 20515.

4. Kuznetsov and Dymshits were later sentenced to 15 years' imprisonment and in 1979 were sent to the West along with three other Soviet political prisoners, in exchange for two convicted Soviet spies. On the early years of the Jewish emigration movement, see Leonard Schroeter, *The Last Exodus* (Seattle, WA: University of Washington Press, 1979).

5. The journal is available through Cahiers du Samizdat asbl, Anthony de Meeus, 48 rue du Lac, Bruxelles 1050, Belgium.

6. Alexeyeva's book, *Soviet Dissent: Contemporary Movements for National, Religious and Human Rights* (Middletown, CT: Wesleyan University Press, 1985), is a comprehensive account of organized dissent in the Soviet Union.

7. Alexander Nekrich, *The Punished Peoples* (New York: Norton, 1978), is an account of these events by a distinguished Soviet historian who now lives in the West.

8. Copies available, in English, from the Lithuanian Roman Catholic Priests League of America, 351 Highland Boulevard, Brooklyn, NY 11207.

9. Elena Bonner, *Alone Together* (New York: Knopf, 1986).

10. See Martin Gilbert, *Shcharansky, Hero of Our Time* (New York: Viking, 1986), for an account of his case and efforts to gain his release.

7

The KGB

JOHN E. CARLSON

The term "the KGB"—*Komitet Gosudarstvennoi Bezopasnosti,* or Committee for State Security—comes up frequently in these pages, as it does in virtually any book on the Soviet Union. Indeed, if we are to understand the Soviet system and Soviet society as they are today it is important to understand what the KGB is. But our curiosity in this instance cannot, of course, be fully satisfied.

Recent years have witnessed the defection to the West of a number of KGB agents as well as the arrival of rather more Soviet citizens who had suffered at the KGB's hands. To be sure, the testimony of both former agents and former victims—testimony that is often, by its nature, unverifiable—has enhanced Western appreciation of the KGB's significance particularly in two areas: Soviet covert operations abroad and the suppression of dissent at home.[1] Yet nothing like a clear picture of its overall organization and range of activities is available—in part, obviously, because of the clandestine nature of some of those activities, and in part because of the habitual secretiveness of Soviet officialdom in matters large or small (itself a function, at least in part, of the continuing official cover-up of past abuses of power). Moreover, while Soviet scholars have been prohibited, not surprisingly, from freely working in this field, their Western counterparts, less understandably, "have devoted scant attention to the KGB. . . . There have been no serious attempts to assess its impact on the Soviet political process," an American specialist has observed, "or to examine its role in Soviet society."[2]

Still, there can be no doubt that the KGB is an important institution in the Soviet Union and one without parallel in the West. Its uniformed armed forces alone number as many as 250,000 men, the largest component of whom, the Border Troops (including the Maritime

Border Troops, or coast guard), are estimated to total about 200,000: their olive-drab uniforms with green flashings are seen at passport control by every visitor to the country. The Signal Troops are responsible for all high-level communications in the Soviet Union, while soldiers of the KGB's special guard units, with their bright blue flashings, are on duty in all important government and Party buildings and at monuments such as the Lenin Mausoleum in Red Square. The KGB troops see to the security and secrecy of Soviet military research and production and to the handling and storage of nuclear weapons. These uniformed forces should not be confused with the Internal Troops of the Ministry of the Interior, which number another 250,000 or more and are considered the ultimate bulwark of the regime. Similarly, the regular police of the Soviet Union—the "militia"—come under the ministry's control, although the latter appears to have close ties with the KGB as a result of personal links at the top and repeated campaigns against official corruption.

But it is the KGB's plainclothes forces, engaged in the work of foreign intelligence, domestic counterintelligence, and internal security, that raise the most questions. And here, numbers are still harder to come by; even former KGB officers have said that they could not make meaningful estimates because the organization is compartmentalized into so many different directorates, services, and departments, each largely or wholly ignorant of the other's activities.

In 1973 two Western intelligence services estimated that the KGB then employed about 90,000 career officers and another 400,000 technicians, secretaries, clerks, security and border guards, and special troops. Since, as was just noted, the latter total perhaps 250,000, this would leave about 150,000 technical and clerical workers, a number that has no doubt grown. Other sources suggest that the total of KGB operatives (officers and auxiliaries) deployed abroad is over 250,000; that the total of all KGB officers, agents, and informants working within the country is roughly 1.5 million; and that the KGB's total annual budget is anywhere from $6 billion to $12 billion.

We might compare these figures, to gain some perspective, with those concerning the respective U.S. agencies. In 1986 the Federal Bureau of Investigation employed about 23,000 people (about 10,000 special agents, the remainder support personnel) and its annual budget was nearly $2 billion.[3] The FBI is responsible for enforcing a wide variety of Federal laws in the United States, including those relating to internal security and counterintelligence; and its resources in this respect are clearly inferior to those of the KGB. On the other hand, the KGB's evident mandate in the field of internal security and counterintelligence is obviously much broader than that of the FBI, a fact that, in itself, points to a fundamental difference between the two countries.

The field of foreign intelligence is another matter, however. Between 1975 and 1985 the overall annual intelligence budget of the United States apparently tripled, to about $25 billion, a total that includes appropriations for the Central Intelligence Agency, the National Security Agency (in charge of spy satellites, code-breaking, etc.), and the various military intelligence services. (In the Soviet system the functions of the NSA and the CIA fall under direct KGB purview, as we will see, whereas those of military intelligence do not.) Further information is nearly as hard to obtain in the American case as it is in the Soviet. But basing his inferences on both confidential interviews and published sources, one student of the matter concluded in 1984 that U.S. intelligence agencies employed more than 150,000 people, primarily in technical surveillance (electronic eavesdropping and communications intercepts as well as photoreconnaissance), with the result that the United States had "surrounded its perceived enemies, notably the Soviet Union, with a vast electronic eavesdropping web whose size, complexity, and thoroughness remain unmatched in the history of espionage."[4]

Nevertheless, the suggested analogy between American and Soviet foreign-intelligence efforts should not be carried too far. For one thing, apart from its much greater reliance on technical rather than direct human means of gathering data, the U.S. side is manifestly not engaged in a clandestine campaign to acquire Soviet technology. Equally, it does not enjoy the opportunities for covertly influencing policymakers or public opinion in the largely closed society of the Soviet Union that the Soviet side exploits in the largely open society of the United States. Nor does any single U.S. government agency active in the security and intelligence fields exercise anything like the degree and range of authority wielded by the KGB. In fact, from its relatively modest beginnings under Lenin (as the *Cheka*) through its years as the instrument of Stalin's terror and its consequent decline under Nikita Khrushchev,[5] the KGB emerged in the 1980s as one of the main power blocs in the Soviet Union, rivaling in this respect the military establishment and even the Party bureaucracy.

As for its internal organization, the KGB appears to be divided into the five main directorates of "the Center" in Moscow, which are subdivided in turn into an undetermined number of directorates, services, and departments. The First Main Directorate conducts KGB operations abroad through dozens of "residencies" located in the regular Soviet embassies, consulates, and trade missions; the Second Main Directorate is responsible for counterintelligence and internal security; the name of the Border Troops Directorate speaks for itself; the Fifth Main Directorate is charged with eliminating overt manifestations of dissent and with infiltrating religious, ethnic, and other potentially dissident groups; and the Eighth Main Directorate is responsible for communications security and signals intelligence. Other independent directorates include the Third Directorate, whose agents closely watch the armed forces from the General Staff down to company level; the Seventh Directorate, with more than 3,000 personnel engaged in internal surveillance; and the Ninth Directorate, which safeguards the leadership and sensitive installations. Each of the main directorates and perhaps some of their subdivisions maintain their own intensive training programs and special schools. Departments of the KGB also run an extensive network of prisons and labor camps.

We know most about the KGB's First Main Directorate—the CIA of the Soviet Union. It includes a Directorate S, whose job it is to select, train, and plant Soviet illegals in countries throughout the world and to recruit foreign nationals as spies; a Directorate T, the second largest, responsible for collecting scientific and technical intelligence in the industrialized countries in cooperation with the Soviet State Committee on Science and Technology and the Soviet Academy of Sciences; and a Directorate K, which tries to penetrate foreign intelligence and security services, maintains security at Soviet embassies, and watches all Soviet citizens abroad.

Its Service I—the third largest division of the KGB's First Main Directorate and the one responsible for analyzing all of the intelligence that the latter collects—produces, among other things, a daily summary of foreign affairs for the Politburo and regularly submits forecasts of world developments. Its Service A—now called the Active Measures Service but formerly the Disinformation Department—drafts plans for a wide range of covert activities abroad, including disguised propaganda and disinformation, forgery, subversion, and sabotage; it is thought to have a Moscow staff of about 300 people and to make use of as many as 15,000 more (journalists, academics, officials and experts of one kind or another, and ordinary Soviet citizens).[6] Service R continuously analyzes in detail all of the KGB's foreign operations with a view to improving them. Founded in the 1970s, it was modeled on what was believed to be a similar division of the CIA.

Among the First Main Directorate's 18 or so operational departments, organized both geographically (to cover specific areas of the world) and functionally (e.g., for technical support), one, the Eleventh Department, conducts liaison with and penetrates the intelligence services of the Soviet-bloc countries while another, the First Department, runs agents in the United States and Canada. In 1986 the FBI was monitoring some 300 Soviet intelligence agents among the 900 or so Soviet citizens stationed in diplomatic missions in the United States. In addition, the FBI acknowledged that a large number of KGB illegals were living for the most part undetected in the United States and that hundreds, indeed thousands more of Soviet and Soviet-bloc diplomats, commercial representatives, journalists, and others legally resident in the country were probably reporting to the KGB from time to time.

There is a good deal of evidence, in short, that KGB operations abroad are both extensive and increasingly sophisticated. But the success of these operations—whether measured in terms of the Soviet investment of time, personnel, and money or in terms of the results of similar operations mounted by foreign governments against the Soviet Union—is another question. At the same time, Western media reports, often quite alarmist in tone, manage to suggest a record of KGB incompetence, bungling, and plain bad luck in this respect. Between 1970 and 1986, for example, some 500 Soviet officials, all of them positively identified as agents of either the KGB or Soviet military intelligence, were publicly expelled from various countries for their involvement in espionage or subversive activities, while as many as 300 more appear to have been quietly sent home on similar grounds. These figures do not speak well for KGB methods. Moreover, the aggregate cost of such expulsions includes the loss of experienced officers who cannot easily be used in the West again, the need for extreme caution in using agents who may be under surveillance, and the psychological as well as bureaucratic problems entailed in reintegrating expellees from highly desirable assignments in the West into service at home, often in dismal internal security jobs in the Soviet provinces.

KGB defectors were mentioned above. In just one period of two years (1984–86), at least nine senior KGB officers defected to the West. Evidently the most valuable of these was Oleg G. Gordievsky, who at the time of his defection (September 1985) was officially a counsellor of the Soviet embassy in London but actually the chief of the local KGB residency. Gordievsky had reported to British intelligence for 15 years, and his defection broke up the Soviet espionage network both in Britain and in Scandinavia, where he had previously served. He also provided President Reagan with important briefings for his Geneva summit meeting in November 1985 with General Secretary Gorbachev. Moreover, it was later revealed that, having returned to Moscow on orders in the summer of 1985 only to find himself under KGB suspicion, Gordievsky was promptly "exfiltrated" from the Soviet capital by Western agents. In contrast, only one CIA affiliate is known to have defected to the Soviet Union (also in September 1985): Edward L. Howard, a former trainee who was fired by the CIA in 1983 and had been under investigation for possible Soviet connections. Howard's defection led to the arrest of several U.S. Soviet spies in Moscow, including one of the Soviet Union's top aviation-design experts with access to top-secret defense information.

Nor do recent Soviet successes in attracting U.S. spies appear to have been much more than a matter of luck. In the case of the Navy spy ring involving the brothers John and Arthur Walker and their accomplice Jerry Whitworth, who were arrested and then convicted of espionage in 1985–86, it seems that the Americans approached the Soviet side and that their motive was simple greed. That the KGB considered this to have been the most important operation in its history, as was reported at the trial, is a reflection less of the KGB's competence than of the value of the information regarding U.S. naval communications that had fallen into its hands. Much the same can be said, evidently, in the case of Ronald W. Pelton, the former NSA employee who was arrested and convicted at about the same time. Pelton's trial revealed, moreover, that NSA had penetrated the highest levels of Soviet military communications. Indeed, FBI and CIA officials agree that most Americans who spy for the Soviet side are volunteers, not KGB recruits.

The KGB's role in a greatly stepped-up Soviet effort to acquire Western high technology is also much discussed. In 1983 Western intelligence experts were saying that a "technology procurement campaign" was now the primary task of the KGB abroad and that several thousand technology-collection officers, armed with precise shopping lists, were at work under various legal covers; it was thought that as many as 100 such officers were based at the Soviet embassy in Tokyo alone. The effort was said to be very successful. As a result of either direct KGB espionage or illegal trade diversions—that is, the purchase of sensitive, embargoed, or export-controlled equipment through dummy corporations in the West for eventual transfer to the Soviet Union—technology of great monetary and strategic value had been obtained.[7]

But again, a cautionary note is in order. According to a September 1985 U.S. Defense Department report on Soviet acquisition of Western technology, a report based in part on hundreds of internal Soviet documents secretly turned over to the French government, the Soviet Union "obtains 6,000 to 10,000 pieces of equipment and 100,000 documents every year, about one-fourth of them either secret or restricted by export controls."[8] In other words, three-fourths of the Western technology acquired by the Soviet Union is obtained from open sources and by legal means. In fact, the FBI more recently estimated that 90 percent of all U.S. intelligence acquired by the KGB comes from open—that is, public—sources.[9]

It is rather the role of the KGB at home, difficult though it is to assess, that merits for it a chapter of this book. And here, the sheer ubiquity of this crucial component of the Soviet system must be stressed: the fact that a KGB detachment is covertly assigned to watch from within every sizable group or enterprise in the country, from units of the armed forces as small as a company, to factories, schools, hospitals, and even movie studios and athletic teams. It is as if an FBI agent were routinely attached to the Chicago Bears football team—as a physician, say, or an assistant coach—in order to check constantly on their political beliefs, patriotism, and fulfillment of production quotas.

"The KGB, of course, is everywhere in Russia . . . a feared and fearful organization," wrote a British newspaper correspondent, Michael Binyon, after completing a four-year assignment to Moscow in 1982. But ironically, Binyon also observed, this does not mean that the KGB "does not attract some of the brightest talent or number among its members the most urbane, intelligent and sophisticated officials, the kind of people I found stimulating and worthwhile talking to because only they had the self-assurance and authority to speak frankly—or reasonably frankly—and drop the mumbo-jumbo of propaganda cliches." The point is echoed by a leading American correspondent, Serge Schmemann: "Westerners living in Moscow have often noted that the most outspoken, best-informed and least inhibited of their contacts are frequently people reputed to be KGB officials." Indeed, as Schmemann reports, "it is a career that has much to attract a Russian—membership in an elite group, access to information, relative freedom to voice opinions, foreign travel, money, all served up as patriotic duty." And the fact that its officers include some of the most competent members of Soviet society partly accounts, he suggests, for the KGB's influence.[10]

The emergence of a new type of competent, sophisticated, even cordial—if still potentially deadly—KGB officer might be thought to reflect a kind of maturing of the Soviet system as a whole. Much of the credit here seems to belong to the late Yury Andropov, head of the KGB from 1967 to 1982 and then, until his death in February 1984, the top leader of the Soviet Union.

As head of the KGB Andropov accelerated the effort to improve its image that had begun in the earlier 1960s. KGB agents—often called *Chekisty,* after the original *Cheka* of Lenin's time—were given increased attention in the Soviet press and a rash of memoirs, biographies, documentaries, and semifictional thrillers began to appear glorifying them and their exploits. In 1984 a new television series, "TASS is Authorized to State," began, with top Soviet actors depicting a battle of wits between the KGB and the CIA in an imaginary African country. Based on a best-selling novel of 1979, the series projected the image of clean-cut young agents led by a wise and decent KGB general defending progressive humanity from the blackmail, seduction, murder, and other machinations of the CIA. Soon an annual competition was announced to encourage more such books, films, and television shows; the winning entry in 1985 was an hour-long documentary about Andropov himself, many of whose scenes, according to the film's credits, came from the KGB's archives. Andropov was portrayed as an intellectual who wrote poetry, sang in a fine baritone, and kept a large library at his country house.

Andropov is also credited with creating the KGB's notorious Fifth Main Directorate—the "dissident" or "ideological" Directorate discussed above—and with institutionalizing, as a method of dealing with particularly stubborn dissidents, the perversion of psychiatry in the Soviet Union. Without denying the force of the latter charge (it led to the Soviet delegation's virtual expulsion from the World Psychiatric Association in 1983), the reality, viewed from within, is perhaps somewhat more complex. Walter Reich, an American psychiatrist, studied Soviet psychiatry for many years, using such means as personal examination of Soviet émigrés who back home had been diagnosed as mentally ill. And on the basis of his studies Dr. Reich concluded that although in some cases Soviet dissidents were hospitalized as a result of deliberate misdiagnosis (and then variously abused in treatment), in some cases the subjects *were* mentally ill: "Dissent is, after all, a marginal activity in the Soviet Union, with its highly repressive political system, and the margins of any society contain a disproportionately high number of people with mental illnesses." [11] One could only add that, like a study of the KGB itself (or of the laws under which dissidents are arrested), a study of Soviet psychiatry in this connection reveals how profoundly different Soviet society is from Western society.

More to the point now, under Andropov KGB representation in the leading organs of Party and state grew steadily. In 1978 its official status was changed from that of the Committee for State Security "under" the Council of Ministers to that of the Committee for State Security of the Soviet Union, which meant that its head automatically became a member of the Council of Ministers—the body that governs (under close Party supervision) the Soviet Union. Meanwhile, Andropov himself had assumed the rank of full army general and, in 1973, of full member of the Party Politburo, thus cementing his position as one of the country's top dozen or so leaders, a position from which he launched his successful bid for the job of Party general secretary.

Since Andropov's tenure as head of the KGB and then as the Soviet Union's top leader, and owing much, it is thought, to his influence, career KGB officers have openly assumed an unprecedented number of powerful offices. The most prominent of such officers include the current head of the KGB, Viktor Chebrikov, who is also a full member of the ruling Politburo, and Geidar Aliev, a longtime former KGB official (1941–69) from Azerbaidzhan who is both a full member of the Politburo and the First Deputy Prime Minister of the Soviet Union. Moreover, the head of the KGB in each of the Soviet Union's 15 constituent republics is a member of that republic's Party executive bureau (or local politburo).

Will the KGB's enormous power be used to facilitate a wide-ranging reform of the Soviet system, one that would entail sharp restrictions on its own role? Or will the KGB work to frustrate real reform, perceiving it as a fundamental threat to established authority, its own included? At this writing it is impossible to tell.

NOTES

1. For examples of the former, see Aleksei Myagkov, *Inside the KGB* (New Rochelle, NY: Arlington House, 1978; also Ballantine Books, 1981) (Myagkov, a KGB captain on duty with the Soviet army in East Germany, defected to the British in Berlin in 1974); or the testimony of Stanislav Levchenko, a KGB major operating in Tokyo when he defected to U.S. officials in 1979, in *Soviet Active Measures: Hearings before the Permanent Select Committee on Intelligence, House of Representatives* (Washington, DC: U.S. Government Printing Office, 1982), pp. 137–69. For accounts by various of its victims of KGB harassment, see the works cited in chap. 6 (esp. nn. 1, 6, 9, 10).

2. Amy W. Knight, "The Powers of the Soviet KGB," *Survey: A Journal of East and West Studies* (Summer 1980), p. 138. See also the same author's "The KGB's Special Departments in the Soviet Armed Forces," *Orbis* (Summer 1984), pp. 257–80 and "Soviet Politics and the KGB-MVD [= KGB– Ministry of the Interior] Relationship," *Soviet Union* 11, no. 2 (1984), pp. 157–81. Knight's book-length study of the KGB should appear shortly. Meanwhile, Jeffrey Richelson, *Sword and Shield: The Soviet Intelligence and Security Apparatus* (Cambridge, MA: Ballinger, 1986), is a sparse factual outline, while Brian Freemantle, *KGB: Inside the World's Largest Intelligence Network* (New York: Holt, Reinhart & Winston, 1984), and John Barron, *KGB Today: The Hidden Hand* (New York: Reader's Digest Press, 1983), are sensationalist in tone and concerned almost exclusively with KGB operations abroad.

3. *Committee on Appropriations, U.S. Senate, Hearings before the Subcommittee on State, Justice . . . and Related Agencies* (Washington, DC: U.S. Government Printing Office, 1986), pt. 2, p. 314.

4. Ernest Volkman, *Warriors of the Night: Spies, Soldiers, and American Intelligence* (New York: Morrow, 1985), pp. 13–20, 162.

5. On the history of the KGB, see George Leggett, *The Cheka: Lenin's Political Police* (Oxford and New York: Oxford University Press, 1981); Simon Wolin and Robert M. Slusser, *The Soviet Secret Police* (New York: Praeger, 1957); David J. Dallin, *Soviet Espionage* (New Haven, CT: Yale University Press, 1955); and Ronald Hingley, *The Russian Secret Police* (London: Hutchinson, 1970; New York: Simon & Schuster, 1971).

6. See Richard H. Schultz and Roy Godson, *Dezinformatsia: Active Measures in Soviet Strategy* (Oxford and McLean, VA: Pergamon, 1984).

7. *New York Times* (July 25, 1983), pp. 1, 5. See also Linda Melvern, Nick Anning, and David Hebditch, *Techno-Bandits* (Boston: Houghton Mifflin, 1984).

8. *New York Times* (Sept. 19, 1985), p. 7.

9. *U.S. News & World Report* (Sept. 15, 1986), p. 27. The FBI made the same estimate in 1981: see Richelson, p. 120.

10. Michael Binyon, *Life in Russia* (New York: Pantheon, 1983), p. 11; Serge Schmemann, "To a Russian, KGB Offers a Taste of the Good Life," *New York Times* "Week in Review" (Sept. 22, 1985), p. 2.

11. Walter Reich, "The World of Soviet Psychiatry," *New York Times Magazine* (Jan. 30, 1983), pp. 20–27. See also Sidney Bloch and Peter Reddaway, *Soviet Psychiatric Abuse* (London: Gollanz, 1984; Boulder, CO: Westview, 1985).

THE ARMED
FORCES

The expansion and continual updating of the Soviet armed forces over the last 20 years and more has been justified by Soviet leaders largely in terms of national defense. The Soviet armed forces, they have said, are designed to defend the Soviet Union if it is attacked, to hold the "socialist camp" together (the so-called Brezhnev doctrine), and to support Third World struggles of "national liberation" (when it suits Soviet purposes). In particular, the Soviet buildup in nuclear weapons has been justified (since 1977) as necessary first to achieve and then to maintain strategic parity with the United States—a relationship more often known in the West as mutual deterrence or mutual assured destruction (MAD).

The authors of the four chapters that follow are concerned to study this aspect of contemporary Soviet reality, as best it can be done, in a spirit of sober realism, eschewing both the alarmist hyperbole and the facile optimism that infect so much Western comment on this matter. David R. Jones discusses the overall organization and deployment of the Soviet armed forces, concluding that they are sufficient for the defense of the Soviet Union but not much more—given Western, especially U.S., retaliatory power. In the next chapter Mikhail Tsypkin warns against exaggerating either the deficiencies or the strengths of the basic "human factor" in question: the Soviet servicemen, most of whom are short-term conscripts. And Eugenia Osgood points out, in the third of these chapters, that Soviet strategic thought has yet to absorb the doctrine of parity—that indeed the Soviet military establishment still has no clearly enunciated nuclear strategy.

Lastly, David Holloway urges that particularly in recent years the Soviet leadership has sought arms control primarily as a means of both regulating—always on the basis of parity—the strategic relationship with the United States and preventing the nuclear competition from leading to nuclear war. But given the formidable obstacles in the way of reaching significant new agreements even on this basis, the future of arms control, as we go to press, is far from clear.

8

Organization and Deployment

DAVID R. JONES

Wars and the preparation for war have always been central to Russian life. In large part this simply reflects Russia's geographical position. Situated in the midst of the great Eurasian plain, the Russians have no natural frontiers to offer them either protection from attack or hindrance to their expansion east to the Pacific, south to the Black Sea and the Caucasus, or west to the Baltic and Europe. The causes of this expansion are too complex for analysis here. Yet we should note that the Russians have suffered from recurring, deep-rooted, and often justified fears of invasion; these fears, in turn, help explain why maintenance of a military establishment that is capable of ensuring the security of the state has always been among their governments' highest priorities.

The Soviet armed forces retain the essential characteristics of the national mass armies, based on conscription, that grew up in nineteenth-century Europe and took root in Russia thanks to the conscription law of 1874. In short, they depend on a skeleton of regular cadres of long-service professionals fleshed out by annual levies of conscripts in peacetime and by a call-up of reservists in case of war. At present, conscription in the Soviet Union is carried out in accord with the Law on Universal Military Obligation, which is further discussed in the following chapter. All 18-year-old males are considered eligible to serve, and some 76–80 percent are conscripted annually. In 1985 the armed forces probably totaled some 5,300,000 uniformed personnel, including 615,000 railroad and construction troops and 705,000 command and support personnel. At least another 600,000 served in the internal troops of the Ministry of the Interior and the KGB's border units.[1]

Following a conscript's term of service, which normally is two years (three in the Navy and Border Guards), he is assigned to the reserves, there to remain until the age of 50. Thus, theoretically the Soviet Union has some 25 million reservists. But although all are required to attend refresher courses, Western analysts generally agree that only those who have been on active service during the last five years (in 1985–86, about 5,400,000) have any military value.

Apart from those in the frontier or internal formations, all other Soviet military and naval personnel serve under the aegis of the Ministry of Defense. Depending on his experience and qualifications, a conscript will be assigned either to one of the five main combat arms or to one of the ministry's support branches—the Troops of the Rear, Civil Defense, Railroad, Construction, and so on. The latter frequently are involved in work that is not strictly military. As Marshal D. F. Ustinov, the late defense minister, pointed out in 1982:

> A considerable amount of housing and large numbers of buildings used as facilities for social and cultural service are built by military construction workers. A number of important economic projects have been built with their participation as well, and they have aided in the construction of thousands of kilometers of hard-surfaced roads. Railway workers [troops] are involved in the building of a number of rail lines and are at work on the eastern section of the Baikal-Amur Railroad. Soviet military personnel make an active contribution to the harvesting of our country's crops and in performing other tasks for the economy.[2]

Although such functions have considerable value in the Soviet government's view, the armed forces' primary mission is to be ready to wage war in defense of the "fatherland." This is the immediate task of the five regular service arms: the Strategic Rocket Forces, the Ground Forces, the Air Defense Forces, the Air Forces, and the Navy. Soviet sources almost always list them in this order, which reflects their importance in Soviet strategic doctrine. Recently, however, there have been some indications that the Strategic Rocket Forces are losing points to the Ground Forces as a result of the renewed interest of Marshal N. V. Ogarkov and other theoreticans in the growing potential represented by precision-guided conventional armaments. In any case, before looking at these services in greater detail, an examination of the military's command and administrative system is in order.

Soviet sources are very closemouthed when discussing any aspect of defense, including policy-making and the institutional framework through which policy is implemented. Nevertheless, Western ana-

lysts can discern the system's general outlines, even while disa-
greeing on the exact competence or membership of a given agency.
If, for example, Soviet accounts of developments tend to overplay
the "leading role" of the Communist Party in this as in other areas
of Soviet life, they do provide a useful distinction between the "leadership of the country's defense" and the "leadership of the armed
forces."

The first form of leadership takes as its sphere the whole complex
of policies that determine the Soviet Union's defense posture: those
relating to arms production, the preparation of the civilian population for military service (and for mobilization, if necessary), the
basic organization of the armed forces, and the overall focus of
ideological indoctrination. Meanwhile, the second type of leadership is more narrowly concerned with the practical implementation
of such policies in the armed forces themselves, with the details of
military planning, troop organization and training, weapons acquisition, and so forth. It is therefore more military—and less political—
in the professional sense. But if the first realm of leadership is
obviously superior in authority, the input of the second on most
military questions is such that it remains fully involved in the policy-
making process.

Major decisions about defense almost always seem to be made
by the Politburo of the Party, given executive action through the
Party's Secretariat, and simply ratified by its Central Committee,
the periodic Party congresses, and all other Party and state organs.
So the Politburo has the final word on major matters of defense and
military policy. Yet, in large measure, the Politburo's role consists
of accepting, rejecting, or modifying the proposals and recommendations of the two defense leaderships, whose agencies in turn
implement the broader policies. For this reason the latter also play
a vital part in determining those policies, even if the Politburo—
and, through it, the Party—retains the final word.

More precisely, the supreme "leadership of the country's defense" today is vested in the Defense Council of the Soviet Union,
about which little is known. Indeed, although rumors of its existence began circulating in the West late in the 1960s, the Soviet
press confirmed the fact only in 1976, when Leonid Brezhnev was
identified as the council's chairman. Its existence was then formally
sanctioned by the new Soviet Constitution of 1977. In May 1983
Marshal Ustinov confirmed in *Pravda* that Yury Andropov had replaced Brezhnev as the council's chairman, and since him Konstantin Chernenko and Mikhail Gorbachev, in their role as the Party
leaders, have held this position. Otherwise, the council appears to

include the most important members of the Politburo, the head of the KGB, and senior military officials. The successor to such earlier bodies as Stalin's all-powerful Committee of State Defense of World War II, the Defense Council's peacetime role seems confined to examining all major military questions with the aim of making recommendations to the Politburo. Programs for developing and procuring new weapons systems seem to be of prime concern, as does the definition of each of the five service arms' basic mission with reference to overall strategic planning.

The more circumscribed "leadership of the armed forces" is vested in the highest body of the Ministry of Defense, usually known either as the Collegium of the Ministry or as its Main Military Council. It is chaired by the defense minister, who has powers roughly comparable to those of the U.S. secretary of defense and chairman of the Joint Chiefs of Staff combined. Other presumed members include the head of the Main Political Administration, the commanders of the five services (each of whom is a deputy minister of defense), other branch chiefs and deputy ministers, the chief of the General Staff, the commander-in-chief of the Warsaw Pact, and possibly the commanders of the newly established Theaters of Military Operations (TVDS). The Main Military Council's responsibilities include resolving most professional issues that touch on the "development of the armed forces" proper, as Soviet sources put it; the adjudication of major professional rivalries; and the settlement of interservice disputes over the assignment of missions, funds, economic capacity, and manpower. Framing as it does various proposals that will then move up to the Defense Council and on to the Politburo, it also has a major role in resolving just how the latter's decisions will be implemented.

The second agency of the Ministry of Defense intimately involved in leading the armed forces is the General Staff. Modeled on its Imperial Russian predecessor—and thus to some extent on the pre-1914 German General Staff—this body has no U.S. equivalent. It is responsible for basic strategic planning and for working out proper roles for each of the five services. It has 10 subordinate directorates of which the three most important handle intelligence, organization-mobilization, and operations. For the most part, the General Staff is run by officers who have completed courses at its Voroshilov Academy. Since it is responsible for coordinating the work of the main staffs of the services and branches, these latter bodies can be considered subordinate to the ministry through the General Staff. Other important directorates are concerned with "military science" (that is, the further development of military theory), the Warsaw Pact, and, recently, military-assistance programs abroad. Since the 1960s the General Staff has also played a major role in introducing cybernetics and automated systems of planning and command into the Soviet military, and it took the lead in the revision of Soviet doctrine carried out since 1976 by Marshals V. G. Kulikov and Ogarkov (see below).

At roughly the same administrative level as the General Staff but outside the Ministry of Defense in the governmental hierarchy is the Military-Industrial Commission. Despite some opinion to the contrary, it appears unlikely that the commission is directly connected with the Defense Council. At any rate, it is headed by a deputy chairman of the Council of Ministers, and other members probably include representatives from the nine Ministries of Defense Industry, from the State Planning Commission *(Gosplan)*, from the Party, and from the Ministry of Defense and its General Staff. The Military-Industrial Commission deals with technical problems related to the armed forces' requirements for armaments and matérial, with ensuring that sufficient resources are available to meet production targets, and with coordinating the delivery of new equipment with the military's schedules for its introduction. Thus the commission is an essential link between the military establishment and its industrial rear.

The Ministry of Defense itself, then, includes the General Staff and its directorates, the Main Political Administration, the individual commands of the five service arms, and various agencies for administering support services. Of these last, the most important are the Inspectorate and those that manage the Services of the Rear, Armaments, Construction and Quarters, and Personnel. All of these agencies are headed by deputy ministers, who are probably members of the ministry's Collegium or Main Military Council as well. The same is true of the commanders-in-chief of the five individual service arms. But between the commanders and the defense minister stand (1986) the three more senior first deputy ministers: Marshal S. F. Akhromeev, chief of the General Staff; Colonel General A. D. Lizichev, head of the Main Political Administration; and Marshal V. G. Kulikov, commander-in-chief of the Warsaw Pact. Below the remaining deputy ministers are the heads of the lesser directorates—those for highways, tactical rockets and artillery, inventions, military-educational institutions, civilian military training, military bands, and so on. Many of these lesser section chiefs have no seat in the ministry's Collegium, though they may be involved in its discussions if the topic is relevant to their sphere of responsibilities.

One major institutional component of the ministry deserves special comment: the anachronistically labeled Main Political Administration, the chief means by which the Party's Central Committee
guides and controls political indoctrination within the armed forces.
This agency's significance is underlined by the fact that as well as
being a part of the Defense Ministry, it is a department of the Central
Committee, which gives it dual representation. In addition to Lizichev as head, its leading officials include his assistant chief for
Komsomol (Communist Youth League), the secretary of the Party
Commission, the head of the Party-Organization Administration,
and that of the Administration for Agitation and Propaganda. Apart
from indoctrination through its network of political officers (or "deputy commanders for political affairs"), the Main Political Administration is responsible for troop morale and for maintaining the
armed forces' "ideological purity." All in all, this agency is the
conduit for Party control and influence over the rest of the military
establishment at every level. Moreover, since 1960 it has been considered a "collegial" institution that is empowered to issue its own
directives. These directives sometimes require the signature of the
minister of defense as well, but those concerning routine activities
are signed by its head alone. And since all of the Defense Ministry's
leading figures are Party members who frequently hold seats in
both the Central Committee and the Supreme Soviet, the Party's
control of the armed forces is assured.[3]

The central institutions just enumerated are all "collegial" in
nature, which in Soviet parlance means that they are "organs of
collective leadership." To varying degrees this same pattern is rep-
licated in the high commands of each of the five services, in the
military and air defense districts, in the fleets, and probably in the
recently created TVDs. Each is headed by a commander and his
"military council" of deputy commanders, the appropriate political
officer, and sometimes other major figures as well. Theoretically,
this and the other councils "discuss and resolve" major questions
by a majority vote. But in practice they are mainly deliberative,
since the commander-in-chief's position easily allows him to achieve
a consensus.

The doctrinal revision mentioned above has resulted in greater
attention being paid to the operational level of any future war, to
the potential represented by modern conventional systems, to the
increased significance of battles in a conflict's first phase, and to
the wider geographical scope of operations conducted in these conditions. Under Marshals Kulikov and Ogarkov, the General Staff's
planners have devised the concept of "strategic operations." Even

though they may be purely conventional in nature, these operations are expected to have a far-reaching and possibly even decisive impact on a war's outcome. To conduct them, an operational level of command has been created in the form of TVDs, which evidently exist, at least in skeletal form, even in peacetime. Thus, Ogarkov left his position as head of the General Staff in September 1984 to take charge of a Western TVD, and at least four other TVDs (the Northwestern, Far Eastern, Southwestern, and Southern) have apparently also been formed. So, too, may a skeleton Headquarters of the Supreme Command (*Stavka VKG*), although most Western experts consider this unlikely.

With the outbreak of hostilities, this system should convert smoothly into a hierarchy for guiding the armed forces at both the strategic and operational levels. The Defense Council would probably expand in membership and undertake the overall strategic direction of the war and supervise the mobilization of the home front. Military directives as such would be issued by the *Stavka VGK*, which would probably comprise the Defense Ministry's Collegium and employ the relevant sections of the existing General Staff as its executive and operational arm. Unity of front and rear would be guaranteed by the fact that both bodies are directly subordinated to the Party's General Secretary. *Stavka*'s directives to the TVD commands or to specially created commands for operations in a particular "strategic direction" (or axis of attack) would then pass to the Fronts. The latter typically would contain a tank and two combined-armed armies as well as support units, giving it a total establishment of some six tank and eight motorized-rifle divisions.

Let us now examine each service arm in the order of its official ranking.

• The Strategic Rocket Forces were founded in 1959 and are still shrouded in great secrecy. This service includes all medium- and long-range ground-based nuclear-armed missiles—that is, all such systems with ranges over 1,000 kilometers. In the 1960s Soviet military doctrine assigned this force the decisive role in the waging of any future war; but, as mentioned earlier, recent doctrinal developments suggest that this role—and hence the service's status—are being downgraded in favor of the Ground Forces and high-tech, precision-guided conventional armaments.

Commanded by Army General Yu. P. Maksimov, the Strategic Rocket Forces are staffed by some 300,000 military personnel, who may be backed by an additional 50,000 civilians. Those assigned to this premier service constitute an elite. For example, officer recruits must be certified as suitable by the local military commissariat (the induction agency), a procedure not followed by the other four service arms. Such recruits then follow a five-year course at one of the service's four Higher Military Schools before being commissioned. Active personnel serve in six rocket armies, each of which is subdivided into divisions, regiments, battalions, and batteries, with one launcher assigned to each battery. Operational control is achieved through some 300 launch-control headquarters that normally carry out orders issued by the Strategic Rocket Forces' own command and military council. Such operational orders, however, presumably would be sent from the Defense Council to the Strategic Rocket Forces through the General Staff, which could by-pass the Strategic Rocket Forces' command center if necessary. It is possible that any operational push of the button would require KGB sanction as well. Otherwise, the Strategic Rocket Forces control the Soviet Union's three missile-testing grounds and play a major role in the space program.

The International Institute for Strategic Studies in London estimates that in 1985 the Strategic Rocket Forces controlled 1,398 strategic ICBMs, of which 308 are the feared "heavy" SS-18s, carrying some 8–10 warheads each. The Strategic Rocket Forces also were in charge of some 543 intermediate- and medium-range missiles, of which 423 were thought to be deployed in the western part of the country (the most significant of these missiles is the much discussed mobile SS-20, each of which carries three warheads). In the West it is often overlooked that, unlike the United States, Britain, or France, who presumably have only one potential enemy, the Soviet Union has to deal with the strategic forces of all three and to counter a small but growing Chinese capability as well. Having achieved parity with the United States in strategic systems, the Soviet leaders undoubtedly count on their SS-20s to overcome the lesser but much closer threats along their extensive frontiers.

• Although ranking second in official protocol, the Ground Forces continue, through their senior commanders, to dominate the upper echelons of the Soviet Ministry of Defense. This service, headed by Army General E. F. Ivanovskii, is also the largest of the five. In mid-1985 his forces numbered an estimated 1,995,000, of whom as many as 1,400,000 were conscripts. They were enrolled in 51 tank, 141 motorized-rifle, 7 airborne and 8 air-assault (aeromobile) brigades and 16 artillery divisions, as well as in a number of smaller, independent units. Recent reports have also mentioned the creation of two combined-arms formations, each approximately the size of a corps. With some 450 tanks and 600 armored personnel carriers each, these would seem ideally suited to fit the role of the much-heralded "operational maneuver groups" that many believe would act as independent, roving forward detachments at the theater level in the "deep battle" that is now envisaged in strategic operations.

Not all of these divisions are kept at anything like their full strength. In fact, three categories of readiness exist. Category I—in which a unit maintains its full complement of equipment and 75–100 percent of its manpower and can be brought up to full strength in 24 hours—includes the 27 divisions stationed with the four groups of Soviet Forces in East Germany, Poland, Czechoslovakia, and Hungary as well as all airborne divisions and air-assault brigades. About 20 percent of the 68 divisions stationed in the western Soviet Union are maintained at either this or the second (Category II) level of readiness—a full complement of combat vehicles and 50–75 percent of required personnel, with three days required for full mobilization. The rest of the Ground Forces, including the bulk of those deployed in the central, southern, and eastern regions, are in Category III. This means that they function with only 20 percent of their manpower; and even if they have all of their vehicles, some are bound to be obsolescent. These divisions would require eight to nine weeks to be brought up to full strength.

The Soviet Ground Forces have seemingly vast stocks of equipment available: an estimated 52,600 tanks; 70,000 armored personnel carriers, scout cars, and other vehicles; and some 33,000 guns, mortars, multiple-rocket launchers, and antitank weapons, including some 4,700 self-propelled guns and 1,500 nuclear-capable surface-to-surface tactical missile launchers. Yet, in many instances, these numbers reflect the Soviet habit of retaining equipment withdrawn from service during modernization programs, much of which is obsolescent if not obsolete. Thus, the core of any Soviet armor thrust to the West would consist of T-64, T-72, and T-80 main battle tanks—of which a total of 19,100 exist. Indeed, the Western TVD as such has a total of only 13,000 tanks of all types for action on the Central European front. Similarly, as SS-21, SS-22 and SS-23 tactical missiles replace the older Frogs, Scuds, and SS-12s, the latter presumably will be mothballed. This does not make them suitable for immediate use, especially given the slack standards of much Soviet maintenance. As noted above, many reports suggest that much military equipment, especially that found in Category III divisions, is out of date. The same may be true of many of the divisions in the other two categories (particularly those in Category II) that are stationed outside of Eastern Europe, except for those in Afghanistan.

The Soviet leadership continues to modernize the Ground Forces and to prepare them for all possible eventualities. For example, units are being trained to operate in an environment of nuclear-chemical-biological warfare, and equipment is being designed for such use. Changes in Soviet tank design, as well as the growing use of automated or computerized command and control systems, have also been observed. Revised conceptions of the scale of combined operations have led to the formation of units of "army aviation" (helicopters and possibly light aircraft), 16 special artillery divisions for use at the front, and other specialized units. Presumably the programs in the Ground Forces' Higher Military Schools are being altered to train officers capable of employing the new techniques.

Even so, many problems persist. Apart from uncertain morale, obsolete equipment, shortages, and slack maintenance, there is concern with a lack of initiative among subordinate and junior commanders. These factors make any calculations regarding the Ground Forces' effectiveness difficult for Western and Soviet experts alike.

• This observation is equally applicable to the Air Defense Forces. Charged with protecting the homeland against enemy air attack, this service is also responsible for research in ballistic-missile and "antispace" defense. The last, however, was publicly exempted from its responsibilities in the late 1970s, to be relegated to the category of "foreign" concept as part of the Soviet Union's campaign for a treaty banning the stationing of "strike weapons" in space. The American "Star Wars" program has led to an intensification of this campaign, but in fact Soviet fears of American prowess in space date from the U.S. Space Shuttle program.

In any case, the arm's commander-in-chief presumably has charge of the remaining 32 Galosh-B antiballistic missile launchers stationed at eight sites around Moscow and of the development of new defense systems, consisting of missiles, antisatellite interceptors, laser systems, or some form of "beam weapons." Although a new system is replacing Galosh, the threat posed by the enemy's aerodynamic means of delivery—aircraft, cruise missiles or a combination of the two—remains the chief concern. The continuing vulnerability of the Soviet Union to airborne attack seems to have been a factor in the General Staff's rather gloomy assessment of the "correlation of forces" in the mid-1970s.

In 1985 the Air Defense Forces contained an estimated 635,000 men in three main branches: the radio-electronics (radar) troops, the surface-to-air missile (SAM) troops, and the air interceptor forces. The first branch mans the approximately 7,000 early-warning, ground-controlled intercept and antimissile radars, which in turn control the operations of both the interceptors and the SAMs. In all, the SAM forces include some 9,600 strategic defensive launchers (with 14,000 launcher rails) at 1,200 fixed sites within the country. These are backed by 4,300 tactical launchers (in some 440 units) as well as by the antiaircraft guns of the Ground Forces.

Major organizational changes have been introduced into this service since 1978, but their full significance remains unclear. Some Western experts have contended that the Air Defense Forces have become mainly a SAM service, with their interceptors transferred to a reformed tactical air service. In this view, the Soviets' aim was to increase the offensive weight of their air power for the expanded combined-armed battles envisaged in the strategic operations mentioned above. But the continued deployment and development of mission-specific interceptors (the MIG-29 Fulcrum and MIG-31 Foxhound) suggest that a more purely defensive air mission still exists for today's Air Defense Forces. Moreover, the new American tactic of low-level penetration by means of air-launched cruise missiles, along with the demonstrated weaknesses of Soviet SAMs and interceptors at such low levels, suggest that the reorganization reflects serious concern about the Air Defense Forces' ability to meet the challenges of the 1980s.

Further, the Air Defense Forces still lack an efficient airborne warning and control system (AWACS). Whereas American experts consider that a minimum of 50 of these aircraft is required, in 1985 the Soviet Union still fielded only nine obsolescent TU-126 Moss and four IL-76 Mainstay AWACS aircraft. Worse still, Soviet technological backwardness in general (in microcircuits and other important areas) indicates that in spite of high levels of expenditure the Air Defense Forces will be unable to close the gap successfully—and thus counter an aerial onslaught against the Soviet Union—within the forseeable future.

• The Soviet Air Forces also consist of three branches: Frontal (tactical) Aviation, Military-Transport Aviation, and the Long-Range Air Force. Together they numbered about 570,000 men in 1985. Frontal Aviation's mission is to provide direct support to the Ground Forces. It is organized into 17 air forces or armies. One each is attached to 12 of the 16 military districts, to the four groups of Soviet Forces in Eastern Europe, to the forces in Outer Mongolia, and to the contingent in Afghanistan. Although tactical aviation has lost some helicopters and light aircraft to the new army aviation units, it has gained fighters from the Air Defense Forces and can count on more direct operational support from that service arm's interceptors (and vice versa). In 1985 the Frontal Aviation nonetheless had its own, slowly modernizing inventory of 2,650 attack helicopters, 2,360 fighters, 2,350 fighter/ground-attack planes, 590 reconnaissance/electronic-warfare aircraft, and 1,000 trainers.

Because of the Soviet Union's poor highway system, limited railway network, and vast area, Military Transport Aviation is vital in moving troops about the country and in supporting clients abroad. With 65,000 men in 1985, it was, except for some independent regiments, organized into five divisions of three regiments each. It has only 600 aircraft, but in case of war it can count on Aeroflot's 1,400 medium and heavy transport-passenger aircraft as well as some 1,250 transports assigned to the other services.

The role and status of the Soviet bomber forces are not clear. Long- and medium-range units still exist, and the development of a new strategic bomber, known to NATO as the Blackjack or Ram-P, shows that the Soviet military value their service. But although Colonel General (Aviation) V. V. Reshetnikov appears in the press as a deputy commander-in-chief of the air forces, he no longer is specified as chief of the Long-Range Air Force. Even so, in 1985 he undoubtedly commanded the estimated 1,680 aircraft (including 170 long-, 500 medium-, and 450 short-range bombers) that, according to Western analysts, are now divided into five air armies. Yet the operational command of these forces is obscure: it is just possible, in the light of some hints dropped by the Soviet press, that Moscow has decided to consolidate all its strategic weapons—missiles, bombers and ballistic-missile submarines—into a single strategic command.

• The growth of the Soviet Navy since the early 1960s has been so pronounced that many in the West consider the Soviet Union a maritime superpower. Apart from the usual administrative and educational networks (including five regular and five specialist officer schools), in 1985 the Navy comprised 77 ballistic-missile submarines (63 nuclear and 14 diesel), 66 cruise-missile submarines (49 nuclear and 17 diesel), 203 attack submarines (72 nuclear and 131 diesel), 102 submarines used in other roles, the 875 combat aircraft and 310 helicopters of the Navy's aviation branch, 289 major and

700 minor surface combatants, 79 ships and 99 other craft for amphibious warfare, 305 auxiliaries, 60 intelligence-collection vessels,
and 495 oceanographic and research ships. Some 14,000 coastal
artillery and missile troops, with 100 Sepal surface-to-surface
launchers, form a division that protects bases and other vital points
under naval command. In addition, there are 16,000 marines in five
regiments, and four Special Forces *(Spetsnaz)* brigades. These forces
total some 480,000 men, of whom about 75 percent are short-term
conscripts.

In 1985 the Navy had an additional 23 major surface combatants
and numerous small surface combatants mothballed as reserves,
and in a crisis it can press the extensive Soviet merchant marine
into auxiliary service. Its forces soon will be upgraded further with
three to four new Typhoon nuclear-missile submarines, one large
carrier, two cruisers, eight destroyers, and a number of frigates and
corvettes, as well as other vessels. Since these ships are generally
more powerful and efficient than the earlier models that they replace, the overall number of major surface combatants in the Soviet
Navy may drop from 294 in 1981 to roughly 250 by 1990. The
expansion of the surface fleet may also be hindered by the fact
that the commander-in-chief since 1985 is a vocal submariner lacking the personal political influence that seems to have aided his
predecessor, Admiral S. G. Gorshkov, who took charge of the Navy
in 1956.

Apart from the smaller vessels in the Caspian Flotilla, the Navy's
resources are divided among four fleets. Excluding ballistic-missile
submarines, 143 ships were assigned (1985) to the Northern Fleet,
39 to the Baltic Fleet, 34 to the Black Sea Fleet, and 88 to the Pacific
Fleet. The Northern Fleet had one of the three aircraft carriers, and
the Pacific Fleet had two. As for major surface combatants, the
distribution was 74 in the Northern Fleet, 46 in the Baltic Fleet,
74 in the Black Sea Fleet, and 81 in the Pacific Fleet. The last of
these fleet had the strongest amphibious capability, and overall it
and the Northern Fleet were the two strongest. However, the Baltic
Fleet, ranked fourth, is structured to play an important role in any
European conflict.

Such forces are obviously sufficient to protect Soviet home waters
and, if little risk is involved, to support diplomatic goals abroad.
Clearly, Moscow is aware of the possible benefits accruing from the
latter option. Thus, although the buildup of the 1960s and 1970s
was probably a response to the U.S. Polaris missile program, today's
Soviet Navy seeks to maintain, as Gorshkov once pointed out, other,

more general "state interests." By 1981 an average of 140 warships
were forward deployed on any given day, a figure that by 1985 had
risen to between 165 and 180.

Still, the Soviet leadership has shown no willingness to commit
these forces, even diplomatically, in any situation of real danger.
For, as well as the usual caution, considerable doubt remains as to
the Soviet Navy's likely effectiveness in any future conflict with
Western forces. Soviet sailors get less sea-time than do their American counterparts; their fleets are much less experienced in under-
way replenishment than NATO's; and, in recent years, a number of
embarrassing incidents—a mutiny in the Baltic, a nuclear-armed
submarine run aground in neutral Swedish waters, another sunk in
the Atlantic, and a string of accidents with other, nuclear-powered
submarines around the world—raise questions about both morale
and performance. Soviet submarines are noisier than their Western
counterparts and Soviet antisubmarine-warfare capabilities are much
less developed. These factors may help explain why Moscow maintains fewer submarines on regular station in a nuclear-response role
than does the United States.

The quality of any state's armed forces depends largely on that
of their equipment and training. With respect to the former, the
Soviet armed forces have been moving away from technically sim-
pler but generally reliable weapons to more sophisticated ones. Yet,
because of complicated problems of maintenance, their new tanks,
like their new aircraft, have lower readiness levels and in general
remain inferior to their Western counterparts. In some ways, indeed,
the Soviets have obtained the worst of both worlds.

As for the quality of the enlisted personnel, problems of discipline have been referred to above, and the training of the conscripts
is dealt with in the following chapter. It is worth stressing that any
preconscription military training available in the Soviet Union is at
best of very limited value and that the military value of perhaps 80
percent of the reservists—those who have been out of service more
than a few years—is even more dubious.

The Soviet armed forces continue to be plagued by shortages of
both long-service and noncommissioned officers, who are the back-
bone of any military system. Yet the majority of officers have received good education and training in the extensive network of
Higher Military Schools, and senior commanders are usually graduates of at least one of the 17 military academies—of which the
Voroshilov Academy of the General Staff, the Frunze Military Acad-

emy, and the Lenin Military-Political Academy are the most prestigious; it is their professors and graduates who produce most of
the major Soviet works on military doctrine and science, tactics,
history, and military-political themes.

One of the greatest problems facing the Soviet leadership derives
from the demographic trends discussed elsewhere in this book
(Chapter 26). Although the army has always served as a means of
indoctrinating and assimilating non-Russians and especially non-
Slavs, the Russians and their Slavic neighbors have formed the overall majority of the Soviet armed forces' manpower. But the Kremlin
currently faces the dilemma of, on the one hand, a decreasing pool
of young men for use in the military and in industry and, on the
other hand, a rising proportion of non-Slavs within that pool. According to one U.S. estimate, the number of non-Russians among
available conscripts was to increase from 51.7 percent in 1980 to
74.7 percent by the year 2000. The picture is further complicated
by the lower educational levels of non-Russian—and especially non-
Slavic—recruits, who, if present force levels are maintained, must
be trained to use increasingly complex equipment. Given the economy's general stagnation, there are obviously no easy solutions here.

The Soviet leadership does indeed have an impressive military
machine constantly at its disposal. Under a tightly centralized command, it is capable of intervening effectively in Eastern Europe as
well as elsewhere around the Soviet periphery. Yet, in the long
view, there is nothing unprecedented about this fact. Historically,
the Russian armed forces have usually been large, have frequently
had an offensive tactical doctrine, have often required a high level
of expenditure, and have commonly inspired fear in potential enemies. The deployment of a large army near the western frontier by
Nicholas I (1825–55) is but one example reflecting these tendencies. Similarly, the combat potential of Russia's forces has been as
frequently denigrated by outsiders as it has been overestimated—
a result, often, of domestic political considerations in other countries. As usual, the truth probably is to be found somewhere in
between.

The Soviet armed forces are sufficient for the defense of the
Soviet Union—and for external expansion, when that entails little
or no risk. They are hardly sufficient to launch a strike for European
hegemony, let alone world domination. As planners of the Ministry
of Defense know full well, any such course almost certainly would
bring about the destruction of the "fatherland" that they have sworn
to protect.

NOTES

1. Figures from *The Military Balance, 1985–1986* (London: International Institute for Strategic Studies, 1985); and esp. David R. Jones, ed., *The Soviet Armed Forces Review Annual,* vol. 10 (Gulf Breeze, FL: Academic International, 1986), which draws on numerous other sources.

2. D. F. Ustinov, *Sluzhim rodine, delu Kommunizma* (Moscow: Voenizdat, 1982), p. 62 (English trans., *We Serve the Homeland and the Cause of Communism* [Washington, D.C.: JPRSL/10604, 1982], p. 47).

3. KGB supervision of the armed forces also ensures their loyalty (see chap. 7).

9

The Conscripts

MIKHAIL TSYPKIN

Relatively little attention has been paid in the West to the human dimension of the Soviet armed forces. Official Soviet sources emphasize that "no weapon or combat equipment can of themselves replace" the "moral, political, psychological and combat qualities" of a soldier. The huge Soviet military machine is based on conscription, and providing for its smooth functioning involves special arrangements within both the armed forces and Soviet society as a whole. Analysis of this "human factor" is made difficult by the biases inherent in official Soviet publications, however, as well as by the extraordinary secrecy in which the Soviets cloak their military establishment. Still, by combining information contained in official Soviet publications with the accounts of eyewitnesses, recent émigrés, and defectors and by evaluating the results on the basis of our general knowledge of Soviet society, we can form a picture of how the Soviet conscript army works.

In sheer numbers, the Soviet armed forces are impressive, as indicated in the preceding chapter. Such diverse factors as long and exposed frontiers, the need to control a vast empire, relative technological backwardness, ideology, and the experiences of World War II have resulted in an emphasis on mass in manpower.[1] This has led to a reliance on conscription. Conscription is also viewed by the Soviet leadership as an instrument for political socialization, while the abundance of military manpower provides cheap and adaptable labor that can be used on such different priority projects as construction of the Baikal-Amur Railroad and the Olympic Village in Moscow.

The 1967 Law on Universal Military Obligation, amended in 1980, not only deals with conscription but also formulates a program of "military-patriotic" training from elementary school on. Since 1967 each secondary school has hired its military instructor, and millions of school children have taken part in compulsory paramilitary exercises, including trips to battlefields of the Great Patriotic War (the Soviet name for World War II), mock fighting engagements, and visits to military units, where a show of modern weaponry is usually organized for the young guests. A visitor to the Soviet Union can observe uniformed teenagers with dummy submachine guns goose-stepping around the Great Patriotic War memorials erected in practically all major cities. The next stage of military education begins when all 17-year-old males have to show up at their borough military commissariats to receive their draft certificates, after which they are assigned to a local unit of the Volunteer Society for Cooperation with the Army, Aviation and Fleet for part-time training in the basics of their future military specialty.

It is not easy to measure the precise effect of this gigantic attempt at a "military-patriotic upbringing." One remains skeptical about the ability of this program to instill an enthusiasm for military service and self-sacrifice: much of the earlier exuberance, born of Stalin's great industrialization campaign and of victory in World War II, has been eroded by decades of unfulfilled economic promises, widespread corruption, and alcoholism. One also suspects that the pre-draft training conducted by the Volunteer Society cannot provide future draftees with the necessary military skills. For the giant scale of the undertaking ensures inefficiency, good performance is virtually unenforceable, and Soviet secretiveness guarantees that Volunteer Society classrooms are equipped with obsolete military hardware.

At the same time, the "military-patriotic" program has its positive aspects. It accustoms young people to the inevitability of military service and fortifies the lessons of obedience they receive in the highly authoritarian Soviet secondary schools.

Two other factors influence young minds here. First, the massive infusion of the "military-patriotic theme" into literature, cinematography, and the theater incessantly glorifies the Great Patriotic War and the sacrifices and victory of the Soviet people. Second, very few young people are exempt from military service, so almost every young man has the example of an older brother, older friends, or a father who was drafted. The result is that military duty is viewed by future conscripts as normal.

According to the Law on Universal Military Obligation, all 18-year-old males are liable for two years of active duty (three years in the Navy). A 1980 amendment permits exemptions in several instances: when the potential draftee is the only breadwinner for dependents incapable of working; for health reasons; for "reasons of state," which implies work in a priority branch of the defense industry; and to full-time students at a few select colleges and universities, institutions that in turn have compulsory reserve officers' training programs. There is no conscientious objector status under Soviet law.

Conscripts are usually sent thousands of miles from home. Of course, geography has some bearing here. But this policy also reflects a general effort to maintain control over the conscript force by isolating soldiers from the civilian world. Proximity to family and friends might lead to drinking and going AWOL (absent without leave). Even more important, in case of civil unrest servicemen without local roots would be more reliable for crowd-control operations. This isolation is particularly noticeable in Soviet troops stationed in the Warsaw Pact countries, where the fear of "ideological contamination" and of conflicts between the local population and unruly soldiers keeps the conscripts virtually confined to barracks throughout their term of duty.

Conscripts accept military service but usually without enthusiasm. The enlisted men's pay is negligible, usually not more than about $30 a month, and most conscripts are not interested in possible careers as noncommissioned officers. To overcome this problem, a number of formal programs and informal arrangements have been devised. Political indoctrination is an example of the former. But a necessary precondition for political indoctrination is a cutoff of unauthorized sources of information. Thus, like the great majority of Soviet citizens, servicemen have no access to nontechnical Western publications. To prevent enlisted men from listening to foreign radio broadcasts they have to surrender their radios to their noncommissioned officers, who return them on Sundays and holidays. The prohibition against listening to foreign radio broadcasts is such that even radio operators are afraid to receive anything but Soviet broadcasts.[2]

No precaution is considered excessive. Television sets in the barracks of the Group of Soviet Forces in East Germany are specially outfitted *not* to receive West German programs. Possession of such a nonpolitical Western publication as *Playboy* magazine may be viewed as a serious political offense. KGB officers are assigned to every military unit down to company level and, by developing a network of informers, can acquire compromising information about servicemen and thus considerable power over them.

Yet the effect of the political indoctrination itself is problematical. Regular sessions of political indoctrination contain repetitive harangues against U.S. imperialism or lengthy discussions of the latest Party congress, and the officers conducting the sessions are frequently ill-prepared and bored themselves. Argument is excluded as "politically subversive." The audience of young conscripts, 18 to 20 years old, are tired from the heavy training schedule, and their thoughts naturally gravitate to their homes or girlfriends. Most of them view the sessions as a convenient moment for writing a letter or taking a nap. Even enlisted men who see active participation in political work as a way to promotion and discharge with a good character reference can do no more than recite from their textbooks in order to satisfy the officers.

Moreover, the political indoctrination system often fails to provide plausible explanations of international crises that result or might result in the use of Soviet military might. Thus, at least some Soviet soldiers during the 1968 invasion of Czechoslovakia thought they were in West Germany or even in Israel.[3] During the 1968 crisis a Soviet infantry division was alerted and moved forward to the Sino-Soviet border, but its enlisted men were not told why. Similarly, neither enlisted men nor officers of a surface-to-air missile (SAM) battery alerted during the 1973 U.S.-Soviet showdown were offered any explanation of the international situation.[4]

Discipline, however, was not impaired, and therein lies the paradox of political indoctrination. By its sheer irrelevance to the conscripts' everyday life indoctrination anesthetizes their interest in politics. At the same time, because of its reiteration it imprints on their minds the image of an unreservedly aggressive outside world, an image that surfaces under combat or quasi-combat conditions.

In the early 1970s, seamen on a ship in the Baltic were ordered to stay below decks when passing through the straits near Denmark. The officers explained that they were "in capitalist waters" and could be attacked at any moment by boats spraying their ship with machine-gun fire. Having no basis for thinking otherwise, the seamen obeyed. More recently, we know from interviews with several Soviet prisoners held by the Afghan guerrillas that Soviet soldiers believed it when told that they had to fight "American and Chinese agents" in Afghanistan. In a system where political decisions are made by a small elite, political passivity combined with basic loyalty is, after all, a desirable quality in the conscript.

The ethnic diversity of draftees presents problems in managing the Soviet armed forces. In 1977, Slavs comprised about 69 percent of the draft pool, with Muslims constituting about 18 percent and other minorities about 13 percent. By the mid-1980s, the Muslim share had grown to 24 percent at the expense of the Slavic. Closely related to this development is the problem of language: Russian is the official armed forces language, yet according to some estimates about 15 percent of the current draft pool can speak it only haltingly. Other differences arise between the urban residents, who now comprise more than 60 percent of the draft pool, and the draftees from rural communities, whose educational and technical proficiencies are usually much lower. At the same time, the urbanites have more trouble adjusting to the harsh living conditions.[5]

The military has devised ways to tackle these problems. The unofficial motto of the armed forces is: "If you can't do something, we'll teach you; if you don't want to do something, we'll make you." This reflects two basic realities: a very heavy training schedule and very tight discipline, enforced by various types of punishment. An important informal arrangement here is the practice of giving enlisted men in their second year (third in the Navy) very considerable power over new conscripts (the "young ones"). While officers spend only part of the day with the enlisted men, these "old men," as they are called, who are confined to barracks with the "young ones," enforce discipline and teach them necessary skills.

An "old man" is expected to train his relief before he is discharged, particularly in the Navy, with its greater technical demands. In exchange for such services officers are usually ready to overlook the fact that "old men" often exploit and habitually abuse the "young ones." The abuse ranges from practical jokes and discriminatory treatment in matters of food to extortion of new uniforms and money. The arrangement works because the "old men" are a highly cohesive group ready to protect their privileges against the disunited "young ones," who find consolation in knowing that, if they behave, they will in time become "old men" themselves.

The Soviet approach to training conscripts is characterized by repetitiveness and a heavy load of classes and exercises as well as by narrow specialization and compartmentalization. Soviet military writers ritualistically call for more "initiative" on the part of servicemen, but "initiative" actually means the more precise implementation of orders and regulations—the main requirement of the Soviet enlisted man. The result of such training is well described by a former Soviet seaman: "We were drilled and drilled and drilled, relentlessly. . . . I could undoubtedly do my job, even now, five years later, in my sleep."

This approach to combat training, like the Soviet military's approach to political indoctrination, is reflected in the training of enlisted men for combat under conditions of nuclear (as well as chemical and biological) warfare: servicemen operate their equipment while wearing gas masks and protective coveralls; radioactive decontamination is practiced; and officers are taught to evaluate the possible effects of nuclear blasts on their units or ships in various circumstances. But any discussion of nuclear issues is narrowed to the presumed essentials of survival and implementation of orders at a given level of the military establishment. This "need to know" approach, based on a very narrow definition of responsibilities, is another indication that questions of nuclear strategy are discussed only by those immediately involved in strategic planning. It is also typical of the compartmentalization of decision making and of Soviet secretiveness. Servicemen go through the motions of training for nuclear war but have very little interest in matters over which they have no influence and that they cannot even discuss—not an unwelcome result, obviously, from the point of view of the Soviet military command.

Officers and noncommissioned officers have a whole array of punishments at their disposal to enforce strict discipline. Assignment of extra duties or deprivation of Sunday leaves (these are not granted automatically) are usual for such minor transgressions as a poorly made bed, irregularity in uniform, and attempting to argue with a superior. More serious offenses, such as drinking, rudeness to superiors, or going AWOL for less than 24 hours can be punished by up to 15 days in the guardhouse. Conditions there are usually harsh: it is often cold; there is no stool or chair; the prisoner has to stand for 18 hours a day (his bed is folded up and bolted to the wall); and rations are reduced. Court-martial is reserved for such offenses as desertion, major negligence, assaulting a superior, or mutiny. Offenders at this level are sentenced to confinement in disciplinary battalions, a punishment much feared by servicemen because of the brutality, forced labor, and starvation diet characteristic of the Soviet penal system as a whole.

The two most frequent violations of military discipline are drinking and going AWOL. Enlisted men can be punished for drinking even when on Sunday leave, and sobriety in garrison cities is enforced by military patrols. The men are not allowed to carry any unauthorized bags or parcels in their hands, so smuggling liquor into the barracks is very difficult. Liquor stores are under orders not to sell anything to enlisted men, who are required always to be in uniform. Drinking still persists, a fact that has affected the image of the Soviet armed forces in the West. One should, however, avoid hasty conclusions: for young Soviet males, becoming intoxicated is an act of bravado. It is also inextricably linked with the notion of "enjoying oneself" in a country notorious for its lack of entertainment. This does indeed frequently lead to alcoholism—but not yet in 18- to 20-year-old men. Also, drinking normally takes place when enlisted men are off duty and so does not seriously affect combat readiness. Those who return drunk to the barracks are not given leaves thereafter.

Going AWOL is another serious disciplinary problem. It is frequently related to drinking. But mostly it happens because the sexual needs of soldiers confined to barracks 24 hours a day, without regular leaves, are completely ignored. The AWOL incidence is reduced by such strong preventive measures as military patrols and the ban on wearing civilian clothes at any time. (A recent amendment to the Law on Universal Military Obligation stipulates that, on arrival at the place of service, the civilian clothes of the conscripts be mailed home.) Nor does the AWOL problem seriously impair combat readiness, since soldiers know that after 24 hours AWOL is viewed as desertion and punishable by court-martial.

The same factors help to make desertion exceedingly rare. But here the strongest deterrent is the unlikelihood of success in a society where police surveillance is omnipresent and the state controls everything. Lacking the basic document of every Soviet citizen—the internal passport (which is surrendered at the moment of induction)—a deserter would simply be unable to obtain work, medical care, or even shelter.

Strict discipline and intensive training are instrumental in solving many problems inherent in a multiethnic conscript army. Indeed, ethnic friction is often reduced by the pressure of training and the common feeling of shared and overcome hardship it engenders. At the beginning of their service members of ethnic groups tend to stick together, but friendship patterns soon cross ethnic barriers and common interests and tenure of service become more important.[6]

In top combat-priority sectors of the Soviet armed forces—such as the Navy—the quality of officers and the educational standards of enlisted men are higher, living conditions less harsh, food more abundant, and training more sophisticated. These units appear to succeed better in softening ethnic and other kinds of friction and in achieving good combat cohesion. Moreover, the sheer size of the military allows for flexibility in utilizing the diverse manpower pool: top combat-priority branches—the Strategic Rocket Forces, the paratroops, the combat-ready divisions based in Eastern Europe, the Navy—get a larger share of better-educated draftees. The less combat-ready units have to make do with less qualified conscripts while noncombat branches (the construction and railroad troops) absorb such "undesirables" as soldiers not fluent in Russian, members of "politically unreliable" minorities—ethnic Germans or Crimean Tatars, for example—or even former criminals.

The two most recent examples of the Soviet use of military force demonstrate that the disparity between the top combat-ready units and the rest of the armed forces is consistent with the functions assigned to them. In Czechoslovakia in 1968 and in Afghanistan in 1979 elite paratroops successfully secured the main military and political targets, while the massive invasion force symbolized the irreversibility of the Soviet move. (The symbolism apparently did not impress the Afghans, but it worked with the Czechs—and with the West—both in 1968 and in 1979.)

Although it is too early to assess the impact on the Soviet armed forces of the Soviet involvement in Afghanistan, preliminary observations are possible. First, despite rather serious problems with discipline and morale, the Soviet soldier has performed adequately in the conditions of limited, antiguerrilla warfare for which he was not initially trained. Second, despite the rigidity of Soviet tactical training, the troops in Afghanistan are obviously developing more flexible tactics for that particular war. Third, actual combat experience will help to identify and correct various weaknesses in the combat training of Soviet troops. Just as the confrontation with the Chinese in 1969 brought home the need to improve training for conventional warfare, including such simple skills as proper organization of small-arms fire, so the Afghanistan experience will probably result in more realistic training for the Soviet conscript army.

By the time of his discharge, a typical enlisted man has lost whatever youthful interest in military service he once had, but he still believes in the importance of military service. Although he was often tired and homesick, he returns home physically stronger than he was two years earlier. Sporting a snugly fitting uniform with badges, he is in no hurry to change into civilian clothes. He is a center of attention, respect, and curiosity for his friends and neighbors, a true man who has fulfilled his duty to his country. Nor is his connection with the armed forces over. He is registered in the borough military commissariat as a member of the ready reserves and can be called up for retraining, for as long as three months, at any time. Retraining can take him rather far from home, as it did many a reservist during the invasions of Czechoslovakia and Afghanistan.

Thus the Soviet armed forces have a huge pool of reservists with recent active-duty experience to be drawn on in time of need, as

David R. Jones has shown (chapter 8). Still, the simultaneous rein-
tegration of reservists on a large scale has yet to be tested, and so
it remains one of the major unknowns to be considered by both
Soviet and Western military analysts.[7]

Neither reservists nor present and potential soldiers in the Soviet
Union are motivated by dreams of military glory, adventure, and
conquest: this would be incompatible with the basic thrust of their
training, which inculcates obedience and duty. Rather, they per-
ceive military service as an unavoidable part of life. For them, being
a man includes putting on the uniform whenever one is told to do
so by the authorities.

In this era of nuclear stalemate, with its corresponding emphasis
on perceptions of readiness to apply conventional military might,
the Soviet Union has a definite advantage over the West in its potential for mobilizing its forces quickly and smoothly, without disruption and protest on the part of either the conscripts themselves
or the population in general. This provides the Soviet ruling elite
with credible military muscle that they can flex at will.

NOTES

1. See Rebecca V. Strode, "Soviet Strategic Style," *Comparative Strategy* 3, no. 4 (1984), pp. 11–22.

2. Robert Bathurst, Michael Burger, Ellen Wolffe, *The Soviet Sailor:
Combat Readiness and Morale* (Arlington, VA: Ketron, 1982).

3. Zdenek Mlynar, *Nightfrost in Prague* (New York: Karz, 1980), p. 186.

4. Robert Bathurst and Michael Burger, "Controlling the Soviet Soldier:
Some Eyewitness Accounts," *Occasional Papers* no. 1 (Center for Strategic
Technology, Texas A&M University, 1981).

5. Ellen Jones, "Manning the Soviet Military," *International Security*
(Summer 1982), pp. 346–59.

6. Ellen Jones, "Minorities in the Soviet Armed Forces," *Comparative
Strategy* 3, no. 4 (1984), pp. 28–37; Ellen Jones and Fred W. Grupp, "Political Socialization in the Soviet Military," *Armed Forces and Society* (Spring
1982), pp. 31–42.

7. See John M. Collins, *U.S.-Soviet Military Balance 1980–1985* (Washington, DC: Pergamon-Brassey, 1985); and John L. Scherer, ed., *USSR Facts
and Figures Annual* (Gulf Breeze, FL: Academic International, 1985).

10

Military Strategy in the Nuclear Age

EUGENIA V. OSGOOD

In the compartmentalized edifice of Marxist-Leninist military theory, military strategy occupies a very special place. Together with operational art and tactics it constitutes "military art," the most intuitive and imaginative, as well as the most important, component of military science, which is the "objective" study of warfare.

Owing to the nature of the problems it is required to solve, military strategy enjoys a certain freedom in its choice of means for the achievement of its goals. But it is both circumscribed and governed by the general principles laid down in military doctrine. While military doctrine is the ensemble of official views on the nature of war and represents the essence of the state's military policy, military strategy deals with actual plans and preparations for war, the employment of forces in combat, and the strategic views of any adversaries.

Official Soviet policy has always proclaimed that the Soviet Union is a champion of peace, and its military doctrine has consistently maintained a defensive stance. But Soviet military strategy, which is a tool of policy, has always—both in the prenuclear and in the nuclear age—favored offensive over defensive operations. Most Western commentators view this stance as one largely determined by Soviet capabilities.

Thus, especially since the Soviet acquisition of nuclear weapons, Westerners have taken a dim view of Soviet offensive strategy. Almost inevitably they have drawn the conclusion that a doctrine calling for war-fighting capabilities, when combined with an offensive strategy, translates into an aggressive stance. This, they conclude, makes the initiation of nuclear war likely, if not imminent. But such reasoning omits a very important factor in the formation of Soviet doctrine and strategy: the historical conditioning of a nation's mentality—and the convergence of this mentality with a new set of military options.

A "war mentality" has characterized the Soviet Union from the beginning, the result of a hostile international environment encapsulated in the phrase "capitalist encirclement." Yet the concept of the offensive had been emphasized by Russian strategists as far back as the eighteenth century, when the famous Russian general Suvorov extolled the primacy of the offensive and became a proponent of the strategy of annihilation. In the 1920s the Soviet commander M. V. Frunze, often considered the inventor of Soviet strategy, taught that the offensive was superior to the defensive because it was "good for the morale of the army." Frunze believed that the tactical and strategic concepts of the Red Army should be based on the offensive. Lenin, after all, had said that "the offensive and not the defense should become the slogan of the masses," and Marshal Mikhail Tukhachevsky, victorious Bolshevik commander in the Civil War, had urged that the offensive was the only strategy that could lead to victory. More recently, Stalin was convinced that only an offensive strategy could allow the Soviet army to prevail over its adversary.

So it is ironic that while the Red Army had evolved a fairly coherent and predominantly offensive military strategy prior to World War II, what saved it from defeat in that conflict was a contingency plan based on the Clausewitzian concept of defense in depth. The German thrust deep into Soviet territory, the defense mounted by the Soviet forces, and the subsequent counteroffensive all seem to have been lifted from Clausewitz's book *On War* and to have followed a pattern established by Napoleon's Russian campaign of 1812. Defense and counteroffense, with all that they entailed in terms of extensive destruction on one's own territory and millions of dead, were the Russian experience in World War II—and not the offensive initiated beyond the country's borders. But the "revolution in military affairs" that began in about 1950, with its new atomic and then thermonuclear weapons, promised to change all that. These weapons would make it possible to defend the country with offensive weapons aimed at enemy territory without having first to retreat into the Soviet interior.[1]

Indeed, this revolutionary convergence of theory and weapons meant that the familiar concept of the offensive was now to be implemented by the strategic nuclear missiles that the Soviet Union began to acquire in the 1950s. No grander scenario was ever drawn

up for the delectation of military minds. In the words of a senior
Soviet strategist, the future nuclear world war would encompass all
continents and be waged on the ground, on the seas, in the air, and
in space, where the "incredible spatial expansion of combat action"
would kill hundreds of millions of people and bring about the "simultaneous defeat and destruction of the enemy's economic potential and armed forces throughout its territory."[2]

Such a conflict would embody Clausewitz's dream of the "absolute war" that, "untrammelled by any conventional restraints,"
would break out "in all its elemental fury."[3] Militarily, it would be
an unprecedented feat of arms, for it would bring about a triumph
of pure strategy, accomplishing everything in one fell swoop, without "friction" and without the intermediate stages of operational
art and tactics. This was heady stuff, and it undoubtedly appealed
to military men, many of whom viewed nuclear weapons as simply
the highest achievement in firepower and maneuverability. The
firepower of the nuclear warhead, coupled with the mobility of the
rocket, became the strategic factor that would determine the outcome of war.

Yet the explosive power of the nuclear missile, which seemed to
make it a perfect weapon for a war-fighting strategy, led other Soviet
analysts to an appreciation of its tremendous deterrent value. During his years in office Nikita Khrushchev, having first rejected Georgy
Malenkov's 1954 declaration that nuclear war would be "a catastrophe for all mankind," gradually came to accept this view. Real-
izing that the wholesale destruction resulting from the use of nuclear
weapons could make a general war suicidal for both sides, and that
such a war should be avoided at all costs, Khrushchev formulated
a "minimum deterrence" nuclear strategy.

At the Twentieth Party Congress in 1956 he proclaimed that war
between socialism and capitalism was not inevitable and that a
peaceful transition to socialism would take its place. Khrushchev
thus amended the well-entrenched Soviet dictum that had served
to justify Stalin's massive defense effort. He also implied that deterrence of the capitalist adversary was possible thanks mainly to
Soviet possession of the new "superweapon," as the thermonuclear
bomb was then called.

Then, in January 1960, in a speech before the Supreme Soviet,
Khrushchev formally unveiled his new "deterrence only," one-
weapon strategy—a strategy that relied in essence on the terror-
inspiring might of nuclear missiles. At the same time, he advocated
deep cuts in the ground forces while promising to equip them with

vastly improved firepower. His bold initiative, however, did not please the Soviet military, who rejected the one-weapon strategy as unsound. For while Khrushchev thought of preventing war and believed that a stable nuclear standoff would eliminate or at least minimize crises, the military was concerned with the contingency of having to fight a war and viewed crises as inevitable. Soviet military strategists still doubted that the "imperialists" could be successfully deterred or that they would give up their "aggressive designs." The strategists saw all-out nuclear exchange or surrender as the only alternatives under Khrushchev's new deterrence strategy.

Khrushchev's dictum, that "peaceful coexistence or catastrophic war" are the only choices open to humanity, has remained in force in the Soviet Union and is proclaimed today more loudly than ever before by the leadership. But his pure deterrence stance was quickly discredited after his ouster in 1964, as were the deep troop cuts. In fact, even before Khrushchev's departure a compromise strategic solution had been worked out by a team of military strategists under Marshal V. D. Sokolovsky. Their book, *Military Strategy,* first published in 1962, went to a second edition in 1963, to allow for a critique of the new U.S. counterforce strategy made public in June 1962 by Secretary of Defense Robert S. McNamara.

Sokolovsky's team, authors of the grandiose nuclear scenario quoted above, retained Khrushchev's reliance on the mighty rocket weapons, which were to be employed in massive strikes on both military and industrial-economic targets deep in the enemy's territory. They did not, however, relinquish the traditional Russian emphasis on the role of mass armies. Because of the huge number of casualties to be expected, they argued, even larger armies would be needed in a nuclear war. And while graphically depicting the devastation that would be wrought by it, they steered clear of the notion of "mutual assured destruction." Instead, they foresaw victory for the morally and socially superior socialist camp, which would crush any "imperialist aggressor."

Meanwhile, the Soviet Union began to build up its nuclear component, and in the 1960s and 1970s land-based missiles, both intercontinental (targeted on the United States) and regional (deployed against Western Europe and China), became the mainstay of the Soviet nuclear deterrent. Even today, land-based missiles comprise 75 percent of the Soviet intercontinental nuclear forces, the remaining 25 percent being divided between relatively small fleets of long-range bombers and of submarines equipped with nuclear weapons.

In Soviet eyes deterrence—*sderzhivanie putem ustrasheniia* or "containment through intimidation"—is considered a Western concept. Yet we can speak of a Soviet nuclear deterrent, since, under prevailing Soviet military doctrine, deterrence is the principal mission of their nuclear component, just as it is the principal mission of U.S. strategic forces. We should also remember that the Soviet nuclear stance has often been misinterpreted in the West because it differs from the Western notion of "deterrence through punishment." The Soviet variant, by contrast, implies denial of success to an adversary's plans. It requires massive capabilities as well as reliance on a preemptive or a launch-under-attack posture in response to a nuclear strike, rather than on riding out the attack and then inflicting unacceptable punishment on the aggressor.

Much has been written about the importance of preemption and surprise in Soviet strategy and about the aggressive connotations of these terms. The truth is, however, that in the 1950s, when the fear of nuclear surprise attack in Europe was so acute as to lead to the convocation of the Geneva surprise-attack conference (1958), *both* sides considered preemption as the only viable option for their slowly fired, vulnerable, first-generation missiles. But by the early 1960s improvements in warning technology and in missile design had already begun to make preemption both unnecessary and unfeasible. Today preemption on the intercontinental level simply is no longer a valid option. More survivable warning systems have made it possible for either side to fire its missiles during the 30-minute flight time required by the other's missiles, after receiving unambiguous signals that an attack has been launched.

For a while the surprise factor assumed a disproportionate importance at the strategic level, both in the U.S. strategy of massive retaliation, with its emphasis on seizing the strategic initiative, and in the Soviet option of preempting an impending attack. Strategic surprise became less of a threat during the 1960s when, in addition to improving their warning systems, the Soviets began to acquire their second generation of storable liquid-fuel missiles that could be fired at from four to eight minutes' notice. At the same time, the United States built solid-fuel systems that could be launched practically at the turn of a key. Perhaps for propaganda purposes, or to keep relations at a suitably adversarial level, the Soviets continued through the 1970s to accuse the United States of preparing a surprise attack against them while the United States kept leveling similar accusations against the Soviets, invariably viewing Soviet intentions with suspicion.

To be sure, Western mistrust of Soviet intentions has been exacerbated by the ambiguities surrounding the Soviet force posture, with its preponderance of heavy land-based missiles believed to be targeted on U.S. strategic forces with a potentially "disarming" intent, and by ambiguities in the Soviet view of nuclear war as a possible instrument of policy. Even though Soviet leaders have always assured the world that their nuclear weapons would never be used in a first strike, and even though Khrushchev proclaimed that nuclear war could not serve the purposes of *socialist* politics, the issue remained unsettled.

More exactly, in the middle 1960s a doctrinal debate flared up in the Soviet military centering on the challenge Khrushchev's "revision" posed to the Marxist-Leninist (originally Clausewitzian) dictum that war is a continuation of politics by other means. A nuclear war, it was argued, would be even more "political," for it would be the final confrontation between the two opposed systems, from which socialism would emerge victorious to fulfill its historic mission. This "orthodox" line persisted side by side with the outright condemnation of nuclear war by the eminent Soviet strategist General M. Talensky and others. The debate continued until 1967, when an unsigned article in the January 24, 1967, issue of *Red Star,* the authoritative military journal, put an end to it. There, the orthodox position on the viability of nuclear war as an instrument of policy was repudiated with a quotation from the current Program of the Communist Party of the Soviet Union: "Nuclear war cannot and must not serve as a means towards the solution of a political conflict. All peaceloving and anti-imperialist forces oppose world war as a means for the continuation of politics."

This statement seemed to tally with the Soviet contention that no first use of nuclear weapons would ever be contemplated by the Soviet Union. But in a nuclear war the even more critical question of what victory could mean remained unanswered. Military spokesmen ritually endorsed the triumph of socialism and the final extinction of capitalism. The third edition of *Military Strategy,* published in 1968 with very few changes, again confidently affirmed that a "general victory" was possible in a nuclear war as a result of the simultaneous "application of the entire might of the state."[4] Still, the fact that its authors, like other military theoreticians, never explained how such a victory could be obtained after absorbing either a massive nuclear first strike by an aggressor or a devastating retaliatory blow, gave rise to doubt as to the seriousness of their assertions, no matter how confidently phrased. Indeed, among some analysts the Soviet belief in victory seemed more a patriotic exhortation than a realistic forecast.

When the SALT I interim agreement on offensive arms was signed by the United States and the Soviet Union in 1972, it was based on the principle of mutual assured destruction (MAD): the belief that both sides could completely destroy each other, either in a retaliatory or in a preemptive strike. SALT I also upheld the principle of parity rather than the striving for superiority; and in place of "equal security" and mutual survival, it stressed mutual vulnerability (reinforced by the signing of a separate treaty limiting antiballistic missile defenses). SALT I thus ran counter to some of the most cherished Soviet beliefs in the field of nuclear strategy and contradicted much of official Soviet rhetoric. Not surprisingly, acceptance of the new relationship with the United States—and of its implications with respect to weapons acquisition and nuclear strategy—was a slow and painful process for the Soviet military.

A debate, this time between military conservatives and mostly civilian moderates, flared up in 1973, soon after the signing of SALT I. As did the earlier debate, it concerned the viability of nuclear war and the possibility of victory. The "moderates" (mostly specialists from the Institute for the Study of the United States and Canada of the Soviet Academy of Sciences) underscored the futility of further arms competition, saw victory in a nuclear war as at best Pyrrhic, and pointed to the economic benefits of arms control and stable deterrence. Spokesmen for the military-political establishment, on the other hand, still thought victory in a nuclear war possible and advocated a war-fighting capability to forestall the growing threat of "imperialist aggression." They criticized the "quantifiers" from the Institute for placing too much stress on the material damage that would result from a nuclear war and for discounting the "moral superiority" of the communist side.

In the later 1970s, however, the conservatives softened their stance considerably. A treatise produced in 1977 by members of the faculty of the Lenin Military-Political Academy attested to the shift to a pro-deterrence and pro-detente orientation, at least among the military-political elite (as distinguished from the usually more hard-line General Staff officers). The authors of the treatise took a dim view of nuclear war as an instrument of policy, since it would not be conducive to attaining the dual Soviet political objective: to "topple capitalism at any cost" and to build communism.

Statements by Soviet spokesmen on MAD have been few and far between over the years, at least partly for ideological reasons. Mutual destruction is not seen as part of the Marxist-Leninist historical process, whereas the victory of socialism is. Yet declarations of the "catastrophic" effects of nuclear war, which imply belief in assured destruction, have become common since the later 1970s. Leonid Brezhnev in particular frequently pictured nuclear war as the ultimate tragedy for all humanity—and even expressed the fear that the final "ideological dispute," should it ever arise, would end in catastrophe for both camps, since, along with millions of people, their ideas would also perish.[5]

During Brezhnev's last years in office and now under the new Soviet leadership, high-level Soviet civilian and military spokesmen have been endorsing what amounts to the doctrine of MAD, stressing the unacceptable damage that would result from a general nuclear war. Some Western observers have speculated that this apparent acceptance of MAD may have come about because the Soviet military realized that continued weapons modernization and a qualitative buildup were not hampered by SALT and, equally, that the numerical parity that SALT called for was not the equivalent of functional parity. Thus, while adhering to the "parity" of MAD, so the argument goes, the Soviet Union proceeded through the 1970s to acquire a lead—a strategic edge in some systems—which it could then exploit to gain political leverage. Whether this lead could also be translated into any militarily meaningful results, apart from a more secure deterrence against a first strike, is debatable.

In any case, the Soviet leadership appears more reluctant than ever to fight a nuclear war. Certainly, the solemn Soviet pledge at the June 1982 U.N. Special Session on Disarmament never to use nuclear weapons first must act as more of a constraint on Soviet action than all previous peace campaigns and assurances that nuclear weapons are unsuitable as an instrument of policy. Although dismissed by U.S. leaders as "only words," there is every indication that this pledge carries considerable political weight in the Soviet Union itself, making the deliberate initiation of nuclear war by the Soviet leadership very unlikely.

In June 1982, again, the Soviet leadership allowed the ideas of victory and of survival in a nuclear war to be publicly questioned by a team of Soviet and U.S. doctors. Before a Soviet television audience of millions, the team discussed the incalculable consequences of a nuclear exchange and concluded that even in a limited nuclear confrontation medical help would be almost nonexistent, since doctors would be able to treat only a small fraction of the huge number of casualties. In other words, as Nikita Khrushchev once put it, "the living would envy the dead." The doctors agreed

THE U.S./SOVIET STRATEGIC BALANCE IN 1964 AND 1985

	United States	Soviet Union
July 1964		
ICBMs	834	190
SLBMs	416	107
Bombers	630	175
Total	1,880	472
July 1985		
ICBM and SLBM launchers	1,634	2,338
Bombers	263	170
Total	1,897	2,508
ICBM warheads	2,118	6,420
Total (ICBM & SLBM etc.) warheads	10,600	9,804

Note: ICBM = intercontinental ballistic missile (land-based: range up to 15,000 kilometers); SLBM = submarine-launched ballistic missile (range up to 9,100 kilometers); Bomber = long-range bomber (U.S. range up to 16,000 kilometers; Soviet range up to 12,800 kilometers); and Warheads = independently targetable nuclear weapons.
Source: International Institute for Strategic Studies: *The Military Balance 1977–1978* (London: 1977), p. 80 (for 1964); *Strategic Survey* (London: 1986), p. 57 (for 1985).

in denying the possibility of anything even approaching victory. They stressed the view that a nuclear conflict would inevitably escalate to the global level and asserted that nuclear war could endanger the very survival of mankind.

By allowing the program to air, the Soviet leadership implicitly endorsed its findings, leaving little doubt about official Soviet attitudes in the matter of general nuclear war. This reorientation is noticeable even at the hard core of the military establishment. Compare Marshal N. V. Ogarkov's low-key, cautious, seemingly pro forma formulation in 1979 of an "objective possibility" of the Soviet Union's prevailing in a protracted nuclear war[6] with the brash rhetoric describing socialism's sweeping victory and the catastrophic end of imperialism in Marshal Sokolovsky's *Military Strategy* of the 1960s.

There is a growing consensus in the West that the Soviets may really believe in MAD at the level of general war. But many in the West still suspect that the Soviet Union would consider initiating a *limited* nuclear war, possibly against military targets alone and with smaller, more accurate, and less damage-producing weapons. The Soviet Union, so the theory goes, would then try to blackmail the leaders either of NATO or of the United States into making major concessions, if not surrendering outright, on the principle that such a course of action would be preferable to an all-out nuclear exchange. Or perhaps it is thought that Soviet conventional superiority in some theaters would preclude Western resistance. At any rate, since limited nuclear war has been traditionally a taboo subject in Soviet writings on strategy and doctrine, it is almost impossible to ascertain what the Soviets really think about it—even though their capabilities are now such that limited nuclear use is theoretically feasible.

Still, Soviet military leaders have emphatically denied that limited nuclear-war scenarios have ever been developed by their staffs. They have persistently rejected the Western notion of escalation control or of deterrence and bargaining in the midst of war, perhaps because such views contradict the traditional Soviet image of an apocalyptic clash between two opposed systems. Soviet military writings describe nuclear flexibility as destabilizing—because it may make the use of nuclear weapons more likely—and maintain that nuclear forces exist solely for retaliation on the attacker's homeland with massive counter-military and counter-economic strikes. Nor do the Soviets publicly contemplate a "counterforce" strike aimed at weapons alone. Many U.S. analysts, however, are convinced that selective options are well within the reach of Soviet nuclear forces and that they exist in Soviet war plans—both at the intercontinental level, in the form of a counterforce strike on the vulnerable U.S. Minuteman force, and in the European and Asian theaters, where the new mobile SS-20 intermediate-range missiles have made it possible for the Soviet Union to implement a limited-strike strategy.

Nevertheless, apart from having acknowledged with some satisfaction the newly acquired accuracy of Soviet strategic and regional missiles and their ability to strike a wide variety of targets, Soviet generals have given no indication as to what changes these developments might mean for their nuclear strategy. Rather, new SS-20s, although much more accurate than their predecessors (the SS-4s and SS-5s), are said to have basically "the same mission"—that is, they are aimed at European military targets. And that is as much as Soviet spokesmen will say.

One reason why they are reluctant to make public any contingency plans involving limited nuclear use may be that this would imply the existence of a first-use option, which Soviet leaders have explicitly disavowed. Moreover, it may be that the Soviet Union has less need to retain either a first-use option or plans involving limited nuclear employment than does the United States. Unlike the United States, it is not party to a nuclear contract extending a "deterrence umbrella" to distant allies; nor is it under any obligation to use nuclear weapons first, in a limited way, to prevent a conventional defeat. Even though nuclear use has been fully integrated into the Soviet battlefield posture for years, Soviet strategists are probably more interested in reliably deterring NATO's first use should a conventional conflict break out in Europe. And there is of course the possibility that, should NATO engage in a limited strike on Soviet territory, Moscow would choose an appropriately limited response rather than unleash Armageddon.

Any changes in Soviet nuclear strategy and nuclear employment must remain matters of speculation until the strategists of the Soviet General Staff come forward with a follow-up to the last edition of their *Military Strategy* (1968). So far there is no indication that this is about to happen. Meanwhile, one can only guess that, having officially admitted that meaningful victory through a massive nuclear strike is impossible in a general nuclear war, they will either formally subscribe to the concept of MAD or adopt a strategy of limited nuclear retaliation and intrawar bargaining. Or they might decide in favor of a defensive strategy of "assured survival" by deploying new high-efficiency, antimissile technologies, possibly together with—or in response to—a parallel U.S. move.

On the other hand, recent statements by authoritative military spokesmen indicate that we may be witnessing a real questioning of the utility of nuclear weapons in Soviet military strategy. The prenuclear principles of concentration of forces, economy of force, and partial victory were enunciated in a 1985 study of the military thought of Frunze, thus signaling a preference for the conventional option, especially in a theater campaign. Statements by Marshal S.F. Akhromeev, the current chief of the General Staff, suggest that the Soviet military will augment its arsenal for conventional war fighting by acquiring the latest high-precision technologies.

Soviet interest in solving military problems by nonnuclear means has also led to extensive research on weapons based on new physical principles, such as particle beams and laser rays, which are just as destructive as and potentially much more usable than nuclear-tipped ICBM warheads. This makes one wonder whether the Soviets are not trying to break out of the nuclear stalemate and transcend the nuclear dimension. Drastic cuts in nuclear weapons—or even their elimination by the year 2000—as proposed in 1986 by General Secretary Mikhail Gorbachev would be entirely in line with such a new orientation.

International security would no doubt be enhanced if the Soviet leadership's widely publicized "new political thinking," which advocates among other things nonmilitary solutions to all global problems, had an impact on the substance of Soviet military strategy. Rather than devising operational guidelines for fighting victorious wars without nuclear escalation, the Soviet General Staff could then finally reconcile its strategy with arms control. Whether or not nuclear weapons remain in the Soviet arsenal, a reduction in Soviet military capabilities and the adoption of a genuinely defensive doctrine and strategy would build international goodwill and promote global stability.

NOTES

1. For the Soviet "military revolution," as it is called by Soviet military writers, and related material, see Harriet Fast Scott and William F. Scott, *The Soviet Art of War: Doctrine, Strategy, and Tactics* (Boulder, CO: Westview, 1982).

2. See Marshal of the Soviet Union V. D. Sokolovsky, ed., *Voennaia Strategiia*, 2d ed. (Moscow: Voenizdat, 1963), p. 19.

3. Carl von Clausewitz, *On War* (Princeton, New Jersey: Princeton University Press, 1976), pp. 593, 351–59.

4. V. D. Sokolovsky, *Voennaia Strategiia*, 3d ed. (Moscow: Voenizdat, 1968).

5. *Aktual'nye voprosy ideologicheskoi raboty KPSS*, vol. 2 (Moscow: Politizdat, 1978), p. 564.

6. Marshal of the Soviet Union N. V. Ogarkov, "Strategiia voennaia," *Sovetskaia voennaia entsiklopediia*, vol. 7 (Moscow: Voenizdat, 1979), p. 564.

The views expressed in this chapter are solely those of the author and do not represent the position of the Library of Congress or of any other agency of the U.S. government.

11

ARMS CONTROL

DAVID HOLLOWAY

The Soviet Union sometimes claims a continuous commitment to disarmament since 1917 and points as proof of this to the Decree on Peace, calling for an end to World War I, which the Bolsheviks adopted the day after they seized power. But this claim to continuity is misleading. Soviet policy has changed significantly since 1917 and especially since the advent of nuclear weapons. And it is only by examining this process of change that we can understand Soviet policy on arms control.

The Bolsheviks were not pacifists. They believed that wars were inevitable as long as imperialism existed and that imperialism could be overthrown only by socialist revolution. The revolution would be violent, moreover, because the capitalist ruling class would resist with force the struggles of the working class to seize power. Before World War II, the Soviet Union advanced several major disarmament proposals; but these were not taken seriously by the major powers, which regarded the Soviet Union as a dangerous interloper in the international system. Nor did the Soviet Union itself, if its efforts to build up the Red Army are taken as evidence, believe that its proposals would be accepted. The Soviet leaders viewed disarmament as a useful propaganda weapon and saw the peace movements in the capitalist world as something to be exploited in weakening and confusing the enemy.

World War II was quickly followed by the breakup of the wartime alliance and by the Cold War, which did not create a propitious climate for disarmament. But before the Cold War got under way, talks were started at the United Nations to bring the atomic bomb under international control. The United States already had the bomb, however, and was not willing to give it up until the Soviet Union had agreed to international control; meanwhile, the Soviet Union would not agree to international control until the United States had got rid of its atomic bombs. It is not surprising, therefore, that the talks failed. In August 1945 Stalin had expanded the Soviet program to build the bomb, and in August 1949 the Soviet Union conducted its first atomic bomb test. By the time of Stalin's death in 1953 the Soviet Union and the United States were locked into a nuclear arms race.

Both the Soviet Union and the United States tested hydrogen bombs in the early 1950s. These can have an explosive yield more than 1,000 times greater than that of the atomic bombs dropped on Hiroshima and Nagasaki, and the first Soviet thermonuclear test in August 1953 brought home to Soviet leaders the destructiveness of nuclear war. After he became the first secretary of the Central Committee in September 1953, Nikita Khrushchev was briefed on nuclear weapons. "When I . . . learned all the facts about nuclear power I couldn't sleep for several days," he later recalled. "Then I became convinced that we could never possibly use these weapons, and when I realized that I was able to sleep again." [1]

Khrushchev understood how destructive a nuclear war would be. He also believed that the Soviet Union's growing nuclear arsenal would deter an attack by the United States. At the Twentieth Party Congress in 1956 he declared that war was no longer "fatalistically inevitable." Peaceful coexistence between states of different social systems could now be envisaged as a permanent relationship rather than as a mere breathing space before the next war. But nuclear war, though not inevitable, was not regarded as impossible; and this view has underpinned the Soviet policy of preparing for nuclear war while at the same time seeking to prevent it.

The Soviet Union and the United States, even as they built up their nuclear arsenals and maintained large conventional forces, made far-reaching proposals for disarmament in the 1950s. These did not result in agreements. In 1958, however, an important change took place in the Soviet and American approach to disarmament, when the two sides began talks on a nuclear test ban. These talks marked a shift from disarmament to arms control, from the effort to end the arms race by a comprehensive agreement to the attempt to make it less dangerous by piecemeal measures. This shift carried the unfortunate implication that the arms race could not be stopped, but without it the two sides might not have moved beyond rhetoric and posturing to the agreements of the 1960s and 1970s.

The first practical expressions of arms control came in the wake of the Cuban Missile Crisis of 1962, which had demonstrated just how dangerous the nuclear confrontation could be. In 1963 the Hot Line was set up between Moscow and Washington to make it possible for leaders to communicate in times of crisis. In the same year the Soviet Union, the United Kingdom, and the United States signed the Limited Test Ban Treaty, which prohibits nuclear weapons tests in the atmosphere, in outer space, and under water. Although underground tests continued unabated, the treaty resulted in a considerable reduction in the levels of radioactive fallout in the atmosphere. The Soviet Union and the United States showed again that they could cooperate in limited areas when they negotiated the Nuclear Non-Proliferation Treaty in 1968.

Still, one more condition had to be met before the Soviet Union was willing to make a serious effort to control the competition in strategic arms. Until the late 1960s the Soviet Union lagged the United States in strategic power. From 1945 until the mid-1950s the Soviet Union had no bombers (or at best a very few) capable of delivering weapons against targets in the United States. In 1956 the Soviet Union began to deploy intercontinental bombers, and in 1957 it tested its first ICBM (intercontinental ballistic missile). For about 10 years, from the mid-1950s to the mid-1960s, the Soviet Union had nuclear forces that could strike the United States, but it could not be sure that these forces would survive a first strike by the United States. By the late 1960s, however, the Soviet Union had drawn close to strategic parity with the United States, and on this basis the Soviet leaders were willing to enter into negotiations with the United States to limit strategic arms.

At the opening session of the SALT negotiations in November 1969 the Soviet delegation declared that while mountains of weapons were growing mutual security was not improving but rather diminishing as a result. "Even in the event that one of the sides was the first to be subjected to attack," the Soviet side continued, "it would undoubtedly retain the ability to inflict a retaliatory blow of destructive force. It would be tantamount to suicide for the ones who decided to start war."[2] On the basis of parity the Soviet Union and the United States concluded the ABM (Anti-Ballistic Missile) Treaty and the Interim Agreement on Offensive Missiles, which were signed during Richard Nixon's visit to Moscow in May 1972. For the Soviet leaders, these SALT agreements were the outward and visible sign of the equality with the United States that they had long pursued. They hoped now to derive political and economic benefits from detente, which, they believed, was made possible by their attainment of strategic parity.

The SALT agreements had specific implications for the Soviet Union's strategic relationship with the United States. The ABM Treaty severely limited the development and deployment of ballistic-missile defenses: each side remained vulnerable to retaliatory strikes by the other, no matter which struck first. Parity thus signified not only equal numbers of launchers and warheads but, more importantly, a relationship of mutual vulnerability. The two sides recognized at SALT that if one side deployed ballistic-missile defenses the other would increase its offensive forces in order to defeat the defense: thus, defenses would not only be ineffective but would also stimulate the deployment of offensive systems. The ABM Treaty was seen, therefore, as a prerequisite for restraining the competition in offensive arms.

Only limited progress was made, however, in constraining offensive systems. The Interim Agreement on Offensive Missiles of 1972 set limits on the deployment of ICBMS and SLBMs but did not restrict bombers or multiple warheads. Unlike the ABM Treaty, which is of unlimited duration, the Interim Agreement was to run for five years, in the expectation that it would be replaced in that time by a more comprehensive treaty.

The SALT agreements closed off some areas of strategic competition where the Soviet Union feared that it might find itself outpaced by American technology. They also marked the Soviet Union's attainment of strategic parity with the United States. Soviet leaders have regarded this as a historic achievement, but they have not been altogether happy with parity based on mutual vulnerability. In the early 1970s they signed several agreements with the United States which showed that they believed that other measures were needed to make that relationship safer: the Accident Measures Agreement of 1971, which was designed to prevent accidental war; the Basic Principles of Relations of 1972, which laid down the principles that should govern Soviet-American relations; and the 1973 Agreement on the Prevention of Nuclear War. SALT was a matter not merely of technical decisions about the forces to be permitted on either side; it also implied a certain way of looking at the Soviet-American strategic relationship.

SALT I did not lead to the rapid progress in arms control that many people hoped for, and the SALT II Treaty was not signed until 1979. Soviet-American relations deteriorated in the later 1970s, and this contributed to the delay in reaching a new agreement. But the specific difficulties that arose in the course of negotiations were perhaps more important than the general decline in relations. The strategic forces of the Soviet Union and the United States were not symmetrical, and this made it difficult to agree on what equality really meant for the two sides. Besides, the Soviet Union insisted not only on equality but also on equal security, arguing that British and French forces should be taken into account as well as the American nuclear forces stationed in Europe that could strike Soviet territory. The United States would not accept this argument, and the Soviet Union was forced to drop it at SALT II.

The United States, for its part, sought reductions in the Soviet heavy ICBMs. In the four years after SALT I the Soviet Union deployed three new types of ICBM, the most powerful of which was the SS-18, which carries 10 warheads and is more accurate than earlier Soviet missiles. The United States feared that the Soviet Union might now be able to destroy over 90 percent of the 1,000 U.S. Minuteman silos by launching 200 SS-18s against them. This seemed, to many Americans, to indicate that the Soviet Union was striving for strategic superiority or, at the very least, for a significant preemptive capability. The United States strove mightily to persuade the Soviet Union to reduce its heavy ICBM force at SALT II— but without success.

American critics of SALT began to argue in the mid-1970s that the Soviet Union was using arms control to mask its pursuit of strategic superiority. They claimed that the Soviet Union was not committed to maintaining parity but, on the contrary, was striving to achieve superiority by building up its offensive forces and expanding its civil-defense effort. In support of their case they pointed not only to Soviet military deployments but also to Soviet military writings of the 1960s and early 1970s, which urged that the Soviet Union attain superiority in order to be able to fight and win a nuclear war (see chap. 10). They argued, in short, that the Soviet Union did not accept the premises which the United States thought underpinned SALT and that arms control was thus a snare and a delusion.

Just when these charges were being made, Leonid Brezhnev, the Soviet leader, began to outline a new version of Soviet military doctrine. In a speech in January 1977 he declared that sufficiency, not superiority, was the Soviet goal. "The Soviet Union's defense potential," he said, "must be sufficient to deter anyone from taking the risk of interfering with our peaceful life. Not a policy aimed at superiority in armaments, but a policy aimed at reducing them, at lessening military confrontation—that is our policy."[3] Over the next five years Brezhnev elaborated on this position. The key concept here was parity: Soviet strategic forces were intended to prevent an attack on the Soviet Union and its allies; if such an attack were launched, the attacker would receive a "crushing rebuff"; parity existed with the United States, and neither side could outstrip the other; the Soviet Union was not aiming for superiority and would not allow the United States to achieve superiority; nuclear war would be immensely destructive, and it would be suicidal to start one. These statements ran counter to the earlier calls for military superiority and indicated that military doctrine was being adapted to the relationship of parity. But many observers in the West dismissed these statements as no more than propaganda designed to calm American anxieties about the direction of Soviet policy.

In the American debate about the SALT II Treaty the argument that the Soviet Union was striving for strategic superiority played a crucial role. The treaty, which was signed at the Carter-Brezhnev summit in Vienna in June 1979, was a long and complex document that limited the deployment of launchers and warheads. U.S. critics argued that the treaty was too favorable to the Soviet Union, and the Carter Administration had to abandon its efforts to have it ratified by the Senate after the Soviet invasion of Afghanistan in December 1979.

Soviet leaders evinced no great dismay at Ronald Reagan's election in 1980, even though he clearly had no enthusiasm for arms control. They apparently believed that, once in office, he would come to recognize the realities of power; and he did agree not to undercut the provisions of the unratified SALT II Treaty, even though he had called it "fatally flawed." But Soviet complacency about Reagan was soon replaced by the alarming realization that he was serious in seeking to build up American military power.

One of the chief causes of Soviet concern was NATO's decision of December 1979 to deploy GLCMs (Ground-Launched Cruise Missiles) and Pershing II missiles in Western Europe. NATO asserted that these systems were a response to the buildup of Soviet strategic and theater nuclear forces. The Soviet leaders, for their part, claimed that these missiles, which could strike targets in the Soviet Union from Western Europe, were part of an American drive for strategic superiority. They argued that a balance in intermediate-range nuclear forces (INF) already existed and that the Soviet Union needed the new SS-20 intermediate-range ballistic missiles to counter the British and French nuclear forces in Europe and the Chinese forces in Asia. The Soviet Union was determined to stop the deployment of NATO's new systems and evidently hoped that the peace movements that mushroomed in Western Europe in the early 1980s would help in this. Although it made some changes in its negotiating position in 1983, as the date for NATO deployment drew closer the Soviet Union refused to accept the U.S. offer to forgo deployment of the GLCMs and Pershing IIs if the Soviet Union would destroy all of its medium-range missiles. In November 1983, when the NATO deployment began, the Soviet Union withdrew from the INF talks and also from the Strategic Arms Reduction Treaty negotiations, which had been proceeding without result since June 1982.

Arms control now seemed to have reached an impasse. Yury Andropov, who had become general secretary in November 1982, apparently saw no prospect of an improvement in relations, for in September 1983 he declared that it was an illusion to think that the policies of the Reagan Administration would change for the better. Nevertheless, in 1985 the Soviet Union resumed bilateral arms control talks with the United States, with the object of "preventing an arms race in space and terminating it on earth."[4] Since that time, under the umbrella of the Nuclear and Space Talks, three sets of negotiations have been conducted in Geneva: START, INF, and Space.

The new element here is the space talks, which were put on the agenda by Ronald Reagan's call, in his "Star Wars" speech of March 1983, for the development of defenses that would make nuclear weapons "impotent and obsolete."[5] This speech evoked an immediate response from Andropov, who claimed that the United States was aiming to disarm the Soviet Union by rendering it incapable of dealing a retaliatory blow. Defenses against ballistic missiles, he said, might appear attractive to the layman, but "those who are conversant with such matters" could not view them in the same way. The SALT I Agreements had been based on the realization that an "inseverable relationship" existed between offensive and defensive systems, and the implementation of Reagan's plan would "open the floodgates to a runaway race involving all types of strategic weapons, both offensive and defensive."[6]

It soon became clear that a large-scale research program would result from the Star Wars speech, and before the end of 1984 the Soviet Union informed the United States that it was willing to begin new talks. The desire to restrain Reagan's Strategic Defense Initiative (SDI) was no doubt a major factor in that decision, though the political costs of refusing to negotiate—of allowing the United States to appear more interested in arms control—probably influenced it too. The SDI has played a crucial role in the Nuclear and Space Talks, for the Soviet Union has made reductions in offensive forces contingent on agreement to restrain the development of ballistic-missile defenses. This was made particularly clear at the Gorbachev-Reagan summit in Reykjavik in October 1986, when the

Soviet Union offered significant concessions in START and INF but only as part of a package that would include restraints on the SDI program. The SDI has played a seemingly paradoxical role in arms control, providing the Soviet Union with an incentive to make concessions on offensive forces while making agreement on offensive forces, so long as the Reagan Administration remained committed to the SDI program, more difficult.

Gorbachev has made far-reaching proposals and shown a new flexibility in Soviet policy. In January 1986 he issued a statement proposing the phased elimination of all nuclear weapons by the year 2000. To some observers Gorbachev's statement seemed no more than an exercise in public relations designed to seize the moral high ground from President Reagan. There is no doubt that Gorbachev wanted to seize the initiative, to portray the Soviet Union as more concerned about peace and disarmament than the United States, and to portray the United States as the main obstacle to nuclear disarmament.

But Gorbachev did also make concessions that the Soviet Union had resisted making for many years. He agreed to the American position on INF and said that, on condition that the United States restrain the SDI program, the Soviet Union was ready to cut its strategic nuclear forces by half in five years and to reduce its heavy ICBMs by the same proportion. Gorbachev said that the Soviet Union was willing to consider any methods necessary for verifying agreements, and he made a number of gestures to demonstrate that willingness. The real significance of the new Soviet positions cannot be assessed definitively until an agreement is concluded, but they certainly indicate greater flexibility in Soviet policy. Gorbachev called for "new thinking" about international security, and the flexibility of Soviet policy is said to be a sign of the new thinking. He maintained that in the Soviet-American context security can only be mutual: if one side feels insecure the relationship will be unpredictable and dangerous.[7] Under Gorbachev, the Soviet Union seemed more sensitive to the problems of managing its strategic relationship with the United States than it had been in the 1970s.

Formidable obstacles remained in the way of new agreements, however. In the later 1980s each side harbored deep suspicions about the intentions of the other, and the experience of arms control served to heighten—rather than to reduce—that mistrust. Important issues concerning existing treaties needed to be resolved before further progress could be made. The United States and the Soviet Union disagreed about the interpretation of the ABM Treaty: the United States claimed that the treaty did not cover the exotic technologies that it was developing for the SDI while the Soviet Union said that it did. The United States accused the Soviet Union of not complying with existing agreements, while the Soviet Union made similar charges against the United States. The future of arms control was by no means assured.

Arms control is at once a cooperative venture in which rival states try to lessen the risk of nuclear war and the burden of the arms race and a mechanism whereby they pursue their conflicting interests and ambitions. It is this dual purpose, rather than the technical complexity of the issues involved, that gives arms control its intense and contradictory political character. Arms control has also become an integral part of the Soviet-American relationship. As the Soviet Union learned when it withdrew from the INF and START talks in 1983, a superpower cannot afford to seem uninterested in arms control for fear of incurring the opprobrium of world opinion.

The Soviet leaders have used their arms control proposals over the years as a political instrument with which to influence public opinion in the West and thus exert pressure on the United States. They have also used arms control to try to channel the arms race away from areas in which the United States might enjoy an advantage. But the greatest importance of arms control for the Soviet Union has been as a means of trying to manage the strategic relationship with the United States and to prevent the nuclear competition from leading to the catastrophe of nuclear war.

NOTES

1. Quoted in M. Heikal, *Sphinx and Commissar: The Rise and Fall of Soviet Influence in the Arab World* (London: Collins & Sons, 1978), p. 129.

2. Gerard Smith, *Doubletalk: the Story of SALT I* (New York: Doubleday, 1980), p. 83.

3. *Pravda* (Jan. 19, 1977).

4. "Joint U.S.-Soviet Statement, Geneva, Jan. 8, 1985," *Department of State Bulletin* (Washington, DC: March 1985), p. 30.

5. Quoted in Sidney D. Drell, Philip J. Farley, and David Holloway, *The Reagan Strategic Defense Initiative* (Cambridge, MA: Ballinger, 1985), p. 103.

6. *Pravda* (March 27, 1983).

7. *Pravda* (Feb. 26, 1986).

THE PHYSICAL CONTEXT

We turn now to the physical context of Soviet life today, beginning with the country's basic geography. Chauncy D. Harris reminds us of the Soviet Union's vast extent, extremes of climate, variety of vegetation, and ethnic diversity and indicates some of the economic consequences of its geographical situation. John M. Kramer then discusses major environmental problems that have emerged in the Soviet Union, contrary to communist doctrine: problems that arise from the conflicting demands, familiar enough in the West, of economic development and environmental protection.

Economic as well as technical and aesthetic issues are raised by William C. Brumfield in his discussion of developments in Soviet architecture and urban planning since World War II, when approximately one-third of all Soviet housing (already inadequate by Western standards) was severely damaged or destroyed. Again we see that massive efforts to overcome critical shortages have brought in their train huge new problems, many of them peculiar to the Soviet system. And we see, in the mass construction of monotonous concrete tenements, which now house some two-thirds of the total population, the Soviet commitment to a policy that has been largely discredited in the West.

12

Basic Geography

CHAUNCY D. HARRIS

The important geographical features of the Soviet Union are its immense size; great longitudinal extent; high latitudinal position; large aggregate quantity of forest, energy, mineral and agricultural resources; and the diversity of its peoples. On a per-unit-area basis, however, these resources are moderate. Their location is often unfavorable. Diverse climates, vegetation, and soils form great landscape zones sweeping across the country. The state has asserted ownership of land and all other resources of the country and has pursued a policy of developing an industrial and urban society.

The Soviet Union is such a large country and extends for such a long distance in an east-west direction that it is difficult to depict the country on a map without serious distortion. It is possible to show true area, shape, angle, and distance of the Soviet Union only on the surface of a globe. Any map drawn on a flat piece of paper must distort one or more of these qualities.

• Figure 1 is drawn on a sinusoidal projection to make possible easy comparisons of northerly position or distances from the equator. It is also an equal-area projection on which the parallels, or lines of latitude that measure distance north of the equator in degrees, are drawn as horizontal. But the angles—and therefore the shapes and distances—are badly distorted on the edges of the map.

• Figures 2, 4, 5, and 7 are drawn on a conic projection, commonly used in Soviet atlases to show the entire country. Its key quality is the representation of true shapes because the meridians and parallels cross each other at right angles, as on the globe. Since the parallels are circles and the meridians diverging straight lines, apparent directions change in different parts of the map. In following a horizontal line at the top of the map from left to right one is

137

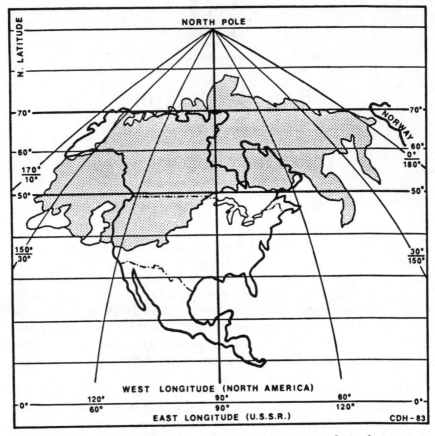

Fig. 1. Relative size and location of the Soviet Union and North America. The Soviet Union lies in high latitudes and extends for 170° of longitude. It thus has a cool or cold, generally dry, extreme continental climate degrees that limits agriculture. (Islands omitted.)

traveling first northward (in the upper left) and then southward (in the upper right). Comparisons of latitude and all features associated with it—such as length of day, temperatures, seasons, climate, and vegetation—are more difficult on this projection than on the sinusoidal, but the shapes are far superior.

• Figure 3 is drawn on Lambert's azimuthal equal-area projection in which both the meridians and parallels are curved lines. On it shapes, angles, and distances are all only moderately distorted.

In looking at any map of the Soviet Union, one should bear in mind that the meridians run true north-south and the parallels true east-west. The lettering on the maps in this chapter generally follows the orientation of the parallels and thus helps the reader in

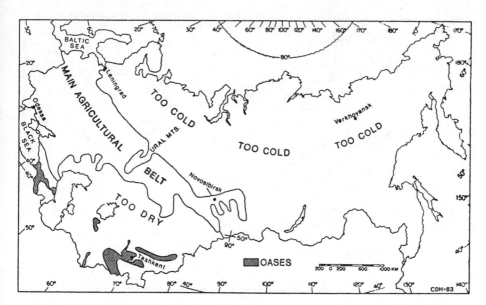

Fig. 2. Main agricultural belt of the Soviet Union and areas generally too cold or too dry for agriculture. For climatic data of five cities named on map, see table. (Generalized from distribution of state farms depicted in *Atlas SSSR*, 1st ed., pp. 112–13, and 2d. ed., pp. 114–15, and from sown area depicted in *Atlas Razvitiia Khoziaistva i Kul'tury*, pp. 62–63, and *Atlas Sel'skogo Khoziaistva SSSR*, pp. 102–3.)

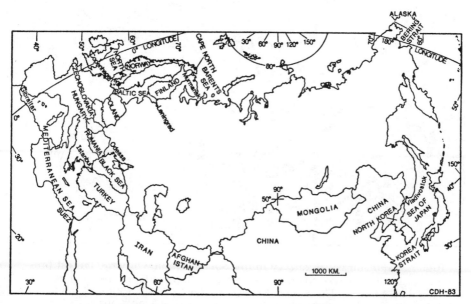

Fig. 3. Boundaries and bordering seas of the Soviet Union. (Based on *The Times Atlas of the World*, comprehensive ed., 5th ed., 1975, plate 16.)

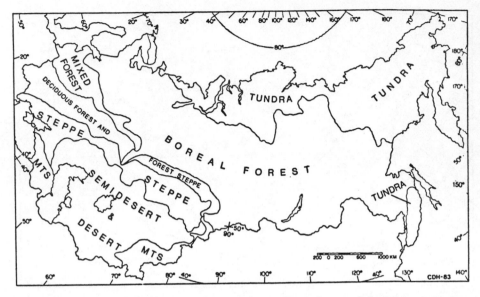

Fig. 4. Vegetation belts of the Soviet Union. (Greatly simplified from *Atlas SSSR*, 2d. ed., pp. 90–91.)

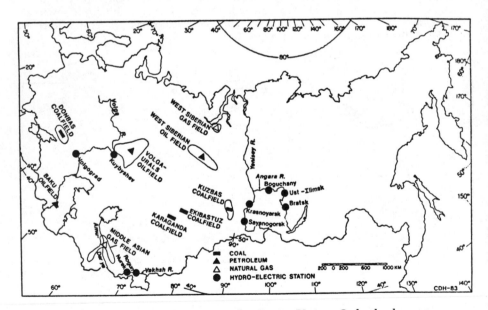

Fig. 5. Major sources of energy in the Soviet Union. Only the largest producers are shown. (Based on *Atlas SSSR*, 2d ed., pp. 105; Leslie Dienes and Theodore Shabad, *The Soviet Energy System,* pp. 45–150; and Paul Lydolph, *Geography of the USSR: Topical Analysis,* pp. 261–301.)

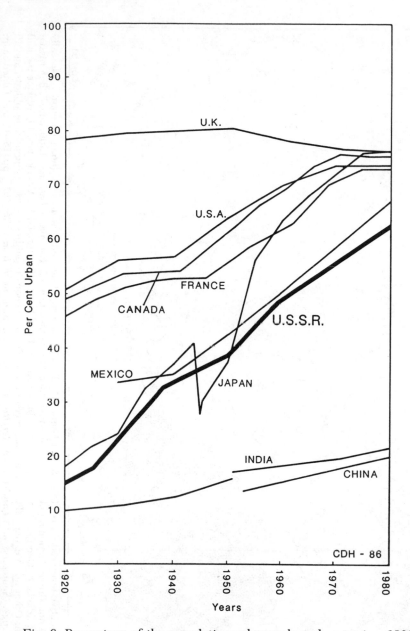

Fig. 6. Percentage of the population urban, selected countries, 1920–80. (Sources: *Narodnoe Khoziaistvo SSSR v 1980g.: statisticheskii ezhegodnik,* p. 7; United Nations, *Demographic Yearbook* 1955, pp. 510–73, 1960, pp. 373–95, 1972, pp. 296–327, 1973, pp. 666–85, Historical suppl., special issue, 1979, pp. 189–209, 1984, pp. 169–86; 1980, pp. 159–96, and official statistics of individual countries, partly estimated.)

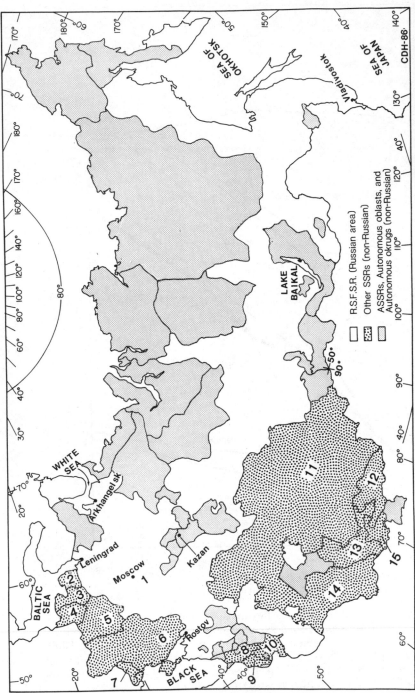

Fig. 7. Administrative-territorial units of the Soviet Union. Of the 15 union republics only the R.S.F.S.R. (no. 1 on map) is basically Russian. The 14 non-Russian union republics (SSRs), from northwest to southeast, are: 2, Estonia; 3, Latvia; 4, Lithuania; 5, Belorussia; 6, Ukraine; 7, Moldavia; 8, Georgia; 9, Armenia; 10, Azerbaidzhan; 11, Kazakhstan; 12, Kirgizia; 13, Uzbekistan; 14, Turkmenia; and 15, Tadzhikistan. Other non-Russian ethnic groups are recognized in 20 autonomous republics (ASSRs), 8 autonomous oblasts, and 10 autonomous okrugs. (Source: *SSSR. Administrativno-territorial'noe Delenie Soiuznykh Respublik, 1977*, pp. 15–16 and folded map; and *Narodnoe Khoziaistvo SSSR v 1984 g.: statisticheskii ezhegodnik*, p. 10).

sensing directions on a map. If in examining maps of the Soviet Union on a conic projection one turns one's head so that the parallels are horizontal in the field of vision, the head is tilted to the right in looking at the western part of the country, with the result that the Baltic Sea appears to run north-south (as it does on the Earth); if the head is tilted to the left in looking at the eastern part of the country, the Bering Strait appears to run north-south, as it does in reality.

The Soviet Union is a giant among the countries of the world. Of continental dimensions, it is larger than South America, only slightly smaller than North America (figure 1), and almost three times the size of the conterminous 48 states of the United States. It covers 22.4 million square kilometers, compared with 17.8 for South America, 24.3 for North America, and 7.8 for the conterminous United States. It includes about one-sixth of the land surface of the globe, excluding areas covered by continental ice sheets.

The Soviet Union extends nearly halfway around the globe in an east-west direction, or some 170 degrees of longitude (from 20 degrees east longitude eastward past 180 to 170 degrees west longitude), through 11 time zones, or nearly 10,000 kilometers. (The east-west distance around the globe is 40,000 kilometers at the equator and 20,000 at 60 degrees north latitude). This is equivalent to stretching from the west tip of Alaska across North America and the Atlantic Ocean to Norway. As a result of this great longitudinal extent the Soviet Union has the most continental climate of any country in the world.

Most of the Soviet Union lies between 50 degrees and 70 degrees north latitude, farther north than any part of the conterminous 48 states of the United States. (The east-west segment of the United States-Canadian boundary is 49 degrees north latitude). The north-south extent of the Soviet Union is about 3,000 kilometers in the western part of the country and about 2,500 kilometers in the eastern part.

As a result of its high latitude most of the Soviet Union has a cool or cold climate. More than half of the Soviet Union lies north of the band of land that has continuous agricultural settlement. On figure 2 this area is marked "too cold."

Because of its great longitudinal extent, most of the Soviet Union lies deep in the interior, far from the western ocean that provides moderating influences and moisture through the "Prevailing Westerlies." The Arctic Ocean on the north is frozen much of the year. The Pacific Ocean on the east affects only a narrow band of Soviet territory. As a result, the climate is continental and generally dry. Much of the interior of the country in Soviet Central Asia consists of vast desert or semiarid stretches marked "too dry" on figure 2; only where rivers issue from high mountains and bring life-giving waters for irrigation are there oases, agriculture, and dense settlements.

The core of the Soviet Union, the main agricultural belt, occupies only about a sixth of its territory but contains most of its agriculture, people, industry, and cities (figure 2). This belt has a broad base along the western border of the Soviet Union, south from Leningrad and the Baltic Sea to Odessa and the Black Sea. It then extends eastward to the Ural Mountains, around the southern Urals and, in a narrower belt, to just beyond Novosibirsk—to the boundary of western and eastern Siberia and of the Soviet Union with China and Mongolia, near 90 degrees east longitude and 50 degrees north latitude.

Expansion of farming to the north and northeast of this core territory is prevented by a combination of unfavorable character-istics: short growing season, cool summer, irregular weather (with danger of unseasonable frosts), infertile podsol soils, generally poor drainage, and, in the eastern part of the country, permanently frozen subsoil (permafrost). At the same time, expansion of agriculture on the dry margin to the south and southeast is discouraged by the low annual rainfall, irregularity and undependability of rainfall, and occasional desiccating winds, called *sukhovei.*

Partly as a result of its huge size, the Soviet Union has the longest land frontier in the world. It has boundaries with 12 countries, more even than Brazil or China, which also border many countries, and far more than other large countries, such as the United States, which borders only two countries, or Australia, with no land frontier at all. Since the Soviet Union stretches across eastern Europe, middle Asia, and the Far East, it has boundaries with Norway, Finland, Poland, Czechoslovakia, Hungary, and Romania in the West, with Turkey, Iran, and Afghanistan in the south and with China, Mon-golia, and North Korea in the southeast. The boundary between the Soviet Union and China is comparable in length to the one between the United States and Canada, and that between the Soviet Union and Mongolia to the line between the United States and Mexico. In general, the southern boundaries of the Soviet Union lie in sparsely settled areas of deserts or mountains; but in the west the border areas are open and densely settled.

The Soviet Union has the longest coastline of any country—and the most useless. In the north the entire Arctic coastline is largely blocked by ice for most of the year. The major ports lie not on the open ocean but on seas, which can be blockaded in time of war. Ships from Leningrad in the west must go through the Baltic Sea and past Copenhagen. Ships from Odessa in the southwest must go through the Black Sea and past Istanbul to reach the Mediterranean, a closed sea except for the Strait of Gibraltar. Ships in the east from Vladivostok must go through the Sea of Japan and out through the Korea Strait, while ships from Murmansk in the extreme northwest must exit through the Barents Sea around Cape North. In peacetime these sea lanes are open; but in wartime they may become choke points controlled by a foreign power.

The extreme continentality and general low precipitation of the Soviet Union are revealed by the accompanying table.
• Odessa, on the Black Sea, in the extreme southwest of the country (figure 2) has a climate much like Chicago (−3 degrees centigrade mean January temperature, 22 degrees centigrade mean July temperature), but with less than half as much precipitation.
• Leningrad, on the Gulf of Finland (an arm of the Baltic Sea), is among the least continental places in the Soviet Union. The city has as great a temperature range from summer to winter as does Chicago, 26 degrees centigrade (between the mean January and mean July temperatures); but it is about four degrees centigrade cooler both in summer and winter. Leningrad, compared to other Soviet cities, is rainy and cloudy, but it still has only two-thirds the precipitation of Chicago.
• Novosibirsk, near the eastern tip of the main agricultural belt, has a mean January temperature of −19 degrees centigrade (15 degrees colder than Chicago), a mean July temperature only three

Climatic Data for Selected Stations

	Mean Centigrade Temperature			Mean Precipitation in Centimeters
	January	July	Range	
Odessa	− 3	22	25	39
Leningrad	− 8	18	26	56
Novosibirsk	−19	19	38	42
Verkhoyansk	−49	15	64	16
Tashkent	− 1	27	28	42
Chicago	− 4	22	26	86

Source: Paul E. Lydolph, *Climates of the Soviet Union* (Amsterdam-Oxford-New York: Elsevier Scientific Publishing Co., 1977); *World Survey of Climatology*, vol. 7, climatic tables, pp. 363–427.

degrees below Chicago's, but an annual range of temperature of 38 degrees, about 50 percent greater than Chicago's. Its precipitation is less than half that of Chicago.

• Verkhoyansk in northeast Siberia, in the heart of the area too cold for successful general agriculture, has a mean January temperature of −49 degrees centigrade, some 45 degrees colder than Chicago's. The difference between the January temperatures of Chicago and Verkhoyansk is almost twice as great as that between January and July in Chicago. The mean July temperature of Verkhoyansk is 15 degrees, about the same as May in Chicago. The annual range of temperature (between the means for January and July) is an incredible 64 degrees centigrade, or two-and-a-half times the range in Chicago. Extreme continentality, indeed! Located deep in the interior of the continent, it receives little moisture, only 16 centimeters a year, less than one-fifth that of Chicago. If it were not so dry, northeast Siberia would be covered by a continental ice sheet. Extinct mammoths from the Ice Age have been discovered with the flesh intact frozen in the permafrost of northeast Siberia.

• Tashkent, in Soviet Central Asia, in an area generally too dry for agriculture without irrigation, is warmer, with temperatures generally three to five degrees centigrade higher than those in Chicago but with less than half the precipitation. Because of the high temperatures and low relative humidity, this precipitation is insufficient for agriculture, even though Tashkent itself, at the base of the high mountains of Soviet Central Asia, receives more rainfall than the desert or semidesert regions proper.

Because of its huge size, the Soviet Union extends not only over many climatic zones but over many vegetation belts as well. The whole northern coast, for example, is bordered by tundra, where the summer months are not warm enough to sustain the growth of trees. A low vegetation consists of mosses, lichens, and dwarf willows only a few inches tall.

To the south of the tundra lies the boreal forest (taiga), occupying nearly half the Soviet Union, with a vegetation of coniferous trees such as pine, spruce, firs, and larch together with broad-leafed deciduous birches and aspens. This zone, larger than all of Canada, is generally hostile to human settlement or agriculture, but it is the source of timber and, locally, of minerals. It covers most of the European north, western Siberia, eastern Siberia, and the Soviet Far East. Its eastern part is underlain by permafrost, which poses difficult conditions for farming, mining, and forestry and for the construction of roads, railroads or buildings.

The ancestral home of the Russian people is the mixed forest zone, with both broad-leafed deciduous trees such as oak, beech, and hornbeam, familiar in central and western Europe, and coniferous trees typical of the taiga. This zone forms a triangle with a base along the western edge of the Soviet Union on the Baltic Sea and the land frontier with Poland, Czechoslovakia, and Hungary, and extends eastward to a tip at the southern part of the Ural Mountains. It is traditionally the land of rye, potatoes, and flax. It has adequate rainfall and moderately fertile soil that is improved by liming and fertilization.

To the south of the mixed forest lies a strip of deciduous forests, forest-steppe, and meadow-steppe—good agricultural land with rich soils and adequate rainfall in most years. It is the land of wheat and sugar beets, extending from the western border of the Soviet Union eastward across the southern edge of western Siberia to the base of mountains near 90 degrees east longitude and 50 degrees north latitude.

The next belt to the south is the famous steppe proper, with its grassy and herbaceous vegetation, fertile black-earth soils (among the best in the world), and low and irregular rainfall with occasional catastrophic droughts. The northern margin of the steppe usually has adequate rainfall for a good crop of wheat and sunflowers, but toward the south agriculture becomes increasingly precarious.

Yet farther to the south and inland lie semideserts, deserts, and mountains. They are the home of non-Slavic peoples. Here are the mountains and fertile valleys of the Trans-Caucasus, with a variety of humid and dry climates, subtropical to alpine vegetation, and agricultural production in favored places. Soviet Central Asia contains great deserts but also oases along rivers, at the base of the mountains, or in mountain-girt valleys. Here cotton is produced.

These great vegetation belts or landscape zones formed the basis of a major contribution by Russian and Soviet scholars to the development of modern soil science. In western Europe, with its relatively uniform climate and complicated geology, early soil scientists classified soils by their parent materials. Russian scientists noticed, however, that soils such as the fertile black earths extended over vast stretches, regardless of parent material, and throughout areas with similar vegetation and climate, such as the steppes. Thus was born the modern field of soil geography, which emphasizes the role of climate and vegetation in the development of the major soil groups of the world.

Soviet agricultural production has regularly fallen far behind the goals of the successive Five-Year Plans. It has not kept pace with the growth in other sectors of the economy, particularly in heavy industry, and has lagged increasingly the improvement of agriculture in other countries. Three factors have been involved: low investments in agriculture, inefficient management, and poor physical conditions. In recent years the first deficiency has been largely overcome, as D. Gale Johnson points out (chapter 17). However, the system of overly centralized direction of farming remains a strongly negative factor.

Yields per hectare in the Soviet Union are roughly comparable to those in climatically similar parts of North America. Within the main agricultural belt of the Soviet Union conditions are much like those in the Prairie Provinces of Canada or the northern Great Plains of the United States. Compared with areas having warmer and moister climates, average yields per hectare are lower, yields fluctuate more from year to year, possibilities of increasing yields are less favorable, and the range of crops that can be grown is more limited. As a result, Soviet agriculture is heavily dominated by grains. Fruit production is hindered by the very cold winters. Vegetables are relatively less important than in the United States. The diet of the average Soviet citizen is more dominated by grains than is that of the average citizen of any other major industrial country.

The Soviet Union has an arable area about as large as that of the United States and Canada combined, yet total production is insufficient for Soviet needs and is much below that of the United States alone. In the Soviet Union the isotherms (lines joining points with the same mean temperature) and isohyets (lines of equal rainfall) are parallel but increase in opposite directions. As one goes northwest the rainfall increases but the temperature decreases, whereas to the southeast it becomes warmer but drier. Thus the areas warm enough for production of maize for grain are too dry, while the areas with enough moisture are too cool for the maize to mature as grain. Hence it is cut green for silage. The Soviet Union lacks those large areas with a combination of adequate moisture, a long, warm growing season, and rich soil that account for the high productivity of the Corn Belt of the United States, with its vast acreage of high-yielding corn and soybeans. Large areas in the production of hay or forage crops in the Soviet Union have low yields.

We know that the Soviet government has placed a high priority on the development of energy and that the country now produces almost as much energy as the United States. The Soviet Union has some of the world's largest reserves of petroleum, natural gas, and

coal as well as abundant water power. But these are generally remote from centers of population and distribution. Their utilization
entails high costs of long-distance overland transport. Of the energy
content of fuels produced in the Soviet Union in 1984, 42 percent
was accounted for by petroleum, 33 percent by natural gas, and 23
percent by coal.

The Soviet Union is now the world's largest producer of petroleum. Exports of petroleum provide a significant fraction of the
earnings of foreign exchange in hard currency, utilized largely to
purchase imports of grain and of up-to-date technology. In recent
decades, huge new oil discoveries in western Siberia have provided
a large and cheap source of energy. This energy, however, must be
transported by pipeline or railroad over long distances.

Until World War II more than three-fourths of Soviet oil production came from the Baku region in the Trans-Caucasus, west of the
Caspian Sea (figure 5). With the postwar discovery of new deposits,
production increased rapidly. The Volga-Ural fields, originally called
the "Second Baku," generally accounted for about 60 percent of the
total Soviet output from the 1950s to the 1970s. The discovery of
gigantic new fields in west Siberia in the 1970s made possible
further expansion. As other fields are either declining or stagnant,
western Siberia has increasingly dominated production, now accounting for more than 60 percent of the Soviet output.

Many Western experts now predict a slowing of the rate of increase and a peaking of oil production in the near future, with
possible limiting effects on the growth of industrial production in
the Soviet Union, on its ability to provide petroleum to the politically and strategically important countries of Eastern Europe, or on
the country's capacity to maintain high levels of petroleum exports
to Western Europe to earn hard currency. It is well to note, however,
that geological conditions in the Soviet Union favor the possible
discovery of major large new petroleum deposits. Improved technology may also make possible utilization of much deeper sources,
as it has in the United States.

Natural gas has only recently come to be used in considerable
quantity in the Soviet Union. As late as 1955 it produced only about
half as much energy as did peat, about a third as much as firewood,
and less than three percent as much as coal. Successful geological
prospecting, a realization that natural gas was by far the cheapest
energy to produce, and the construction of natural-gas pipelines
resulted in significantly greater production. Natural gas quickly
passed peat and firewood as an energy source, and in 1980, for the
first time in Russian or Soviet history, outstripped coal. Production

promises to increase as rapidly in the years ahead and, with the provision of capital, pipeline, compressors, and other technical equipment by Western Europe, Soviet export of natural gas promises to increase substantially in the decades ahead. But again, the larger reserves and the source of rapidly increasing production lie far from the markets, either domestic or foreign. The largest known reserves lie under the cold, bleak forests and the marshes and tundra of the northern part of western Siberia, and under the deserts of Soviet Central Asia.

In total resources of coal the Soviet Union rivals the United States. There is enough to last centuries. Coal production reached a peak in the proportion of Soviet energy supplied in 1950–52, when it provided almost two-thirds of Soviet fuel energy. But the proportion, as already noted, has been dropping because of the increase in petroleum and natural gas. Absolute total production of coal continued to rise for many years, reaching a peak (in standard units of 7,000 kilocalories) in 1978. Since then production has been about level, even though the Five-Year Plans continued to call for substantial increases.

The Donets coal basin (Donbas) in the southwestern part of the Soviet Union has been the main coal producer for more than a century, but costs of mining in this old field have been rising. The Kuznetsk Basin (Kuzbas) in western Siberia has easily mined, high-quality coal. Although it is far from the main markets, it is increasingly supplying coal to much of the Soviet Union. Other large deposits in Kazakhstan are being developed at Karaganda and Ekibastuz, the latter producing a cheap but low-quality fuel. The enormous coal deposits in eastern Siberia are little developed, either because of their remoteness from transportation lines or because of problems with quality.

The largest waterpower potential in the Soviet Union occurs on the Yenisei River and on its eastern tributaries, which run off the central Siberian plateau. Here gigantic hydroelectric projects have been constructed at Bratsk and Ust-Ilimsk on the Angara River, which runs from Lake Baikal to the Yenisei River, and at Krasnoyarsk and Sayanogorsk on the Yenisei River itself. These are in eastern Siberia, far from markets. The electricity must be utilized locally, largely in power-intensive industries. Better located projects have been constructed on the Volga and other rivers, as at Volgograd and Kuybyshev. Two spectacular large projects in Soviet Central Asia on the Vakhsh River (a tributary of the Amu Darya), which flows along the edge of the Pamir Mountains, have very high dams—335 meters at Rogun and 300 meters at Nurek.

Party and government in the Soviet Union have always stressed industrialization, which has prompted geological prospecting over wide expanses of the country. As a result, the Soviet Union is now the world's largest producer of iron ore, manganese, pig iron, and steel among the metals; of mineral fertilizers in the chemical industry; and of petroleum among the fuels. The Soviets have also greatly increased the production of machinery, and the country is now the largest producer of diesel locomotives and of tractors. It lags the United States, Western Europe, and Japan, however, in many branches of light industry and in the production of consumer goods. For example, Soviet production of automobiles per capita is only about a tenth that of Japan, France, or Germany, or a fifth that of the United States.

Urbanization, a phenomenon closely related to industrialization, came later to the Soviet Union than to Western Europe or the United States and has not proceeded as far. The proportion of urban to total population rose from only 18 percent in 1926 to 65 percent in 1985 (figure 6). Yet this figure remains substantially below that of the United Kingdom, Japan, Canada, the United States, or France. In fact, the Soviet Union has closely paralleled Mexico in this respect over the past 60 years. It is, of course, far more industrialized and urbanized than countries such as India or China, where the proportion of population living in cities still remains very low.

Finally, there is the matter of human geography. The Soviet Union is a multinational entity, the product of outward expansion over the centuries. Recognition is given to the various peoples by a series of ethnic-political administrative units, the most important being the 15 union republics, which together constitute the Union of Soviet Socialist Republics. These are in turn subdivided into 20 autonomous republics, eight autonomous "oblasts," and 10 autonomous "okrugs" (figure 7). The western, southern, and northern margins of the country are largely non-Russian in population.

The Russian is by far the largest of the union republics, extending from the ancient home of the Russian people in the mixed forest lands around Moscow northwest to Leningrad on the Gulf of Finland; northward to Arkhangelsk and the White Sea; southeastward to Rostov, the coast of the Black Sea, and the Caucasus; and eastward across the Urals to the Soviet Far East and Vladivostok. But there are notable clusters of other peoples concentrated at the bend of the Volga around Kazan or scattered across Siberia, particularly near Lake Baikal and along the southern boundary of the Republic.

In 1979, 137 million Russians constituted 52 percent of the over-all Soviet population of 262 million. Other Slavs made up 20 percent or 52 million; Turkic and other peoples of largely Moslem tradition, 16 percent or 41 million; and a great variety of yet other peoples, 12 percent or 32 million. (For a more detailed discussion of ethnicity in the Soviet Union, see chapter 26.)

The major ethnic groups, those recognized at the level of a union republic, are being maintained with only moderate assimilation. Ethnic groups of lesser political units are showing higher rates of assimilation. Individuals retain the right to use their national languages only within the political unit that recognizes that group. When members of ethnic minorities migrate to other parts of the Soviet Union, they typically must use Russian. Among the groups that are relatively resistant to assimilation are the peoples of the Baltic (Estonians, Latvians, and Lithuanians), who retain the Latin alphabet in their languages; the ancient Christian peoples of the Caucasus (Georgians and Armenians), who also have their own scripts; the peoples of Moslem heritage, especially the Turkic-speaking peoples of the Trans-Caucasus (Azerbaidzhanis) and of Soviet Central Asia (Uzbeks, Kazakhs, Kirgiz, and Turkmen); and the Tadzhiks. Peoples speaking other Slavic languages—Ukrainian or Belorussian—and those with Christian backgrounds assimilate to the dominant Russian culture much more readily than those with Moslem backgrounds and/or speaking non-Slavic languages. More-over, urban inhabitants assimilate more rapidly than do rural dwellers.

Even in areas that give political-administrative recognition to non-Russian groups, the Russians form a very significant element, typically as a minority in the rural population but forming a large fraction, often a majority, of the population in the cities. The cities thus represent Russian points in non-Russian rural expanses. The Russians are particularly important in administration and industry in, for example, Soviet Central Asia.

Nevertheless, owing to the demographic trends discussed in chapter 26, the non-Russian peoples of Soviet Central Asia will furnish a disproportionate share of births, entrants into the labor force, and recruits into the army in the years ahead. In the industrial core of the Soviet Union, as a result of reduced birth rates, an acute labor shortage is developing, while in the rapidly growing popu-lation of Soviet Central Asia there is a large surplus with rural underemployment. The 1979 census indicates negligible outmi-gration of Turkic people from Soviet Central Asia between 1970 and 1979. (In 1979 less than one percent of Uzbeks, Kirgiz, Turkmen, and Tadzhiks lived outside their republics.) Thus, because of labor shortages in Russian areas and a labor surplus in Soviet Central Asia, Russians may well begin leaving the latter area to return to their homelands, vacating jobs that can be filled by the indigenous Turkic peoples. And such a trend would only work to enhance ethnic diversity in the Soviet Union.

13

Environmental Problems

J O H N   M.   K R A M E R

As long as private ownership of the means of production exists, there can be no conservation and efficient utilization of natural resources. Capitalism is pushing society towards an ecological catastrophe and is threatening many important aspects of the lives of the people. True harmony between nature and society can be achieved only under conditions of socialism with its integral humane social relations.—*Kommunist Ukrainy*, No. 4, 1979.

Only since the mid-1960s has environmental protection drawn considerable attention from the Soviet authorities. Friedrich Engels once warned that man should not be "very hopeful about our human conquest over nature," since "for each such victory nature manages to take her revenge." But in general, Marxism has imbued the Soviet elite with optimism concerning man's ability to transform the physical environment and create a communist society. Political and economic considerations have also impelled the elite, until fairly recently, to view economic development as sacrosanct.

Nevertheless, in its early years the Soviet regime did initiate some measures to protect the environment. By 1920, it had passed laws regulating the use of land, timber, wildlife, fish, and water resources; several of these laws contained provisions to control pollution. In February 1919, the regime established the Central Committee of Water Protection, whose duties included combating water pollution. But since the Soviet state faced acute political and economic problems during these early years, the implementation of conservation laws was often sadly inadequate.

The environment received even less attention during the Stalin years. The Council of Ministers did issue a decree in 1947 outlining measures to reduce water pollution, and in 1949 it established the Sanitary-Epidemiological Service, creating at the same time a commission to elaborate norms for the permissible concentration of pollutants in the atmosphere. Yet these were isolated acts. With the initiation of the Five-Year Plans in the late 1920s, the regime repeatedly stressed the need to surpass economically the developed capitalist countries as quickly as possible. Propaganda extolled the achievements of Soviet industry, and smoke-belching factory chimneys became the symbol of Soviet industrialization. Such priorities did not facilitate the pursuit of sound conservation policies.

Concern for the environment has become more evident since Stalin's death. On June 7, 1957, the Estonian Republic passed a law "for the Protection of the Environment," and by 1963 all of the union republics had promulgated similar legislation. The mid-1960s also witnessed the Soviet Union's first public controversy over the status of the environment. A campaign was waged to protect Lake Baikal—the world's largest repository of fresh water—and its environs from the industrial development that threatened the unique ecology of the region.[1]

More recently, environmental protection has become an issue of national concern. Numerous publications dealing with the environment have appeared, and threats to the ecology of the Caspian Sea and of the Volga-Ural Basin have received extensive press coverage while generating considerable public debate. The government has demonstrated its concern by promulgating an impressive body of environmental protection laws.

Presumably, the Soviet leadership recognizes that past policies have engendered substantial environmental disruption and that it must now strike a better balance between the exigencies of the environment and the imperatives of economic development. Several factors, however, prevent a precise determination of the overall extent of—and costs associated with—environmental pollution.

In part, the problem arises from the nature of pollution itself, since levels may fluctuate rapidly as other factors, such as the weather, also fluctuate. Further, the Soviets have only begun to establish a nationwide system for gathering data on levels and sources of environmental pollution. It is said that current measurements yield only the most general idea about the condition of the environment and provide no data for a whole series of air pollutants, including copper, lead, and zinc.

Finally, the Soviet government has not been completely forthcoming in disseminating available data on environmental conditions, presumably because these may prove politically embarrassing or may undermine ideological claims regarding the superiority of socialism to capitalism in protecting the environment.

Yet, available evidence makes it clear that high levels of environmental pollution do exist in the Soviet Union and that they have entailed considerable costs for the society. One estimate, purportedly based on suppressed official data, reports that air and water pollution inflict upwards of 20 billion rubles (nearly $30 billion at official rates) annually in damages to the economy; unofficial sources place these damages even higher. These costs include the many valuable resources lost through emissions, massive fish kills, accelerated corrosion and decay of buildings and other structures, higher labor turnover in intensely polluted areas, and the economic and public-health costs associated with the increased incidence of pollution-related afflictions such as respiratory diseases.

One Western expert concluded that by the later 1970s water pollution in the Soviet industrial heartland was as pervasive and serious as in the continental United States. A study by the Soviet Academy of Sciences estimated that polluters yearly dump 36 cubic kilometers of contaminated sewage into Soviet waters. The impact of these emissions on water quality is staggering, since they pollute from 12 to 15 times their volume of pure water. According to a "conservative" Soviet estimate, more than half of the country's annual total water runoff is polluted to some degree. Overall, the "absolute amount" of water pollutants is "constantly increasing" and their presence "frequently approaches the assimilative capacity of the water sources." On the other hand, some success in controlling water pollution has been noted. Water quality in the Moscow River, which runs through the capital, has improved dramatically in recent years. The river's soluble oxygen content has increased substantially, and in 1978 it was reported that fish appeared in the river "for the first time in a long time."[2]

Air pollution has only begun to assume the critical levels that water pollution has already reached in many regions of the Soviet Union. Two factors have traditionally limited air pollution—a minuscule number of motor vehicles and an energy balance that relies heavily on liquid fuels, which are less polluting than solid fuels such as coal. Official data, however, reportedly show that air pollution levels in the next few years may approach those found in the United States.

The rapid expansion in the number of automobiles is a primary cause. Although the figure is still small by U.S. standards—approximately 18–20 million in 1980 compared to over 100 million in the United States—these cars are almost entirely concentrated in a few urban centers. Further, poor maintenance and the absence of pollution-control devices make Soviet automobiles far more intensively polluting than their current U.S. counterparts. Consequently, automobiles are already responsible for 25 percent of the air pollution in large cities, and in Moscow the figure is 50 percent.

Predictions are that air pollution levels in the Soviet Union may double by 1990, with the automobile responsible for almost 70 percent of total emissions. Atmospheric quality will probably diminish even further if ambitious plans to increase reliance on heavily polluting coal for generating electricity are realized. In 1982, emissions of sulfur dioxide (which in large part derive from the burning of coal and other fuels with a high sulfur content) exceeded 25 million metric tons—approximately 40 percent of all such emissions in Europe in that year—and studies estimate that by 1992 these emissions could reach 30 million metric tons, primarily because of increased utilization of coal.[3]

In one sense, of course, the same processes of modernization and economic development that disrupt the environment in all industrialized countries account for the now considerable pollution in the Soviet Union. Befouled air and polluted water seem to be among the inevitable—if undesirable—concomitants of modern societies, whether socialist or capitalist. Yet political, economic, and technological factors peculiar to the Soviet Union also contribute to its pollution problems.

First, the government has not committed the political and economic resources necessary to undo past neglect. As have many of its capitalist counterparts, the regime has made rhetorical commitments to enhance environmental quality, but it has not made the difficult and costly decisions necessary to implement these commitments. Thus, the Eleventh Five-Year Plan (1981–85) actually allocated less for environmental protection than did the Tenth Five-Year Plan; nor did the Twelfth Five-Year Plan (1986–90) do much better. Further, the funds allocated to pollution control comprise only a relatively small segment of the total funds for environmental protection, which are dispersed among many projects, such as land improvement.

Second, industrialists exhibit little interest in controlling pollution. Their attitude derives from the emphasis in Soviet economic planning on the production of goods, which leads to bonuses, premiums, and other perquisites for production personnel. Thus, a low priority is assigned to any activity, including pollution control, that detracts from this pursuit. The typical view among Soviet industrialists toward environmental protection is found in the comment of the enterprise manager who admitted that "there really is a lot of smoke from our work, but the plans must be fulfilled. The plan and the rates—these are the main things. The rest can wait."[4]

Such attitudes help explain why many enterprises, despite explicit legal regulations to the contrary, operate without—or with inadequate—waste treatment facilities. For example, between 1975 and 1985 the Soviet Ministry of Power and Electrification failed to install a single installation to abate emissions of sulfur dioxide at its thermal power stations, which annually emit over 9 million tons of this pollutant. And even in Moscow, where the authorities have pursued with some success well-publicized campaigns to control pollution, a large number of pollution sources are still not equipped with treatment facilities.[5]

Part of the problem, as we have seen, lies in the inadequate funds available for pollution control. Between 1976 and 1980 annual appropriations to control air pollution averaged only 260 million rubles, with Moscow receiving almost half of this amount. Nor are all of these funds actually utilized for this purpose, because industrialists divert some of the money to production activities. Moreover, many existing treatment facilities are technologically backward and are poorly operated and maintained. To be sure, one can also find examples in the Soviet press of enterprises successfully controlling their pollution, but careful reading suggests that these accounts are exceptions.

Indeed, the behavior of industrialists has prompted numerous criticisms in the Soviet press and at times even a grim humor. Industrialists are accused of a narrow "departmental" attitude that subordinates society's interest in a clean environment to the pursuit of immediate economic gain. While this criticism has merit, it ignores the circumstance that impels polluters to behave as they do. So long as industrialists find it more profitable to pollute than not to pollute, they will continue to do so. As one source colorfully explained it, forcing enterprises without economic incentives to control pollution is like "getting a cat to eat cucumbers by giving it a lecture on the benefits of vegetarianism."[6]

The legal system has also failed to deter polluters. Most environmental legislation is hortatory, containing general principles but lacking detailed provisions. The Soviet Union still lacks a nationwide law on nature conservation, despite repeated calls by environmentalists for such an act, and it was not until 1980 that national air pollution legislation was promulgated.

The absence of such legislation permits many enterprises to pollute with legal impunity, since they are attached to central ministries and not subject to local legislation. Criminal liability for water pollution exists in all 15 union republics, but for air pollution in only eight; fines imposed for such crimes rarely exceed 300 rubles. Administrative penalties—the most common sanction imposed on polluters—are even more lenient. For example, public-health physicians, the officials most directly involved in regulating polluters, may levy fines of up to 10 rubles for violation of air pollution regulations. The chief public-health physician of the Soviet Union may impose fines of no more than 50 rubles for similar violations. Such fines are even less of a deterrent than these modest sums suggest, since enterprises simply budget for them in their operating expenses.

Deficiencies also exist among the numerous agencies responsible for monitoring adherence to environmental regulations. Coordinating their activities is difficult since they are attached to various ministries at the national and republic levels. As an editorial in *Pravda* explained, this situation stimulates "interdepartmental skirmishes" that engender "unhealthy competition." Then, too, these agencies typically cannot identify those guilty of a particular pollution discharge, since they lack the necessary measuring equipment.

Even more serious, environmental agencies in the Soviet Union have little incentive to pursue their duties vigorously. Not only do they lack political power, but they are usually attached to the very production ministries whose activities most pollute the environment. Consequently, as articles in the press complain, polluters are rarely punished, and when "somewhere, somebody, somehow" is convicted, "it is found that the punishment is purely symbolic and no more annoying than a mosquito bite."[7]

The Soviet Union has responded to its pollution problems primarily through legal and organizational measures. There is All-Union legislation on land use (1968), public health (1969), water (1970), and air (1980). In both 1973 and 1978 the Council of Ministers and the Party Central Committee issued joint decrees to control pollution and protect the environment of specific waterways, including Lake Baikal, the Baltic Sea, the Black and Azov Seas, the Caspian Sea, and the Volga-Ural Basin.

Yet legal measures, as we have seen, have done little to deter polluters. Many Soviet sources, particularly in the academic world, now acknowledge this and argue (as Western economists have long done) that enterprises will control their emissions only when given sufficient economic incentives to do so. The major impediment to the creation of these incentives is the fact that the Soviet Union does not place a price on such natural resources as water and land. This circumstance derives from the Marxist law of value, which considers "free" any goods—such as natural resources—not created by human labor. Unless the regime can overcome its ideological scruples and impose a price on natural resources, enterprises will continue to lack economic incentive to conserve "free" goods.[8]

Soviet authorities have taken several steps to enhance urban environments. They are establishing an automated network in 350 cities to monitor atmospheric quality. Cities have planted vast areas of greenery, in part to purify the air by absorbing carbon monoxide while giving off oxygen. Measures to combat motor-vehicle emissions include the development of computerized traffic-control systems, pedestrian underpasses, and limited access superhighways to facilitate vehicular movement and reduce air pollution, since motor vehicles markedly increase their emissions when breaking and accelerating. The substitution of liquid for solid fuels as a source of power for industrial and residential units has noticeably reduced air pollution in many urban centers, particularly Moscow. However, the current plans calling for a substantial increase in the utilization of solid fuels may reverse this trend.

Soviet officials frequently have justified plans for the large-scale development of nuclear power—including nuclear plants to generate electricity and to provide heat to urban centers—by claiming that nuclear power inflicts minimal (if any) damage on the environment. But the accident in April 1986 at the Chernobyl nuclear plant in the Ukraine, which contaminated extensive regions in both the Soviet Union and eastern and western Europe, seriously damaged these claims. A particular area of concern for environmentalists is that many nuclear reactors in the Soviet Union are built without containment structures and other safety features standard in the West. Soviet officials insist that the incident at Chernobyl will have no impact on their plans to have nuclear power generate approximately 20 percent of indigenously produced electricity by 1990 (versus approximately 11 percent in 1985), although they have pledged to take additional measures to ensure the safe operation of nuclear power plants and to protect the environment.[9]

The Soviet Union also has participated in international efforts to protect the environment. Soviet and American cooperation in this field dates from agreements reached during President Nixon's trips to Moscow in 1972 and 1974 and reaffirmed at the Geneva Summit in 1985. The 1972 agreement included projects devoted to air and water pollution control, urban environmental problems, and scientific research on environmental issues of mutual interest. The 1974 agreement provided for the establishment of "biosphere preserves" in each country as part of a worldwide UNESCO project, wherein Soviet and U.S. scientists could jointly study the impact of man's activity on the biosphere.

The Soviet Union was also an active participant in preparations for the 1972 U.N. Conference on the Human Environment held in Stockholm, Sweden. Although boycotting the conference itself (to protest East Germany's inclusion only as a nonvoting participant), the Soviet Union does support the resulting program and is represented on the governing board designed to coordinate its activities.

Other Soviet positions have not been as helpful for international cooperation. The Soviet Union consistently opposed—as have most countries, including the United States—any international regulation of domestic sources of pollution as an infringement on national sovereignty. Again like the United States, it has demanded exemptions for its warships from the provisions of international conventions to regulate pollution. On balance, its record of international environmental cooperation is probably as good (or bad) as that of most other industrial countries.

An examination of Soviet environmental pollution must evoke *déjà vu* among Westerners. Not only are the problems themselves similar, but so too are many of the factors promoting them. *Homo economicus*, whether socialist or capitalist, seems far more concerned with maximizing production and profit than with minimizing environmental damage. And the same factor in each system—that it is cheaper to continue than to abate pollution—impels *Homo economicus* to behave as he does.

Homo politicus, like his economic counterpart, also manifests seemingly universal traits, including an unwillingness to implement a rhetorical commitment with the requisite political and economic resources. Americans can readily empathize with another trait of the Soviet political system: the problem of coordinating policy among numerous bureaucracies subordinated to different administrative and political jurisdictions.

To be sure, there are important differences between the Soviet and Western systems. Ideological strictures against putting prices on natural resources are an obvious example. The Soviet system also creates a collusive relationship between polluters and the nominal protectors of the environment, because both are government agencies. This circumstance is not unknown in private-ownership systems, but would U.S. environmentalists willingly emulate the common Soviet practice of having both the polluters and protectors of the environment in the same agency?

Conversely, Soviet environmentalists must envy the numerous opportunities that a democratic political system affords Western environmentalists to pursue their goals. Many tactics of U.S. or West European environmentalists, such as the mobilization of political and fiscal resources to elect favored candidates, are simply unavailable to their Soviet counterparts. On the other hand, at public meetings and in the press, Soviet writers and other groups have become increasingly vocal on environmental issues, an outgrowth, evidently, of the policy of "openness" or "publicity" adopted in 1985 by the new Gorbachev leadership.

The extent to which the Soviet political and economic system can respond to environmental pollution is arguable. The ambitious economic plans announced by the Twenty-seventh Party Congress in 1986 made little headway on the problem. Yet the Soviet experience in combating pollution, like the Western, confirms an observation that Thomas Jefferson once made about political corruption: "It is better to keep the wolf out of the fold than to trust to drawing his teeth and talons after he shall have entered."

NOTES

1. For a discussion of the controversy, see Marshall I. Goldman, *The Spoils of Progress: Environmental Pollution in the Soviet Union* (Cambridge, MA: MIT, 1972), pp. 177–210. See also Boris Komarov, *The Destruction of Nature in the Soviet Union* (White Plains, NY: M. E. Sharpe, 1980).

2. W. Douglas Jackson, ed., *Soviet Resource Management and the Environment* (Washington, DC: American Association for the Advancement of Slavic Studies, 1978), p. 103; *Priroda* (December 1969); *Materialnotekhnicheskoe snabzhenie* (December 1978); *Gorodskoe khoziaistvo Moskvy* (August 1978).

3. Komarov, p. 30. Among numerous accounts of the impact of the automobile on the environment, see *Izvestiia* (July 3 and July 4, 1985). Data on emissions of sulfur dioxide are from N. H. Highton, "The Effects of Changing Patterns of Energy on Sulfur Emissions and Depositions in Europe," *Ambio* no. 6 (1982), p. 326.

4. *Zaria vostoka* (Jan. 9, 1980).

5. *Pravda* (July 3, 1985).

6. Komarov, p. 95. John M. Kramer, "Environmental Problems in the U.S.S.R.: The Divergence of Theory and Practice," *Journal of Politics* (November 1974), pp. 886–99, provides a detailed discussion of "departmentalism" and the environment.

7. *Pravda* (Oct. 29, 1980; June 22, 1981); *Sotsialisticheskaia industriia* (July 12, 1980).

8. See John M. Kramer, "Prices and the Conservation of Natural Resources in the Soviet Union," *Soviet Studies* (January 1973), pp. 364–73.

9. *Pravda* (July 19, 1986).

14

Architecture and
Urban Planning

WILLIAM C. BRUMFIELD

"Soviet architecture" is a slippery designation, not only because of zig zags in official policy concerning permissible styles—constructivist, functionalist, neoclassical, bureaucratic pompous—but also because the Soviet Union is such a diverse aggregation of nationalities and cultures.

If one speaks of the architecture of Soviet Estonia or of Soviet Uzbekistan, does this imply a subdivision within a larger category known as Soviet architecture or a distinctly national architecture? In fact, for reasons of cultural policies, the Soviets have tried to have it both ways: public buildings and housing developments in Tashkent and Dushanbe are likely to have "Islamic" decorative motifs incorporated into the design; recent architecture in Estonia shows the influence of neighboring Finland; and in the Caucasus the rough terrain has been exploited to achieve striking forms unknown in other parts of the Soviet Union. Climatic differences, geographical features, and distinctive cultural legacies unquestionably contribute to variations in architectural practice in the 15 union republics.[1]

Yet there can be little doubt that overall architectural policy is directed from Moscow. Moscow's influence extends to the setting of construction goals and the allocation of budgetary resources in the Five-Year Plans, as well as to more specific questions of design and construction technology. The capital contains the headquarters of all major institutions concerned with architecture, planning, and construction—including the state construction agencies (*Gosstroi* and *Gosgrazhdanstroi*), the Union of Architects (with over 13,000 members), and numerous research institutes, such as the Central Scientific Research Institute of Experimental Projects. Local autonomy may be tolerated and even encouraged; but most large projects, be they in Tallinn or in Tashkent, utilize similar construction techniques and frequently the same basic designs.

The centralization of architectural planning—to be expected in a highly centralized state—has been intensified by the top priority assigned to rapid construction according to standardized plans and materials. In explaining this "industrialization" of construction, Soviet writers have noted the pressing need to rebuild the enormous amount of housing and industrial space destroyed during World War II. Yet the large-scale application of rationalized construction methods actually began some 10 years after the war's end. The immediate postwar decade was characterized by a number of grandiose projects (such as the seven "Stalinist Gothic" towers that still dominate the Moscow skyline; see, e.g., figure 1); but the larger needs of society, particularly in housing, were being addressed by construction methods of pre-Revolutionary origins. Furthermore, economic considerations received inadequate attention, so that large sums were expended on prestige buildings, while the majority of the population lived in overcrowded communal apartments or in hastily built barracks.

In 1955 the Central Committee of the Communist Party and the Council of Ministers responded to the housing crisis by adopting a series of measures aimed at transforming the Soviet construction industry. Its thrust involved the implementation of industrialized construction methods based on the prefabrication of standardized parts and modules for assembly on site. In a process called *tipifikatsiia* (typification), architects and designers produced a catalog of building types and interior arrangements that could easily be adapted to large-scale, multistoried housing projects in a variety of settings. Such a system provided an effective means for constructing millions of square meters of housing and factory space quickly, at low cost, and without need for sophisticated technology. With a crane for lifting reinforced-concrete beams and panels into place and a welder's torch to fasten the sections, the shell of an apartment building could be completed within a few months.

The results of industrialized construction on a broad scale have been impressive—at least in quantitative terms. For example, during the Ninth Five-Year Plan (1971–75) some 544 million square meters of housing space were constructed, thus providing new apartments for 56,000,000 people (the rule of thumb is roughly 10 square meters per person). During the same period, around 100 new towns were founded, many of them in the Soviet Far East. More recently, from 1975 to 1979 Moscow added 17.7 million square

Fig. 1. Ministry of Foreign Affairs, Moscow. Completed 1954. Architects: M. Minkus and V. Gelfreikh.

meters of living space (for 1.7 million people, most of whom were resettled from older parts of the city), completed 4 million square meters of industrial space, and built 82 schools and over 1,000 stores and restaurants. The same tempo of construction proceeds today.

  These and other figures spew forth from the planning agencies and are announced with a boosterism that would do credit to any

U.S. Chamber of Commerce. To appreciate the results, however, one must wander among row after row of buildings—newly completed or still under construction—on the outskirts of Moscow, Leningrad, Kiev, or Vilnius. Any of these cities provide excellent examples of industrialized construction, and the Lazdinay region of Vilnius combines efficiency with a concern for aesthetic planning.

But Moscow's projects, by virtue of their scale and use of innovative building methods, are the most impressive. The names of old country estates, formerly on the outskirts of the city, now designate gargantuan new developments within the city limits—an area of 878 square kilometers defined by the Moscow Ring Road. These projects (Chertanovo, Troparyova, Konkovo, Strogino) are called "living massifs," and they are indeed massive: Strogino, nearing completion, will be home to over 150,000 people, many of whom have been moving in during the past two years despite the area's lack of adequate transportation and services. (This is a minor shortcoming for people who have been on a waiting list for years.)

The extent of new construction poses a number of problems for planners and architects, and again Moscow provides the best example, although its problems are shared by Leningrad, Kiev, and other major urban areas. In the early 1970s, there were thoughts of limiting the city's population to 7 million, but it is now over 8.5 million and will continue to increase. To accommodate this number, planners have adopted a radial plan, with eight super zones extending from the city's core. Parks and green areas are interspersed among the zones; and beyond the ring expressway is a green belt, within which are located satellite communities.

This general plan, the formulation of which began in 1961, was approved by the Council of Ministers of the Soviet Union in 1971 with the express purpose of transforming Moscow into a "model communist city." In its second phase, 1976–90, particular attention is to be devoted to the formation of ensembles both in the central city and in the surrounding zones. In specific terms this will mean the integration of "microregions" into a comprehensive plan for land use within the eight major zones. Each planning region is allotted space for social and commercial centers, whereas other areas of the city have been designated as general, "city-wide" centers (for educational, administrative, and research complexes). In addition, the plan projects 46 "production zones" to regulate and contain the city's industrial apparatus (in most cases this will mean the improvement of existing developments).

Essential to the functioning of such large-scale projects is Moscow's rapid transit system, which had reached some 220 kilometers in length by 1985. Other Soviet cities with subway trains include Leningrad, Kiev, Tbilisi, Tashkent, Kharkiv, and Baku. Most regions of Moscow are already efficiently served by a subway system with several radial lines and a ring line connecting them; but the pace of subway construction is not sufficient to meet the needs of a city overwhelmingly dependent on public transportation. Tram lines and an overloaded and frequently dilapidated bus system must fill the gap for hundreds of thousands of residents in the outlying areas. The growth of the number of private automobiles, modest by Western standards, has only served to create new problems by overloading the street network, particularly in the central city.

Moscow's demand for new housing and services is therefore restricted to an area sufficiently compact to be served by public transportation: suburban sprawl is not an option for Soviet developers. The available building space is further restricted by the need to provide open space, all the more essential as population density increases. The solution has been to design taller apartment buildings. At the beginning of the 1960s, the greater part of Moscow's living space consisted of buildings of five stories or less. With improved techniques of construction, the heights of mass-produced buildings increased: 10, 12, 14 stories. By the late 1970s apartment rows of 16–20 stories were not uncommon; and during the current Five-Year Plan such buildings are expected to comprise 65–70 percent of all new housing construction in Moscow. A similar trend has occurred in Leningrad: apartment towers in both cities now frequently exceed 20 stories.

The increase in height has required an increase in technological sophistication, extending from such basic matters as structural integrity to such details as the design of efficient, reliable elevators. More care must now be given to the siting of buildings, in order to achieve the required minimum levels of sunlight exposure and open space. In fact, such requirements are not always faithfully maintained, and in some cases land allocated for open space by the planner has been taken by the builder to meet construction quotas.

The disparity between plan and implementation has created a number of deficiencies, particularly in the area of services to the new regions. With an overriding concern to provide housing space, builders often lag in completing basic service facilities such as schools, clinics, stores, and restaurants. For example, in June 1982 at the Iasenevo project—one of the city's more innovative—the percentages of completion were: housing, 94 percent; schools, 58 percent; stores, 31 percent; restaurants and cafes, 5 percent. The problem has been attributed not only to the lack of integration among planning organizations but also to the lack of penalties against builders who neglect even the insufficient amounts allotted to service facilities in the rush to fulfill construction targets for housing space.

If the lack of coordination within housing projects has elicited complaints from citizens and Party officials, its absence on a broader, interregional level has raised questions among city planners concerned about the "seams" between microregions. In their view, individual developments have been planned with too little concern for the nature of their relation to adjoining developments. As one architect noted: "The basic problem of such projects is that these territories are built up as isolated fragments, developed only in and of themselves. As a result, the city's appearance is formed haphazardly, and the creative architect is pushed into the background."[2] The lack of coordination on this scale can produce an aesthetic disaster, particularly at major points of intersection where no attempt has been made to effect a transition between two (or more) developments.

The very success of Soviet industrialized construction—above all in the area of housing—has created a momentum that does not always respond to redirection or modification. For example, some planners in Moscow have suggested that the ground floor of new apartment buildings be adapted for commercial use, thus alleviating the lack of service facilities mentioned above. But builders with standardized plans for towers are reluctant to introduce modifications for which they are not equipped and that would slow the all-important tempo of construction. Furthermore, the momentum of standardization encourages uniformity in building height, particularly in housing developments, where a frequent pattern has been 12-story rows of blocks with 16-story towers. These figures are now moving to 16 and 22 stories, respectively, and it has been suggested that a less monotonous effect would be obtained by varying the height, with the standard figures used as an average for construction goals. One current adaptation of standardized models to relieve the monotony of the building silhouette is the "block-section" method, a form of horizontal variation consisting of a series of attached towers, or sections, that can be bent as the terrain or planner dictates. This "curtain" effect has been impressively demonstrated in Moscow's Iasenevo region.

Whatever the variations in placement and height, new projects must make some effort to address the problem of design monotony in industrialized construction. Architectural publications frequently contain discussions of this problem in regard to both out-

Fig. 2. Apartment complex, Vasilevsky Island Harbor Development, Leningrad, 1985 (under construction).

ward appearance and interior design. Partial solutions include the use of colored ceramic panels on the exterior, structural modification in the basic box design, and greater variety in the arrangement of interior space. Most new projects are still characterized by ranks of buildings stamped from a few standard models, but the goals of construction can no longer be defined by the speed with which a certain number of square meters are enclosed. New approaches are developed primarily in "experimental housing regions" that display greater creativity in the design of large housing masses (figure 2).

One such region is Chertanovo-North, designed for 22,000 inhabitants and located in south Moscow. In terms both of innovative design and land use and of such conveniences as underground parking complexes and shopping malls, this project offers a view of the latest concepts in Soviet urban planning. The project is dominated by a complex 30-story tower overlooking a small lake. The area around the tower leads to an esplanade and central plaza containing buildings for educational, social, and commercial use. Beyond the plaza are three tower clusters (21–25 stories) visually linked by three additional apartment blocks, whose greatly extended horizontal facades are bent at oblique angles. Interior traffic arteries are underground. The development has a subway station and such futuristic technological services as a central waste-compacting station attached to collection points in the various buildings by underground pneumatic pipes.

Whatever the project—be it for housing, administration, education, entertainment, or trade—Soviet architects are usually constrained by rather limited technological and financial resources and by the narrow range of options presented by industrialized, mass-construction methods. These limitations can, however, serve as a spur to the architect's ingenuity—as in the Children's Music Theater, one of the best of Moscow's recent buildings (see figure 3).

In a booklet devoted to the new theater, the project's designers— V. Krasilnikov and A. Velikanov—comment on the problems of working with prefabricated materials: "Architects are forced to use methods and construction materials worked out by construction and architectural practice, and this places its mark on the architecture

Fig. 3. Children's Music Theater, Moscow. Completed 1979. Architects: A. Velikanov and V. Krasilnikov.

of a building, especially under conditions of industrialized construction."[3] A close inspection of the theater's exterior gives one example of what the architects are talking about. Wishing to create a monolithic structure of simple geometric contrasts but unable to use the techniques of poured, textured concrete that characterize Western "brutalism," the architects have sheathed the facade in textured stone and concrete panels. The seams that mark so much of contemporary prefabricated Soviet architecture are here integrated into the rough surface, thus adapting standardized components to a boldly sculpted design.

The pervasiveness of prefabricated materials in Soviet building does not imply that the architects are locked into patterns of industrialized conformity. New techniques are being introduced, particularly in the development of poured ferro-concrete structures. In 1980 poured concrete comprised almost half of the concrete used in the Soviet Union; and while much of this can be accounted for in foundations, dams, and certain industrial structures, poured concrete (or "monolithic" concrete, as the Russians call it) is being used with increasing sophistication and with some awareness of its aesthetic properties. The most notable structure in this material is the Moscow television tower at Ostankino. In recent years, a number of high-rise buildings have been constructed by raising a central concrete shaft from which the rest of the structure is draped. Space-frame construction is also increasingly in use.

Other innovations in design and materials have appeared in cantilevered structures, covered stadiums, and buildings composed of complex geometric forms. A new biochemical institute in the south of Moscow, for example, resembles a diagram of a compound molecule (the return of *architecture parlante*). Furthermore, the legacy of Russian architecture's great experiment in modernism during the 1920s is being cautiously resurrected, as architectural journals include sketches and quotations from Lissitzky, Melnikov, and the Vesnin brothers.[4] Yet the results of the attempt to create—or revive— a modernist aesthetic in Soviet architecture are mixed. There is no clearly discernible movement or school; and although buildings of distinction have risen in Moscow, Leningrad, and in the Caucasus during the past decade or so, much of what passes for "modernist" architecture is overbearing and awkward.

The problem is compounded by the fact that even showcase buildings in the Soviet Union do not achieve the luster of, say, the best American corporate headquarters. On this point a telling contrast is provided by Moscow's new center for international trade, designed and constructed under the supervision of Western firms. Although not particularly remarkable in conception, the building's sleek gray frame and large window panels of tinted glass stand out in its Soviet context. Indeed, when Soviet planners wish to build a structure intended to accommodate—and impress—capitalists, they will often hire a capitalist firm. The Finns have built a hotel tower in downtown Tallinn, the Swedes have built a large hotel on Vasilevsky Island in Leningrad (see Figure 4), the French have built the grand Hotel Cosmos in Moscow, and in 1980 the West Germans finished the new (second) international terminal at Sheremetevo Airport. In some cases the entire work force has been imported, as have the materials.

In the future, Soviet leaders may also decide to buy abroad rather than depend on the local product. Yet there is little of the interchange between Soviet and Western architects that characterized the vital period of the 1920s, when Le Corbusier, Frank Lloyd Wright, and the architects of the Bauhaus and of *de Stijl* knew their Soviet colleagues and occasionally collaborated with them. Perhaps this will change. In architecture, as in so much else, Russia has frequently assimilated ideas from the West and recast them in re-

Fig. 4. Hotel "Pribaltisky," Vasilevsky Island, Leningrad. Built 1976–78. Architect: N. Baranov. Built by: Skanska Cementgiuteriet, Stockholm.

markable form. If the past decade in Soviet architecture has produced little that is remarkable, its accomplishments in mass planning and construction are impressive and warrant our close attention.

NOTES

1. This essay draws on the author's personal observations of building in the Soviet Union as well as on various Soviet sources, particularly articles published in the journals *Znanie* (architectural series) and *Stroitel'stvo i arkhitektura Moskvy*. For a helpful introductory guide to the literature, see Paul M. White, *Soviet Urban and Regional Planning* (New York: St. Martin's, 1980).

2. M. Shapiro, in a round-table discussion reported in *Stroitel'stvo i arkhitektura Moskvy* no. 11 (1982). The central city has its own problems of aesthetic and design integration, particularly in the wake of devastating urban renewal projects of the 1960s and 1970s. This problem and some solutions are discussed in *Stroitel'stvo i arkhitektura Moskvy* no. 6 (1982). One discussant speaks of the danger of creating "dead zones" by moving people out of the center city, which then becomes a purely administrative center.

3. *Moskovskii gosudarstvenii detskii muzykalnii teatr* (Moscow: Nauka, 1979).

4. See S. Frederick Starr, *Melnikov: Solo Architect in a Mass Society* (Princeton, NJ: Princeton University Press, 1978), for a well-illustrated study of this early leader in Soviet architecture whose work was later repudiated.

THE ECONOMY

Soviet economic growth since World War II has been steady, and Soviet economic performance has frequently been impressive. But in the past two decades the rate of growth has declined, difficulties have multiplied (in part the result of earlier successes), and a kind of stagnation has set in. The Soviet economy is not on the verge of collapsing. Yet by all indications it is in serious trouble—more serious, in several critical respects, than is that of the West.

James R. Millar surveys the current situation in the light of both developments since the 1950s and the economy's future prospects, emphasizing in the process the many dilemmas and hard choices facing the leadership. Marshall I. Goldman focuses on the plight of Soviet consumers, who have money enough to spend but find little that is desirable to buy. D. Gale Johnson, also going back to the 1950s, discusses the difficulties of Soviet agriculture, while Perry L. Patterson, in the last of the chapters in this section, looks at the Soviet approach to foreign trade.

Whether the subject is agricultural imports, technology transfer, improving the range and quality of consumer goods, or raising the hard currency needed to facilitate these vital transactions, it seems clear that Soviet economic interdependence with the rest of the world is growing irreversibly.

15

An Overview

J A M E S R. M I L L A R

Comrades, the Communist Party is advancing a great task—to achieve in the coming 20 years a living standard higher than that of any capitalist country and to create the necessary conditions for achieving an abundance of material and cultural values.

—Nikita Khrushchev[1]

In the 1980s the Soviet Union may pass through the worst period since the death of Stalin. Growth rates will be the lowest ever, and the population can expect a stagnating or even declining standard of living. The very stability of the social system may be in question.

—Seweryn Bialer[2]

Three years after announcing the heady goals quoted above at the Twenty-second Party Congress, Nikita Khrushchev was deposed. That same year, 1964, the Soviet Union imported a large volume of grain on a net basis for the first time since World War II, a policy that was continued in ever-increasing volume throughout the Brezhnev years. The high rates of growth in gross national product and of per-capita consumption achieved during the 1950s began to decline immediately following the congress, and they have continued in systematic decline ever since. Seweryn Bialer's prediction for the 1980s, quoted above, was based on projections to the end of the decade of declining and/or stagnant rates of economic growth.

What happened to undermine Khrushchev's confident, sunny forecast of 1961? Is the current picture as gloomy as Bialer suggested? What are the leadership's economic alternatives? My purpose here is to describe and evaluate briefly the principal structural

177

and performance changes that have taken place in the Soviet economy since Stalin's death in 1953. I will then examine the policy options currently available to Soviet policymakers and speculate about the course of the economy in the next decade.

Soviet history is replete with abrupt, traumatic changes in social and economic conditions. World War I, the Revolution of 1917, the Civil War, collectivization and rapid industrialization, the great purges, World War II, and postwar reconstruction all demanded considerable personal sacrifices and caused significant structural changes in the economy. Change has been more gradual since Stalin's death, but the cumulative effect of reform and policy revision during the 30 years of Khrushchev and Leonid Brezhnev was greater than may be generally realized. The current leadership confronts an economy that is quite different in both structure and performance from the one that faced Khrushchev in 1953 or Brezhnev in 1964.

Structurally, between 1928 and 1953 Soviet economic development represented a variant of the "classical" model. Growth was achieved by mobilizing under- and unemployed labor and by shifting labor from low- (or zero-) productivity sectors into sectors where productivity was relatively higher (or positive) or increasing at a relatively high rate. A large share of the resulting increase in final product was reinvested in the growth sectors, thereby providing still more employment opportunities in high-productivity sectors. In general, labor moved out of rural nonagricultural as well as agricultural employment into industrial occupations. About 15 million people migrated from the countryside between 1928 and 1940. Labor also moved from activities not valued in the measurement of gross national product into those that are "counted." The largest single component of the latter flow was made up of women moving mainly into the lower-productivity jobs abandoned by men—that is, into agriculture, light industry, and retail sales.

The Soviet model differs from other classical cases of economic development, such as that of Japan, chiefly by the degree to which heavy industry was accorded priority. World War II and the Cold War that followed accentuated this priority in the Soviet Union, for conventional warfare requires a heavy industrial base above all else. Autarkic development of domestic raw materials and natural resources was another response to the Soviet Union's international situation. Thus, unlike Japan, it did not develop a comparative advantage in exportable consumer goods. It did so in energy, raw materials, and armaments.

The principal structural changes in the Soviet economy *since* Stalin's time have been modifications designed to accommodate a higher priority for consumer goods and, perforce, a higher priority for agriculture, light industry, and residential construction. This has required changes in the leadership's long-standing preferences for industry over agriculture, for the urban worker over the rural—for, in short, the hammer over the sickle.

Khrushchev and Brezhnev were favored by several circumstances in seeking to revise priorities. Khrushchev obtained relatively quick, if somewhat transitory, returns by bringing 36 million hectares of virgin land under the plow and by improving incentives in agricultural production. Brezhnev benefited from the surge in employable population resulting from the country's postwar baby boom. The rural sector also provided a substantial flow of labor. Thus, although resources were gradually shifted away from previously preferred sectors, the availablity of new supplies of land and labor helped to cushion both a decline in the rate of growth of total investment and the shift of an increased share of total net investment to agriculture and related industries.

Even so, the trend in the growth rate of the gross national product declined in the early 1960s (table).[3] The sectors into which resources were rechanneled were those of relatively lower productivity, while the increase in total factor productivity—that is, the increase in output not attributable to quantitative increases in inputs of capital and labor—also declined after 1970. Agricultural output after 1958 grew at a healthy, although slackening, rate. Unfortunately, the real resource cost of agricultural output rose continuously because productivity did not.

AVERAGE ANNUAL GROWTH OF SOVIET GROSS NATIONAL PRODUCT

	1956–60	1961–65	1966–70	1971–75	1976–80	1981–84
Average annual growth (percent)	5.9	5.0	5.3	3.7	2.6	2.7

The problems of the Soviet consumer and of Soviet agriculture are dealt with specifically in the chapters that follow. But here a few generalizations are in order. Consumption per capita increased at an impressive rate during the post-Stalin period taken as a whole, averaging in excess of 3 percent per year for 1951–80. This performance was better than that of the United States, Canada, Sweden, Switzerland, and the United Kingdom. France, Italy, and West Germany performed somewhat better, averaging 3.9, 4.0, and 4.6 percent, respectively, over the same period, and Japan attained a phenomenal annual rate of 6.6 percent.

At the same time, the composition of Soviet personal consumption expenditures changed in accordance with the profile typical of industrialized countries, if at a more gradual rate than in most other developing economies. Food declined as a portion of total personal consumption, from 60 percent in 1951–55 to 45 percent in 1976–80, and durables increased from 2 to 11 percent. But services remained essentially constant at about 23 percent.

Thus Khrushchev and then Brezhnev did succeed in raising the priority of the consumer sector in the Soviet economy. But three serious and related problems remained:

• Attainment of a relatively high rate of growth of consumption per capita was more costly in real resources than had been anticipated.

• The rates of growth in all consumption subseries began high but have been declining since. Although the Brezhnev government succeeded in reversing the downward trend in 1966–70, immediately after assuming power, the downward trend reasserted itself thereafter. The 1980s have been characterized by stagnation.

• Khrushchev committed himself to a policy of retail price stability, which Brezhnev followed. As agricultural production costs and money payments to farmers increased, nominal retail prices on a multitude of products, especially foodstuffs, came to bear little relationship either to cost of production or to each other. This continues to be the case.

Competition among increasingly affluent consumers for underpriced goods has perpetuated queuing as a major activity of adult Soviet citizens and fostered a wide range of illegal and quasi-legal private dealings (sometimes called the "second economy"). As rates of growth in output decline or stagnate at low levels, the hope of meeting effective demand at existing consumer prices in state retail outlets is clearly doomed. Elimination of queues and of black- and gray-market opportunities would unavoidably require price adjustments—all upward. To raise prices, however, has been considered politically risky. Scattered evidence of food riots in the Soviet Union suggests that this is not an idle consideration, as does the experience of the Polish leadership in recent years.

Irrationally low official prices create consumer expectations that are certain to be frustrated, and these frustrations are blamed on the government. Raising prices generates immediate protest. This is a dilemma no Soviet government since Stalin has been prepared to resolve. Thus, the annual state subsidy of consumer goods continued to grow, increasing from 35 billion rubles in 1981 to an estimated 50 billion in 1983.

During the rapid industrialization of the 1930s, procurement of adequate food grains to provision urban workers was the primary index of the success of Bolshevik agricultural policy. Since Stalin, the index has increasingly been the provision of animal husbandry products, particularly red meat. This was demonstrated by the Brezhnev government's willingness to expand greatly the use of hard currency to purchase large quantities of grain in the West. These purchases were not made to supply food grains for Soviet dinner tables; rather, they were needed in order to meet the goals set for livestock herd expansion, for which domestic grain and fodder production was inadequate. With the help of imports, animal husbandry expanded substantially: total meat production rose by approximately 4 percent a year between 1951 and 1979, and milk output by about 3.5 percent. Success in this endeavor may also be measured indirectly, by an increasing incidence of coronary-artery disease, with attendant morbidity, among Soviet citizens.

The Brezhnev regime benefited from two windfalls that helped to finance the shift in priorities. The price of gold soared as a result of floating the dollar and other "hard" currencies in the 1970s; and the formation of OPEC drove petroleum prices up beyond any expectation. As a major producer and exporter of both gold and petroleum products, the Soviet Union enjoyed a substantially improved foreign position.

These windfalls were not sufficient, however, to offset completely a growing conflict of priorities during the 1970s and early 1980s. Sometime late in the Khrushchev period a decision was made to increase the share of gross national product devoted to defense expenditures, most probably as a response to Khrushchev's humiliation in the Cuban Missile Crisis of 1962. During Brezhnev's time, the Soviet Union achieved parity with the United States in military strength for the first time. This absorbed about 12–14 percent of Soviet gross national product, a proportion that rose to 15–17 percent thereafter. The implication is that an increased share of final product will continue to be required for military purposes in order to maintain parity.

The current Soviet government therefore faces direct competition between the goal of increasing per-capita consumption and that of maintaining—let alone expanding—the Soviet military establishment. Unless a breakthrough is achieved that will accelerate technological innovation in Soviet industry and agriculture, or unless augmented supplies of labor and capital are obtained to continue the traditional pattern of growth, the regime will face a direct trade-off between producing red meat and maintaining, so to speak, the red menace. The Soviet leadership cannot determine defense policy unilaterally. It is determined by reactions to perceived external threats as well as by domestic considerations. Thus continuation of the arms race may lead to a degree of disappointment of consumer expectation that could threaten "the very stability of the social system," as Bialer, quoted above, suggests. The alternative is to seek arms limitation or, better, arms reduction.

No help can be expected from the growth of employment, which has declined from 2 percent per annum during 1965–70 to about 0.05 percent per annum currently. Projections suggests a constant labor force through the year 2000. Since labor participation rates are already high for women as well as men, when compared to those of other developed economies, there is no obvious reserve to tap. Agriculture still employs a great deal of manpower, but outmigration is being discouraged for the sake of agricultural output. Only a sharp reduction of the large standing army would supply a significant new source of manpower.

Meanwhile, gross national investment has been one-third of gross national product in the 1980s, up from one-fourth in 1960. This share is already high, cross-nationally, and is unlikely to increase further. The rate of growth of investment has slowed to less than 3 percent per year, down from 7.6 percent in 1965–70. Further sources of investment capital, in short, are not likely to appear.

Imports of capital embodying new technology represent a potential source of growth, but imports have not composed a large share of total Soviet investment in machinery and equipment (only about 3 percent recently), and expansion is constrained by limits on hard-currency earnings. Recent declines in the price of oil do not help. Imports of grains, meat, and other consumer-related items compete directly for foreign exchange with imports of investment goods.

Innovation by Soviet enterprises has been slow and uncertain, and this has inhibited economic growth. Moreover, costs of most raw materials have been rising because of quality decline in mined-out regions and because of the increased cost of locating, recovering, and transporting resources from sites that are increasingly remote from traditional population centers.

To top it all off, maintaining control in Eastern Europe is increasingly costly. Intervention in Afghanistan is proving an expensive exercise, and relations with China are unlikely to improve sufficiently to permit reduction of military power designated to protect the long common border.

The economic situation looks difficult indeed for the current Soviet leadership. A number of hard choices must be confronted, and soon.

Although the troubles and restraints enumerated above are real and serious, it does not follow that Soviet policymakers consider the situation to be as bleak as do most Western analysts. It is easy to exaggerate the long-term consequences of today's ills, and much that is completely unexpected can happen between now and the end of the century. Besides, the fundamental strength of the Soviet economy, like that of the American, resides in its size, in the skills of its population, in the extraordinary richness of its natural resources, and in the proven ability of the leadership to respond effectively to problems old and new.

The Soviet Union has experienced victory in the most ferocious and devastating war in history; a rise during the postwar years to military parity with the largest economy in the world; a doubling of the living standard of the population as a whole over that same quarter of a century; and its transformation into a modern industrial state surrounded by a large, relatively prosperous empire. Moreover, year in and year out the Soviet economy is still growing more rapidly than the U.S. economy, which means that the gap between them continues to narrow, albeit more slowly than before. Why should Soviet leaders conclude that the problems they face today are fatal?

It would be wise to discount predictions of imminent Soviet economic collapse. But how might the performance of the Soviet economy be improved over the next decade or two? Can acceptable rates of growth in the non-defense components of the gross national product be reestablished for a decade or more? The problem is at base one of stagnation, and its solution requires searching for ways to increase the supply of final products and/or to reduce final demand. Let us consider demand management first.

The most obvious solution is a reduction in the share of gross national product absorbed by defense expenditures. As we have seen, this share is currently estimated at more than 15 percent. A slowdown in the rate of increase in military expenditures from 4–5 percent per annum to, say, 1–2 percent would allow for increased rates of growth for both investment and consumption. Observers of

Soviet affairs agree that the leadership is ripe for serious arms talks for this reason, but successful negotiation requires readiness on the part of the United States and its allies, which is what makes this alternative problematic from the Soviet standpoint.

There are two broad schools of thought in the West about the potential usefulness of arms limitation agreements with the Soviet Union. One holds that fundamental change in the nature of the Soviet political system must precede any significant agreement. Otherwise, the Soviet leadership would merely exploit the agreement to its own advantage, one way or another. The other school operates on the assumption that the leadership is willing and able to conduct—and to adhere to—an arms-limiting agreement. Favorable change in the nature of the Soviet system would, in this view, be fostered by the agreement itself. Meanwhile, careful verification and vigilance would be required to ensure against cheating.

Appraisal of these two views is beyond the scope of this essay. What is significant is that from the end of 1979 or so, the United States has favored the first view. In fact, some members of the Reagan Administration have suggested that acceleration of the arms race by the United States would foster favorable change in Soviet domestic and foreign policies by increasing the competition for domestic resources, as defense absorbs an ever-increasing share of Soviet output.

But from the Soviet point of view, as we have seen, the constraint on a policy aimed at deceleration of the arms race is its dependence on the other side. Insofar as Soviet leaders sense that U.S. disarmament policy is aimed at forcing change in Soviet domestic policies, they are certain to move slowly and with extreme caution. On the other hand, deceleration of the nuclear arms race, attractive as it must seem, does not offer them a reliable way to free resources to support a new economic policy. A more reasonable goal would be to attempt either to contain their military spending at current levels—so that the crunch does not get worse—or to reduce conventional armaments. All other economic-policy options involve finding ways to increase the growth rate of the Soviet gross national product and thus the supply of final product. There remains, to be sure, the possibility of improving the way in which consumer demand is managed centrally.

There can be no doubt that demand exceeds supply for most quality commodities and services in state-operated retail outlets. This is because many of the most desirable goods and services— such as red meat, vegetables and fruits, quality apparel and state-of-the-art durables—are underpriced by very large margins. Underpricing leads not only to queuing, but to "scarcity mindedness." Runs on periodically scarce commodities in retail outlets tend to make these items scarce all the time. Underpricing must, in addition, tempt many Soviet citizens into undertaking illegal middleman activities in black and grey markets in order to collect the difference between actual and equilibrium prices. Deficit supplies of goods have a deleterious effect on total employment and on incentives to work hard and advance professionally. Time is better spent in queues or at leisure. Elimination of supply shortages would have a beneficial effect on productivity and thus on output.

Consumer demand management could be greatly improved—and illegal, petty private enterprise diminished—if flexible prices were used to a greater extent. But this would require raising prices on many goods—a process that would, in turn, redistribute income among Soviet citizens in a significant but not entirely predictable way. People with more time than money would surely lose out. And if prices were also raised in the special stores open to privileged groups, those outlets would be effectively closed. Better demand management alone, then, might do as much political harm as economic good and so is unlikely to be seen, by itself, as a way of making friends or encouraging productivity. Yet some realignment of retail prices and a consequent reduction in the huge subsidies that now support many commodities represent essential first steps toward any fundamental reform of the Soviet economy.

Soviet leaders and economists have been considering and implementing structural reforms in planning and management since the early 1960s. But if periodic reform has become institutionalized by now, thoroughgoing reform has yet to be undertaken. Nor are radical changes likely to be introduced by the leadership. The degree of centralization of the economy is unlikely ever to be reduced sufficiently to permit a significant exercise of discretion at the enterprise level. Recently the tendency to write tight plans has been curbed somewhat, but it remains a standard central management tool. The amount of detail in Soviet plans is also likely to be reduced only gradually and marginally.

A wholesale reform of Soviet central planning and of managerial incentives—a prospect that has excited the attention of many Western observers for almost two decades—does not appear to be in the making. Rather, the fundamental paradigm of central planning remains intact and, like other paradigms, will not disappear until replaced by a new conception of planning. Market socialism has, to date, been rejected by dominant Soviet economists and policymakers. And although much has been written in the West about the possible applicability of the "Hungarian model" to the Soviet economy, what is often overlooked is the fact that since its introduction in Hungary itself, the rate of increase in gross national product in that country has not risen significantly. Besides, Hungary is too small and too export-oriented to serve as a model for the Soviet Union.

This does not mean that serious economic reform in the Soviet Union is out of the question; but it is more likely to happen somewhere other than the central planning and management institutions. If the reform movement of the past two decades has produced any consensus, it is that policy on consumer prices in state retail outlets must be changed before any other reforms can be expected to work properly. In short, the present price system is perceived by all concerned as capricious and inequitable and as an invitation to citizens to participate in black, gray, and other illegal marketeering.

Soviet leaders had hoped that with increased output economies of scale would eventually permit satisfaction of demand at 1953 prices. This expectation has clearly and unambiguously failed for all agricultural products. But how are anxious Soviet consumers to be persuaded, after repeated promises of stable prices, that they cannot have their cake and eat it too? Consumers complain about queues, but they complain even more loudly about price increases.

Nonetheless, Soviet authorities may seriously consider retail price reform as a component of a major economic reform program. It would not suffice by itself but would have to be part of a package that would not only make more palatable the bitter pill of income redistribution but also lead to a sustained period of improved growth performance. The appeal of price reform to Soviet leaders is obvious: it would decrease queuing and complaints about special privileges and it would help stamp out economic crime. The danger is that consumers would not stand for it.

Price reform could be accompanied by the large-scale—but short-term—import of consumer goods. This policy would minimize the price increases required to eliminate queues in individual markets and at the same time increase total satisfaction, offsetting somewhat the impact of redistribution on the losers. Price reform would also require some wage adjustments. My guess is that the result would be greater inequality in income distribution, which might in turn have a favorable impact on incentives. Moreover, unfavorable comparison with imported consumer goods might help to improve the quality of Soviet goods. And once retail prices were better adjusted, wholesale prices could be adjusted also, giving managerial incentive reform experiments a better chance of success.

A minor but potentially significant component of reform was announced in 1986. The aim was to facilitate small-scale private enterprise in urban areas, especially in services, a region that has been dominated by "second-economy" activities. The fostering of repairs of durable goods and autos, hairdressing, and similar economic activities by the private sector, accompanied by provision of the necessary tools, parts, and other supplies through state outlets, will no doubt reduce economic crime and improve the efficiency of these activities for the benefit of all—as some very limited moves in this direction in the earlier 1980s tended to show. The same holds true for permitting greater enterprise by farmers on private account. Willingness to tolerate such petty private enterprise is a victory of economic rationality over hidebound ideology.

With better management of demand and three to five years of increased imports of consumer goods, the government could buy time to focus on ways of regaining some of the dynamism of earlier growth. One possibility would be to find a way to offset the decline in the rate of growth of both manpower and capital stock. A second would be to achieve a reasonable rate of growth of total factor productivity—perhaps of 1.5–2 percent per annum.

Restructuring prices and wages ought to make material incentives work better all around, but even this would not be sufficient to achieve what is needed. Relatively unproductive labor, labor that could be shifted to better uses, does exist in the Soviet Union, but it is located far from the more industrialized regions. Restructuring of wages could be done in such a way as to attract workers from Central Asia and elsewhere to the industrial regions or to resource-rich Siberia.

Some Western specialists believe that cultural barriers limit voluntary outmigration from these areas. There is considerable countervailing evidence from elsewhere, however: in the movement of Pakistanis to England, for example, of Turks to West Germany, or of Algerians to France in the 1950s and 1960s. In the Soviet Union such a policy has never been tried with comparable incentives. The barriers may reflect racism more than cultural preference.

Internal migration is not the only possibility. The Soviet Union might decide to use foreign workers on a greater scale, adopting one of the tools of successful growth in Western Europe. There are, however, two main constraints on such a policy: (1) obtaining, or creating, currency that is "hard" enough to be an incentive and (2) policing a large number of foreign workers. Either obstacle is probably sufficient to rule out this option.

Another possible reform would be to encourage foreign investment in the Soviet Union and to rely more heavily on foreign borrowing to finance inputs of capital. The Soviet Union has always been a very conservative debtor country, and its current debt-service ratio is relatively low. A more aggressive policy of risk taking would find lenders. Careful choice of capital imports designed to maximize desirable technological features would help generate growth of factor productivity. This option shows some promise.

Japan, for example, represents an ideal trading and venture-capital partner for the Soviet Union. Japan's technology is well developed in many of the areas where the Soviet Union is particularly weak: high technology, the production of high-quality consumer durables, and the use of robots to minimize the demand for labor in the modern industrial sector. The Soviet Union, on the other hand, has the vast natural resources that Japan lacks. There are similar possibilities with other countries, and European nations appear prepared to continue to expand economic relations with their Soviet neighbor.

Finally, if retail prices could be set at clearing levels and used flexibly to bring supply and demand into equilibrium, a solution to the food problem could be found. Because retail prices are kept artificially low to subsidize the urban dweller, producer prices also tend to be set too low to serve as adequate incentives to farmers. Besides, a wide gap between the two would cause farmers to buy at retail to deliver wholesale. Countries that subsidize farmers rather than consumers, such as the United States and France, usually face agricultural surpluses. In seeking to subsidize consumers, however, the Soviet Union perpetuates shortages. A major restructuring of retail and wholesale prices for agricultural products could break the vicious circle and go far toward generating both the resources and the incentives required to stimulate higher productivity more generally.

Some combination of the policies described above could alleviate the resource crunch that the current Soviet leaders face. But there are other factors that could make these alternatives easier or harder to implement, factors over which they have no real control. A recurrence of better weather conditions for a decade or more could greatly ease things; two or three good harvests per Five-Year Plan would raise the rate of growth a percentage point or two and reduce competition for foreign exchange between investment and consumption.

Full economic recovery in the West would also be helpful. Rising world industrial production and a growth in international trade would help firm the prices of petroleum and natural gas. It would also help Eastern European economies, which depend heavily on exports to the West for prosperity. Greater prosperity in Eastern Europe might dampen political discontent there and thus reduce demands for Soviet economic assistance and for Soviet forces to cope with social unrest.

Speeches by Soviet leaders over the last several decades have often featured calls to Party members for a return to the ideological dedication of the halcyon days of the 1930s and to the populace as a whole for a return to the moral commitment of wartime Russia. Thus far, they have generated little more than nostalgia. There is no evidence that the Soviet leadership or the Party that it speaks for knows how to rekindle these emotions, but there is little doubt that doing so would work miracles in the economy. What seems to be needed is a "moral rearmament" movement: the creation, somehow, of born-again communists. Although its seems an unlikely prospect, we should not overlook the possibility of a rededication to Marxist goals among Party members or a resurgence of long-standing populist ambitions.

The best of all possible worlds for the Soviet leadership would include a series of excellent harvests, a deceleration of the arms race, quietude in Eastern Europe, and full economic recovery in the West. Were it to adopt policies leading to an end of the war in Afghanistan, increased rationality in setting retail and wholesale prices, and the mobilization of new and/or more productive labor and capital, the Soviet gross national product could grow at a rate that would satisfy most members of society and help foster ideological and spiritual commitment to the regime and its goals.

Of course, the worst may happen instead. Climatic change may contribute to more poor harvests; the arms race may accelerate; and Eastern Europe, Afghanistan, and other parts of the Soviet Union's empire may become even more unstable and costly to discipline and police. Price reform may backfire, causing domestic unrest. Both labor and capital productivity may decline further because of the resulting economic disarray, leading to general political instability.

Usually, in history, neither the worst nor the best happens. Early indications of Soviet economic growth in 1986 are encouraging, and the prospects for success in stabilizing growth at a level tolerable to the leadership are quite good. The big question is whether the leadership has the power, the courage, and the foresight to develop and implement a well-wrought, rational policy—or whether, instead, it will hesitate before the risks that such a course of action poses and decide to follow the example set by Brezhnev at the end of his career, which was to coast, leaving the hard choices to his successors.The jury is still out on this question.

NOTES

1. *Report on the Program of the Communist Party of the Soviet Union* (Moscow: Novosti, 1961), vol. 2, p. 85.

2. Seweryn Bialer, *Time* (November 22, 1982), p. 26.

3. The performance data cited here and elsewhere in this chapter are based on the following computations and estimates: USSR: *Measures of Economic Growth and Development, 1950–1980*. Report of the Joint Economic Committee, U.S. Congress. (Washington, DC: Government Printing Office, 1982); *Soviet Economy in a Time of Change*. Report of the Joint Economic Committee, U.S. Congress. (Washington, DC: Government Printing Office, 1979); *Allocation of Resources in the Soviet Union and China in 1984*. Report of the Joint Economic Committee, U.S. Congress. (Washington, DC: Government Printing Office, 1985); *Economic Survey of Europe in 1981* (New York: Secretariat of the U.N. Economic Commission for Europe, 1982); and *Handbook of Economic Statistics, 1985* (Washington, DC: Directorate of Intelligence, September 1985). See also James R. Millar, *The ABCs of Soviet Socialism* (Urbana, IL: University of Illinois Press, 1981).

16

The Consumer

MARSHALL I. GOLDMAN

In the Stalinist model of economic development, the consumer generally comes last. The highest priority is placed on heavy industry. The hope is that by initially giving priority to heavy industry and capital accumulation, overall economic growth in the long run will be faster than if light industry had been stressed. Then, once the economic foundation has been created, the expectation is that economic planners will be able to switch their priorities and pay more attention to consumption. Because the economic base is larger than it otherwise would have been, the planners promise to increase the production of consumer goods rapidly. Thus, before too long, consumers will be better off than they would have been if a more traditional strategy had been followed.

Pacified by the promise of an abundant tomorrow, Soviet consumers for decades have patiently endured the diversion of the country's resources into the building of industrial and military might. But after so many years of such promises, more and more Soviet citizens are beginning to wonder whether tomorrow will ever come. Indeed, to coin a phrase, in the Soviet Union "tomorrow" has become the "opiate of the people." Unfortunately for Soviet leaders, there is evidence that, just as in Eastern Europe, the impact of the drug may be wearing off. Signs of protest have begun to increase, and friction has occasionally given way to violence.

Soviet leaders are not insensitive to popular discontent. At a meeting of the Central Committee of the Communist Party in November 1981, Leonid Brezhnev, the late Party leader, acknowledged that "food is economically and politically" the central problem of the Eleventh Five-Year Plan (1981–85). As we shall see, he had cause to be concerned. But it will take more than acknowledging it to remedy the problem. For that matter, merely increasing the allocation of resources to food and consumer-goods production is not enough. As it is, the share of the country's national investment going to agriculture has grown to 27 percent of the total.[1] The difficulty is that this newfound concern for agricultural investment has come too late to produce a quick improvement.

Until the mid-1950s, agriculture in the Soviet Union was treated as the economic sector from which resources were to be taken. Under Stalin, investment in agriculture was held to as low as 13 percent. Moreover, procurement prices paid to the peasants were more often than not inadequate to cover operating costs, so that an unusually large number of farms operated at a loss. On top of everything else, a very large turnover tax of about 86 percent was added to the price of bread.[2] Agriculture had become a source of primitive accumulation.

The situation improved markedly under Nikita Khrushchev, when investment in agriculture was increased from 13 percent to 17 percent of the country's total investment package. However, resources invested later are not the equivalent of resources that might have been invested at the beginning of the process. It is not just a matter of making up for lost time by providing compensatory funds. A ruble's worth of investment at the early stage of Soviet development would have been much more critical to increased production than an equal investment 50 years later. In fact, agricultural and consumer-goods production suffered so during the Stalinist days of stringency that the shortages have had lasting impact on incentives and morale. Eventually workers in both industry and agriculture discovered that the money they earned for their work had little real meaning, since there were seldom enough high-quality goods in the stores to buy with that money. What was the sense of working hard once it was discovered that there was no real compensation beyond the money facade? A partial demonitarization of the economy ensued. Workers became much more responsive to in-kind or barter transactions than to payments in money. Thus the system of salary incentives broke down, at least in part.

Once such a breakdown occurs, the system is not easily reconstituted. It is not enough to announce that more resources will be devoted to producing consumer goods. It is also necessary for the planning authorities to regain their credibility and to convince the workers that they mean what they say. This is very hard to do. Efforts at increasing investment generally turn out to be less effective than originally anticipated because the population has become so skeptical that it usually fails to respond properly even when the authorities are sincere. The danger is that in time the whole system will become demonetarized and demoralized and thus unresponsive to official incentives.

Although there is no denying that consumption has lagged in the Soviet Union and that Soviet workers and peasants have become dispirited, it is also true that living conditions have improved markedly from what they were in the 1940s and early 1950s. One indication of how far the authorities had neglected urban housing during the period of industrialization is reflected in statistics showing that the amount of such space per capita fell from 5.7 square meters in 1926 to 4.5 square meters in 1940. To be sure, the wholesale destruction of World War II did not help the situation. By 1950, the per-capita figure had increased only minimally, to 4.9 square meters. But by 1958, the average had increased to 5.8 square meters, which was equal to the 1926 level. There were further improvements throughout the 1960s and 1970s, so that by 1977 the comparable figure was 8.2 square meters—which was still below the legal norm of 9 square meters per person, the equivalent of a room measuring 10 feet by 10 feet.[3]

Nonetheless, as much as housing has improved for the majority of the population, there remain serious complaints. Perhaps the most telling reflection of the problem is that in 1985 20 percent of the Soviet urban population still lived in communal apartments.[4] This means that one or more families each have a room in what would normally be a one-family apartment and that toilets and kitchens are shared. Certainly the reduction in the number of communal apartments is an improvement over conditions that prevailed as recently as 1971, when as much as 40 percent of Moscow's population lived in such apartments. Yet the move to a private apartment does not always mean that housing worries are over. Even new apartments often appear to be in poor condition as well as poorly equipped. In short, by Western standards the quality of housing in the Soviet Union leaves much to be desired.

The availability of consumer goods reflects much the same pattern. Although there has been a very marked increase in the production and sale of most goods, supplies are still generally inadequate. At the same time, the quality of goods is generally poor. This is seen not only in the relatively short service life of many items but in a lack of innovation and style. Naturally, the size of Soviet apartments puts a limit on how much the Soviet family can use. Even so, Soviet workers find few desirable goods to buy.

The food situation reflects a different set of problems. The generally poor supplies are not so much a question of storage (the majority of Soviet homes now have refrigerators) or quality but of low levels of production. Beginning in 1979, as will be seen in the following chapter, the Soviet Union had several bad harvests in a row. This inevitably has affected the country's ability to feed itself. Fortunately, the Soviet Union has been able to supplement much of its harvest shortfall with grain imports from the United States, Canada, Australia, and Argentina.

Yet, in spite of poor harvests, for the past two decades the Soviets have always had enough bread. The impact of the poor harvests has primarily affected meat supplies. Never overabundant, meat commonly becomes extremely difficult to find after the slaughter that follows a bad harvest. Feed for livestock is almost always cut back first. This is reflected in table 1, which shows that following the bad harvests of 1976 and 1983, for example, meat imports rose markedly.

Nor have meat imports been high enough to satisfy the appetites of most Soviet consumers. This is evident from the length of shopping lines after even the best of harvests. After the poorer harvests, especially when they come two or three in a row, the lines become ubiquitous, and waiting in them becomes the chore of everyone lacking access to the special shops set aside primarily for Party functionaries. All too often, moreover, supplies run out before everyone in line has had a chance. In Moscow, normally better provided than elsewhere in the Soviet Union, shopper frustration is compounded by the fact that shoppers from as far as 150 miles away come early in the morning to buy meat and other products that are almost never available in their own communities. Not surprisingly, there is not much left for Muscovites unable to go shopping until after work.

Similar experiences plague most large Soviet cities. In several instances, the local authorities have limited the purchases any one customer may make. In more extreme cases, rationing has been instituted. Volodga, Irkutsk, Kazan, Naberezhnye Chelny, and Tbi-

TABLE 1. MEAT AND MEAT PRODUCT IMPORTS (THOUSANDS OF TONS)

Year	1971	1972	1973	1974	1975	1976	1977
Imports	225	134	129	515	515	361	617
Year	1978	1979	1980	1981	1982	1983	1984
Imports	183	386	576	651	938	985	805

Source: Ministerstvo Vneshnei Torgovli, *Vneshnaia torgovlia SSSR: Statisticheskii sbornik* (Moscow), vols. 1971–1984.

lisi are among the cities in which rationing was reported in late 1981 and early 1982, and there was a similar report about Volgograd in 1986. That the authorities should find it necessary to institute rationing 35 years after ending it in 1947 is a serious indictment of Soviet agriculture and marketing.

The supplies of other consumer goods are usually more dependable. Still, there are occasions when such basic products as matches and toilet paper will simply disappear from store shelves. The more typical complaint about nonfood goods, however, is that both quality and distribution facilities are almost always poor. In part the dearth of stores and marketing facilities is a reflection of Marxist ideology, which regards marketing as a nonproductive, even parasitic activity. More basically, the low priority assigned to distribution is usually predicated on the rationalization that capital investment allocated to production and construction will result in a higher overall output in the long run than if those resources were devoted to such activities as services. An underlying assumption is that holding back on investment in the distribution sector will not significantly affect the ultimate supply of goods; that, if anything, it will eliminate the waste of unutilized capacities so often found in the West. Admittedly, there will be longer lines and the consumer will have to spend several hours more each week in line, but presumably the consumer would rather have more money spent on production than on building more stores where the clerks would stand idle a portion of the day. Or so the planners have reasoned. Yet even if the state's costs are reduced by not having to build so many stores and warehouses, the cost to the consumer of standing in line or of running around town in search of goods is very real—and expensive as well as demoralizing.

The downgrading of service activities affects not only capital but also human allocation. The personnel working in the service sector of the economy are thought of as less able and honest. The Soviet press is filled with stories of store and warehouse clerks who have been arrested for diverting state supplies of goods to their friends for sale on the black market. "Why else," asked a Soviet official, "does a qualified worker making 250 rubles a month seek the job of a sales clerk who makes only 90 rubles a month?"[5] Economists call the Soviet case a classic seller's market.

Seller's markets, particularly those of long duration, are seldom if ever noted for their solicitous treatment of customers. The customer comes to be regarded as a nuisance, and service, in the fuller or better sense, all but disappears. An attitude of "take it or leave it" is almost inevitable. We discovered this ourselves, in the United

States, during the gasoline shortages of 1973 and 1979. Thus, not only are there complaints about the availability and quality of the goods being sold in Soviet stores; there are also complaints about *how* the goods are sold.

In view of what has been said, it will be understandable that Soviet consumers frequently find it difficult to spend all their money. Just how serious the problem has become in recent years is reflected in table 2. Unlike consumers elsewhere in the world, Soviet consumers frequently increase the money value of their savings faster then they increase the money value of their retail purchases. Thus savings-bank deposits increased by 15.2 billion rubles from 1983 to 1984 while retail sales increased by only 10.1 billion rubles. Since the savings figures presented in table 2 reflect only savings flowing into Soviet savings banks, actual savings, including those held in liquid form, were undoubtedly considerably higher. For that matter, even in 1981, when the ruble increase in savings-bank accounts appears to have been lower than the ruble increase in retail sales, the percentage increase in savings still exceeded the percentage increase in retail sales. This increase in the disposable income of Soviet consumers not only reflects a lack of satisfaction with the goods that are available; it also measures how much Soviet consumers have come to downgrade the purchasing capabilities of the ruble. No wonder more and more transactions are made through barter.

Satisfying consumers in the Soviet Union has become a very serious concern to the authorities. Nonetheless, there is little to indicate that Soviet leaders are contemplating any measures that will significantly alter the situation. Initially, the Eleventh Five-

TABLE 2. CHANGES IN SAVINGS-BANK DEPOSITS AND RETAIL SALES (BILLIONS OF RUBLES)

Year	Total Savings	Increase	Retail Trade Volume	Increase
1985	220.8		. . .	
		18.7		
1984	202.1		324.6	
		15.2		10.1
1983	186.9		314.5	
		12.6		10.1
1982	174.3		304.3	
		9.2		16.1
1981	165.7		294.1	

Year Plan (1981–85) called for a faster rate of growth for the production of consumer as compared to capital goods, but whenever similar promises were made in the past they were almost always revised downward. True to form, such a revision was made in the final version of the Eleventh Five-Year Plan, when the target for the increase in consumer-goods production was set at an average of 4 percent a year instead of the 4.9–5.2 percent first projected.[6] And even if the target were not further diminished, merely increasing the physical output of consumer goods would not, in itself, solve the problem. The goods would have to be of a higher quality than has been the case in the past, and they would have to be properly distributed. More than that, something has to be done to stimulate industry to more innovative and service personnel to provide better service.

There is no doubt that the Soviet economic system has become particularly vulnerable. That should be reassuring for those in the West who worry about which system is doing better. But given that economic conditions in the West are not all that good, we should not become smug. Nor should we forget that the Soviet Union seems to have solved the problem of unemployment and held inflation below what we have seen in the West. We are faced, in sum, with a kind of basic paradox: the Soviet system has perhaps settled some of the major problems besetting modern economies—but only to create still others.

NOTES

1. Figures here and below, unless otherwise indicated, are from *Narodnoe khoziaistvo sssr*, published annually by the Central Statistical Administration, Moscow.

2. Franklyn Holzman, *Soviet Taxation* (Cambridge, MA: Harvard University Press, 1955), p. 153.

3. Henry W. Morton, "The Soviet Quest for Better Housing—An Impossible Dream?" *Soviet Economy in a Time of Change*. Report of the Joint Economic Committee, U.S. Congress. (Washington, DC: Government Printing Office, 1979).

4. *Pravda* (May 14, 1986).

5. *Pravda* (December 15, 1981).

6. *Radio Free Europe–Radio Liberty Research Bulletin*, 496/81 (December 11, 1981), p. 2.

17

Agriculture

D. GALE JOHNSON

The performance of Soviet agriculture for the past several years has been dismal. Since 1970 total agricultural production has barely kept up with the slow growth in population, and numerous food products have disappeared from the shelves of the state stores. During this period the Soviet Union has changed from being a significant net exporter to being the world's largest importer of grains. Starting from a rough balance between the value of its exports and imports of agricultural products in 1970, by 1985 annual Soviet imports exceeded the value of exports by $16 billion.

Before looking ahead, however, it would be useful to compare recent performance with the past record. By 1950 Soviet agriculture had recovered from World War II—except for the greatly reduced farm labor force, a result of the enormous wartime casualties. During the 1950s the farm labor force consisted very largely of women, older men, and young boys and girls. Given this composition, agricultural production in that period was quite remarkable. Output grew by about 4 percent annually, nearly double the rate of growth in Western Europe or North America.

As was indicated in the preceding chapter, with the death of Stalin in 1953 the rapacious exploitation of rural people by their government was largely brought to an end. Prices paid to farms in 1958, compared to those paid in 1952, were increased severalfold— the grains by six times, livestock by 11 and sunflowers by eight. Sugar beet prices doubled, and milk prices in 1958 were four times those of 1952.

Between 1953 and 1964, Nikita Khrushchev undertook several bold and risky agricultural ventures. His New (or Virgin) Lands Program brought 36 million hectares of marginal land under cultivation. The corn program increased the planted area of corn from 4 million to 37 million hectares in 1962 (although the maximum area harvested for grain was just 7 million hectares). The Machine Tractor Stations were abolished. And a single procurement price for each product was introduced. Although Soviet agriculture in general responded positively, it may have been success that undid Khrushchev.

In part because of the measures adopted and in part as the result of favorable growing conditions, 1958 was a bumper-crop year. It was then that Khrushchev abolished the Machine Tractor Stations, in the expectation, widely shared outside the Soviet Union, that this would significantly improve productivity by making the collective farms more responsible for the use of their resources and by providing greater incentives. Like all too many agricultural reforms, this one was poorly planned and executed. Repair services were inadequate, and the machinery was transferred to the farms under unfavorable terms for them. A new burden replaced an old one, and farm incomes declined after what could have been a constructive move.

Agriculture performed far below Khrushchev's bellicose claim that the Soviet Union would catch up with and overtake the United States in meat and milk production by 1965. Several of the goals for 1965, announced in 1958, still have not been met, including the critically important one for meat. Farm output grew by 43 percent between 1952 and 1958, but for the next six years the output increased by just 17 percent. At least in part as a result of the poor performance of agriculture and the need to import 10 million tons of grain in 1963–64, Khrushchev was replaced by Aleksei Kosygin and Leonid Brezhnev in 1964.

The new administration instituted important agricultural reforms. Farm prices were increased, an enormous fertilizer-production program was inaugurated, investment in agriculture was increased sharply, wages were introduced for farm workers, and a pension system for members of collective farms was introduced. These were clearly sensible measures and were expected to result in a revitalization of agriculture. But hardly any other aspect of the agricultural policy inherited from Khrushchev was changed. Moscow still maintained tight control over the minutest details of farm operations: extent of crop areas, plowing dates, seeding dates and rates of seeding, harvesting, delivery quotas, and the annual and Five-Year Plans for each farm. Nothing was done to gain the respect of the farm people for the planners or other government officials. Indeed, confidence in those officials remained minimal.

Still, given the material resources devoted to agriculture, it would have been reasonable to expect a rapid and continuing increase in production. And for a time, from 1964 to 1970, it appeared that the program was succeeding, since agricultural output grew at an annual rate of 3.9 percent. But the 1970s saw an annual growth rate of only 1.2 percent, with an even lower rate after the mid-1970s; and the 1980 output was the same as in 1973 and 1976.

The shift in resources to agriculture under Kosygin and Brezhnev can only be described as enormous. From 1961 to 1965 some 19 percent of national investment was allocated to agriculture; between 1976 and 1980 this figure increased to 27 percent. If the investment in agriculturally related industries is included, the allocation increases to 33 percent for 1976–80. Annual rates of investment increased from 9 billion rubles in 1961–65 to 34 billion in 1976–80 (and to 39 billion in 1980–85). There were significant increases in the delivery of farm machines, but, owing to high scrappage rates, inventories rose slowly during the 1970s and early 1980s. Yet, for all the high investment in agriculture, returns were disappointing, to say the least.

Some of the recent output performance of Soviet agriculture can be attributed to poor weather: thus, grain production from 1979 to 1981 might have been 13 percent less than it would have been with normal or average weather. But the effect of the relatively low production of grain and other feed supplies was partially, if not wholly, offset by grain imports averaging 36 million tons for those three years. The level of grain imports was greater than the shortfall in grain production from trend levels for that period. Thus, the fact that per-capita meat output in 1981 was the same as that in 1975 cannot be attributed primarily to poor climatic conditions. In Moscow, lately, meat seems to have disappeared from the state stores; elsewhere it is available either in the collective-farm markets at two or three times the official prices (so much for stable prices!) or in newly devised distribution systems at places of employment.

The costs of livestock production have increased sharply since the consumer price policy was adopted in 1962. Thus, in 1965 the Soviet government inaugurated a policy of increasing prices paid to farms, making up the difference by subsidies. In 1981 the cost of food subsidies, primarily for meat and milk, came to about 35 billion rubles. Further increases in prices of agricultural products, taking effect in January 1983, increased subsidies by 16 billion rubles. The 1983 subsidy bill had already exceeded the total retail value of all meat, milk, potatoes, and grain products sold in the state stores.

The relatively poor performance of agriculture in recent years and its low aggregate level (approximately 80 percent of U.S. output) are often attributed to the poor climate that prevails over most of the agricultural acres of the country. It is true, as noted above, that climatic factors have had an adverse effect on grain production from 1979 on. Yet the impact of the weather on grain production is often exaggerated: the output levels for the past few years appear very low at least partly because climatic conditions from 1969 to 1978 were *favorable*.

The effect of climatic conditions on farm production in a single year—or over a short period of years—is one thing; more important is their effect in the long run. A relatively small area of the Soviet Union is similar in climate to the American corn and cotton belts. But it is an enormous country with a huge arable area—as much as those of Canada and the United States combined. Regions in North America with climatic conditions similar to those in the Soviet Union include the Great Plains; the Great Lakes states of Minnesota, Wisconsin, and Michigan; and the southwestern states of Arizona, New Mexico, and Utah.

Comparing grain yields in climatically similar areas, then, one finds that yields in the Soviet Union are nearly the same as those in North America. To be sure, the yield relationship depends on the method used to calculate yields. When calculated per harvested hectare, Soviet yields averaged 84 percent of the yields in five U.S. states plus the Prairie Provinces of Canada; when calculations were based on harvested areas plus land in fallow, the Soviet yields were 114 percent of those of North America for 1975–79. These comparisons exclude corn in the North American area. If corn is included, the relative Soviet grain yields on a harvested-area basis were 68 percent; and, on a harvested-plus-fallow-area basis, 88 percent. Also, the figures for the Soviet Union are on a bunker weight basis and need to be discounted by 10–15 percent. Thus, when fallow is considered, corn is excluded, and Soviet yields are discounted appropriately, yields in the Soviet and North American areas are approximately equal.

Excluding corn from the North American data, we find that grain yields in the 1960s and 1970s increased at a slightly higher rate in the Soviet Union: 0.3 centners (300 kilograms) per hectare compared to 0.26 centners for North America. When the fallow area is included in the calculation of yields, the annual yield increase in North America is reduced to 0.18 centners per hectare. Since the amount of fallow actually declined in the Soviet Union, both absolutely and as a percentage of the grain area, its inclusion actually results in a small increase in the Soviet yield trend.

Similarly, cotton yields in the Soviet Union were higher than those in the American Southwest, and the trend was positive until the early 1980s, when average annual yields began to fall.

Sunflower seeds were for a time one of the agricultural success stories in the Soviet Union. Plant breeding resulted in a marked increase in the oil content and in relatively high yields. But more recently yields have fallen far below expectations. During the late 1960s sunflower yields in the Soviet Union were about 25 percent higher than those in the United States; from 1976 to 1980, U.S. yields were 15 percent higher. In addition to unfavorable weather, factors such as disease; poor-quality seeds; inadequate supplies of fertilizer, herbicides, and defoliants; and faulty rotation practices have been identified as causes of recent yield declines. Certainly, the Soviets have failed to follow through on their earlier successes in breeding improved varieties by means of hybridization. At the same time, sugar-beet yields have increased very little over the past 20 years, losing ground relative to those in the United States. Yields are now two-thirds or less those of Minnesota or North Dakota. In the late 1960s, the difference was a little less than one-fifth.

Grains, cotton, sunflowers, and sugar beets have enjoyed high priority in Soviet agricultural policies. Consequently, it is not too surprising that in at least some instances yield levels compare favorably with those in North American areas having similar natural conditions. There are, however, large—even enormous—yield differences for crops that have not had high priority, namely forage crops such as hay and silage.

Forage crops are important to plans for achieving a significant increase in livestock output, and the Soviets have depended primarily on the increased use of grain for feed to achieve their livestock goals. Between 1966 and 1981, for example, livestock production increased by about 32 percent while the use of grain for feed increased by about 80 percent. This means that other sources of feed supply increased relatively little during these 15 years.

What are the forage yield differences between North America and the Soviet Union? Hay yields in the latter averaged 2.04 tons per hectare between 1975 and 1979. This is a little more than half the average yield in the Canadian Prairie Provinces, about 60 percent of the average for three U.S. Northern Plains states, and a third of the average for three Great Lakes states. Thus, on average, Soviet hay yields were only 45–50 percent of those achieved in climatically similar North American states in the later 1970s.

The Soviet yields were so starkly low, in fact, that further analysis was called for. Since it is reasonable to assume that hay and grain yields are correlated, hay yields were related to wheat and corn yields in the United States. Thus figuring I found that based on the average Soviet wheat yield of 1.64 tons per hectare for 1976–80, the expected hay yield would be 3.6 tons per hectare; instead, the actual yield was 2.04 tons. For the Ukraine, with its average wheat yield of three tons per hectare and a hay yield of three tons as well, the predicted yield was six tons per hectare, exactly double the actual yield. In Estonia, recent hay yields have been 3.8 tons per hectare with a grain yield of 2.5 tons; the predicted hay yield was five tons, or just one-third above the actual. For Latvia, the difference between the actual and predicted hay yields was about the same: predicted at 4.9 tons, actual at 3.5 tons. For the Russian Republic, the predicted yield was more than double the actual hay yield of 1.6 tons.

Silage yields were also significantly below those of the comparable North American areas: 15 tons per hectare compared to 30–35 tons in the Great Lake states and 20 tons in the Northern Plains states.

In sum, the low levels of Soviet hay and silage yields must be attributed to policy factors rather than to climatic or soil differences. The yield comparisons for climatically similar areas establish this beyond any doubt. And if more evidence is required, one need only look at forage yields in areas of Europe with either similar or no more satisfactory conditions for the production of forage crops.

Let me explain some of the important policy factors that, as my research indicates, have reduced the level of agricultural production in the Soviet Union while increasing its costs. One such policy factor, as we have seen, is the low priority given to the production of forage crops, resulting in abysmally low yields. If hay yields could be brought up to the level indicated by the American comparison— an increase of 1.5 tons per hectare—the feed value would be equal to 25–30 million tons of grain, or more than the average annual grain imports of 20.5 million tons for 1975–80. If the quality of the hay were significantly improved, as it could be, the feed gain would be even greater.

Grain production varies substantially from year to year. In such circumstances North American farmers seed most of their wheat and other grains on land that has been fallowed. In the Soviet Union, instead of fallowing one-third to one-half of the land devoted to grain, the clean fallow land has been reduced both absolutely and relatively. In 1940 the clean fallow area was 26 percent of the grain-sown area of 111 million hectares. By 1975 the sown area had increased to about 128 million hectares, but the fallow area had been cut back to 11 million hectares or just 9 percent of the sown area. Since then, fallow land has increased slightly, to 11 percent.

The Soviet practice of reducing the fallow area has had two important effects. It has increased both the variability of production and costs of producing grain. North American farmers use a lot of fallow primarily because it lowers costs per unit of output. Soviet planners impose little fallow on the farms in the mistaken notion that the result will be increased output, even though some Soviet experimental data support the contrary view. And this is not counting the savings of seed, which could be significant.

Soviet farms use more than twice as much seed per hectare of land seeded to wheat and other small grains as do farms in the United States. In the Soviet Union grain used as seed is about 16.5 percent of the production of clean grain; in the United States, seed wheat is 4 percent of wheat production. If the current seeding rate of 200 kilograms per hectare were reduced by half (still above the U.S. rate for comparable areas), the grain saving would be 12.5 million tons.

Not only grains have high seeding rates. In one important potato-producing province of the Soviet Union it was reported that the amount of seed potatoes used was one-third of the output in an average year. The seeding rate on socialized farms was three times what it was on the farm workers' private plots: 4.7 tons compared to 1.6 tons per hectare. Climatic factors cannot explain this enormous difference; only policies can. In the United States, approximately 2.3 tons of seed is used per hectare; because of higher yields, this is only 7 percent of output.

Why are Soviet seeding rates so high? Primarily because the rates are established officially and not by the farms. Evidence of meddling by planning officials is overwhelming. Of course, there are some reasons for setting seeding rates at such high levels: low rates of germination, seed stock that includes a substantial fraction of extraneous material, late planting, or replanting. But whatever the problems, they could all be corrected by modifying policies and improving farming practices.

Two kinds of waste in Soviet agriculture are conspicuous, one in the handling of farm inputs and the other in the harvesting, transporting, processing, and selling of farm output. A recent Soviet article estimates that 9 million tons of fertilizer—some 10 percent of fertilizer production—is wasted between the factory and the field.

If each ton of fertilizer properly applied increased grain output by just one ton (the Soviet author argues that the increase would be 1.5–2 tons), grain production could be increased by nearly 10 million tons. And further: "We lost approximately one-fifth of the gross harvest of grain, vegetables, fruits and berries during the harvesting itself, in transportation and storage, and during industrial processing." So wrote V. Tikhonov, a prominent agricultural scientist, early in 1982.

Owing to the poor quality of farm machinery and inadequate maintenance, the average service life of a machine in the Soviet Union is significantly less than that in the United States. The annual scrappage rate for grain combines was 11 percent for 1980–85, compared to 8 percent in the United States; for tractors it was between 12 and 13 percent, compared to 4 percent in the United States. Between 1971 and 1975, the scrappage rate for such a simple machine as a windrower was 18 percent, an average life of little more than five years, while a farm truck has a life expectancy of less than six years. This is not only because of the poor quality of the trucks but also because of poor maintenance, the abysmal state of rural roads, or a combination of these factors.

Still other factors are important in explaining the recent relatively poor performance of Soviet agriculture. Soviet agricultural price policies, for instance, suffer from two main deficiencies. First, prices paid to farms are used as a means of equalizing incomes within agriculture by differentiating prices regionally. In the process, this policy encourages production in high-cost areas and on high-cost farms while discouraging production under low-cost conditions. Second, the relative price structure favors grain and field crops at the expense of livestock products. This seems nonsensical, since, officially, priority is given to increasing per-capita meat production.

Perhaps the major adverse policy factor affecting Soviet agricultural performance is that farm managers and workers are not given the opportunity to direct their skills, knowledge, and capacities to efficient farming. In part, this is due to a price system that does not provide the appropriate signals. But, perhaps more important, the Soviet bureaucracy does not trust farmers; it does not believe that farmers have either intelligence or initiative. Farmers are told what to plant, when to plant, how much seed to plant, when to cultivate, when to harvest, how many livestock to maintain (even if there is not enough feed), and when to fertilize and how much fertilizer to apply. For example, in the socialized sector milk production per cow in 1980 was even less than that in 1970, when it was nearly the lowest in Europe. Why is output so low and declining? One reason may be that the number of cows is imposed on farms by the central planners.

In October 1981 Brezhnev called attention to the central role of food in Soviet planning; it was both "economically and politically the central problem of the whole Five-Year Plan" (1981–85). But in May 1982, in announcing the much-heralded new Food Program, scarcely anything was said about transferring authority to the farms.

The Food Program was, in fact, shockingly unimaginative. It appears that general agreement could not be reached on what was required to improve agriculture. Instead, what emerged was the creation of two new levels of bureaucracy, a further sharp increase in prices paid to farms and, given the policy of fixed retail prices, an increase in food price subsidies of almost 50 percent. Hardly a word was spoken about the initiative or independence of the collective and state farms themselves. Yet, recalling that in all of the Soviet Union there are only 46,000 such farms with a total of about 24 million members and employees, it would seem reasonable to assume that organizations of such large average size could well manage their own affairs.[1]

In a typical year, the United States and the Soviet Union produce about one-third of the world's grain. The United States is the world's largest grain exporter and the Soviet Union—a significant net exporter of grain in the early 1970s—is now the world's largest grain importer.

In my judgment, there is no way that the Soviet Union can avoid high levels of grain imports except by reducing the volume of livestock products in the Soviet diet. The annual grain goal for the Eleventh Five-Year Plan (1981–85), 240 million tons, was not met; the annual shortfall was 60 million tons or 25 percent. Production during the latter half of the 1980s may well average at least 50 million tons below the annual goal of 250–255 millions tons (see table). Thus, if the livestock goals for the 1980s are to be met, annual Soviet grain and feed imports must average as much as 40 million tons for the decade. But the ability and willingness to import such large quantities were adversely affected after the mid-1980s by the fall in the prices of oil and natural gas. Petroleum products have been the Soviet Union's major source of hard-currency earnings.

I have followed Soviet agricultural developments for somewhat more than three decades. And although there is much that continues to puzzle me, I am firmly convinced that Soviet agriculture could be much more productive than it is—and that it could be so as a socialized enterprise. With appropriate policy setting, good perfor-

SOVIET GRAIN IMPORTS AND GRAIN PRODUCTION AND U.S. SHARE OF SOVIET GRAIN
IMPORTS, 1975–76 TO 1985–86.

Crop Year	Soviet Grain Imports (Million Tons)	Percentage from the U.S.	Soviet Grain Production[a] (Million Tons)
1975–76	25.7	54	140
1976–77	10.3	72	224
1977–78	18.3	78	196
1978–79	15.1	74	237
1979–80	29.7	55	179
1980–81	34.0	24	189
1981–82	45.0	34	160[b]
1982–83	31.5	20	180[b]
1983–84	32.0	44	190[b]
1984–85	55.0	28	190[b]
1985–86	28.0	15	190[b]

Source: U.S. Department of Agriculture, Foreign Agricultural Circular, various issues.
a. Production occurs in the first calendar year of the crop year. Thus, for 1975–76 the production occurred in 1975.
b. U.S. Department of Agriculture estimates. No official Soviet data were available.

mance by those sectors of the economy that furnish the products
needed for agriculture, and the necessary marketing, processing,
and transportation services, socialist agriculture could be highly
productive. After all, private agriculture cannot succeed without
supportive governmental policies and an assured supply of appropriate inputs and marketing services.

All of this is not to suggest that minor changes in policy can make
Soviet agriculture much more productive. But it is to say that policy
changes are possible that would retain the critical features of socialist agriculture—including either collective or state ownership
of the land and even some significant elements of central planning—
yet would result in substantially greater productivity. The crucial
change would be to give the farms much greater authority to make
their own decisions, not only with respect to what to produce and
how to produce it, but also with respect to relating reward to effort.
But even major changes in agricultural policy will not be enough
unless the rest of the economy functions much better than it now
does.

The price system, in particular, has largely lost its ability to guide
producers, workers, or consumers. No outsider could have been
more precise or eloquent in criticizing the ineffectiveness of the
Soviet price system than the drafters of the 1982 Food Program.
One of the measures announced there—and anticipated by Brezhnev in his speech of May 1982—was "to increase the amounts of

payments in kind to collective and state farm workers, above all in grain, fruits, vegetables, and feed." This measure was designed to improve work incentives. What it also signifies is that the ruble has lost much of its value as a reward for effort because goods and services of a kind that people, especially in rural areas, wish to buy are not available at the official prices. Most such goods and services *are* available in the collective-farm markets, but at two to three times the official state-store prices, or in the growing black markets, where barter and foreign currency prevail.

A lesson historians and economists thought they had learned was that as economic growth occurs—as real per-capita incomes increase over time—wages in kind decline in importance and eventually disappear (except as a means of tax avoidance). But the Soviet Union has demonstrated that this principle is not universally valid. There, the bureaucracy has proven that you can so mismanage a productive economy that it becomes desirable to resort to measures that you had long since tried to eliminate or minimize. The increase of payments in kind to collective- and state-farm workers is evidently viewed as a necessary evil, as a kind of bribe calculated to offset some of the advantages of those personal plots assigned to farm workers that currently account for a quarter of all Soviet agricultural production.[2]

For six years before he became the Party's general secretary in 1985, Mikhail Gorbachev was the Politburo member responsible for agriculture. There were no major changes in farm policies during these years. Thus, it should be no surprise that there were few significant changes in agricultural policy after he took office. He supported the expansion of the so-called contract system to improve the relationship between effort, productivity, and reward. The contract system involves assigning certain resources—say, land and machinery—to teams of workers and compensating them on the basis of their output. There is little evidence that it has been effective in increasing output or in containing rising costs of production. One problem with the system is that it reduces the authority of the farm directors while making no change in their responsibilities or rate of reward. It is most puzzling why the reward structure for farm managers was left unchanged when the contract system was introduced. The failure to change the structure of incentives, both positive and negative, offsets whatever positive merits the system may have.

The effectiveness of the contract system cannot be improved only by removing the conflicts between farm managers and the teams; the system also requires a functioning price system for both outputs and inputs. The members of the team must be induced through the price system to produce the correct things in the proper way—namely, at lowest cost for a given level of output. With the present price structure and the failure to supply all the inputs demanded at the established prices, the contract system cannot contribute to increased productivity and lower costs. At this writing, the problems of Soviet agriculture remain far from solved.

N O T E S

1. In the spring of 1983 it was reported from Moscow that Brezhnev's successor as Party leader, Yury Andropov, "has put the Food Program at the head of his list of goals." Measures were being undertaken "to provide greater autonomy and greater incentives for the farm workers, and to give them greater responsibility for organizing the entire productive enterprise." It was, in short, "a major effort by the state to get farm labor to work better and harder." *New York Times* (May 30, 1983).

2. See also D. Gale Johnson and Karen McConnell Brooks, *Prospects for Soviet Agriculture in the 1980s* (Bloomington, IN: Indiana University Press, 1983).

18

Foreign Trade

PERRY L. PATTERSON

The Soviet Revolution of 1917 brought the world a new perspective on the management of foreign trade. Faced with armed aggression on the part of both Western powers and domestic foes and remembering past foreign domination of Russian commerce, the new Bolshevik rulers decided to place all power for regulating and conducting export, import, and credit operations directly in state hands. This new style of economic management, now imitated to a greater or lesser extent by many nations, brought with it a variety of political and economic questions of vital importance both to the Soviet Union itself and to its trading partners, particularly those in the capitalist West.

Can government traders make economically sensible decisions, or will political concerns rule? Is it possible for individual Western firms to trade on a fair basis with a state-controlled trade monopoly? Should Western governments, in order to counteract Soviet government control of exports and imports, participate directly in trade themselves? How do planned economies reach sensible trade decisions? And how do political and strategic considerations affect Western trade policy toward the Soviet Union?

The foreign trade system that provokes such questions has changed relatively little since its inception. Its distinctive feature is its comprehensive, consciously coordinated, and highly centralized nature. Although direct government participation in international trading is common in certain markets throughout the world, only the Soviet Union and similarly structured planned economies produce a centrally coordinated trade plan that encompasses the vast majority of traded products.

To say that Soviet foreign-trade planning is centralized does not, however, mean that one person or one bureau makes all the decisions. In fact, owing to the complexities of linking foreign-trade plans to domestic production and financial plans, a large number of agencies must participate in policy coordination (see figure 1). These agencies include the policy-making organs of the Communist Party itself, the Council of Ministers, *Gosplan* (the central economic-planning agency, responsible for compiling use and supply balances for some of the most important products), and *Gossnab* (another acronym, this one standing for the materials-supply agency, which is responsible for compiling balances for a great number of relatively disaggregated commodities and for the actual allocation of industrial supplies). The Ministry of Foreign Trade, of course, also takes part, as does the State Committee on Science and Technology (high-technology imports and purchases of foreign licenses), the Ministry of Finance, the State Price Committee (domestic price setting), various industrial ministries, and, finally, the individual FTOs (foreign-trade organizations, 64 in number in 1980), which do the actual buying and selling of the products over which they have jurisdiction. It is the FTOs that make actual contact with foreign traders, since Soviet firms generally do not take an active role in direct negotiations.[1]

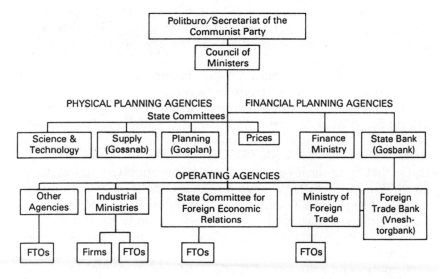

Fig. 1. The Soviet Foreign-Trade Bureaucracy. FTO = foreign-trade organization.

Although the concept of a foreign-trade monopoly has remained constant throughout the Soviet era, the importance and goals of state control have passed through several distinct phases. The early years of the monopoly saw efforts to import advanced industrial products in order to spur growth, and a certain decentralization of trade authority that extended even to some of the remaining Russian capitalist firms. The Stalinist period, however, brought an end to all private trade and a near halt to foreign trade in an effort to insulate the domestic economy from outside influence and to generate homegrown technologies. But Stalin's successors, especially Leonid Brezhnev, brought the Soviet Union back to a considerable level of trade with both Eastern-bloc and capitalist partners. Much as in the early period of Soviet power, the recent emphasis has been on imports of equipment and technology for industrial modernization, with major imports from the West going, for example, to the Soviet automobile and chemical industries. Many consumer products are now imported as well, including grain from the West; sugar, fresh fruits, and tea from less developed countries; and shoes and consumer durables from Eastern Europe.

The Soviet Union's most important trading partners in the years since World War II have always been the countries of Eastern Europe, particularly the European members of the Council for Mutual Economic Assistance (CMEA): Poland, Hungary, East Germany, Bulgaria, Romania, and Czechoslovakia. Yet the share of trade with Eastern Europe has declined in recent years—from 56 percent of Soviet exports and 58 percent of imports in 1965 to 42 percent and 43 percent, respectively, in 1980—as the Soviets have turned increasingly westward.

Soviet trade with Eastern Europe is conducted on a bilateral, country-by-country basis. Trade between any two of these nations must be balanced, for their national currencies cannot be used on international markets and a trade surplus with, say, Poland could not be directly used to buy goods in, say, Czechoslovakia. Soviet trade with other CMEA countries is also conducted on a planned basis; that is, trade levels and items to be imported and exported are defined in both long-range and yearly national plans, thus removing some of the uncertainties generated by freely fluctuating market forces. Occasionally, sales of petroleum to Eastern Europe, especially above-plan sales, have been made in exchange for hard currencies.

A continuing criticism of Eastern European–Soviet trade relations has been that the Soviet Union, as the dominant military and economic power of the group, could unilaterally extract greater benefits from intrabloc trade than could its partners. This accusation was particularly relevant in the years immediately following World War II, when the Soviets engaged in wholesale confiscations of Eastern European factories and equipment in an effort to rebuild quickly the war-ravaged Soviet economy. More recently, it has been pointed out that transfers of modern plants and technology within CMEA still run almost exclusively in an easterly direction, the result largely of Soviet attempts to develop the natural resources of Siberia.

On the other hand, it has also been shown that the Soviet Union provides major subsidies to Eastern Europe through CMEA pricing policies.[2] Attempting to set prices that would simultaneously conform roughly to those on world markets and eliminate violent price swings commonly encountered on these markets, the CMEA states adopted rules that calculate intrabloc prices as a weighted average of current and past world prices. In consequence, when world energy prices skyrocketed in the 1970s, the Soviets found themselves selling oil to Eastern Europe at below-market rates. Thus, Eastern Europe's energy bills and Soviet revenues were both lower than if price had been determined exclusively by world market conditions. The resulting implicit losses for the Soviet Union ran into billions of dollars a year. Still, in a period of falling energy prices, such as the earlier 1980s, Eastern Europe has had to go along with a scheme that tended to benefit the Soviets.

The most dynamic sector of Soviet foreign trade in recent years has been that with the West. Trade with the industrialized capitalist countries increased dramatically during the 1970s, registering a 55-percent jump in export volume from 1970 to 1980. Imports rose at an even faster pace—by 207 percent—over the same decade, leading to an increase in hard-currency debt as well. Some of this growth came at the expense of Eastern European partners, whose share of Soviet foreign trade, as mentioned above, sharply declined. The share of less developed countries remained fairly constant. Growth in trade with the West also resulted from the increased overall Soviet participation in world markets.

Western trade with the Soviet Union has occurred in a number of forms. In addition to simple purchases and sales on a cash or credit basis, Soviet planners, faced with hard-currency deficits, have often preferred trade by means of two kinds of non-monetary transaction. The first of these, barter or countertrade, involves direct exchanges of one type of good for another: say, vodka for Pepsi. A second arrangement, industrial cooperation agreements, typically allows foreign firms to participate in the construction of new plants within the Soviet Union and to receive payment in the form of the new plants' output. Probably the best known of these agreements was the 1973 deal with Occidental Petroleum under which Occidental built an ammonia-processing plant in the Soviet Union (and provided shipments of superphosphoric acid) in exchange for part of the plant's ammonia output (as well as urea and potash).

A great variety of new opportunities and new trading modes emerged in the 1970s, in the wake of detente. But hopes of further large increases in East-West trade in the 1980s were dashed by a variety of factors, including the organizational structure of the Soviet economy, international institutional arrangements, changes in world prices, and interactions between politics and economics. Let us consider each in turn.

The Soviet planned economy presents a variety of special inhibitions to increased trade. The fact that foreign trade decision making is not conducted at the level of individual enterprises has often meant that Western firms have had little direct contact with Soviet buyers and suppliers. This has often made for frustrating delays in the specification of technical details, especially in the case of complex manufactured goods. A large bureaucracy both inhibits the rapid negotiation of contractual agreements with foreigners and stalls the diffusion of new technologies throughout the domestic economy. An organizational reform to be implemented in 1987 might well improve East-West commercial communication, however, since 70 major Soviet firms and more than 20 ministries are to receive permission to negotiate directly with foreigners, thus bypassing much of the bureaucracy.

The Soviet domestic-planning structure has also frequently hindered a furtherance of East-West commercial ties. For instance, the notorious deficiencies in the quality of Soviet products, while suffered by Soviet consumers, naturally make it difficult to sell these products on Western markets. Since these deficiencies are most glaring in manufactures, the Soviets have been forced to rely to a great extent on raw-materials exports, despite stated desires to diversify.

Then too, imports of Western technologies and know-how have often proved ineffective. Strategies of buying single units of a given technology for "reverse-engineering" aimed at producing similar items domestically have not worked, frequently because of an environment that encourages caution rather than innovative (disruptive) changes in output mixes or in process technologies. Both export revenues and the impact of many imported goods are thus diminished by the system itself. A relatively low trade volume with the

West, measured as a percentage of gross national product, could therefore be regarded as a sensible Soviet policy.

Another stumbling block to East-West trade arises from the institutional and legal differences between the two blocs. For example, Soviet foreign-trade officials are members of the government (Ministry of Foreign Trade) and, as such, demand the credentials and perquisites of diplomats when traveling abroad. But Western private traders are not generally accorded the same status while working in the Soviet Union.

Additional problems occur in the context of integrating the Soviet Union into international regulatory agencies such as the General Agreement on Trade and Tariffs (GATT) and the International Monetary Fund (IMF). Among GATT's obligations is the prevention of dumping, that is, the predatory selling of exports at prices below production costs. Unfortunately, both the official ruble exchange rate and Soviet internal price structures are set administratively, often on a non–cost basis, by Soviet agencies. Thus, the determination of true Soviet production costs tends to become an intractable problem. Again, for purposes of making loans the IMF often requires high levels of financial disclosure on matters (gold stocks, for instance, or indebtedness) that the Soviets have traditionally classified as state secrets.

As seen from the Soviet side, a further deterrent to greater trade with the West derives from the extent of Soviet dependence on sales of petroleum products and natural gas (51 percent and 12 percent, respectively, of hard-currency earnings in 1980). Although the Soviets benefited directly from price rises in both commodities in the 1970s, the induced recessions in the West of the later 1970s limited sales volumes for all products. More recently, the drastic decline in world energy prices, combined with the exhaustion of many of the Soviet Union's relatively low-cost sources of oil, have placed Soviet export earnings in serious jeopardy.

Since it may no longer be possible to export more oil to make up for falling energy prices, it seems that increasing reliance on gold sales—and increasing indebtedness—will be required if the Soviet Union is to increase its trade with the West. Weakness and uncertainty in gold prices would seem to tip the scales in favor of increased indebtedness. This possibility is bolstered by the fact that the Soviet Union's credit history is quite strong and its debt burden modest.

But the thorniest question of all regarding the future of East-West trade concerns the role of politics. As is true for all sectors of

Soviet foreign commercial operations, trade with the West is inextricably linked with politics. Indeed, Marshall Goldman has suggested that the Soviet Union "continues to place politics at the center of its trade policy . . . . In a sense, everything in the Soviet Union is subjected to political considerations since for them, there is no such thing as a private profit motive."[3] Goldman cites cases in which the Soviets have cut off trade flows with Yugoslavia (1948), Israel (1973), Finland (1958), China (1964), and Cuba (1968) owing to a variety of ideological, political, and military disputes with those countries. At the same time, recent years have seen major, politically motivated disruptions of Soviet trade originating primarily within the Western bloc, where government policy, particularly that of the United States, has often used trade as one of the weapons in a broader political game.

The great upsurge in U.S.-Soviet trade (see figure 2) that accompanied political detente was surely the result of careful calculation on both sides. If the Soviets foresaw gains to be had from high-technology imports, leaders in the West envisaged a world in which Soviet dependence on East-West trade would be such that temporary trade cut-offs—or threats to that effect—could be used to modify Soviet aggressiveness abroad and the treatment of dissidents and minorities at home. It was hoped, more idealistically, that increased cross-cultural contacts would by themselves eventually facilitate a lessening of superpower antagonism.

Such long-range aims were quickly overtaken, however, by direct attempts at short-term behavior modification. As early as 1974, the Jackson-Vanik amendment to the Trade Reform Act linked most-favored-nation status (which provides for minimum U.S. tariffs on goods imported from the nation concerned) to the right of Soviet Jews to emigrate. An amendment offered by Senator Adlai Stevenson simultaneously restricted Soviet access to Export-Import Bank loans. In 1978 export controls were placed on U.S. sales of oil and gas equipment to the Soviet Union, following Soviet and Cuban intervention in African affairs; internal Soviet human-rights violations were at issue in this instance, too. The Soviet invasion of Afghanistan in December 1979 provoked U.S. embargoes on grain exports and on phosphates used in fertilizer production, along with tighter controls on high-technology exports, including oil and gas equipment. The 1981 imposition of martial law in Poland brought credit controls and even more severe export-licensing procedures, but the grain embargo was not renewed. By 1982 the U.S. State Department had concluded that the embargo had "unfairly damaged one sector of the U.S. economy [agriculture] and was ineffec-

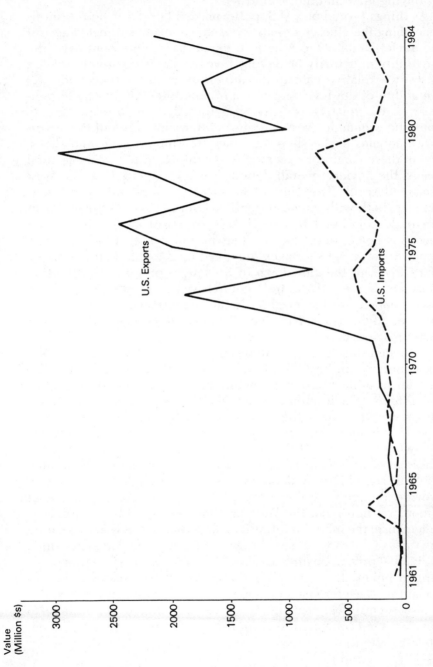

Fig. 2. U.S.-Soviet trade, 1961–84: value of U.S. exports to the Soviet Union and value of U.S. imports from the Soviet Union (constant 1977 dollars). (*Source:* U.S. Department of Commerce, *Business Statistics 1984*).

tive insofar as the Soviets were able to satisfy their import needs by buying grain in other countries."[4]

As things turned out, U.S. policymakers faced vexing questions concerning the efficacy of *most* economic sanctions directed against the Soviet Union. One American expert has pointed out that "the possibility of actually achieving leverage ... is positively related to: (1) the relative gain to the adversary from bilateral trade; (2) the ability of the leveragor to coordinate internally its trade policies; (3) the relative sensitivity of the adversary's leadership to domestic economic pressures; and (4) the mutability of the adversary's policies in the short- and medium-run."[5] In the mid-1980s, few of these conditions seemed to obtain. Despite certain sectoral needs, the Soviets' overall dependence on imports from the West remained small. The United States often quarreled over export policies, both with its Western allies (whose share of Soviet-Western trade continued to rise at U.S. expense) and with affected sectors at home. In retrospect, it seems unlikely that the relatively minor Soviet meat shortages provoked by the U.S. grain embargo of 1979–80, or the slowdown of Soviet gas-pipeline construction caused by U.S. export controls, could have been expected to change Soviet policies of the magnitude and importance of the decision to enter Afghanistan. Nor does it appear that such a decision is easily rescinded.

Although short-term embargoes have come and gone, a relatively constant factor in East-West trade has been the attempt to slow the transfer of militarily related technology and material to the East. Such items, which often either embody advanced microtechnologies or would facilitate the development of Soviet natural resources, have long figured at the top of Soviet import priorities. In the years following World War II the West responded to Soviet initiatives in this respect with the establishment of the Coordinating Committee for Multilateral Export Controls (COCOM). COCOM has attempted to provide a unified set of restrictions on Western sales to the Soviet Union. Yet here, too, the West has not spoken with one voice—a reflection of the inherent interest of all parties to COCOM in violating the rules of the cartel and of disagreement over the degree to which individual private businesses should bear the costs of their nation's foreign policy. It seems clear that some COCOM restrictions will remain in place for years to come, with attendant controversy. But it also seems clear that the West will be obliged to continue to develop non-economic levers for the management of East-West political relations.

The picture before us of Soviet foreign trade contains possibilities both for growth and for a retreat into commercial isolation. The West offers a variety of advanced technology and know-how to a country rich in the natural resources needed to fuel industrial growth both domestically and abroad. Opportunities thus abound for trade in these goods and for financing Soviet development projects. On the other hand, a number of factors will probably limit U.S. enjoyment of these opportunities. Foremost among such factors are the hindrances arising from the Soviet central planning apparatus, differences between the institutional structures of the two countries, and, most important, the influence of politics on trade decisions. Barring new political breakthroughs, the combination of U.S. insistence on at least some trade restrictions and of Soviet reluctance to deal with an uncertain supplier seems likely to depress U.S.-Soviet trade for years to come.

NOTES

1. H. Stephen Gardner, *Soviet Foreign Trade: The Decision Process* (Boston: Kluwer-Nijhoff, 1983). This book contains a much more detailed account of the interrelationships among the various agencies than can be presented here.

2. Michael Marrese and Jan Vanous, *Soviet Subsidization of Trade with Eastern Europe: A Soviet Perspective* (Berkeley, CA: University of California Press, 1983).

3. Marshall I. Goldman, "Interaction of Politics and Trade: Soviet-Western Interaction," *Soviet Economy in the 1980s: Problems and Prospects.* Report of the Joint Economic Committee, U.S. Congress. (Washington, DC: Government Printing Office, 1983), pt. 1, p. 119.

4. Goldman, pt. 2, p. 399.

5. Thomas A. Wolf, "Choosing a U.S. Trade Strategy Towards the Soviet Union," *Soviet Economy in the 1980s*, pt. 2, pp. 400–401.

SCIENCE AND
TECHNOLOGY

Soviet achievements in science and technology since World War II have been spectacular on occasion, have generated widespread alarm in the West (particularly in the United States) at times, and have fundamentally influenced Western perceptions of the Soviet Union as well as Western policies. To illustrate the point, we need think only of Western reactions to the Soviet development of nuclear weapons and to the successes of the Soviet space program, beginning with the launching of the world's first orbiting satellite, Sputnik, in 1957. Indeed, in recent decades no aspect of Soviet life, apart from foreign policy and military matters, has given rise to more comment in the West.

But how good are Soviet science and technology? How effective is Soviet education in this respect? How is Soviet science organized? And what can be said of its future prospects? These and other questions are discussed in the following three chapters, which also refer to political and economic issues raised in earlier sections of the book.

The picture that emerges is a decidedly mixed one, with the implication that although there is something for the West to learn from Soviet science and technology—and from Soviet education—there is much that the Soviet Union could gain from more contact with the West.

19

Science Policy and Organization

LOREN R. GRAHAM

During the past 20 years the Soviet research-and-development community has become, in number of personnel, the largest in the world. The moment when the Soviet Union quantitatively surpassed the United States in number of research personnel is debatable, since the relevant Soviet statistics are not compiled by the same criteria as the American ones. But in a careful analysis Murray Feshbach and Louvan Nolting have concluded that the "numerical crossover occurred toward the end of the 1960s" and that by 1978 the Soviet total was "nearly 60 percent greater than the U.S. total."[1]

Further study of the statistics soon demonstrates, however, that the disparity between the sizes of the two research establishments is not quite as large as this figure suggests. If only researchers with the doctoral equivalent are included, the sizes of the two groups are very close. On the other hand, if one subtracts from these totals the degrees in the social sciences and humanities (included as scientific degrees in Soviet statistics), the Soviet Union jumps ahead again by about a third. In other words, the Soviet Union is comfortably ahead of the United States in the number of advanced researchers in the engineering and natural sciences, but the greater U.S. effort in the humanities and social sciences brings the total sizes of the two research communities closer together.

In the early 1970s the impressive expansion of Soviet science and technology slowed markedly, and it would seem that the heroic period of building the Soviet scientific establishment had come to an end. In the 1960s the average annual rate of increase of scientific workers in the Soviet Union was around 8 percent; in the early 1970s it was about 6 percent, and by the late 1970s had dropped to 3 percent; and in the period from 1981 to 1984 it was only slightly above 1 percent. During the past 15 years, moreover, the number of graduate students in the Soviet Union has been approximately stable; in 1984 the total was actually almost 2 percent lower than it had been in 1970.

Statistics on the financing of Soviet research present a roughly similar picture. In the late 1950s and early 1960s the annual funds in the Soviet budget allocated to science grew at phenomenal rates, in excess of 15 percent a year. By the mid-1960s the annual increases were around 8 percent. By 1976 the rate had dropped to 1.7 percent, after which it picked up a bit, only to drop again to 1.2 percent a year between 1981 and 1984.[2]

What about quality? How good are Soviet scientists and engineers? Overall, U.S. analysts judge U.S. science and technology to be superior to Soviet science and technology, although they find that in certain fields, such as theoretical physics and mathematics, Soviet specialists are among the very best in the world. Soviet strength tends to be in fundamental rather than in applied areas, but there are some exceptions, such as metallurgy. On the commercial level, U.S. industrialists do not worry about Soviet technology (they have enough anxiety about Japan); but in military technology the received opinion in Washington is that the Soviets will be able to do anything that the Americans can do, albeit with a considerable time lag.

Finally, under the general rubric of recent achievements in Soviet science, we should remember that it was only in 1965 that the scandal of Soviet biology, Lysenkoism, was eliminated. Nikita Khrushchev, who was in power until 1964, was a strong supporter of T. D. Lysenko. The prominent Soviet émigré scientist, Zhores Medvedev, has written that Khrushchev's support of Lysenko was a major reason for the premier's ouster.[3] Although that claim may be somewhat exaggerated, Khrushchev's successor, Leonid Brezhnev, followed a very different policy by sharply reducing ideological interference in the content of scientific work.

This relaxation of philosophical restrictions was more than matched, however, by a tightening of political controls over the extra-scientific activity of scientists. Although Soviet scientists today (with a few exceptions) do not have to worry about the interference of ideologists in their technical work, their concerns about orthodoxy in the political and social realm have increased. Under Brezhnev and his immediate successors, a scientist could easily get into trouble because of his political views and activities, as the case of the eminent Soviet physicist Andrei Sakharov illustrates.

The traditional organization of Soviet science and technology, as it developed under Stalin, was in three administrative pyramids: the Academy of Sciences of the Soviet Union and the regional and specialized academies; the industrial ministries with their associated institutes for research and development; and the higher educational system. In number of researchers involved, the Academy of Sciences was the smallest of these pyramids; but it had the greatest authority and prestige. The industrial ministries had the most research-and-development personnel, but usually they did not challenge the authority of the Academy as the court of last resort in scientific and technical questions. Research in the university system was, under Stalin, markedly undeveloped, although there were a few fields, such as mathematics, where the universities were strong.

During the last 20 years this pattern has changed in a number of ways. Research in the universities and in the industrial ministries has become stronger. Regional associations of industrial research and production facilities have developed. The most important event, in terms of the organization of science and technology, was the rise to power of the State Committee on Science and Technology, established in 1965. At present, the State Committee is still relatively small compared to the Academy of Sciences, but it is already a major competitor in terms of influence and prestige. In its system of scientific councils (*nauchnye sovety*) the State Committee obtains the assistance of thousands of Soviet scientists, including almost all the members of the Academy of Sciences.

The advisory role of these scientific councils resembles that of the committees of the U.S. National Research Council, but there is an important distinction. In the Soviet Union, the State Committee has executive authority above this advisory function, particularly when a jurisdictional conflict over technology arises among several industrial ministries. The State Committee has a unique responsibility for planning applied research. Moreover, it approves the entire research-and-development budget, including the gross figures for the Academy of Sciences' budget, the internal structure of which is left to the Academy. Finally, the political strength of the State Committee is revealed by the fact that its chairman until 1986, G. Marchuk, was also deputy chairman of the Council of Industrial Ministries, outranking the president of the Academy of Sciences, who was only a member of the Council of Industrial Ministries. In October 1986 Marchuk was elected president of the Academy of Sciences, replacing the aging A. P. Aleksandrov.

A major question in Soviet science policy is whether the State Committee will add to its present small set of research institutes—

most of which are informational or policy oriented—other institutes that actually do research and development in "hard" science and technology. If that happens, the academy will face the greatest challenge in 50 years to its authority as the supreme scientific institution of the Soviet Union. Proposals for such a change have been made, but we do not yet know if they will be accepted.

Before describing those proposals, I shall review briefly the history of the Academy in the last two or three decades in order to see how it reached its present dilemma.

Under Stalin the Academy was the seat not only of fundamental research but also of a great deal of applied research, centered in its Department of Engineering Sciences. Emphasis on applied work in the those years was seen by many Soviet scientists as regrettable but unavoidable, an integral part of the Stalinist dogma of "the unity of theory and practice." After Stalin's death the ideological thaw in science was equated by many scientists with the freedom to give much more attention to pure science. These fundamental scientists thought that by the late 1950s the most strenuous period of Soviet industrialization was over and that, as a result, they would be permitted to free themselves from narrow industrial concerns.

A few years after Stalin's death an influential group of scientists in the Academy of Sciences mounted a large effort to change the orientation of the Academy by putting much more emphasis on fundamental research. They managed to get Khrushchev's support during one of his moments of zeal for administrative reform and were successful in their campaign. The most important result was the elimination of the Department of Engineering Sciences from the Academy, and the transfer of many of the institutes working on applied sciences from the Academy to the industrial ministries.

These changes in the Academy's priorities, which occurred 25 years ago, are in part responsible for the major problem in the present organization of Soviet science and technology. It soon became clear that if the Academy was not going to take major responsibility for coordinating applied research, then some other body would have to do so. It is no accident that only a few years after the Academy divested itself of much of its responsibility for applied research the State Committee assumed the responsibilities the Academy had spurned, and it is now powerful enough to be in direct competition with the Academy.

During the past 25 years it has also become clear that those fundamental scientists of the Academy who thought that in the post-Stalin era they could devote their time to pure science, without much concern about governmental priorities or industrial needs, were mistaken. In the past decade, the need of the Soviet economy to increase productivity through technological innovation has grown tremendously; so have the pressures on the Soviet Union to keep up with the West in high technology. The result has been that Soviet political leaders have become more and more insistent that research efforts have practical effects. The Academy of Sciences has, in fact, often been accused by economic planners of lacking interest in industrial technology.

As these challenges multiplied, the Academy's own leaders were divided in their response. Some of them, particularly a few influential physicists and chemists, continued to insist that the Academy concentrate on what it does best, fundamental research. Others, concerned that the Academy was being bypassed by the State Committee and the industrial ministries, called for the Academy to move back into industrial research. The latter camp has had some significant successes in recent years.[4] The share of the Academy's research devoted to industrial applications has grown appreciably. Many of the Academy's institutes now have contracts with industrial ministries to do applied research. The Siberian division of the Academy of Sciences and the Ukrainian Academy have been leaders in the creation of centers of research with strong industrial connections. These two parts of the Academy system are often cited as models for the integration of fundamental and applied research. Still, the problem of how to improve applied research in the Soviet Union remains the major worry of managers of the Soviet research-and-development community. There seems to be an essential incompatibility between the existing organization of research and development and the requirements of technological innovation.

At the beginning of the 1980s the Academy of Sciences had the necessary talent but few pilot plant production facilities. Furthermore, it was not clear that the Academy wanted the responsibility for all high-technology research and development. The State Committee for Science and Technology had great political authority but did not possess institutes of its own working on these problems. Meanwhile, the industrial ministries had demonstrated that they usually paid attention only to their own narrow interests, placing more emphasis on short-term production goals than on long-term innovation. What seemed to be needed was a drastic reorganization of Soviet science and technology—one that would either give much greater authority to one of the existing bodies or create an entirely new body with the necessary authority to transcend the rivalries of existing organizations.

A number of proposals for such reforms were published. M. L. Bashin suggested that the Academy of Sciences be given much greater authority and that experimental production bases be subordinated to it. This would enable the Academy to do the original research behind an innovation and also to test it in production.[5] Such a reform would represent a great change in the role of the Academy and would put it in the middle of industrial concerns to a much greater degree than it was even in the days of Stalin.

A sharply different proposal by V. P. Rassokhin called for a "fourth system of research and development organizations" (in addition to the Academy, the universities, and the ministries) that would be subordinated to the State Committee for Science and Technology.[6] This new system would include most of the applied-research institutes removed from the Academy in the early 1960s. For the first time, the State Committee would have its own research base, and it would be directly challenging the Academy of Sciences as the leader of Soviet science.

The unanswered question is whether the members of the Academy wish to take on greater responsibility for high-technology research. Will the fundamental scientists who called for the expulsion of engineering institutes in the early 1960s still carry the day? Or has the Academy learned that if it does not fulfill the functions that the government and Party expect of it, it will be replaced in prestige and authority by a competitor? This question will surely be answered in the next few years.

Many of the pressures on science and technology that occur in the Soviet Union are also present in the United States. To be sure, there is no single U.S. equivalent of the Soviet Academy of Sciences, but the National Science Foundation has been under great pressure to put less emphasis on fundamental science and more on research promoting industrial innovation. There have even been proposals to create a National Engineering Foundation that would support applied research. The National Science Foundation, seeing such proposals as a threat to its own authority, has assured Congress that it will give more attention to applied research. Thus, U.S. and Soviet leaders in science-policy questions have some common worries, worries which stem from the increasingly intense worldwide competition in high technology.

The Soviet economy faces major problems, as various of the preceding chapters have pointed out. Industrial growth rates have dropped dramatically, and the demographic statistics show that growth cannot be invigorated in the old way—that is, simply by bringing in more workers. The single most important means by which the Soviet Union can hope to energize its economy is by improvements in productivity, boosting the capacity per worker.

Improvements in productivity come from scientific and technological innovation. Soviet economic planners are putting more pressure on the scientific establishment to speed innovation than at any time in recent Soviet history. It is being emphasized to the Academy of Sciences that economic growth can no longer depend on extensive factors but now must rely on intensive development—and that this situation puts a heavy responsibility on Soviet scientists and engineers. Before his retirement Academy president A. P. Aleksandrov focused on energy issues, problems in computer technology, the rapid pace of genetic engineering, and the need for scientific aid to agriculture. His last speeches were remarkable in their emphasis on industrial and agricultural applications rather than those areas of the the Academy's work that had been so important in the past: fundamental research in physics, astronomy, mathematics, and chemistry.

At a special joint meeting of the Academy of Sciences and the Academy of Agricultural Sciences in September 1982, the leaders ·of both institutions underscored the need for science to improve Soviet nutrition.[7] And in an article published in April 1983, Aleksandrov asked Soviet scientists to find and eliminate "the bottlenecks" that hold back technical progress in the Soviet Union.[8] Aleksandrov thus served the Academy notice that industrial and agricultural problems would have top priority throughout Soviet science.

The problem of increasing industrial productivity is only one of the serious issues facing Soviet scientists today. Other increasingly sharp issues concern the adverse effects of science and technology, particularly on the environment (see chapter 13). The days of undiluted optimism about scientific progress are over in the Soviet Union. More and more articles are being published, often written by biologists, that describe the effects of pollution on the biosphere— and even on human beings—in alarming terms.

The "scientific-technical revolution," so often praised in Soviet publications, is now getting its share of criticism. Biologists point out that this revolution is creating a new environment, in which radiation from nuclear power stations and mutagens from the chemical industry are having a deleterious effect on people. Some Soviet scientists had begun to criticize nuclear power well before the accident at Chernobyl in 1986. A 1979 article in the influential Party journal *Kommunist* called for future nuclear power stations to be

built in the sparsely populated regions of the Soviet Union. Academician N. P. Dubinin, one of the Soviet Union's senior geneti-
cists, even indicated that a dramatic increase in genetic defects in
children may be due to higher radiation levels.[9]

This comment relates to yet another problem in science and
technology that the Soviet Union faces. And it is perhaps the most
serious of all, since it suggests a major decline in the quality of
Soviet life. According to published Soviet statistics, between 1971
and 1974 infant mortality rose by more than 20 percent; between
1960 and 1974 death rates for people in their fifties rose by almost
20 percent; and death rates for people in their forties rose by more
than 30 percent.[10] Although attempts have been made, in both the
West and the Soviet Union, to explain these alarming statistics, there
is still no persuasive hypothesis. Even if better reporting of relevant
statistics is partially responsible—as several Soviet officials have
suggested—the fact would still remain that, when compared with
those of other developed nations, the Soviet Union's infant mortality
in the 1970s was one of the highest. Soviet medical health specialists regard this as an urgent problem.

A final problem concerns international science exchanges and
technology transfers. Under Stalin, Soviet leaders expressed confidence that their country would soon surpass the United States in
achievements in science and technology. In the 1970s and 1980s,
as the research-and-development communities of Japan, Western
Europe, and the United States continued to display impressive vitality, Soviet confidence in quickly becoming the dominant research-and-development force in the world diminished, and Soviet
leaders began to put more and more emphasis on cooperation and
trade in technical areas.

The ebbing of detente at the end of the 1970s, however, impeded
Soviet access abroad to high technology and cooperative projects in
science. Science contacts between the United States and the Soviet
Union declined sharply from the high reached around 1975. American disapproval of Soviet treatment of dissidents and Jews has been
one of the reasons for the cooling of scientific relations. The U.S.
scientific community as well as U.S. political leaders must determine how much and what kinds of scientific exchange with the Soviet Union are desirable. The Soviet Union would clearly prefer to
have more rather than fewer contacts, but, if this path does not seem
to be open, they will once again take a more independent road.

I have no crystal ball for reading the future, but I would venture
a few observations about probable developments in several of the

areas I have discussed: the growth of Soviet science and technology, the organization of Soviet science, and particular problems that the leaders of Soviet science and technology face.

It seems clear that the period of tremendous expansion of Soviet research and development has ended. The emphasis in the near future will be on qualitative improvement. A vice-president of the Academy of Sciences, V. A. Kotelnikov, observed in 1980 that now that the Soviet Union had as many scientific workers as the United States, there were no plans to increase the number rapidly. In the area of science and technology, the Soviet Union measures itself by reference to the United States. Nonetheless, science budgets are likely to continue to grow by one or two percentage points a year.

Tremendous pressure will continue to mount for improvements in Soviet industrial productivity through more technical innovation. It is difficult to imagine great breakthroughs here, since the major obstacles seem to be systemic, but it would be a mistake to under-rate the ability of Soviet scientists and engineers. They are getting better and better in important areas such as computer technology and genetic engineering, where truly enormous efforts are being made.

In the organization of Soviet science, the Academy of Sciences continues to face major competition from the State Committee on Science and Technology, and, as we have seen, there are proposals to give the State Committee even greater advantages. In the short run, however, it seems very unlikely that the State Committee will be able to supplant the Academy, and there are even some trends in the Academy's favor. So long as detente was in force and the Soviet Union was able to buy large amounts of technology from the West, the State Committee was able to improve its stature steadily, since it had responsibility for technology transfer from the West. Such men as V. A. Kirillin, head of the State Committee for the first 14 years of its existence, and G. M. Gvishiani, deputy chairman, made their reputations by promoting good relations with the West and trade in technology.

Kirillin often talked of "complementary development" in science and technology, concluding that no one nation could be autonomous in these areas and that therefore the leading nations should trade with each other to their mutual benefit. That viewpoint no longer seems as persuasive to Soviet leaders as it once did. The State Committee, known as a proponent of trade and exchange with the West, is suffering a slight diminution in its status with the decline of scientific exchanges and technology transfer.

The problems of improving industrial productivity and public health are the most serious ones facing Soviet science and technology. It seems doubtful that productivity and health can be radically improved in the near future. Both reorganization and major investment would be required, and at a time when the arms race remains intense such investment funds are very scarce. Therefore, I expect the Soviet research-and-development community to be burdened for a considerable period of time with these difficulties.

One can conclude that although Soviet science and technology are now stronger than at any other time in the history of the Soviet Union, the problems they face are also more intractable. One of these problems—trying to increase productivity—is common to both the Soviet Union and the United States. The other—health—is one in which the Soviet dilemma is more difficult. We should notice, however, that the Soviet Union can serve as an object lesson in what may happen to a nation's health if, over a long period of time, funds are taken from medicine and health care and devoted to the military. Indeed, if the United States and the Soviet Union continue to engage in a strenuous arms race over a long enough time, it is likely that their internal problems will become more similar.

NOTES

1. Louvan E. Nolting and Murray Feshbach, "R&D Employment in the USSR," *Science* (February 1, 1980), pp. 493–503.

2. See Louvan E. Nolting, *Sources of Financing the Stages of the Research, Development, and Innovation Cycle in the USSR*, Foreign Economics Report, no. 3 (Washington, DC: U.S. Department of Commerce, 1973); and *Narodnoe Khoziaistvo SSSR 1984* (Moscow: Statistika, 1985).

3. Zhores Medvedev, *The Rise and Fall of T. D. Lysenko* (New York: Columbia University Press, 1969).

4. Simon Kassel and Cathleen Campbell, *The Soviet Academy of Sciences and Technological Development*. R-2533-ARPA. (Santa Monica, CA: Rand, 1980).

5. M. Bashin, "Priblizit effekt ordachi," *Khoziaistvo i pravo*, no. 4 (1980), pp. 63–67.

6. V. P. Rassokhin, "Nuzhna chetvertaia sistema nauchnykh uchrezhdenii," *Ekonomika i organizatsiia promyshlennogo proizvodstva*, no. 1 (1980), pp. 13–22.

7. See A. P. Aleksandrov, "Zadachi nauk v realizatsii prodovol'stvennoi programmy SSSR," and Iu. A. Ovchinnikov, "Prodovol'stvennaia programma i zadachi sovetskoi nauki," *Vestnik akademii nauk*, no. 2 (1983), pp. 3–26.

8. A. P. Aleksandrov, "Vstupitel'noe slovo," *Vestnik akademii nauk,* no. 4 (1983), p. 8.

9. See Loren R. Graham, "Biomedicine and the Politics of Science in the USSR," *Soviet Union* 8, pt. 2 (1981), pp. 147–58; and N. P. Dubinin, "Genetika i ee znachenie dlia chelovechestva," *Vestnik akademii nauk,* no. 6 (1980), pp. 73–81.

10. Christopher Davis and Murray Feshbach, *Rising Infant Mortality in the USSR in the 1970s* (Washington, DC: U.S. Bureau of the Census, 1980).

11. V. A. Kotel'nikov, "Razrabotka kompleksnoi programmy nauchno-teknicheskogo progressa na 20 let," *Vestnik akademii nauk,* no. 5 (1980), pp. 37–43.

20

Soviet Science in Practice: An Inside View

VLADIMIR Z. KRESIN

The number of scientists in the Soviet Union is enormous—approximately 1,300,000—and to direct this army a peculiarly Soviet scientific system has evolved. Research is carried out primarily in the approximately 1,500 state-supported institutes run by the Soviet Academy of Sciences and by the affiliated Academies of Sciences of the individual Soviet republics: the Ukrainian, Lithuanian, Georgian, and so forth. Many state agencies—the Committee on Atomic Science and Technology, the Committee on Chemistry, the Ministry of Electrical Industry, and others—also maintain scientific institutes. The Kurchatov Institute of Atomic Energy, for instance, comes under the state's Committee on Atomic Energy; the Karpov Institute of Physical Chemistry is responsible to the Committee on Chemistry. Scientific research is conducted in the universities and higher technical schools as well. Moscow University maintains very large laboratories, as do the Moscow Institute of Physics and Engineering, the University of Gorky, and the Moscow Institute of Steel and Alloys, among others. But on the whole, as Loren Graham has already pointed out (chapter 19), fundamental scientific research in the Soviet Union is carried out under the auspices of the Academy of Sciences and its affiliates.

Basically, there are two kinds of Soviet research institute. Some are wide profile, such as the Lebedev Institute of Physics in Moscow, the Kurchatov Institute of Atomic Energy, the Leningrad Physics and Technology Institute, and the Institute of Physics of the Georgian Academy of Sciences. Others, by contrast, concentrate in one scientific area. Examples include the Acoustics Institute of the Academy of Sciences, the Solid State Physics Institute, the Physics and Technology Institute of Low Temperatures of the Ukrainian Academy of Sciences, and the Institute of Crystallography.

Thus, a fundamental difference between the organization of scientific research in the Soviet Union and in the United States is immediately apparent. In the latter, basic research is carried out mostly in universities, often by scientists administering federal or other outside grants; and scientific work is combined with education. In the Soviet Union, on the other hand, such work is done principally in institutes that are entirely state supported and by people occupied solely with research.

The achievements of Soviet scientists—the level of their research and the value of its results—should not be underestimated. I have often encountered such a tendency in the United States, be it a direct underrating of Soviet science or an insufficient knowledge of its activities, which is, in fact, another form of underrating. I will return to the causes of this tendency, but first let me describe the strengths of Soviet science.

The work of many Soviet scientists is up to the latest standards of research. A number of excellent scientists are employed at the Physics and Technology Institute of Low Temperatures in Kharkiv, for example, whereas the Institute of Physical Problems of the Academy of Sciences in Moscow, long headed by Nobel laureate P. L. Kapitsa (he died in 1984), is indisputably one of the leading such centers in the world.

More specifically, scientists at the Kharkiv institute experimentally discovered the nonstationary Josephson effect. Their work led to the creation of a new field of scientific and technical research and to the development of a wide range of equipment used in electronics, computer science, and military technology. Organizationally, too, this institute is unusual in the Soviet Union in that it contains shops in which various kinds of industrial equipment are manufactured as well as laboratories for the pursuit of basic research. In this respect, it is patterned after such Western companies as IBM Research or Bell Laboratories.

The method of colliding beams developed at the Nuclear Physics Institute of the Siberian Division of the Academy of Sciences under Academician G. I. Budker is now widely used in high-energy physics and other accelerator-related research. In the field of experimental optics, a special effect discovered by E. V. Shpolsky (and named after him) led to the development of a process now widely used in optical laboratories for studying complex molecules. Investigations led by V. L. Ginzburg, L. D. Landau, A. A. Abrikosov, and L. P. Gorkov gave birth to a theory (now called, after them, the GLAG theory) that permitted the creation of superstrong magnetic fields. Today magnets based on this principle are in laboratories throughout the world.

It is generally agreed that Lev Davidovich Landau (1908–68), who was awarded a Nobel Prize in 1962, was one of the greatest theoretical physicists of the twentieth century. To a great extent the high level of Soviet physics today, especially of theoretical physics, is due, I believe, to that unique phenomenon known as "Landau's school." For Landau spared no effort in the creation and strengthening of his school, at whose core was "Landau's Minimum," a series of nine examinations. The first was Math I, which was always given by Landau himself. He considered it necessary to get to know everyone who started the Minimum—some 300 students all told—and any student, whatever institution he attended and wherever he lived in the Soviet Union, could telephone Landau in Moscow, express his wish to begin taking the Minimum, and arrange a day for the first exam.

In the fall of 1955, trembling with excitement, I myself dialed Landau's number and asked him to let me begin. He was very friendly, saying that unfortunately he was busy the next day but that at two o'clock the following afternoon he would be happy to meet me in his office. When I came he led me to the adjacent room, where I spent the next three hours on the mathematical problems he gave me. During this time Landau came into the room several times to see how I was doing. Finally, after the closing conversation, I went home in a semiconscious state, infinitely happy for having successfully passed Math I.

After Math I the Minimum was structured to include Classical Mechanics, Classical Electrodynamics and the Theory of Relativity, Math II, Quantum Mechanics, Statistical Physics, Quantum Electrodynamics, Hydrodynamics and the Theory of Elasticity, and Macroscopic Physics and Solid State Theory. Except for Math I, the exams were also given by Landau's closest colleagues, E. M. Lifshitz and I. M. Khalatnikov. But Landau alone gave one other, the seventh in the series, on Quantum Electrodynamics, which was therefore a kind of milestone. To the student who passed it Landau became a kind of scientific father, and there was no limit to his willingness to discuss scientific problems with his newest "son." One of his closest collaborators would be appointed the young man's research director, Landau would think about his future employment, and so on. And having passed the entire Minimum, the student was allowed to study the notebook in which Landau listed what he considered the most interesting unsolved problems in physics and his own ideas about them.

Landau was probably the last universal theoretical physicist. For him physics was a single science with general principles, and more than once he demonstrated the effectiveness of using methods from one field for solving problems in other, seemingly unrelated fields. His 10-volume *Course in Theoretical Physics*, written with E. M. Liftshitz, is famous the world over, and for many years his Thursday morning seminar at the Academy's Institute of Physical Problems was the leading one of its kind in the Soviet Union. His students include many distinguished scientists who today occupy key posts in Soviet physics. The Landau Institute of Theoretical Physics near Moscow is now the foremost Soviet center in this field.

The Soviet system allows scientists to study highly problematic questions—those about which it is difficult, if not impossible, to say how long it will take to solve them, or indeed whether any solution even exists. The system of research grants, so dominant in the United States, does not operate in the Soviet Union. And in spite of its positive features, the grant system sometimes restricts opportunities for pursuing fundamental research, especially in these problematic fields. A ready example is the search for high-temperature (that is, room-temperature) superconductors.

Electric current flowing in a wire conductor experiences resistance, which leads to a heating of the wire and therefore to a loss of energy. But when cooled to a very low temperature (-500 degrees Fahrenheit), many metals cease to offer resistance and no energy is lost. About 20 years ago William Little of Stanford University first suggested that it might be possible to produce a substance that would remain a superconductor up to room temperature. Obviously, if this could be done it would lead to a revolution in technology. Making power lines out of such a substance, for instance, would eliminate enormous losses of energy.

It is equally clear, however, that the task of finding high-temperature superconducting materials is both complicated and problematic, since it is unclear in principle whether such materials could even exist. In the Soviet Union, a special session of the Presidium of the Academy of Sciences declared this problem *second* in importance after the problem of regulated nuclear fusion, and many Soviet scientists are working intensively in this field. The Institute of Steel and Alloys in Moscow alone maintains a laboratory employing some 80 people in this connection. Yet in the United

States, as far as I know, only Little and his group, supported by a grant, are working on the problem. Nor do the Soviet scientists work under the pressure of deadlines. Perhaps a high-temperature superconductor will never be found, but if it is, it will most likely happen in the Soviet Union.[1]

Or take the case of metallic hydrogen. If hydrogen, the lightest element, could be transformed into a metal, we would possess the lightest metal possible. Numerous practical applications would follow. Yet this is also a very problematic question. In the Soviet Union it is under intensive investigation, with large groups of scientists working at the Institute of High Pressure Physics near Moscow and at the Institute of Physics and Technology of the Ukrainian Academy of Sciences in Donetsk. In the United States, to the best of my knowledge, this field is not being experimentally developed.

Scientists working in the Soviet Union enjoy a well-developed system of contacts. All-Union scientific conferences take place frequently and, more important, there is a wide network of regular seminars. In Moscow, every Wednesday, scientists from many institutes come to the seminar chaired by Academician Kapitsa at the Institute of Physical Problems. Regular seminars in theoretical physics include the Thursday seminar at the same Institute and Academician Ginzburg's Wednesday seminar at the Lebedev Institute. Such regular meetings promote that interchange of ideas necessary for productive scientific work.

There is, to be sure, a lot of deadwood in Soviet science, a point to which I shall return. But many research groups work very hard and are highly productive—a matter of both personal devotion and a very effective system of incentives. For many scientists in the Soviet Union science is their whole life. I think especially of A. Larkin at the Landau Institute, I. K. Ianson in Kharkiv, and N. E. Alekseevsky at the Institute of Physical Problems, among others; they come to their laboratories early in the morning and often do not leave until after midnight. Moreover, Soviet scientists earn relatively high incomes and benefit from a series of academic degrees and ranks, each of which corresponds to a higher degree of financial well-being. The most important degrees are candidate of sciences, roughly equivalent to the American Ph.D., and doctor of sciences. The salary of the former is approximately twice the average wage; that of the latter, three times or more. From being a corresponding member of the Academy of Sciences (about 480), one advances to the rank of full member (about 300), to enjoy a standard of living considerably higher than that of the other professions. The Academy of Sciences pays its members simply for being members, and its prestige in the Soviet Union is unmatched by any single scientific body in the United States.

It is true that Soviet industry has not been equal to the task of producing adequate scientific equipment, especially vital in the experimental fields. But a number of Soviet institutes have been able to acquire excellent equipment in the West. For example, the Academy's Institutes of Solid State Physics and of Bio-Organic Chemistry are two centers that are thus able to pursue high-quality scientific work and do not suffer from the lack of adequate domestically produced equipment.

Among the weaknesses of Soviet science, the first involves certain moral or personal failings. A 1979 book on the state of Soviet science argued, correctly, that many heads of Soviet scientific organizations are manipulative, venal, or otherwise morally objectionable.[2] Yet, as Lydiia Chukovskaia remarked when Dmitry Shostakovich signed a widely publicized letter against Andrei Sakharov, "villainy and genius" are quite compatible. A number of leading Soviet scientists are known to be anti-Semitic, for example, or crassly political in their careerism. But a scientist's moral qualities should not be confused with the quality of his work, and the fact is that major moral failings and high scientific productivity often go together.

A related weakness of Soviet science is the reverse of one of its strengths. Compared with their Western counterparts, Soviet scientists enjoy relatively greater prestige and material rewards. Moreover, the nonpolitical nature of science attracts many able people who find scientific work compatible with their moral, and possibly anticommunist, convictions. By the same token, however, science attracts bureaucrats who zealously believe in Marxism-Leninism—supposedly *the* scientific theory—and in the Soviet system. These bureaucrats enjoy the aura of respectability and infallibility conferred by academic degrees and memberships. The prestige and material rewards of Soviet science also attract cynical careerists, of course.

The weaknesses of Soviet science are often a direct consequence of its bureaucratization. An obvious case in point involves the movement from basic to applied science and the implementation of their findings in industry. Here the Soviet Union is very backward. The introduction of new methods or technologies is usually an agonizingly slow procedure, one complicated by an enormous amount of red tape. (The Institute at Kharkiv, described above, is only an outstanding exception to this rule.) The problem of implementing the results of basic and applied research in industry is one of the weakest links in the whole Soviet system.

Another fundamental factor impairing scientific development in the Soviet Union is the low level of computerization. In the United States the ability to use computers in everyday work is as normal to a scientist as driving a car, whereas for Soviet scientists it is far from common. Undoubtedly this will soon change, given the Soviet Union's proven capacity for producing major advances in selected fields of endeavor—the space program, for example. But meanwhile computers are not adequately used, and this slows down progress in theoretical chemistry, solid state physics, and other fields.

In addition to the poor quality of Soviet scientific equipment, and the problem of insufficient contact with the outside scientific world (which I shall deal with below), another difficulty lies in the large size of Soviet scientific organizations. Laboratories are often staffed by dozens, and institutes employ hundreds, even thousands, of scientific workers. As a result, the heads of these organizations become so enmeshed in administration that they lose touch with their science and are gradually disqualified. This does not prevent them from claiming authorship of scientific papers, however. By the age of 45 a recent vice-president of the Academy of Sciences and director of its Institute of Bio-Organic Chemistry, for example, was the ostensible author of more than 300 publications, most of which, in all probability, he had not even read. By the end of his life another Academician had published more than 1,200 papers— an average of one every two weeks from the time he was 20 years old!

The large number of poorly qualified scientists attracted by the profession's prestige and material rewards, combined with Party interference in scientific appointments, constitutes a major weakness of Soviet science. With the partial exception of the Ukrainian Academy of Sciences, the academies of the individual Soviet republics are mostly staffed by such people, and their productivity is practically nil. The heads of the Solid State Physics Department of Moscow University and of the Institute of Atomic Energy owe their appointments to Party politics. Nor does the system, for various of the reasons already noted, give adequate attention to university teaching in science, where unqualified teachers are but one of its grave shortcomings.

For many years I taught at Moscow University and other institutions of higher education in the Soviet capital and was a member of committees on physics curricula for schools and colleges. Soviet secondary schools, in my opinion, give a better technical-scientific education than do their U.S. counterparts, although recently they have begun to deteriorate in this area. But at the university level, as I have observed here at the University of California, Berkeley, the U.S. system takes a giant step forward. For one thing, the Soviet Union does not have a system of computerized testing in the selection of students comparable to the Scholastic Aptitude Tests and various other standardized examinations—a system remarkable for its objectivity. Instead, every Soviet university conducts its own entrance examinations, which are mostly oral. Given the intense competition for admission, especially to the top universities, this leads to arbitrary decisions based on subjective criteria—in short, to corruption.

Another reason for the comparative inferiority of Soviet higher education lies in its excessively structured nature. Students have practically no freedom of choice in their programs and must attend many strictly required lectures. Little attention is paid to developing creative skills. At Berkeley, students are given a great deal of work intended to do just that, whereas at Soviet universities great emphasis is placed on mechanically stuffing the memory.

It is well known that talented Jewish men and women are now, in practice, precluded from entering the leading Soviet universities. The system of oral entrance examinations works to this end.[3] Moreover, Jews are being eliminated from the scientific community as actively as they are from student life. One example is my friend Michael Reyzer, the author of many excellent works in theoretical physics, who looked for a job for over a year. At dozens of laboratories he was met with enthusiasm and told that positions were available, only to be turned down when it became clear from his application (which requires a declaration of one's official "nationality") that he was Jewish. In 1979 he gave up the ordeal and applied to emigrate. He is now a "refusenik." Another young man I knew was among the winners of the All-Union Mathematical Olympiad but later, because he is Jewish, was not admitted to Moscow University. After much difficulty he entered the Institute of Oil Engineering. He will probably become a good engineer, but his remarkable scientific talents are clearly being wasted.

Today it is possible to encounter Jews only among older and middle-aged physicists, and it would seem that in the future Soviet science is to be cleared of all Jews. Such policies can only lower the scientific potential of the Soviet Union.

Why is Soviet science underrated in the West, particularly in the United States? Two reasons seem to me the most important. The first is the infrequency—even the complete absence—of contacts between Soviet and Western scientists, a situation that has worsened in recent years. Only a few Soviet scientists have been permitted to visit foreign countries regularly, to attend international conferences, or to visit universities. I took part, in 1981, in the International Conference on Low Temperature Physics held in Los Angeles; more than 40 papers had been submitted by Soviet scientists, but only three of the authors could come and only two made presentations. In this way, the Soviet authorities drastically curtail opportunities for Soviet scientists to present their work to Western colleagues and to establish contacts that could prove useful to both sides. At the same time, there has been a big drop in the number of Western scientists visiting the Soviet Union; and this, too, has contributed to a breakdown in scientific communication.[4]

My second reason is more specific. Many scientific journals are published in the Soviet Union, and a number of these are translated into English; but some U.S. scientists have told me that they are often difficult to read. It is clear, they say, that an interesting result has been obtained—but not how or why; all the intermediate equations have been left out. This happens owing to an acute shortage of paper in the Soviet Union, and leading scientific publications impose strict limits on the length of their articles. The *Journal of Experimental and Theoretical Physics*, for example, requires that submitted papers be no longer than 15 typed pages. It specifies that the account of the experiment must be very concise and that descriptions of intermediate calculations or other details may be omitted. Hence the difficulty in reading such articles.

In the United States, however, the situation is quite different. When I first submitted a paper to a U.S. journal, it was in the Soviet style; but the editor asked me to write in more detail, not to worry about its length, and to give all my attention to making the paper readily comprehensible. At the same time, Soviet scientists who might want to publish in a Western journal find the way impeded by so much Soviet red tape that only a very few are able to overcome it. Practical difficulties such as these contribute further to a breakdown in scientific communication.

Since the advent of the new leadership in the Soviet Union in 1985, there has been much talk about radical change and about freedom of criticism and discussion. Yet so far Soviet scientists are still unable, by and large, to travel to other countries at their own discretion for the purpose of meeting their colleagues or taking part in scientific conferences; they are still considered the government's property.[5] As far as real events in the world of Soviet science and technology are concerned, there have been two major ones: the disaster at the Chernobyl nuclear power station in 1986 and the change in leadership at the Academy of Sciences that same year.

A lot has been said and written about the Chernobyl accident. It vividly illustrated the insufficient level of safety management in the Soviet nuclear power program. The closed nature of Soviet society and the mania for secrecy led to inadequate safety controls. In the West, the activities of environmentalists, medical professionals, and others, together with a high level of technology, promote a much more responsible approach to the question of safety.

As for the new president of the Soviet Academy of Sciences, it must be emphasized that since the Academy is the main Soviet organization sponsoring scientific research, this position is of the utmost importance. But the ascent of the new president was not the result of a free discussion and election by the members of the Academy themselves. A senior official of the Party Secretariat came to the general meeting of the Academy and informed the assembled members of the Party leadership's choice. This candidate, G. Marchuk (see the preceding chapter), was immediately elected. All previous presidents of the Academy, without exception, were people with considerable scientific reputations; now, for the first time in Soviet history, the Academy is headed by a typical bureaucrat who has not made any sizable scientific contribution. It is difficult to expect positive changes from such an appointment.

In conclusion, it can be said that science in the Soviet Union has both strengths and weaknesses.[6] It is important that we maintain a realistic picture of it.

NOTES

1. Also see Vladimir Kresin, *Low Temperature Physics Research in the Soviet Union* (Falls Church, VA: Delphic Associates, 1985).

2. Mark Popovsky, *Manipulated Science* (New York: Doubleday, 1979).

3. Grigori Freiman, *It Seems I Am a Jew* (Carbondale, IL: Southern Illinois University Press, 1980). This book contains, among other things, examples of special "Jewish problems" (problems virtually impossible to solve) given to Jewish applicants in entrance examinations to universities.

4. See Loren R. Graham, "Scientific Exchanges with the Soviet Union," *Bulletin of the Atomic Scientists* (May 1983), pp. 2–3. Graham points out that in 1975, at the height of detente, over 2,000 U.S. and Soviet scholars and officials participated in scientific exchanges under 13 different agreements; by 1982 this number had dropped to about 300 under eight agreements.

244 Vladimir Z. Kresin

5. For example, at an international conference of mathematicians at Berkeley in the fall of 1986, 36 Soviet mathematicians had accepted invitations to deliver major addresses and were listed in the program; but 17—or nearly half—did not appear. As an American participant further complained, "this was no different from the last regularly scheduled international congress of mathematicians in Helsinki in 1978, when half of the invited Soviet speakers were not permitted to attend." *New York Times* (September 20, 1986), p. 18.

6. Compare G. Taubes and G. Garelik, "Soviet Science: How Good Is It?" *Discover* (August 1986).

21

Education, Science, and Technology

HARLEY D. BALZER

When the Soviet Union launched the world's first orbiting satellite in 1957, Americans undertook a major reevaluation of both countries' educational and technical capabilities. The United States responded to the challenge sufficiently to maintain a commanding lead in most areas of scientific research and technical application. Yet, in retrospect, it can be seen that continued U.S. preeminence results only in part from any actions taken after Sputnik. Sputnik was, in fact, an impressive piece of showmanship rather than a major scientific breakthrough.

Early in the 1980s we again heard warnings about competition from Soviet achievements in science and technology.[1] But precisely at a time when some Western analysts were touting the strengths of Soviet education in this respect, the Soviets themselves were undertaking sweeping reforms of their general and higher educational systems. It might be possible to argue that these reforms were intended to make a good system even better. However, the sharp criticism accompanying the educational reform legislation leaves no doubt that the Soviet educational system had failed to meet the demands of political leaders, economic administrators, faculty, parents, and students.[2]

This chapter seeks to assess the major strengths and weaknesses of Soviet education, primarily with regard to science and technology, while providing a summary of the major changes introduced in the recent reform legislation.

Many major characteristics of contemporary Soviet life were forged during the reign of Joseph Stalin. But we often fail to appreciate the degree to which the Stalinist system reinforced attributes of

245

pre-Revolutionary Russian society. This was certainly the case in education.

Russia's educational system was built from the top down. An Academy of Sciences was created before the first permanent university was established, and the university preceded the creation of a system of public schools. Institutions at the upper levels remained qualitatively superior to schools on the lower rungs of the educational ladder. Money and attention were lavished on elite institutions while other schools led a precarious existence. Moreover, in the best institutions prestige accrued to theoretical investigations; applied research occupied a distinctly secondary position.

The orphan of Russian education was the nonclassical secondary school, especially the technical school. Although managing to train a certain number of scientists, engineers, and workers, educators never resolved the problem of generating middle-level personnel. Secondary specialized schools manifested the most serious drawbacks of Russian education: shortages of staff and equipment, poorly prepared entering students, a high drop-out rate, and the failure of many graduates to seek employment in the geographic locations and particular specialties intended by government planners.

Specific social policy goals sought by education officials in tsarist times were, of course, very different from those of Soviet bureaucrats. Most pre-Revolutionary education ministers wished to reserve higher education for children from the privileged social strata. Soviet leaders have sought to use the schools as mechanisms of social mobility for politically correct social groups, mainly workers and peasants. Yet in both cases the need to train skilled cadres necessitated compromise.

Today, demographic trends are perhaps the strongest influence moving Soviet education officials to adjust their policies. In the past, economic growth was achieved in large part by adding to the labor force. Now, the pools of potential workers are being depleted, overall population growth is declining, and the Soviet Union faces critical labor shortages. This is not a new phenomenon in the Soviet economy. Managers have frequently hoarded workers, maintaining large staffs so as to have personnel available if needed. The negative impact of such practices can no longer be ameliorated simply by adding new groups to the labor force. In the absence of a thoroughgoing economic reform, Soviet planners will have to resort to piecemeal solutions to manpower and training problems.

One solution to the labor problem that appeals strongly to Soviet planners is to increase labor productivity by improving the education and performance of workers. But the era of relatively inexpensive gains derived from quantitative improvements is past. Almost everyone who can receive a basic secondary education already does. Additional returns from education will have to come from qualitative improvements, which are not only expensive but also require proficiency in areas where the Soviets have traditionally done least well—planning and fine tuning.

Each solution they might attempt involves a trade-off. One remedy might be to encourage young people to enter the labor force at an earlier age. But with the scientific-technical revolution, workers need both a higher level of general education and advanced vocational training, which means more time in school. Another course might be to reduce enrollment in secondary and higher education, but, again, the demand for educated personnel—not to mention the interests of students, parents, and the institutions themselves—makes this option difficult.

Before surveying Soviet specialized education, it is important to look at the system of secondary education that prepares students for advanced study. Universal secondary education has been a major goal of Soviet educators for decades, and at the Twenty-sixth Party Congress, in 1981, it was announced that the goal would be realized during the current Five-Year Plan—an impressive accomplishment. Yet the Nineteenth Party Congress, in 1952, predicted that universal secondary education would be achieved by 1960. Which is more significant—that the Soviets are approaching the goal 20 years late or that they are now on the verge of doing so?

The Soviet Union presents a somewhat confusing array of secondary-educational institutions. Most students now spend eight years in general education secondary school. They may then choose from among a number of options in completing their secondary education:

• two additional years of general secondary education, preparing them for the intensely competitive examinations to enter higher educational institutions;

• three to four years in a specialized secondary school (technicum) providing additional general education along with technical training for a middle-level job;

• two to four years at a vocational-technical school offering practical training preliminary to entering the labor force;

• entering the labor force and completing one's education in an evening or correspondence division of a secondary school.

Officially, the system is "unified," with access to higher education open to graduates of any secondary institution. In practice, however, most of those entering higher education do so after completing a

10-year general secondary school. A core curriculum of general education for all types of secondary schools has been promised for the near future.

American visitors who place their children in Soviet schools generally return with stories of mathematics classes far more advanced than those in U.S. schools. The official Soviet mathematics curriculum does indeed go beyond what most U.S. schools offer. But how does the reality of Soviet education nationwide compare both with the schemes of the planners and with the achievements of the best Moscow schools?

Outside the major urban centers secondary schools do not always conform to the standards set in the capital. There are shortages of supplies and equipment and, most notably, of qualified teachers. Many secondary-school teachers do not have a higher degree—and in some cases have received no specialized pedagogical training. Even the vaunted mathematics curriculum has been subject to criticism, some educators arguing that the "new math" overtaxes students and confuses teachers. The mathematics curriculum is now also under revision.

The Soviet system excels at identifying talented individuals and channeling them to the best schools. An extensive system of "mathematical olympiads" and science competitions works to this end. But although many students receive excellent grounding in mathematics and basic science, overall the system does not appear to be meeting the demands of economic and education planners.

Soviet educational officials have not resolved the basic question of whether secondary schools should provide general education or produce skilled workers. Post-Stalin reforms have alternatively stressed labor training for production (1956), science-oriented basic education (1966), and labor training again (1977). Each strategy has its costs. Nikita Khrushchev's program of production education in the 1950s and the early 1960s caused serious disruptions. In the late 1960s and early 1970s a stress on mathematics and science increased the demand for higher education while discouraging young people from seeking jobs in production. At the same time, the curriculum proved too demanding for many students and even for some teachers. Emphasis on labor training since 1977 has failed to deliver immediate economic benefits, since, according to accounts in the Soviet press, 80–90 percent of students receiving such training do not use it on the job.

The most recent answer to the question of whether to have general education or labor training appears to be, "both." The 1981 Party congress proposed improving the quality of general education while reducing the number of hours devoted to it, thus permitting more time for labor training. The general education reform announced in 1984 goes even further in this direction, assigning increased importance to general education, to labor training, and to vocational education.

The inability to solve the labor problem by general-education secondary schools had led to a renewed emphasis on specialized secondary schools, historically the weakest rung on Russia's education ladder. Recent Soviet writings on the subject suggest that educators have failed to eliminate the long-standing problems while encountering new ones created by the economic system.

Specialized secondary schools have difficulty attracting and retaining qualified teachers, administrators, and students.In some instances these schools are affiliated with industrial enterprises and become a dumping ground for undesirable personnel. While planners in Moscow discuss the computerized classroom of the future, local school officials complain about shortages of such basic supplies as chalk. Annual plans for textbook publishing are only two-thirds fulfilled. There is also a dearth of basic teaching materials, such as syllabi, maps, and other visual aids.

Organizational difficulties are endemic. As are workers in other enterprises, students are withdrawn from school to perform "voluntary" social labor, such as helping with sowing and harvesting in agricultural areas. Practical work experience, which constitutes an important element of the curriculum, also presents problems. Industrial managers are frequently tempted to exploit unsalaried helpers rather than to focus on purely educational goals. A 1977 reform called for improving the quality of such on-the-job training while simultaneously decreasing the amount of time allotted to it.

Local organizational problems are in part a reflection of central administrative disorder. The delineation of responsibility for these schools between branch industrial ministries and the Ministry of Education has never been clear, and cooperation is still problematical. There remains a welter of competing administrative entities, some operating only two or three schools. In the Ukraine, for example, as of 1978 there were 71 different government departments and ministries administering 725 technicums! Nationwide, more than 200 administrative agencies are involved in administering such schools.

Problems in secondary schools are reflected in students' poor performance on annual state examinations and in a high drop-out rate. Educational quality in these institutions is also undermined by a heavy burden of paperwork and other administrative pressures. The performance of school administrators is measured by the number of students enrolled and graduated. This can create situations in which school and students become partners in fraud, the school certifying skills and the students happily accepting sham diplomas. There are also instances of outright corruption.

The poor quality of specialized secondary education may be one of the reasons for the surprisingly low ratio of technicians to professional workers in Soviet enterprises. The trouble is exacerbated by the fact that large numbers of individuals with specialized education do not work in the fields for which they were trained. Despite much discussion about scientific planning in manpower allocation, effective correlation of students' specialties with the needs of the economy has remained elusive.

Soviet educators have called for a massive program of guidance at all levels of the system to reduce labor turnover and the consequent waste of educational resources. But to provide even one guidance counselor for every 1,500 students in grades 5–10 by 1985 would have required training over 33,000 specialists—a task for which neither the financial nor the human resources were available.

A persistent difficulty in secondary specialized education has been the quality of students. Since Soviet youth evince a strong preference for higher education, secondary technical schools are left with those who fail to gain admission to the more desirable institutions.

Every survey conducted in the Soviet Union has shown that a great majority of children hope to attend college. Increasing enrollments at general-education secondary schools have exacerbated this problem. In 1960, over 41 percent of secondary-school graduates were able to enter higher education. In 1978, although there was an increase of nearly two-thirds in the number of students entering higher education, the total represented less than 21 percent of secondary-school graduates. That the situation may be changing is indicated by recent reports that some colleges, particularly in engineering, are not filling their entering classes. Still, the pyramids of official social needs and student preferences are almost exactly inverse, suggesting continued intense competition for places in higher education.

Increased competition could result in improvements derived from increased selectivity—but not without putting great pressure on those aspiring to higher education. Students often hire tutors to prepare for entrance examinations, seek to exploit personal connections, and even engage in fraud. Recently cases have been reported of young people faking careers as workers to gain admission to college under special programs for outstanding workers.

Soviet higher education, like any large system, is characterized by enormous diversity and unevenness. The system numbers about 65 universities and over 800 *vuzy* (higher technical-education institutions), which include technical and polytechnical institutes as well as factory-affiliated programs conferring institute degrees. There are likely to be significant differences between an engineer trained at Leningrad Polytechnical Institute, however, and one with a diploma from the Kurgan Machine-Building Institute. Universities manifest a similar range. In 1977 10 large universities each had more than 10 independent research laboratories while more than 30 others had no such affiliated facilities.

The great number of Soviet *vuzy* has permitted the Soviet Union to develop the largest scientific-technical intelligentsia in the world. Studies completed early in the 1980s comparing research-and-development personnel in the Soviet Union and the United States found the Soviets ahead in the total number of scientific personnel, largely because of the enormous body of engineers trained in the previous three decades.[3] But, once again, we must question the quality of the Soviet achievement.

Beyond doubt, many Soviet institutions conduct world-class research while training first-rate specialists. However, Soviet strength is concentrated in specific fields, especially (but not exclusively) those in which theoretical ability is most important, as both Loren Graham and Vladimir Kresin point out (chapters 19 and 20). Work in many applied fields is of lower quality. Although this may reflect shortcomings in the economic system rather than in education, it appears that the weaknesses have been mutually reinforcing. The best students often prefer to specialize in fields where neither a lack of laboratory equipment nor the pressures of restrictive censorship will hinder their scientific work.

Shortages of supplies and equipment, plus a drop-out problem, affect virtually all higher educational establishments. One striking point to emerge from interviews with recent Soviet émigrés is the extent of such drawbacks even at the best institutions.[4] Conditions at less prestigious institutions—and especially in evening and correspondence divisions—are generally worse, although the latter still confer about 40 percent of higher degrees.

In short, marked success in increasing the number of students in higher education has been accompanied by a dilution of quality. Interviews revealed major differences between generations in evaluating their educational experiences. Émigrés educated before World War II have much higher opinions of their teachers than do those who attended college after 1960. The younger group is less likely to state that they were taught by leading specialists, and more of them believe that religious and ethnic prejudice influenced admissions and grading. Clearly, among those who have left the Soviet Union there is a perception of declining educational quality. At the same time, most of the émigrés interviewed retain a healthy respect for the Soviet Union's achievement in science.

The most vexing problem in Soviet higher education today, as in secondary specialized education, is that after students receive their diplomas a significant percentage do not work in their specialties. Graduates of higher educational institutions are required to serve three years in jobs assigned by the state, often in less desirable parts of the country. However, interviews with émigrés and accounts in the Soviet press indicate that the young have become adept at manipulating the job assignment process. Increasingly, they simply ignore their obligation and fail to report.

Excess demand for higher education affects career choices. The desire for higher education and the upward social mobility that it can bring outweigh the attraction of a particular subject or field. The huge number of engineers in the Soviet Union—40 percent of higher education graduates—may be explained in part by the ease with which students are admitted to engineering institutes compared to other higher institutions. Yet young people who choose institutions and specialties on the basis of admission prospects rather than aptitude are less likely to make careers in those fields after graduation. Instead, they swell the statistics on labor turnover that are so disturbing to Soviet economists.

The large number of graduates working at jobs below their officially defined skill level suggests that at least in some cases the quality of their education fails to meet standards set by employers. The idiosyncrasies of Soviet economic planning, salary scales, and individual preferences for geographic locations or particular types of work also account for some of this variety of underemployment.

Thus, Soviet claims about scientific manpower planning under socialism are dubious. Estimates of future needs are produced by enterprises that often grossly overstate their requirements. This is rational behavior by industrial managers in a system that does not penalize for inflated estimates but does punish for failure to fulfill production plans. Should central planners allow for overestimates when developing national requirements? Scholarly journals are full of discussions of the relative merits of various forecasting methods.

Complaints in the Soviet popular press, however, suggest that a practical resolution of this fundamental problem of manpower allocation is still in the future.

An enormous percentage of people with higher education in the Soviet Union are trained, as mentioned, as engineers. Western analysts characterize Soviet engineering education as narrowly specialized. Émigré engineers, on the other hand, have frequently stated that they received broad training preparing them for diverse technical responsibilities. Which is the correct interpretation?

Description of Soviet engineers as narrow specialists has been based in part on official Soviet lists of specialties, with technical fields divided into very detailed subcategories. These categories are important, but it must be noted that Soviet higher education normally consists of a five-year course, with specialization beginning only after intensive grounding in basic science, particularly mathematics and physics. Engineers graduating from good Soviet schools may well receive a broader education than do typical U.S. engineers. The success of many émigré engineers in finding jobs in the United States supports this conclusion. At the same time, students of some industry-administered specialized institutes in the Soviet Union and those in many evening and correspondence institutions receive less basic science education and may well represent the underemployed or underutilized group.

The character of individual institutions and their degrees is particularly important in graduate education. Soviet advanced degrees are organized differently from U.S. masters and doctorates. The basic Soviet postgraduate degree is the *Kandidat Nauk* (candidate of sciences), conferred on the basis of graduate study and/or a dissertation. The Soviet doctor of sciences degree, which resembles the doctorate in European academic systems, is awarded to established scholars well along in their careers. Many observers equate the *kandidat* degree with the U.S. Ph.D., and émigrés have an obvious interest in establishing such equivalence. In many cases this appears to be fully justified; but again, questions must be asked about the type of institution conferring the degree.

In sum, training enormous numbers of engineers and other specialists has not alleviated the chronic impediments to innovation in the Soviet economy. Even when Soviet scientists achieve breakthroughs in fundamental research, applications are likely to be developed elsewhere. In the past decade a solution has been sought in establishing science-production associations responsible for managing the entire research-to-production cycle. Attempts have been made to experiment similarly in higher education institutions, building on the growing amount of research done by these institutions under contracts from industrial enterprises. In 1980, for instance, a group of 73 higher schools in the Moscow region was organized as a Contractual Science Association, officially described as a "joint scientific research, experimental construction and economic complex." Now these experimental arrangements are to become standard for all educational institutions.

Extension of the association reform to higher education may bring significant improvements but only if the difficulties that have impeded such projects in the past are avoided. (A previous association reform in the Stalin era was unsuccessful.) Creating quasi-independent administrative entities could sever institutions from their traditional sources of supplies—and can complicate the tasks of central planners. Research incentives may divert attention from teaching. There is also a real danger that too-close ties between schools and economic enterprises will result in an emphasis on meeting immediate production needs; school administrators may find it difficult to protect fundamental research from demands for direct application.

At least in the short run, a major effort will be made to expand the system of contract associations. But even if the experiment is successful in Moscow, there are serious questions about its viability in regions where the schools, rather than representing a valuable resource, might be seen as a drain on the funds and equipment allotted to industrial enterprises.

Extension of association-style reforms throughout the school system and arrangements for each educational institution to be affiliated with a "base enterprise" constitute only one facet of the far-reaching education reforms announced in 1984 and 1986. Conforming to the Gorbachev leadership's emphasis on intensive development, these reforms propose to make Soviet schools more efficient and better suited to the demands of a technologically advanced society. The stumbling block will come from the fact that the Soviet Union is in many ways *not* a technologically advanced society but rather a society in which islands of modern technology coexist with more backward systems.

The most sweeping changes affect general education—the primary and secondary schools. An eleventh year is being added to the general school course by having students begin their education at the age of six (rather than seven). The addition of this extra year will be accompanied by curriculum revision designed to increase significantly labor and vocational training, to introduce new social studies and citizenship courses, and to begin a program of universal computer education. At the age of 15 a greater number of students will be tracked to vocational-technical schools rather than to a college-preparatory curriculum.

In higher education, the focus is on training specialists for specific jobs in particular locations through more individualized instruction and through contractual arrangements between educational institutions and enterprises. Emphasis on specifics is reflected in a new admissions process. The process includes a personal interview in which candidates must demonstrate their knowledge of and commitment to their proposed field of study. Once enrolled in *vuzy*, students are to participate in research and practical activity and will be monitored more closely than in the past. Some of the administrative mechanisms that frequently resulted in automatic passing grades are being eliminated.

Beyond higher education, the reformers envision a vast system of retraining as well as programs to raise the qualifications of individuals already on the job. The goal is to have all specialists participate in an extended program to upgrade skills at least once every five years. "Intensification" is also the goal for advanced-degree programs, with regulations making it simultaneously less attractive to write traditional dissertations on theoretical topics and easier to defend a "practical" thesis. *Vuzy* have been called on both to perform more practical tasks in the economy and to raise the level of their contribution to theoretical sciences.

These changes will cost a great deal of money. An increase of 11 billion rubles in the general education budget announced in 1984 is a good beginning, but it does not cover all the needed outlays. Most of the additional resources are to come from the ministries that employ workers and specialists, making success of many of the reforms dependent on the willingness of various administrators to invest in future manpower. Once again, the results are likely to be uneven.

Reforms as sweeping as those proposed for Soviet education must perforce be contradictory. They are attempting to do a great many things at one time, and many of the attempts are at cross purposes. One example: the educational reform has been undertaken largely in response to an acute shortage of adequately trained labor; yet it is also intended to promote the spread of advanced technology, which supposedly reduces demand for labor. Similarly, the goal is to make education more vocational at the same time that it becomes better suited to the scientific-technical revolution. The progress of these reforms will merit careful monitoring. Although the problems are daunting, the Gorbachev leadership is demonstrating a determination that suggests that at least some progress will be made in priority areas.

The Soviet Union, of course, is not the only country experiencing problems in education. Many of the difficulties are familiar enough to Americans—and may be characteristic of advanced industrial societies. Nor should the United States take too great comfort in the difficulties of the centralized Soviet system as against America's diverse educational network. A young person with scientific aptitude in the Soviet Union is more likely to make science a career than is a young American so endowed. Such a student will receive a complete scientific education at state expense and is thereafter guaranteed a job. But, to repeat, such students are likely to study theory rather than its practical applications. Enormous quantitative gains in Soviet education have not brought the anticipated qualitative improvements on the technical side.

The Soviet system excels at concentrating resources on priority projects and providing opportunities for large-scale research in important areas, particularly in military-related fields. Yet even in the military sphere the impetus for new technology often comes from the West, implying a built-in time lag before others' achievements can be duplicated.

The strengths of Soviet education may offer only limited lessons for America, given the differences in the two social systems. Soviet weaknesses show what can happen when centralized bureaucracy and political controls become excessive. Although no responsible observer would discount the Soviet challenge, the evidence suggests that the United States should be less concerned with scientific and technical competition from the Soviet Union and more intent on ensuring that its own educational system is not allowed to decay from within.

NOTES

1. See, e.g., Richard B. Foster's "Introduction" to Catherine P. Ailes and Francis W. Rushing, *The Science Race: Training and Utilization of Scientists and Engineers, U.S. and USSR* (New York: Crane Russak, 1982); or Izaak Wirszup, "Soviet Secondary School Mathematics and Science Programs" (paper read at the NATO Science Committee Symposium on Soviet Scientific Research, Brussels, September 1986).

2. The major reform legislation is outlined in *Pravda* (April 15, 1984; June 1, 1986). For analysis, see John Dunstan, "Soviet Education Beyond 1984: A Commentary on the Reform Guidelines," *Compare* 15, no. 2 (1985),

pp. 161–87; Beatrice Beach Szekely, "The New Soviet Educational Reform," *Comparative Education Review* 30, no. 3 (1986), pp. 321–43; Delbert Long, *Educational Reform in the Soviet Union.* Special Studies in Comparative Education, no. 14 (Buffalo, NY: SUNY Buffalo, 1985); and Harley Balzer, "The Soviet Scientific-Technical Revolution: Education of Cadres" (paper presented at NATO Science Committee Symposium on Soviet Scientific Research, Brussels, September 1986).

3. Louvan E. Nolting and Murray Feshbach, "R&D Employment in the USSR," *Science* 207 (February 1, 1980), pp. 493–503; and Ailes and Rushing, *The Science Race.*

4. Harley Balzer, *Soviet R&D: Information and Insights from the Third Emigration* (Washington, DC: National Council for Soviet and East European Research, 1986).

CULTURE

Western readers are often surprised to discover that despite continuing political and economic restraints Soviet culture over the past two decades or more has displayed considerable vitality and variety as well as a lively critical spirit. This has been particularly true of literature and the cinema, as Geoffrey Hosking and Ian Christie make clear in two of the chapters that follow. But it is also true of music, the theater, and painting, a point brought out in Irwin Weil's introductory survey of the Soviet (or Russian) cultural scene. Nor have the Soviet mass media, especially radio and television, remained untouched by the recent winds of reform, as Ellen Mickiewicz tells us. It would seem that at both the elite and the popular level Soviet culture is at once mirroring and promoting far-reaching changes in Soviet society, changes whose political consequences remain as yet matters of speculation only.

22

A Survey of the Cultural Scene

IRWIN WEIL

Moscow has become a huge urban center, with millions of people spread over vast distances that can entail long bus and subway rides. It is easy to form the impression of a hard, drab accumulation of stone and of unsmiling, hurrying people. Yet those who know and love Moscow find the city a veritable mother hen, sheltering her chicks under her wings; and a little careful attention soon rewards the observer with startlingly beautiful sights.

Amidst those stone piles—and sometimes hidden by them—lovely churches and buildings dating from the fifteenth century are to be found, buildings exhibiting the warmest and most charming connections of brick, mortar, and wood and combinations of color and shape. The old Novodevichii Convent, for example, is a movingly beautiful sight, especially early in the morning under the slanting rays of the sun. There are also tens of thousands of people who react with an equally startling and arresting sensitivity to wide aspects of the world around them. Their intellectual interests are catholic, whether their work be in the humanities, the sciences, or engineering.

The Soviet cultural scene in many ways runs parallel to the physical and human map of Moscow, so unlike the Petersburg that became Leningrad, and whose proud and sublime vistas are all on open display—"dusha na rapashku," as the Russians like to say. To those who see it from the outside, Soviet culture has often seemed to be a juggernaut of harsh ideological assertions, of self-satisfied purveyors of art boasting of quantity, purity of attitude, and the athletic heroism of muscle-bound defenders of the faith. The Russians themselves laugh at this affectation with a Soviet-style anecdote:

Naive Moscovite: "Well, comrades, how are things, culturally speaking, in the Tula District?"
Ministry of Culture Representative: "Oh, wonderful! In the Tula Writers' Union alone we have over 100 members—that's 100 times better than it was 80 years ago, when we had only one writer in the whole Tula District: Lev Tolstoy."

From the inside, however, Soviet culture looks as different from this standard Western view as does the mother hen of Moscow from its drab exterior. A vibrancy and joyous energy often produce admirable artistic and cultural results. An outstanding example of this truly Russian phenomenon took place in the spring of 1982: the memorial celebration of the one-hundredth anniversary of the birth of Kornei Ivanovich Chukovsky, who died in 1969.

Chukovsky is known in the West among psychologists and linguists for his highly original work on children's language. He is also known, to a lesser degree, for his sparkling children's poetry and his literary criticism. In the Soviet Union, it was impossible to grow up without his rhymes and rhythms on your lips, and Chukovsky's literary work and judgments helped to form more than one generation of writers and critics. His country house at Peredelkino, the writers' colony outside Moscow, was adjacent to a special children's library built and stocked by him. The house was also the gathering place of some of the best creative talent among the Moscow intelligentsia. Like the great nineteenth- and early twentieth-century Russian writers to whose memory and principles he remained faithful, Chukovsky knew how to bring talented people together in an at-home atmosphere and to elicit from them imaginative literary efforts in both prose and poetry. He was also gifted in dealing with children and in encouraging them to become interested in the arts.

The celebration of Chukovsky's hundredth birthday was an event whose various manifestations involved many of the most noteworthy representatives of Soviet culture. At two of the most important Muscovite gathering places for the intelligentsia, the Library for Foreign Literature and the Central Literary Museum, hundreds of people listened to an evocation of his remarkable personality and a reevaluation of his work and influence. Right after the Revolution Chukovsky had participated in Gorky's project to make good translations of the best of world literature available to a large readership; and throughout his life he worked unstintingly to strengthen Soviet literary culture. His critical eye, moreover, did not spare foreign specialists in Russian literature, as I can testify from personal experience.

Those evenings in honor of Kornei Chukovsky provided excellent insight into the interests and preoccupations of the Soviet intelligentsia. Writers and critics described in detail the care he took in reviewing their work. Audiences crowded around displays of his writings in both Russian and foreign-language editions. Leading Russian authors gave readings from their own works. In short, these Russians of the 1980s were looking back over 70 years or more and once again drinking in that great tradition of literature and poetry that is the subsistence and patrimony of their language and culture. The tradition is as alive today as it was at the beginning of the century. Contemporary Soviet citizens can spout reams of this poetry by heart, and the editions containing it are sold out as soon as they hit the bookstore counters. Ironically, one can buy such works most easily at the foreign-currency stores, and they are always welcome gifts to one's Soviet friends.

Several evenings after the Chukovsky celebration at the Moscow Central Literary Museum a television program devoted to his work and influence was broadcast to an audience of many millions. In addition to the commentary and the documentary pictures, interviews with some of the leading figures in Soviet culture touched on many of the issues that Chukovsky had dealt with during his long life. Again, the program provided a vast panorama of the cultural scene over the last four generations of Russian and Soviet history, and the Soviet viewers with whom I watched it expressed both fascination and pride. One's reactions, of course, were inevitably also affected by the knowledge that Kornei Chukovsky's daughter, Lydiia, has been one of the most courageous of the literary dissenters as well as a gifted writer and critic in her own right. Her voice has always defended freedom of speech, attacked literary censorship, and offered sympathy to those who suffered repression.

Many who took part in the Chukovsky anniversary observances themselves make important contributions to Soviet culture, as I indicated. The sponsor of one entire event was Liudmila Gvishiani, the daughter of Aleksei N. Kosygin, the late Soviet prime minister. She supports a great deal of cultural work in Moscow and can take considerable credit for encouraging many truly creative aspects of Soviet culture. The moderator of another event is connected with the Gorky Institute of World Literature in Moscow, a branch of the Soviet Academy of Sciences that enjoys great prestige and influence.

The Gorky Institute has a scholarly staff of several hundred, all of whom are involved in projects of literary theory and criticism as well as in publishing texts important for the understanding of literature. The moderator of the Chukovsky evening is concerned with, among other things, a major Chekhov project. Apart from a new, multivolume collection of Chekhov's complete works and correspondence (whose chief editor recently attended an international symposium on Russian literature at Northwestern University), there are in preparation several volumes covering Chekhov's influence on many different countries and languages.

These latter volumes will appear in a series called *Literaturnoe nasledstvo* (*Literary Heritage*), which has for decades been publishing important materials by and about major authors. A valuable collection of literary sources, the series is typical of the best work done at the Gorky Institute, which strongly encourages Soviet study of—and reaction to—contemporary Western literary criticism and theory. At the same time, the institute is trying to increase the scope and number of its international symposia involving Soviet and foreign scholars and specialists. Many of its representatives have visited the United States in recent years to participate in a series of U.S.-Soviet literary conferences that are stimulating much discussion.

Speaking of the institute's work on Chekhov, considerable interest has been shown in a new production of *The Three Sisters* at the Taganka, one of Moscow's most interesting and controversial theaters. While he was its director (until 1984), Yury Liubimov staged productions that have become fixtures in Soviet cultural life, including several of Shakespeare's plays as well a dramatization of Bulgakov's *The Master and Margarita*. This outstanding novel, combining the Faust legend, a redoing of the Gospel of St. Matthew, and a raucous satire on Soviet life in the 1920s, remained "in the drawer" until 26 years after Bulgakov's death. Its publication (1966–67) was a major event in both Soviet and Western literature, and it has been a favorite rallying point in Soviet literary circles ever since.[1] Liubimov's dramatization has become a consistently popular staple of the Taganka Theatre, always sold out far in advance.

Predictably, Liubimov's version of Chekhov's *The Three Sisters* is radically different from that created by Stanislavsky and lovingly preserved to this day by the world famous—but by now slightly musty—Moscow Art Theater. And it set the Moscow theatrical world's teeth on edge. The very walls of the Taganka come down (on hydraulic lifts) for a few moments to expose the city itself and its freezing temperatures behind a Russian army band dressed in pre-Revolutionary uniforms (the device suggests the sisters' repeated exclamation: "To Moscow, to Moscow!"). Upstage is a tinny cyclorama, with military barrack spigots and iconic representations, against which the actors noisily bang and bump. At center stage is a crude platform of unfinished wood that the actors mount when speaking internal thoughts. Downstage left are the sisters' rooms and, far downstage, with backs to the audience, sit the soldiers of the local garrison. Chekhov's order of lines is changed, masks are pulled out of pockets and worn—some in the form of round "smiling faces." It seems that everything possible is being done to disorient the spectator, comfortably used to the traditional notion of how Chekhov should be produced.

Predictably, again, all hell broke loose. Some critics loved it; others despised it. Many concerned individuals, including literary specialists of the Gorky Institute, expressed their feelings, some of them aggrieved, to Liubimov. I am in no position to attack or defend this interpretation of Chekhov. But I can testify to the intensity of the feelings aroused among both actors and spectators. For them, Chekhov is a living part of their emotional and intellectual lives. Such identification with an important writer is itself characteristic of Soviet cultural life.

Another aspect of the Taganka Theater that says much about Soviet culture is the corner devoted to the memory of Vladimir Vysotsky, who died in 1980 and is now the object of an extraordinary cult. Vysotsky played Liubimov's Hamlet, among other leading roles, and was also a balladier who in private performances touched on themes of great power and moment to all levels of society: the clumsy pomposity, favoritism, and corruption in high places, the miseries of prison camp life (which he had known firsthand), the futility of war, the tribulations of everyday Soviet life. Unfortunately, Vysotsky was a heavy drinker, and the habit hastened his death at the age of 42. All too many Russian artists and writers suffer from this malady—a theme, again, of Vysotsky's lyrics.

Cassette tapes of Vysotsky's private performances are prized among the Soviet intelligentsia, and his earthy poem-songs are widely known. They always provoke lively discussion among listeners: I have sat through many such an evening with Soviet friends, and I know that Vysotsky leaves no one indifferent to what he has to say. In this respect, he is comparable to Bulat Okudzhava, another popular balladier of the 1960s and 1970s who later turned to writing highly ironical historical novels.[2]

An extremely popular novelist and short-story writer who died recently was Yury Trifonov. Two of his works have been staged at the Taganka: his chilling *House on the Embankment,* a document of betrayal and cowardice during the Stalin purges, and *The Exchange,* whose plot revolves around the imminent death from cancer of the protagonist-narrator's mother. He watches with increasing horror the progress of her disease and the greed of those around them, mostly family and in-laws, who see her approaching death only as a chance to grab her apartment (through the usual official—but largely fictitious "exchange")—an apartment being, of course, a most valuable commodity in the Soviet Union.

The growing horror and pain of the protagonist are deftly understated—and thereby emphasized—by Liubimov's theatrical art. The play's irony and sarcasm provide considerable comic possibilities, and the skilled Taganka actors make the most of them. In one memorable scene, a drunken worker blindly bumps into a tree, becomes angry, and works his way into a mighty argument—with the tree; the actor makes the tree come to life with rare talent. At another point, an old actor mimes with his hands the creation of a vegetable garden; he does it so successfully that the spectator can almost smell the tomatoes and cucumbers. The quality of the art and the actors' concentration are truly impressive, and the theatrical and literary issues are sharply focused. Whether Liubimov's and Trifonov's views are excessively gloomy and misanthropic is a question ardently debated among the Taganka audiences, whose awesome seriousness is recognizable to patrons of small, dedicated theater companies around the world.

The same kind of audience can be seen at classical music concerts in Moscow and Leningrad. The two major Muscovite centers of music are the Tchaikovsky Conservatory and the Gnessin State Musical Pegadogical Institute, both located in lovely areas of the city. The conservatory is near the stately eighteenth-century buildings of Moscow University and the former Manège of the tsar, now devoted to art exhibits. The Gnessin Institute, a haven especially for chamber musicians and practitioners of folk music, is located near the Arbat district, in the midst of older mansions. The latter stand in sharp contrast to the modernistic glass, aluminum, and steel high rises of the nearby Kalininskii Prospekt, a contrast that can be seen as symbolic. For although the excellence of the leading Soviet conservatories and musical institutes is unquestioned, one admiring foreigner has observed that within them "the most modern and the most obsolete teaching techniques exist side by side."[3]

Some concerts take place in halls made venerable by generations of great artists, and today's performances are followed and criticized as vehemently as ever. When the late Leonid Kogan, the well-known violinist, with his son Pavel conducting, gave a concert that combined German Romantic music and a semipopular piece in the main hall of the Tchaikovsky Conservatory, I could hear murmurs of shock at the mixture of styles. The reactions to the violin playing and the conducting were as varied as those in any concert hall whose listeners have been brought up on good performances and passionate musical debate. But in this instance, the great tradition of string playing in Russia made the polemics both sharper and more intense.

Russian musical influence has spread throughout the world, including, most emphatically, North America; this fact hangs over the Soviet musical scene almost palpably. Soviet music lovers are well aware that Soviet-born composers, conductors, and performers are now located in many foreign music centers and that they have made the Russian musical tradition a living presence everywhere. When foreign orchestras and individual performers come to the Soviet Union, they almost always receive a strong response. Listeners are eager to hear what is being done elsewhere and to learn how the Russian tradition has been mixed with others to produce new styles. Thus the New York Philharmonic Orchestra generated tremendous excitement among Soviet musicians and music lovers when it performed in the Soviet Union a few years ago. Soviet concertgoers knew perfectly well how deeply their tradition had influenced the New Yorkers something that is also true of the orchestras of Chicago, Boston, and other leading American musical centers.

This point was quite literally and most poignantly brought home to Muscovite music lovers by the extraordinary concert given in 1986 by the great pianist Vladimir Horowitz. Horowitz had returned to his native land from his home in New York for the first time since 1925, and he performed in the packed main hall of the Tchaikovsky Conservatory to a deeply appreciative—and at times tearful—audience that included hundreds of music students who had evaded police at the last moment to cram the balconies, back wall, and aisles. No doubt everyone at the concert, like the audience of millions watching on international television, hoped that it was a harbinger of a more open era to come.

It is noteworthy that within the past two decades a small group of avant-garde composers has arisen in the Soviet Union. The best of their output has been judged, in the words of one Western critic, "very good indeed—so good, in fact, that its originality and power far transcend national differences or political ideology."[4] Perhaps the leading figure here is Alfred Schnittke, who is being hailed as the greatest Soviet composer since Shostakovich. Since the 1970s his music has been played in well-attended concerts at home and in New York, London, and other Western centers, where it has been welcomed "for its instrumental skill, its haunting sonorities and power to seize and sustain a mood"—thereby leaving the impression, in the words of another critic, "of a questioning, technically very adept expressionism with a twist of surrealism."[5]

Unfortunately, vocal music is not as well represented in the Soviet Union today as it was a generation or two ago. The fabulous art of the traditional Russian bass—of Reizen and Pirogov, not to mention Shaliapin (still a much-loved figure)—has not been maintained, with the possible exception of Boris Shtokolov's mighty renditions. Today's opera companies and choral ensembles can still provide wonderful spectacles and sounds, but they do not have the outstanding voices that once thrilled the musical world. Nor have they been noticeably innovative in their programming—a characteristic, too, of Soviet ballet and dance, in which the power of a glorious tradition in technique and training seems to have inhibited further development.

At a more popular musical level, Western specialists as well as ordinary visitors and travelers have noted with interest and surprise the now thriving worlds of Soviet rock and jazz. Concentrated in the larger Soviet cities, particularly Leningrad, and inspired by touring Western groups as well as the ever-growing volume of records and tapes in circulation, Soviet pop music, both official (officially sponsored groups, concerts, and recordings) and unofficial, has become a major cultural phenomenon.[6] One such group, the Ganelin Trio, named after its pianist, Viacheslav Ganelin, has played with great success in Europe and the United States, mixing jazz, rock, and classical techniques in music that has been found at once enthralling and original.

A kind of hiatus still obtains in Soviet painting and sculpture. The fierce campaigns against modernism, "formalism," and abstractionism launched by officialdom as recently as 1974 have ceased, but the new latitude accorded writers, theatrical producers, and filmmakers since 1985 has yet to reach graphic artists. On the other hand, even in officially sponsored exhibitions one finds paintings in which approved themes are handled in entirely individualistic ways, often to the point of counteracting the simplistic optimism and political piety of the official canon. Indeed, one can see reflected in countless private experiments, and in the sometimes officially sponsored fiddling with traditional Russian folk and religious themes, an intense interest in the possibilities of nonrepresentational art. Any exhibition offering even a hint of novelty is jammed with eager spectators, and foreign exhibitions are especially crowded.

In recent years, large numbers of people in both the Soviet Union and the West have become acquainted with those remarkable movements in early twentieth-century Russian art that are still called the "avant-garde."[7] Although it was sadly ignored (if not repressed) for decades in its own country, despite its associations with the Revolution, a major collection of this art was brought together with examples of its French counterpart and shown first in Paris in 1979 and then, with some alterations, in Moscow in 1981. Hundreds of the Russian works had never been seen on public display, and the effect of the exhibition on the tens of thousands of Soviet citizens who saw it during its four-month showing was said to have been electrifying. Since then, a whole new section of Moscow's Tretiakov Gallery of Russian Art has been opened to exhibit these works, which are now regarded as an accepted part of the Soviet cultural heritage.

Moreover, since 1978 Soviet nonconformist artists have been regularly exhibiting their work in a small basement gallery on Malaia Gruzinskaia Street in Moscow. Their themes are openly religious, surrealist or superrealist, symbolic or semiabstract—anything but the long sacrosanct "socialist-realism" first imposed under Stalin. That these and other avant-garde artists have survived and even prospered outside the official unions, through which so much of Soviet cultural life has been controlled, can be attributed to the patronage of established musicians and other cultural figures, various senior officials and leading scientists, and Western diplomats and businessmen. And with the relaxation of restrictions on individual enterprise introduced in 1987, the market for their work is bound to grow.

Official attitudes aside, the real public for modern or avant-garde art in the Soviet Union, as in the West, is probably quite limited. Equally if not more evident is a fond interest in the art of the past—indigenous, often humble, and decorative. Hundreds if not thousands of gifted, energetic, and dedicated craftsmen are at work in the Soviet Union today, and their sensitivity to and knowledge of the art of former times can be seen in the frescoes, icons, and architectural details of the old churches that they have restored all over the country. The respect—even veneration—felt for these artifacts of Russian culture can hardly be exaggerated; indeed, it constitutes a veritable cult, one that parallels a growing devotion to the masterpieces of Old-Russian literature. This is not mere nostalgia but a kind of cultural nationalism, one which combines on occasion with that Soviet interest in Western art and fashion that is the subject of so much more Western comment.

I have concentrated here on only one nationality within the Soviet Union, the Russian. I do so largely, of course, because it is so dominant. Also, I do not know the languages of the other Soviet nationalities and so cannot read their literatures in the original. Yet, it should be noted that major works in other languages are usually translated into Russian and have an all-Soviet appeal. One of the most acclaimed writers in the Soviet Union today is Chingiz Aitmatov, a Kirgiz author of high standing in the Communist Party who in a series of works has dealt with the painful themes of Stalinism, social callousness, national identity, and the morality of international politics.[8]

At the same time, theaters in such cities as Riga, Tallinn, and Vilnius vigorously uphold the local culture and language (Latvian, Estonian, and Lithuanian, respectively) while maintaining a high level of polish and sophistication. This is also true of the Rustaveli Theater of Tbilisi, the capital of the Soviet Republic of Georgia, which has played Brecht in Berlin and Shakespeare in London to critical acclaim. The international reputation of various other Soviet opera and ballet companies, dance and choral ensembles, and individual and group instrumentalists is familiar enough to need no further mention.

Indeed, a review of cultural life in the Soviet Union today prompts one to hope not only that it may freely flourish but that exchanges between that country and the West, particularly the United States, may be allowed to develop fully. There is much to be learned—and much to be enjoyed—on both sides.

NOTES

1. Mikhail Bulgakov, *The Master and Margarita*, trans. Mirra Ginsburg (New York: Grove, 1967) (also translated by Michael Glenny [New York: Harper & Row, 1967]). See also A. Colin Wright, *Mikhail Bulgakov: Life and Interpretation* (Toronto: University of Toronto Press, 1978).

2. See the extended discussion of both artists in Gerald S. Smith, *Songs to Seven Strings: Russian Guitar Poetry and Soviet "Mass Song"* (Bloomington, IN: Indiana University Press, 1984).

3. Fred Hechinger of the *New York Times*, quoted in Boris Schwarz, *Music and Musical Life in Soviet Russia* (Bloomington, IN: Indiana University Press, 1983), p. 305.

4. John Von Rhein, *Chicago Tribune* (May 23, 1982), p. 10.

5. "Schnittke Premiere," *New York Times* (September 28, 1985), p. 27; Paul Griffiths, "Revelations of Secret Soviet Modernism," *The Times* (London: November 3, 1986), p. 17.

6. See S. Frederick Starr, *Red and Hot: the Fate of Jazz in the Soviet Union* (Oxford and New York: Oxford University Press, 1983), which includes a chapter on "The Rock Inundation, 1968–1980."

7. See Camilla Gray, *The Russian Experiment in Art: 1863–1922* (New York: Abrams, 1971); A. Z. Rudenstine, ed., *Russian Avant-Garde Art: The George Costakis Collection* (New York: Abrams, 1981); John Milner, *Vladimir Tatlin and the Russian Avant-Garde* (New Haven, CT: Yale University Press, 1983); and Christina Lodder, *Russian Constructivism* (New Haven, CT: Yale University Press, 1983).

8. His major novel is available in English translation by John French, with foreword by Katerina Clark: Chingiz Aitmatov, *The Day Lasts More than a Hundred Years* (Bloomington, IN: Indiana University Press, 1983).

23

The Politics of Literature

GEOFFREY HOSKING

When Mikhail Gorbachev, on his accession to power in 1985, began to reveal the extent of the evils besetting Soviet society—the bribery, corruption, petty crime, drunkenness, slovenly work attitudes, environmental pollution, and so on—he was broaching themes already thoroughly familiar to regular readers of Soviet fiction. Indeed, with increasing urgency over a period of about two decades, novelists—at least the best and most discussed of them—had been warning of these evils and more, had been treating them not as superficial, readily correctable flaws in Soviet society but as symptoms of fundamental disorders with deep historical roots.

Valentin Rasputin, for example, in his novel *Farewell to Matyora* (1976), implied that thoughtless technological progress was to blame for the moral degradation of contemporary man and instead proposed as an ideal the traditional outlook and religious beliefs of an old woman. Yury Trifonov, in *The Old Man* (1978), portrayed a society fraught with corruption, careerism, and petty intrigue and traced back its moral decay to the arrogant inhumanity of the Bolsheviks themselves, beginning in the Civil War (1918–20). Chingiz Aitmatov, in *The Day Lasts More Than a Hundred Years* (1980), pilloried the secrecy and obsession with technology of both the Soviet and the American leaderships and accused them of pursuing great-power politics of a kind that dehumanizes man by cutting him off from his past and traditions. Vasil Bykov, in *The Mark of Doom* (1983), portrayed the harshness and arbitrariness of the "dekulakization" program implemented in collectivizing agriculture in the early 1930s and suggested that the social fissures created then were partly responsible for some peasants collaborating with the German invaders 10 years later. Yury Bondarev, in *The Wager* (1985), de-

272

picted a middle-aged film director stifling amid the petty intrigues of his colleagues and taking as his ideal the seventeenth-century Old Believer Avvakum, martyred by the government for refusing to recant his faith.

Although not exactly typical of recent Soviet fiction, these novels were by no means isolated, and they exemplify trends that gained strength throughout the 1970s. Under Stalin—and, by and large, under Nikita Khrushchev as well—fictional heros were strong, energetic characters, confident of the rectitude of their cause and oriented toward a future to be built by science, technology, and industry. In tricky situations, they were clearheaded and resolute, able to make difficult decisions and to lead the mass of the people to victory in metaphorical or actual battles against natural obstacles and the enemies of progress. Such fiction still exists today, and the writers who produce it receive praise in official statements. But it is not their works that are the most widely read and discussed.

At the center of readers' and critics' attention today in the Soviet Union are works of a very different kind, works that spring from a divergent perception of Soviet society—and, indeed, of human nature. The precursors of the trend were works of "village prose" appearing in the late 1960s and early 1970s (indeed the first "swallow" may have been Aleksandr Solzhenitsyn's story *Matryona's House*, first published in 1963); these described a dying rural way of life in loving detail, with elegiac intensity and an authentic feeling for the peasant outlook. The ever-clearer implication of these works was that something essential to man's nature had been lost in the headlong rush to the cities, that technology and industry might bring material comfort but also undermined man's sense of community and his closeness to nature. The heroes of such works were often old people, passive and accepting by nature; far from urgently seeking change, they usually wished to avoid it and saw their ideal not in the future but in a past solidarity that they felt was being betrayed. In due course this mood began to convey itself to other kinds of fiction as well. Writers concerned with urban life, notably Yury Trifonov, began to write of the city as a setting where human relationships were fragmented and unsatisfactory, threatened with the loss of values and with what the sociologist Émile Durkheim termed *anomie*.

The new current of thought brought with it an increasing concern for man's inner life, for his moral and spiritual being. The implication of this concern (sometimes pointed out by hostile critics) was that "moral principles" and "spiritual values" (terms frequently used in the debate) were not wholly derived from social reality and

the current stage of the class struggle, as Marx would have it, but
were absolute categories, applicable to all men at all times. The
fantastic and the supernatural began to be explored in an open-
minded manner. This was done under the influence both of past
Russian writers such as Mikhail Bulgakov (the posthumous publication of his novel *Master and Margarita* in 1966 was itself an
influential and much-discussed event) and of contemporary foreign
novelists such as Gabriel Garcia Marquez, who as a Latin American
socialist was a cult figure acceptable to the authorities. Even religious experience, the search for God (usually but not invariably
spelled with a small "g"), was evoked as a positive force not merely
for past unenlightened peoples but for modern Soviet man.

Naturally enough, all this alarmed orthodox Party ideologists,
who were not prepared to take it lying down. Thus a Party resolution
of July 1982—not the first of its kind—complained that "some authors display a confused world outlook and an incapacity to examine
social phenomena historically, from clearly defined class positions."
It called on writers, critics, and literary journals "to march in step
with the times, to single out and support what is new and advanced
in the life of Soviet society, and to be unfailingly guided by the
principles of *partiinost* [party spirit] and *narodnost* [national
character]." [1]

The curious thing is that such resolutions seemed to have very
little effect: works of the kind that I have mentioned went on being
published. In view of the continuing tight censorship and high
degree of Party control over culture, how was this possible? To
understand it, we must look at the role of ideology in Soviet society
and at the way it interacts with the institutions responsible for
literature.

Since Khrushchev's time, and certainly since the death of Stalin
in 1953, the core meaning of Soviet ideology seems to have changed
considerably. Economic stagnation, ideological supersaturation, and
the arms race have combined to produce a situation in which, in
the eyes of most Soviet people, the term "communism" no longer
denotes an ideal society of the future but rather a great power bloc
of the present. The impetus is no longer toward building what is
new but toward defending and perhaps extending what is already
held. This has produced a psychological change: the leaders have
become conservative and militarist in outlook in a way that one
might characterize as "great-power chauvinist." It was already partly
true in Stalin's time, although at that stage some of the dynamism
of economic growth still remained. Under Khrushchev an attempt

to return to the idealism of communism's early days was made, but this proved too disturbing for most of the political elite; and Brezhnev, following him, allowed a gentle consolidation of the present attitude.

There are two main varieties of this great-power chauvinism: Russian nationalism and multinational Soviet imperialism. Recent research by two émigré scholars, Alexander Yanov and Mikhail Agursky, has done much to elucidate the two varieties in their relationship to politics and culture, although the two scholars take opposite views of their significance. Yanov regards Russian nationalism as an expansive and dangerous force, whereas Agursky concludes that it is the multinational imperialists who are more threatening, since they are in alliance with the Soviet military-industrial complex.[2]

Whichever variety one sees as dominant at any given juncture (and probably they are both strong), there are certain tendencies in contemporary Soviet society that must seriously worry anybody concerned about the economic and military strength of the country. There is the growth in corruption and criminality, which undermines the productivity of the economy. There is the trend toward poorer health and shorter life expectancy among the male population, which, coupled with very high rates of alcoholism, clearly undermines both the growth and the efficiency of industry (see chapter 30). There are the environmental problems, which, as we have seen (chapter 13), often lead to moderate gains in one sector of the economy (usually the industrial) being heavily outweighed by horrifying losses in another (usually agriculture or fisheries). Also worrying are the demographic developments discussed elsewhere in this book by Ralph Clem, which project a continued low birthrate in the European and urban parts of the country in contrast with the high rates in Asia and the Caucasus. This is precisely opposite to the needs of the army and industry and seems to result from persistent difficulties in housing, income distribution, welfare services, and family life.

These, then, are all problems that must worry the leaders of a great power; they have, moreover, a strong moral dimension (family stability, honesty at work, and so on) that official Soviet ideology is ill-equipped to deal with. It is precisely in this area of doubt and bewilderment, I suggest, that literature has established an insecure and vulnerable bridgehead.

In his study *Reform in Soviet Politics* Thane Gustafson showed that expert opinions tend to be fed into the Soviet political system only when one political faction has an interest in them or when there is deadlock and uncertainty.[3] The same may apply to literary works, where their areas of concern overlap those of the political leadership—as they probably do when matters such as family morality, economic probity, and the degradation of the environment are at issue.

But good writers tend to take their explorations much further than the politicians find comfortable. And this is where the heavy bargaining comes in, a process that is, by all accounts, a crucial aspect of the Soviet literary scene. The leading participants in this area are the censorship, the editors of journals and publishing houses, the officials of the Writers' Union, the Party (in serious cases the Cultural Department of the Central Committee) and, of course, the writer himself.

The official state censorship organ, *Glavlit* (acronym for the Chief Administration for Press and Literary Affairs), has an important regulatory role. Its job is to prevent unmentionable subjects and people from appearing in print, or to ensure that they do so only in certain narrowly defined ways. It is negative censorship. The writer also performs a kind of censorship on himself when he sits at his desk, calculating what has the remotest chance of being acceptable and what is not worth wasting time over.

The really decisive role, however, belongs to the editors. Editorial boards are appointed by and are answerable to the Writers' Union, and in the Writers' Union itself the top appointments are almost certainly in the *nomenklatura* (appointments list) of the Party Central Committee (see chapter 4). There is thus a straightforward hierarchy of patronage, reinforced by the regular visits made by senior editors and Writers' Union officials to the Central Committee's Cultural Department to receive the latest authoritative directives.

Editors and union officials, then, are in close touch with the "Party line," the current campaigns and taboos; and these have a decisive impact on their thinking. Much of what they have to decide, however, does not belong so much to the realm of politics as to that of literary taste. Probably the most important factor here is that many editors and virtually all officials are themselves second-rate writers at best. They have never enjoyed a reputation of their own and are dependent on official favor for respectable print runs of their own writings. Their tastes, especially as they get older, tend to be conservative and anti-experimental. They have a natural suspicion of the young, talented, and innovative, whose writings they do not fully understand and whose popular success they resent.

All this induces a stereotyped drabness in official taste that has little to do with ideology; elderly bureaucrats given a monopoly over culture in *any* political system might well produce similar results. The tight grip that such men have on the Soviet publishing world is very disheartening for young writers. At the Seventh Writers' Union Congress in 1981, the proportion of delegates under 40 years of age was just 3 percent; and the same was true at the Eighth Writers' Union Congress in 1986.

A few editors, however, have succeeded in assuming a bolder and more creative role. This is important, since it is the editors who convey to writers the prohibitions of *Glavlit*. It is the editors who discuss with them the necessary rewriting and bargain with them over questions of language, style, and taste as well as over the subtler political implications of what they have written. Solzhenitsyn's autobiography contains long and vivid descriptions of his negotiations with Alexander Tvardovsky, the editor of the journal *Novyi mir* (*New World*).[4] Similar scenes, with less momentous results, are daily reproduced in editorial offices all over the Soviet Union. It is at these sessions that the final product, the published text, takes shape. An editor of honesty, good literary judgment, determination, experience, and cunning can make a great difference at this stage.

From this point of view, Tvardovsky was probably the most remarkable editor Soviet literature has ever known. During his stewardship (1950–54 and 1958–70) *Novyi mir* published many outspoken works, penetrating in their portrayal of the realities of Soviet society and sometimes disruptive to official ideology in their implications. Solzhenitsyn's novel of the Stalinist labor camps in *A Day in the Life of Ivan Denisovich* (first published in *Novyi mir* in 1962) was only the best-known example. Tvardovsky's boldness cost him his position in the end; he was bitterly criticized by some of his more timid colleagues from other journals, and in 1970 he had to resign his editorship. The struggle, however, had been a long one. In the course of it some fine works of literature were published, and some first-rate young authors managed to establish themselves.

There has never been a wholly worthy successor to Tvardovsky, at *Novyi mir* or at any other journal. Still, since 1970 some journals have managed to establish a reputation for publishing interesting works fairly regularly. The two most notable are *Nash sovremennik* (*Our Contemporary*) and *Druzhba narodov* (*Friendship of the Peoples*). It is probably no coincidence that both of them, to some

extent, can be identified with the two varieties of great-power chauvinism I singled out earlier: the first of them with Russian nationalism, the second with multinational Soviet imperialism. In case of
need, that is to say, each journal probably has its protectors at the
very highest levels of the Party.

In 1981 I was able to visit the editorial offices of both journals
and to discuss with some of the editors their perceptions of their
aims and problems. In spite of the different orientations of the two
journals, the editors' attitudes had a great deal in common. In both
I found a concern for literature as a socially responsible force. While
remaining loyal to the political leadership, the editors felt that literature played a very special role since writers could afford to take
a longer and more radical view of social problems than could politicians, who by the nature of their trade have to react quickly and
offer immediate solutions. Writers, therefore, must sometimes be
controversial. "Literature must contribute an element of creative
friction," as someone said, "so conflicts are inevitable." Thus, the
editors to whom I spoke were proud of their occasional struggles
to get published those works in which they believed, though they
were not willing to give me a detailed account of their battles with
any particular higher authority.

There is in both journals a feeling that the Soviet Union is threatened by a faceless international technocracy, vaguely identified as
American in origin, that undermines people's roots as embodied in
their language, folklore, history, and traditions. *Nash sovremennik*
is, of course, particularly keen to revive elements of Russian national tradition, especially those associated with the village. This
has been apparent in its publishing policy for many years. Its authors include the leading exponents of "village prose": Vasily Belov,
Valentin Rasputin, Vladimir Soloukhin, Fyodor Abramov, Viktor Astafyev, and Vasily Shukshin.

Another element of the Russian national tradition that *Nash sovremennik* has helped to revive is religion. As its editors confirmed
to me, they were not interested in any particular denomination but
felt that in a world torn from its moorings a religious outlook could
strengthen man's sense of solidarity with his fellows, his self-
discipline, his devotion to duty, and his readiness to sacrifice himself for a worthy cause. Indeed, much of what they said seemed
to imply that the materialist atheism of the West was a threat to
the Soviet way of life! When I asked if their outlook was not
contrary to Marxism, they replied that they were opposed to "crude
Marxism." Lenin, I thought, must be turning in his mausoleum.

Druzhba narodov takes its material from very different sources. Its mission has been to promote awareness of non-Russian cultures. In practice, however, its outlook has much in common with that of *Nash sovremennik*. Much of the best non-Russian literature is of course concerned with the history and traditions of the non-Russian peoples, many of which are rural and often tinged with religious values. In addition, *Druzhba narodov* has promoted some of the best Russian writing of recent years, notably the later novels of Yury Trifonov, who, though not himself a believer, was strongly influenced by the Christian personalism of Dostoevsky.

To return to the five novels I mentioned at the beginning of this chapter, Rasputin's was first published in *Nash sovremennik*, Trifonov's and Bykov's in *Druzhba narodov,* and Aitmatov's and Bondarev's in *Novyi mir.* From the evidence they offer, it appears to be sometimes possible for an established author, backed by a strong and experienced editor, to publish works that to some extent implicitly conflict with the official ideology. This probably occurs, however, only after a long struggle, often with severe damage to the text on the way and provided that certain conditions pertain:

• The style and language of the work must be neither too innovative nor too obscure, since this would arouse suspicions that the author was trying to hoodwink the censorship—and would, in any case, offend the taste of responsible literary bureaucrats.

• The work must have *some* positive outlook; nihilist, absurdist works or those that disclaim any moral stance are not generally acceptable.

• Divergence from official ideology must not be too clearly stated. Thus, religious values in general may be evoked as a moral or social force, but the preaching of any particular creed or any sustained philosophical discussion of religion would be unacceptable. In general, implication is preferred to direct statement.

• Similarly, although it is sometimes possible to allude to sufferings imposed by the Soviet government on its own people, no consistent historical analysis is possible. This is doubtless why historians have always feared to tread where novelists have sometimes gingerly tiptoed.

This still leaves fairly narrow boundaries for permissible literature. The list is long of those writers who, deliberately or involuntarily, have stepped across them and thereby lost their native audience—and, in many cases, eventually their homeland as well. It has come to include most of the major names, at least in prose fiction, of the 1950s and 1960s. They all made their name at a time when young talent was being actively sought, during the post-Stalin "thaw." This did not happen in the 1970s. In fact, it was probably more difficult in the 1970s and earlier 1980s for a young writer to establish himself in the Soviet Union than it had ever been before.

To tackle the problem, Vasily Aksyonov, himself the leading "youth" writer of the early 1960s, joined forces in 1978 with two representatives of the current younger generation, Evgeny Popov and Viktor Erofeev, both in their early thirties. Their idea was to bring out an anthology, to be entitled *Metropol*, in which writings of the younger generation would appear along with a few pieces by more established authors. A key element of the enterprise was that the authors should edit the work themselves—thereby bypassing the complex and often harmful maneuvering already described—and present a complete text ready for printing, to be published unchanged. The plan fell through when the Writers' Union prevented publication. A copy prudently sent out to the West, however, was published there. Popov and Erofeev were expelled from the union—or, more accurately, its secretariat vetoed their acceptance, which had recently been voted by the Moscow branch. Aksyonov subsequently emigrated, declaring that he could see no future for himself as a writer in the Soviet Union.[5]

Metropol was a test case. As far as an outsider can judge, some of the items in it could have been published by a strong and experienced Soviet editor through the normal channels. Others would probably have been disqualified because of their emphasis on sexual or religious experience or because of their experimental language. The clearest philosophical statement in the collection is an article by Viktor Trostnikov, who argues that developments in the natural sciences in the twentieth century tend to refute the materialist and atheist understanding of the world and to provide evidence for an idealist or religious outlook. Trostnikov's thesis would probably find a lot of sympathy among some writers publishing regularly in the Soviet Union, but its arguments are too extended and unambiguous for his piece ever to have been acceptable to a Soviet editor.

However, the feature about *Metropol* that probably was most objectionable to the literary bureaucrats was simply that it allowed young and virtually unknown authors a way to avoid the established publishing procedures.

If Gorbachev revealed nothing that some Soviet writers had not been pointing out for years, his accession to power in 1985 did strengthen in many ways the position of the bolder and franker among them. His demands for "openness" (or "publicity": *glasnost*); his obvious concern that literature and the arts should contribute to the process of "renewal"; and, some would add, the literary interests and acquaintances of his wife, Raisa, have all added to the pressures in favor of frank and honest writing. It remained a question, however, whether the permitted frankness was to be merely a weapon manipulated by the Party to help expose the shortcomings of Gorbachev's precedessors or whether it was intended to advance the genuine autonomy of literature.

The prospects offered by these alternative possibilities were obviously in the minds of participants at the Eighth Writers' Union Congress in the summer of 1986, which brought both the moral and the professional concerns of writers sharply into focus and which, to judge even from the abridged official verbatim report, witnessed one of the liveliest debates to take place in the Soviet Union for many years. Not all of it was peaceful. A Georgian roundly upbraided the Russian novelist Victor Astafyev for his "coarse, tactless" attitude toward Georgian customs, for instance, and Boris Mozhaev took the opportunity to complain publicly about the rejection by *Novyi mir* of one of his novels.

On the whole, though, a consensus seemed to emerge at the congress: the Soviet Union was in a state of deep crisis, one that was, above all, ecological and spiritual; some writers had been doing their best to warn of the dangers but had been hampered not only by "ideological bureaucrats" (criticized by the Kazakh writer Olzhas Suleimenov) but also by their own colleagues in editorial offices and the Writers' Union apparatus. Perhaps the most vehemently critical speech was that of Andrei Voznesensky, who warned that a plague of "spiritual emptiness"—engendered partly by writers' negligent custodianship of their own past—threatened the nation. "Our indifference destroys the past," he declared, urging that various major twentieth-century Russian writers whose work had been suppressed, in whole or in part, should now be published: "Whose job is it, if not that of the Writers' Union, to stand up for masterpieces and to tend our literary sanctuaries?"[6] His demand would entail the first Soviet publication (now scheduled for 1988) of Boris Pasternak's novel of the Revolution and Civil War, *Doctor Zhivago,* and of Anna Akhmatova's *Requiem,* a poetic elegy in which she described her own sufferings and that of so many Soviet women whose fathers, husbands, brothers, and sons were imprisoned and killed in Stalin's purges. Yevgeny Yevtushenko supported his colleague by submitting to the congress presidium a petition, signed by 40 delegates, calling for the opening of a Pasternak museum in the poet's former dacha to mark the centenary of his birth in 1990.

Voznesensky also criticized the procedures of the Writers' Union. Its electoral practices, he asserted, did not ensure the choice of the most worthy delegates. Where, he asked, were Bella Akhmadulina (the lyric poet), Bulat Okudzhava (novelist and famous guitar bard), and Yury Chernichenko (the controversial essayist on agricultural themes)? The congress confirmed his implied strictures by electing all three of these nondelegates to the union's administrative board.

Perhaps the most important change in personnel was the replacement of Georgy Markov, the conservative first secretary of the Union (who reportedly collapsed while reading his keynote speech), by Vladimir Karpov, the editor of *Novyi mir*. In some ways this was a liberalizing move: himself a victim of Stalin's labor camps, Karpov had been a humane editor and had fought one or two tough battles to get outspoken works published. On the other hand, he also warned the congress against the dangers of unrestrained criticism, against "ignoring the frontiers which distinguish democracy from demagogy."[7] At the same time, his election was accompanied by that of Markov to the post (vacant since 1977) of president of the union. According to some reports, Yegor Ligachev, a senior Party leader, personally persuaded the sick Markov to stand for the office. The significance of this move was not clear, but it seemed intended to ensure some continuing conservative influence in the union's affairs.

The congress also upheld a writers' campaign against the project of reversing the flow of Siberian and northern Russian rivers to irrigate Kazakhstan and Central Asia, and several delegates appealed for the reconsideration of decisions to destroy old buildings to make way for modern concrete boxes. This indicated that writers felt themselves responsible not just for their own heritage but for that of the nation as a whole.

Altogether, the Eighth Writers' Union Congress will probably be seen as a landmark in the cultural and intellectual history of the Soviet Union. Not that it heralded the end of Party tutelage over literature. Far from it. The conservatives have not been routed. But a new mood of outspoken—almost brutal—frankness does seem to have taken hold. It now appears that adherents of different views are likely to express themselves more freely in literature, and controversy should therefore flourish. Even if the Party hopes to manipulate the results, it probably will not be able to do so satisfactorily, for the reasons I have indicated above. And given the importance of literature in the Soviet Union, the long-term effects of this frankness on the way the Soviet people see themselves and the world beyond them could be considerable.

NOTES

1. *Literaturnaia gazeta* (August 4, 1982), p. 1.

2. Alexander Yanov, *The Russian New Right: Right-Wing Ideologies in the Contemporary USSR*, trans. Stephen B. Dunn (Berkeley, CA: University of California, Institute of International Studies, 1978); Mikhail Agursky, *The Soviet Military-Industrial Complex* (Jerusalem: Hebrew University, Magnes Press, 1980). See also John H. Dunlop, *The Faces of Contemporary Russian Nationalism* (Princeton, NJ: Princeton University Press, 1983).

3. Thane Gustafson, *Reform in Soviet Politics: Lessons of Recent Policies on Land and Water* (Cambridge and New York: Cambridge University Press, 1981).

4. Aleksandr Solzhenitsyn, *The Oak and the Calf: Sketches of a Literary Life in the Soviet Union*, trans. H. T. Willetts (New York: Harper & Row, 1980).

5. V. Aksyonov et al., *Metropol: Literaturnyi almanakh* (Ann Arbor, MI: Ardis, 1979). An English-language edition later appeared: Aksyonov, *Metropol: Literary Almanac* (New York: Norton, 1983).

6. *Literaturnaia gazeta* (July 2, 1986), p. 6.

7. *Ibid.*, p. 10.

24

The Cinema

IAN CHRISTIE

There is a grimly ironic story to the effect that Stalin refused to have certain uncooperative directors arrested at the height of the purges in 1937 because they were "the only filmmakers we have." Perhaps apocryphal, the story underlines the fact that few if any notable film personnel suffered the fate of their fellow artists in almost every other field at that time. Indeed, it was during this dark period that the cinema first achieved the unique status it still enjoys in the Soviet Union. For when Lenin made his celebrated remark in 1922—that "of all the arts the most important for us is cinema"— the infant Soviet film industry had produced little to justify his confidence.

Lenin's remark became a formidable reality only in the mid-1930s. Under the supervision of Boris Shumyatsky, Soviet filmmakers were given the official recognition they had craved as well as the resources they needed to convert to sound production. But there was a price to pay for the new prestige and genuine popularity they had gained. Entrusted with the responsibility for communicating Stalin's vision of the Soviet achievement, of Russian history, and of himself, Soviet filmmakers found themselves in the uncomfortable position of latter-day court artists, subject to their patron's whims and dependent on his approval.[1]

The legacy of this crucial pre–World War II period has been paradoxical. On the one hand, ever since Nikita Khrushchev's "secret speech" to the 1956 Party Congress, in which he singled out cinema as the prime instrument of Stalin's self-glorification and self-delusion, Soviet cinema has been marked by a genuine desire to end its close identification with the state and leadership. Filmmakers were quick to take advantage of Khrushchev's cultural thaw in order to explore more personal and lyrical themes. The international acclaim that greeted Mikhail Kalatozov's *The Cranes Are Flying* of 1957 was to herald a second renaissance of Soviet cinema, with striking debuts by such young directors as Tengiz Abuladze (*Someone Else's Children,* 1958), Marlen Khutsiev (*Two Fedors,* 1959), Georgy Danelia (*Seryozha,* 1960), Andrei Tarkovsky (*Ivan's Childhood,* 1962), Larissa Shepitko (*Heat,* 1963), and Vasily Shukshin (*There Was a Lad,* 1964) as well as the first of Sergo Paradzhanov's visionary masterpieces to be seen abroad, *Shadows of Our Forgotten Ancestors* (1964).

On the other hand, despite the evident popularity of the new films with domestic and foreign audiences alike, Soviet cinema had inherited both a mission still couched in Stalinist terms and an authoritarian bureaucracy that discouraged initiative and was liable to interfere arbitrarily at all stages of production and release. Throughout the later 1960s and on into the earlier 1980s filmmakers continued to receive regular exhortations on the need to "expose imperialism and promote communism" by concentrating on the exploits of "positive heroes," even though an increasing number of their films dealt with quite different subjects or were frankly critical of Soviet life. The rationale for tolerating this apparent indiscipline was signaled by a significant change of official metaphor: no longer Stalinist "engineers of the soul," artists were now to be regarded as "physicians" licensed to diagnose social ills and recommend treatment. Still, until the dramatic developments of the Gorbachev era, the prescriptions of filmmakers could be brusquely rejected, their work interrupted, and their films "arrested" (withheld indefinitely from distribution), and troublesome directors—such as Tarckovsky—in effect banished abroad.

In 1986 Soviet filmmakers launched an unprecedented attack on the whole apparatus of political control that had survived, virtually unchanged, from the 1930s. First, they challenged the principle of control through the Filmmakers' Union: the controversial director Elem Klimov was elected head of the union to replace a long-serving bureaucrat, and younger, bolder colleagues took two-thirds of the 213 seats on the union's secretariat. Next, the newly invigorated union established a Disputes Committee chaired by a leading *Pravda* critic, which was to investigate an estimated 60 cases during the past two decades in which films (including at least three by Klimov) had been arbitrarily "arrested." *Goskino,* the state committee or ministry responsible for cinema, found itself obliged to cooperate in this radical display of retrospective "openness." It then had to acquiesce in the union's call for a drastic curtailment of the powers of *Glavrepertkom*, the organization responsible for deciding how—or whether—films are released. Within months of the film-makers' congress in May 1986 a first selection of 17 "arrested" films began to appear in Soviet movie theaters; and by year's end the boast that the union had ended film censorship seemed almost credible.

The long-term impact of these reforms on Soviet cinema is ob-viously difficult to predict. What is certain is that the vast Soviet domestic audience (cinema attendance is still three times more common per capita than in the United States—and 15 times more frequent than in Britain) will not allow Soviet filmmakers to change course suddenly or drastically. To understand this point we need to remember that cinema in the Soviet Union, as elsewhere, is not simply an art but also an industry and, even more important, a social institution. Indeed, neglect of this point has led many Western com-mentators to concentrate on the negative (from an aesthetic or po-litical point of view) aspects of Soviet cinema's evolution under Stalin as a truly popular art medium,[2] an oversight that makes it difficult now to connect those years with recent developments.

The career of just one leading Soviet filmmaker, belatedly dis-covered by Western students, illustrates the underlying continuities of Soviet cinema that need to be stressed. Yuli Raizman (born 1903) began in the late 1920s as an assistant to the pre-Revolutionary veteran Protazanov and is still active as a director and senior ad-ministrator at Mosfilm studios. One of the favored young men who accompanied Shumyatsky on a tour of Western studios in 1935, Raizman was quick both to grasp the potential of the new realism to be found there and to employ it in such sophisticated productions as *Pilots* (1935) and *The Last Night* (1937). In these films Soviet cinema virtually for the first time moved beyond the rhetorical tra-dition inherited from its silent, montage period to create complex, convincing characters and engage the audience with fully fledged narrative. Prestige projects inevitably followed, such as *Virgin Soil Upturned* (1940), based on Mikhail Sholokhov's novel about col-lectivization in the Don area, and the commemorative *Fall of Berlin* (1945). But Raizman was one of the first established Soviet directors to exploit the thaw after Stalin's death with a series of outspoken contemporary dramas on social and moral issues, starting with *A Lesson of Life* (1955) and culminating in one of the most candid studies ever attempted of Soviet industrial policy, *Your Contem-porary* (1967).

A decade later, Raizman narrowed his focus to embark on a cycle of case studies that would explore the dilemmas facing typical, apparently successful members of the generation that came to maturity after World War II. *A Strange Woman* (1977) traces a professional woman's disillusion with her marriage to a high-level official and her subsequent, equally unsuccessful search for fulfillment with a younger man. The hero of *Private Life* (1982) is a factory manager whose enforced retirement plunges him into self-examination and the discovery that his career has been at the expense of his family life. In *A Time of Wishes* (1984), Raizman returned to the theme of women's subordination with an acerbic comedy of determined courtship, in which an ambitious Muscovite deploys her full arsenal of tactics to snare a suitable husband. The cumulative picture to emerge is one of an increasingly materialistic and corrupt society, a society that has long abandoned the revolutionary idealism celebrated in Raizman's earlier film *The Communist* (1957), depicting the construction of a power plant in 1918.

Instead of the "new man" beloved of Party ideologists, Raizman finds only the survivors and casualties of a society ravaged by war and deformed by years of repression, survivors and casualities who warily reach out to reestablish personal relationships amid a pervasive opportunism. The sober economy and precision of his mise-en-scène in these later works (equal to the best of American classical filmmaking), together with his superb direction of actors, adds authority to what would be a remarkable feat of social and psychological analysis in any cinema. It is certainly an analysis that rings true for Soviet audiences: with some embarrassment Raizman recalled for me how hundreds of women responded to the rare insight into their frustrations displayed by *A Strange Woman*—even to the extent of seeking his advice on their own problems!

Raizman's seniority and undoubted integrity have lent weight to his critique of contemporary Soviet society, just as his position as head of one of the Mosfilm production units has enabled him to defend the work of younger and even more outspoken filmmakers. Indeed, for anyone who still believes that Soviet filmmakers are the hapless servants of their political masters, it is a salutary experience to be reminded—as Raizman himself reminded me during a series of interviews in Moscow and London in 1984—that *he* is one of those who gives the orders and thus helps to shape both the content and the direction of Soviet cinema.

Official statistics concerning the scale and organization of the Soviet film industry are impressive. In 1980 there were said to be 37 studios producing every year about 230 feature films (80 for television) as well as 1,000 documentaries and 100 animations. In reality, both resources and achievements are almost certainly more modest (a 1986 estimate offers a total of about 120 feature films made that year). Moreover, there is an enormous imbalance between the level of activity concentrated in Moscow and Leningrad and the contribution of the non-Russian republics. Mosfilm alone employs some 5,000 staff, including a permanent company of 270 actors who are regularly lent to the other 18 studios engaged in dramatic production. Next in importance come the Gorky Studio, also located in Moscow and concentrating on films for young audiences, and Lenfilm, in Leningrad; the Dovzhenko Studio in Kiev, the Georgian studios in Tbilisi, and much smaller production facilities in the other republics.

A master production plan is negotiated annually between *Goskino* and the Filmmakers' Union, with the necessary resources allocated to the studios, which actually employ all production personnel and are responsible for delivering their quota within budget. (As a result of the reforms initiated in 1986, studios are assuming from *Goskino* still more authority over the financial and creative aspects of filmmaking—and are thus also incurring, for the first time, the risk of going under should their films fail at the box office.) This same basic structure is reproduced on a smaller scale in each of the republics, whose studios may enter into co-productions with the central institutions when greater resources are needed. On completion, films enter a complex process of assessment: first by the artistic council of the studio, which may order revision or additional work; then by *Glavrepertkom*, in order to determine which of three levels of release a film is to receive (although, as mentioned above, this agency's power is now declining); and also by a "quality"-judging body whose verdict determines what percentage of box-office receipts the main creative personnel will receive as an addition to their basic studio salary.[3]

Much less is known about the other aspects of Soviet filmmaking, although scripts are unquestionably subject to approval before being accepted for production and there appears to be considerable regional variation in patterns of distribution and exhibition. But two general points should be stressed. First, contrary to some Western assumptions, Soviet cinema is—and always has been—expected to pay its way. Soviet administrators have to give as much attention to production costs in relation to likely revenue as do producers elsewhere, which, of course, means taking account of audience preferences. The implications of this basic requirement are considerable, even if it may often be overridden by ideological and other priorities. Directors and writers of proven mass appeal will tend to be treated more favorably and, if they wish, can use their earning potential to win concessions. Unexpected and perhaps ideologically unwelcome successes can survive official disapproval by the very fact of their box-office success. And the always strong pressure to recover production costs no doubt partly explains why relatively few "arrested" films have remained permanently shelved.

A second factor shedding further light on how Soviet cinema routinely functions has to do with quality. The supply of materials, equipment, and technical skills is notoriously erratic in the Soviet Union, with the result that a significant proportion of completed films are simply unreleasable—a fact candidly admitted by the new Disputes Committee when it announced that not all "arrested" films would automatically be made available. Ambitious and influential filmmakers are usually able to secure the best materials (often imported from the West), but there is a vast undergrowth of inept, substandard productions—now termed "grey films"—that few outsiders ever see. This remains a more serious problem than any supposed ideological deviance, and it also helps to keep Soviet cinema isolated from the rest of the world.

The actual practice of Soviet cinema, I have suggested, has frequently been out of step with official guidelines: indeed, it probably conformed closely to the guidelines only during the last, paranoid decade of Stalin's rule. Personal influence, artistic prestige, and both the relative autonomy of the industry and its need to attract audiences have all combined over the past 20–25 years to give Soviet filmmakers considerable latitude in fulfilling their brief. Numerous films particularly of the last decade could be cited as evidence of this trend. Georgy Danelia's *Autumn Marathon* (1979) shows the contemporary Leningrad intellectual as a harassed confidence trickster constantly on the run from wife to mistress and moonlighting on lucrative sidelines while neglecting his official job. The central couple in Mikaelyan's *Love By Request* (1982) are a divorced former sports star turned alcoholic and a spinsterish librarian whose experiment in mutual self-help speaks volumes about the gulf between the ideal and the real in everyday Soviet life. The consequences of a soaring divorce rate for both individuals and families are explored sociologically in *Don't Part from Those You Love* (directed by Pavel Arsenov from a script by the prolific playwright Aleksandr Volodin) and, more expressionistically, in Nikita Mikhailov's remarkable *Without Witnesses* (1984), with its searing performances by Mikhail Ulyanov and Irina Kupchenko. In his earlier film *Kinfolk* (1983), Mikhailov, who has been the most officially favored of the younger generation of directors, treats family disintegration and the lack of communication between generations with such hysteria that it was effectively banned from exhibition abroad.

Films about young people, in fact, have moved rapidly from their former paternalistic complacency toward a radical, often despairing realism. Where Ilya Frez, a director of the early thaw generation, could tackle the agonies of school-age romance in relatively conventional, almost literary terms (*You Wouldn't Dream of It*, 1982) and still be forced to soften his shock ending, Dinara Asanova, whose premature death in 1985 sadly depleted the small number of first-rate women filmmakers, dealt boldly with pervasive juvenile delinquency and social anomie in her last two films (*Tough Kids*, 1982; and *My Dearest, My Love, My Only One*, 1984). Most shocking of all—and the subject of much earnest debate among teachers and parents—has been *Scarecrow* (1985), directed by the well-known actor Roman Bykov, which shows a group of teenagers sadistically persecuting—and nearly killing—a newcomer to their small-town school. In the published correspondence about this controversial film, a recurrent issue is the unaccustomed lack of a clear moral resolution. One otherwise admiring letter ended on a note of bewilderment: "But then where does such cruelty come from among Soviet children, brought up in a humane society, reading humane books? To this the film gives no clear answer."[4]

A link can probably be traced between the emergence of this new critical realism in Soviet cinema and certain of the literary trends discussed in the preceding chapter. A renewal of interest in rural themes, for instance, can be related to the popularity and cautious official endorsement of the "village prose" movement. Thus, Elem Klimov's *Farewell* (1981–83), based on Valentin Rasputin's much-praised story *Farewell to Matyora* and taken over by Klimov after the death of his wife, the equally acclaimed Larissa Shepitko, mourns the destruction of a village to make way for a dam. The film "failed to make its way to the screen" (in the words of another standard Soviet euphemism) for several years, no doubt because of its frankly hostile portrayal of the march of progress and its elegiac, almost religious treatment of the peasants' traditional way of life. As in Klimov's other works, the full rhetorical power that in Soviet cinema is more normally deployed for affirmative purposes is here used to question some of the most sacrosanct values of Soviet culture, with profoundly disturbing effect.

A similar revisionism can be seen at work in the literary adaptations by several recent productions. Thus, Mikhailov's version (1979) of Goncharov's famous nineteenth-century novel *Oblomov* clearly finds its eponymous hero's embodiment of traditional values—friendship, simplicity, love of nature—more sympathetic than the dynamic Western modernity of his half-German friend Stoltz. More controversially, *Vassa* (1983), Gleb Panfilov's new version of Maxim Gorky's classic play *Vassa Zheleznova*, takes a radically new view of this redoubtable capitalist matriarch, showing her more sinned against by her family and the demands of business than the evil tyrant of Soviet tradition.

All of the achievements mentioned here took place before the May 1986 Congress of the Filmmakers' Union and its dramatic aftermath. They are evidence that Soviet cinema, despite the demands placed on it by Party ideologists, bureaucrats, and a massive audience, had already succeeded in freeing itself from a narrowly political definition of its role as the major cultural institution binding together the diverse peoples and regions of the Soviet Union. For all its inefficiency and frequent crassness, it could boast a seriousness of artistic and social purpose unequalled by the cinema of any other country. But how will it fare in the new era of "openness"? The early signs, apart from the release of "arrested" films and the tentative organizational changes mentioned above, are that filmmakers will be encouraged to tackle previously taboo subjects and that administrators will be expected to take more responsibility for potentially controversial decisions.

However, it may also be true that Soviet cinema has passed the peak of its dominance and is about to suffer a decline in influence similar to what is already happening in the United States and, to a much greater extent, in Europe. The main forces at work here, in the Soviet Union as in the West, are the advent of home video and, above all, the saturation of television (which is discussed in the following chapter). *Pravda* reported in 1986 that only six years previously every eighth film produced in the Soviet Union had drawn more than 50 million viewers, but that currently an audience of even 20 million was a rarity.[5] And Soviet filmmakers could well find that the price of true openness in Soviet cultural life—namely, better television programing and greater access to desirable videocassettes (almost all of which now come from the West)—will result in a further decline of their still vast market.

NOTES

1. See Richard Taylor, "Boris Shumyatsky and the Soviet Cinema in the 1930s: Ideology as Mass Entertainment," *Historical Journal of Film, Radio and Television* 6, no. 1 (1986), pp. 43–64; Ian Christie, "Soviet Cinema:

Making Sense of Sound," *Screen* 23, no. 2 (1982), pp. 34–49; and Taylor and Christie, eds., *The Film Factory: Russian and Soviet Cinema in Documents, 1896–1939* (London: Routledge & Kegan Paul; and Cambridge, MA: Harvard University Press, 1987). For the history of Soviet cinema, see also Richard Taylor, *The Politics of the Soviet Cinema, 1917–1929* (Cambridge and New York: Cambridge University Press, 1979); and, more generally, Jay Leyda, *Kino: A History of Russian and Soviet Cinema* (Princeton, NJ: Princeton University Press, 1983).

2. See, e.g., Annette Michelson, *Kino-Eye: Writings of Dziga Vertov* (Berkeley, CA: Universtiy of California Press, 1985); or Herbert Marshall, *Masters of Soviet Cinema: Crippled Creative Biographies* (London: Allen & Unwin, 1983).

3. See also Val S. Golovsky, *Behind the Soviet Screen* (Ann Arbor, MI: Ardis, 1986).

4. Quoted in Nancy P. Condee and Vladimir Padunov, "Children at War: Films by Gubenko, Evtushenko and Bykov," *Framework*, no. 30/31 (1986), pp. 16–34.

5. Serge Schmemann, "Winds of Change Stir Soviet Film," *New York Times* (Oct. 12, 1986).

25

The Mass Media

ELLEN MICKIEWICZ

The Soviet Union was one of the first modern states to understand the potential of the mass media. Very soon after the Bolshevik Revolution of 1917, the development of radio became a high priority. Here was a medium of mass communication that did not depend on literacy (in 1920, only 40 percent of the population was classified as literate) and that could traverse the vast distances that separated a linguistically, ethnically, and politically divided country. Roughly half a century later, a second massive effort would begin. This one had, by the mid-1980s, brought television to virtually the entire Soviet population, producing a network that covered almost nine-tenths of the country's territory, and left only a few sparsely settled rural areas unable to receive signals. The introduction of television on such a scale has created a mass public, a public that is more diverse and larger than any in history, a public created by television.

The media have a particular function in the Soviet political system. They are educators, just as are the schools, courts of law, the family, and the many organizations of youth, women, veterans, and others. Because the Revolution that Lenin led took place before the conditions that Marx had imagined—namely, universal rejection of bourgeois values and the productive capacity to overcome scarcity—were actually in place, it fell to the state to effect those changes. Thus, the new Bolshevik regime was obliged not only to integrate the country over which it took charge but also to change the attitudes of the population. It was necessary to persuade the masses to internalize the values of the "new Soviet man" in cooperation and collectivism and to achieve the economic and political goals of the Party. Media messages were to present models to emulate and ways

293

toward self-improvement; even entertainment was to provide constructive use of free time. To achieve these goals and to prevent
other, competing messages from entering the communications system, a highly centralized organization of the media was established.

Centralized control of the media is effected in three ways. The
first is the operation of censorship. Since 1922 the key agency here
has been the Chief Administration for Press and Literary Affairs
(known by its acronym *Glavlit*), which recently has declined in
importance. All publications in excess of nine copies must still be
approved by *Glavlit;* but with the passage of time the role of the
censorship agency, as Geoffrey Hosking points out (chapter 23), has
been replaced by a self-censorship system. This works in two principal ways: first, writers (including journalists) understand what is
prohibited and seek to avoid difficulties with the authorities and,
second, the editorial staffs of newspapers and magazines, publishing houses or television studios check the material for deliberate
or inadvertent evasions of the censor's guidelines.

Another important control over the Soviet media derives from
the fact that all journalists are gathered into a single professional
union. The Union of Journalists has some 74,000 members—or 70–
75 percent of the country's working journalists. The union is governed by a board representing the most powerful and prominent
media people, and the union as a whole is heavily saturated with
Communist Party members, who make up about 80 percent of its
membership.[1] Ultimately, however, decisive control is exercised
through the *nomenklatura* system of personnel selection described
in chapter 4. Responsibility for media policy is vested in a senior
member of the Politburo and as a practical matter is decided by the
head of the Central Committee's Propaganda Department. Early in
his tenure as Party general secretary, Mikhail Gorbachev appointed
Alexander Yakovlev, a close advisor with years of experience in the
United States and Canada, to this position. Yakovlev has been quoted
as saying that "the TV image is everything."[2] He took charge of a
major reform of Soviet television, the dimensions of which we shall
see below.

The Party's central Propaganda Department is charged with the
overall mobilization of Soviet public opinion. In particular, it selects
editors and provides them with guidelines as to the appropriate tone
and content to be followed. Similar Departments of Propaganda exist
at lower Party levels to maintain coordination and centralized control. On the government side, media affairs are administered and policies implemented by the central and republic-level Ministries of
Culture and by three central state committees: one for publishing

houses, printing plants, and the book trade; another for the cinema (chapter 24); and a third for television and radio (acronym, *Gosteleradio*). TASS (Telegraph Agency of the Soviet Union) also operates under the aegis of the central Council of Ministers and is responsible for the collection and distribution of news both within the Soviet Union and abroad. *Novosti* (News) is the features press agency.

Gosteleradio was given its name in 1970, indicating the preeminence that television was to achieve as a medium of mass communication. It was also in 1970 that Party control over local broadcasting was strengthened. Because not all regions of the country could then receive television signals from Moscow, local programs had been substituted, often in indigenous languages. This kind of localism—and the resultant danger of the centrifugal pull of the nationalities—resulted in a reorganization that abolished the intermediate link between individual studios and the center; and the central administration of local broadcasting was established.[3] With the reorganization came an order that the most important programs on central television must never be "covered" (interfered with) by local studios; and the most important program of all is *Vremya* (Time), the daily evening news that is aired at 9:00 P.M., Moscow time.

The oldest component of the Soviet media system is, of course, the newspaper. The most important newspapers are the central ones, published in Russian and very widely distributed. The largest of these (and the largest in the world) is the trade union paper, *Trud* (Labor), which has a circulation of over 18.5 million copies daily. But the most important is *Pravda* (Truth), the organ of the Central Committee of the Communist Party, followed by *Izvestia* (News), the organ of the central government, and *Komsomolskaia Pravda*, the organ of the national youth orrganization. The weekly *Literaturnaia gazeta* (Literary Gazette) has the highest proportion of college-educated readers and is preferred by intellectuals. Below the national-level newspapers are those at the republic, province, city, and district levels and the house papers of individual factories and of collective and state farms. There are, in total, roughly 8,000 different newspapers published in the Soviet Union.

Soviet radio, as mentioned, has been left behind in the wake of television and has had to change its role and audience. Although the figures vary, radio listening in the Soviet Union by the mid-1980s did not exceed 30 minutes a day for city residents, and it often was much less. In fact, radio had become a medium of communication primarily for people who are, in sociological terms, overaged, undereducated, and low income. Since radio sets are cheap, the functionally illiterate and poorly educated can be easily reached, and listening can accompany work on the job or at home. Almost 70 percent of the people who listen to Soviet radio regard it as a secondary activity; the radio is on while they are doing something else, and this is especially true for women.[4] Radio has remained an important medium in the countryside, in part because it has taken longer for television ownership to saturate these areas and in part because the function of radio can be directly linked to the utility of its information. Radio provides crop and weather information needed by farmers, for example. However, recent data suggest that significant changes are taking place. Late in 1985 a deputy director of *Gosteleradio* asserted that radio listening in cities was on the upswing. He credited this growth to the development of small radio sets, higher consumption of automobiles (with radios), and the introduction of stereo sound.[5] But there is undoubtedly another reason: radio was much quicker to implement the new Gorbachev policies of responsiveness and openness than was television, with its huge plant, greater visibility, and many thousands of employees. With its focus on more timely news and public affairs and more up-to-date music, radio once again began to attract the attention of the more sophisticated population. Still, radio will never be able to compete with television for the mass audience. During television prime time, radio listening is at its nadir.

Television was slow to develop in the Soviet Union. The political leaders did not immediately grasp its potential to capture the attention of the population and, therefore, to function as an important instrument of persuasion. But perhaps equally critical was the configuration of the country itself, with a vast land mass stretching over 11 time zones. Many areas are thinly populated; many regions are subject to harsh weather and feature terrain that is not easily penetrated. With the development of communications satellites, however, that sprawling, inhospitable territory could be leapfrogged and signals beamed down at relatively low cost. Soviet communications satellites, constituting the densest network in the world, radically altered information diffusion.

The television audience in the Soviet Union is immense. Ninety-three percent of the population watches television, and it is estimated that some 150 million people—or more than 80 percent of the entire adult population—watch the evening news (compare the American figure: just over a third of the adult population watch all three network news programs combined.) Even larger audiences watch movies and pop-music programs. News-analysis programs reach huge audiences eager for information about the outside world.

"Today in the World," a program interpreting foreign events, plays to some 60–90 million people every weekday afternoon. There are two national networks (the First Program and the Second Program), both originating from central television studios in Moscow. Local television stations across the country may have additional local channels or insert their own programming (focusing on local culture and production campaigns) in any "windows" that open in the national broadcasts. Moscow residents have two more choices: an educational channel and a local affairs channel.

Although the Second Program was begun in January 1982 to bring innovation and experimentation to network choice, it has not yet achieved a clear identity or attracted the expected audience, which is less than half that of the First Program. As *Pravda* noted, the First Program carries the most important news and information and events of the "highest significance" (for example, the influential "Today in the World" can be seen only on that network), whereas the absence on the Second Program of "its own timely, as they say 'hot' information on international news events, impoverishes the content." [6] To be sure, the Second Program features certain kinds of programming not found on the First Program, such as advertisements for consumer goods; foreign language, history, and science lessons; a great deal of aerobics (the First Program runs aerobics only on Sundays); and some repeats from the other network. The Second Program also airs considerably more sports events. Yet an indicator of both official interest in the First Program and lack of resolve to upgrade the Second Program can be found in the distribution of articles in the weekly television guide, *Moscow Shows and Speaks,* which devotes about three-fourths of its entire space to the First Program. This problem of how to amplify and diversify Soviet television programming through the use of the second national network needs to be solved if the full potential of television is to be tapped. The problem of regular time slots also demands attention. Very few programs have regular time slots, and many of the most popular ones may be broadcast once every few months. It was only in 1972 that the nightly news was given a fixed time slot, and, with this and some other exceptions, it is very difficult for the viewer to predict what will be on when. To address this confusion, a new program, "The Viewer's Companion," was begun in 1986; broadcast on the First Program on the last day of each month, it covers new and notable programs for the month ahead.

After Gorbachev became general secretary in March 1985, he replaced a number of media officials—newspaper and journal editors, the head of the *Novosti* press agency, and the head of *Gos-*

teleradio, among others. Even before these personnel changes were completed, however, Soviet television had taken on a new look. In keeping with Gorbachev's proclamation of a policy of more publicity or "openness" (*glasnost*), the Soviet viewer began to see opposing points of view. The press conference became much more important: in October 1985 Gorbachev appeared on Soviet television responding to the sometimes sharp questions of French journalists and again in a joint press conference in Paris with President Mitterand. For the first time, Soviet viewers heard their leader take hostile questions on Jewish emigration, the treatment of dissident physicist Andrei Sakharov, or the number of Soviet political prisoners. Shortly after, a "space bridge" (satellite link-up) between Seattle and Leningrad showed Soviet prime-time viewers a series of clashes between Phil Donahue and Vladimir Posner and their studio audiences. Although the edited versions shown in each country differed considerably, there was still a significant overlap. The Soviet audience heard charges that it lacked freedom of speech and that the Soviet shootdown of the Korean jetliner in 1983, the invasion of Afghanistan, and Soviet interference in Polish affairs all reflected fundamental differences between the two societies.

The new policy of openness and responsiveness also resulted in the inauguration of new television programs on the domestic economy, with provision for viewers to call in their grievances to a government official who sat in the studio and was constrained to address them. Gorbachev seems to be convinced that such participation will help bring about greater participation in the workplace and in civic affairs. Problems are to be exposed on television and people are to be shown grappling with them, sternly rooting out the fraud and corruption that pervaded the country under the leadership of Leonid Brezhnev.

The nuclear accident at Chernobyl in April 1986 marked a watershed for the Soviet media. They were confronted by a test for which they were neither prepared nor, apparently, of one mind. After an initial silence, one that was later acknowledged by Soviet spokesmen as damaging, the depth and breadth of the coverage that followed both on television and in the newspapers were unheard of in the Soviet system.

Chernobyl was, of course, a very big event. In one way or another it affected hundreds of thousands of people; and given its international repercussions, it would have been impossible to keep it secret. But the media decisions in response to Chernobyl represented more far-reaching Soviet concerns. The leadership has been increasingly outspoken about what it sees as the Western—and particularly the American—policy of penetrating the information boundaries of the Soviet Union. Gorbachev has referred to it as "information imperialism"—a new, vigorous, technologically advanced campaign to reach Soviet citizens. Soviet officials recognize that information walls are porous, that news travels with tourists, foreign radios, in journals, and through relatives. They regard the Soviet population as more educated, more "mature," and less likely to fall prey to these sources than was the case in the past. But at the same time they are determined to reach their own population more effectively.

It was only in the 1970s that Soviet officials got a direct look at their own media audience.[7] Before that time, they had relied on the numerous letters reaching newspapers and radio and television studios. Their newer information, derived largely from scientifically devised surveys, revealed what is true everywhere—namely, that people who write letters are not representative of the media audience. The real picture of the audience apparently sobered the officials, and they realized among other things that saturation of an audience with consistent, repetitive messages does not guarantee assimilation. They would have to work harder to address the information demands of that audience, and, to be effective, they would have to be the source breaking the story. He who transmits the story first has a decisive advantage, since it is much easier to form opinions than to change them. Timeliness, which had never been an important consideration, was no longer to be ceded to the Western media. In the midst of this long, painfully slow reassessment of Soviet media policy and communication theory, Chernobyl literally and figuratively exploded.

Coverage of Chernobyl and its aftermath represented all dimensions of the new Soviet media policy. First, there was the appeal to an intensified work ethic in the form of contributions to the effort to deal with the disaster (everything from helping to evacuate affected areas to working harder to make up for the produce destroyed). Then there was the control and monitoring aspect, as those who did not perform adequately were publicly stripped of their privileges and responsibilities. Finally, there was the effort to build credibility for the official media in an information environment "contaminated" by hearsay and rumor at home and by broadcast signals from abroad. The Soviet media enjoy an obvious advantage in coverage of foreign news: events are remote from the lives of the public and cannot be independently verified. But in their domestic coverage, regarding events of which people may well have their own versions from other sources, the media enjoy much less credibility. A Soviet survey of the 1970s revealed that 97 percent of respondents believed that the media distorted local events.[8]

In general, media effectiveness is related most strongly to the credibility of the source, the importance of what is covered for the audience, and the utility of the information. Clearly, audience demands and interests are at the center of effectiveness. Moreover, those interests and demands can be and are shaped by the media themselves, most powerfully by television, to which the majority of the Soviet population now looks for information and news. It is an interactive process, the dynamics of which the Soviet leadership visibly has begun to appreciate. But the initiative to meet information demands—and thus to achieve increased effectiveness—remains and always will remain in tension with the requirements of control.

NOTES

1. Thomas F. Remington, "Politics and Professionalism in Soviet Journalism," *Slavic Review* 44, no. 3 (1985) pp. 498–99.

2. Harrison Salisbury, "Gorbachev's Dilemma," *New York Times Magazine* (July 27, 1986), p. 3.

3. V. V. Egorov, *Televidenie i zritel* (Moscow: Progress, 1977), p. 45.

4. *Raionnaia gazeta v sisteme zhurnalistiki* (Moscow: Nauka, 1977), p. 59.

5. G. Iushkiavishius, "Televidenie i radioveshchanie v novykh usloviakh," *Radio*, no. 10 (1985), p. 2.

6. *Pravda* (January 10, 1984), p. 3.

7. See also Ellen Propper Mickiewicz, *Media and the Russian Public* (New York: Praeger, 1981).

8. I. D. Fomicheva, *Zhurnalistika i auditoriia* (Moscow: Nauka, 1976), pp. 110–15, 132.

SOCIETY

The authors of this final section of the book discuss various of the more urgent questions raised by a survey of Soviet society today. Ralph S. Clem, in describing its complex ethnic structure, points out the many problems it has in common with other multi-ethnic societies and reaches the perhaps surprising conclusion that, on the whole, Soviet rule has strengthened the position of the ethnic minorities. The current state of religion is the subject of Paul A. Lucey's essay, which, like the chapter preceding it, abounds in facts not readily available elsewhere. Readers may again be surprised to learn that at least 30 percent of the Soviet population are practicing believers—not as high a proportion as in the United States, to be sure, but considerably higher than in many other Western societies. Mary Ellen Fischer then raises "the woman question"—not just the legal rights and status of Soviet women but the actualities of their situation with respect to both the unfulfilled promises of the past and their future prospects. And Peter B. Maggs, in explaining the workings of Soviet law, provides numerous insights into Soviet society in the larger compass.

In the final chapter of the book, David E. Powell reminds us of the traumatic history of Soviet society; points to the generally beneficial nature, until recently, of social change in the Soviet Union; and expands on certain ominous developments in Soviet society today. His essay may be read as a detailed summary of points raised in various earlier chapters. The picture to emerge is one of a troubled society, its heroic—or tragic—age behind it, its future uncertain. But Powell also notes that much of what he discusses is endemic in modern life. It is right that this book should conclude with a reminder of our common humanity.

26

Ethnicity

RALPH S. CLEM

On April 14, 1978, several thousand people took to the streets of
Tbilisi, the capital of the Georgian Republic of the Soviet Union,
in protest against changes in the republic's constitution that would
have downgraded the official status of the Georgian language. The
next day, the authorities canceled the proposed revisions and restored the indigenous tongue to its privileged position.[1] The significance of this event, probably not fully appreciated in the West,
lies in its dramatic illustration of the salient aspect of contemporary
Soviet reality: that the Soviet Union is an ethnically diverse state,
one in which all of the problems common to multi-ethnic countries
manifest themselves. If one wishes to understand the forces shaping
Soviet society, therefore, the nature and role of ethnicity is a prime
consideration.

The Soviet Union is one of the world's most ethnically hetero-
geneous countries in terms both of the number of ethnic groups
and of their respective sociocultural characteristics. The population
of the country comprises some 100 separate ethnic groups—or nationalities, in Soviet parlance—among which is to be found an extraordinary variety of languages, religions, phenotypes, and the other
attributes, tangible and intangible, of ethnic identity. The Russians
are by far the largest such group numerically, accounting for just
over half the country's population. Minority groups range from several tens of millions to several thousands (see table).

This remarkable assemblage of peoples is the result of a historical
process of territorial expansion that lasted for about four centuries.
During this period the Russians moved out in all directions from
their ethnic hearth in the northwestern part of what is today the

POPULATION OF MAJOR SOVIET ETHNIC GROUPS

Ethnic groups	Population (in thousands)			Average annual growth rate (in percent)		Percent of total Soviet population		
	1959	1970	1979	1959–1970	1970–1979	1959	1970	1979
Russians	114,114	129,015	137,397	1.1	.7	54.65	53.37	52.42
Ukrainians	37,253	40,753	42,347	.8	.4	17.84	16.86	16.16
Uzbeks	6,015	9,195	12,456	3.9	3.4	2.88	3.80	4.75
Belorussians	7,913	9,052	9,463	1.2	.5	3.78	3.74	3.16
Kazakhs	3,622	5,299	6,556	3.5	2.4	1.73	2.19	2.50
Tatars	4,968	5,931	6,317	1.6	.7	2.37	2.45	2.41
Azerbaidzhanis	2,940	4,380	5,477	3.7	2.5	1.41	1.81	2.08
Armenians	2,787	3,559	4,151	2.2	1.7	1.33	1.47	1.58
Georgians	2,692	3,245	3,571	1.7	1.1	1.29	1.34	1.36
Moldavians	2,214	2,698	2,968	1.8	1.1	1.06	1.12	1.13
Tadzhiks	1,397	2,136	2,898	3.9	3.4	.67	.88	1.11
Lithuanians	2,326	2,665	2,851	1.2	.8	1.11	1.10	1.09
Turkmen	1,002	1,525	2,028	3.9	3.2	.48	.63	.77
Germans	1,620	1,846	1,936	1.2	.5	.78	.76	.74
Kirgiz	969	1,452	1,906	3.7	3.1	.46	.60	.74
Jews	2,268	2,151	1,811	−.5	−1.6	1.09	.89	.69
Chuvash	1,470	1,694	1,751	1.3	.4	.70	.70	.67
Latvians	1,400	1,430	1,439	.2	.1	.67	.59	.55
Bashkirs	989	1,240	1,371	2.1	1.1	.47	.51	.52
Mordvinians	1,285	1,263	1,192	−.2	−.6	.62	.52	.45
Poles	1,380	1,167	1,151	−1.3	−.1	.66	.48	.44
Estonians	989	1,007	1,020	.2	.1	.67	.42	.39
Chechens	419	613	756	3.5	2.4	.20	.25	.29
Udmurts	625	704	714	1.1	.2	.30	.29	.27

Mari	504	599	622	1.6	.4	.24	.25	.24
Ossetians	413	488	542	1.5	1.2	.20	.20	.21
Avars	270	396	483	3.5	2.2	.13	.16	.18
Komi[a]	431	475	478	.9	.1	.21	.20	.18
Koreans	314	358	389	1.2	.9	.15	.15	.15
Lezgins	223	324	383	3.5	1.9	.11	.13	.15
Bulgarians	324	351	361	.7	.3	.16	.15	.14
Buryats	253	315	353	2.0	1.3	.12	.13	.13
Greeks	309	337	344	.8	.2	.15	.14	.13
Yakuts	233[b]	296	328	2.2	1.1	.11	.12	.13
Kabardinians	204	280	322	2.9	1.6	.10	.12	.12
Karakalpaks	173	236	303	2.9	2.8	.08	.10	.12
Dargins	158	231	287	3.5	2.4	.08	.10	.11
Kumyks	135	189	228	3.1	2.1	.06	.08	.09
Uyghurs	95	173	211	5.6	2.2	.05	.07	.08
Gypsies	132	175	209	2.6	2.0	.06	.07	.08
Ingush	106	158	186	3.7	1.8	.05	.07	.07
Gagauz	124	157	173	2.2	1.1	.06	.06	.07
Hungarians	155	166	171	.6	.3	.07	.07	.07
Tuvinians	100	139	166	3.0	2.0	.05	.06	.07
Kalmyks	106	137	147	2.4	.8	.05	.06	.06
Karelians	167	146	138	-1.1	-.6	.08	.06	.05
Karachay	81	113	131	3.1	1.7	.04	.06	.05
Romanians	106	119	129	1.1	.9	.05	.05	.05
Kurds	59	89	116	3.8	3.0	.03	.04	.04
Adygei	80	100	109	2.0	.0	.04	.04	.04
Laks	64	86	100	2.7	1.7	.03	.04	.04

Sources: 1959 and 1970 figures from Tsentral'noe Statischeskoe Upravlenia, Itogi Vsesoiuznoi Perepisi Naseleniia 1970 goda (Moscow: Statistika, 1973), IV, pp. 9–11; 1979 figures from Tsentral'noe Statisticheskoe Upravlenie, Naselenie SSSR (Moscow: Politicheskaia Literatura, 1980), pp. 23–26.

[a]Figure for Komi includes Komi-Permyaki.

[b]The number of Yakuts was reported as 236,655 in the 1959 census itself.

Soviet Union to take over neighboring lands inhabited by non-Russians. The empire of the last century was formed, in other words, through the addition of non-Russian territory to the Russian core; and the present Soviet state is, geographically, almost identical to its tsarist predecessor.

Two key elements of the present ethnic situation derive from the manner in which the state took shape spatially. First, it is generally the case that the periphery of the Soviet Union is ethnically non-Russian territory whereas the Russian homeland is geographically the center, a situation fraught with obvious geopolitical significance. Non-Russian lands extend in a vast arc from the shores of the Baltic Sea in the northwest (Estonia, Latvia, and Luthuania); south along the western border (Belorussia, Ukraine, and Moldavia); east across the Caucasus (Armenia, Georgia, and Azerbaidzhan); on to Central Asia (the areas inhabited by Turkmen, Uzbeks, Tadzhiks, and Kirgiz) and the Kazakh steppe; and, finally, across Asia to the Pacific Ocean (homelands of the Buryats, Tuvinians, Altays, Khakas, and other peoples). Sharpening this Russian/non-Russian, center/periphery dichotomy are several irredentist situations in which members of the same ethnic group live on both sides of the Soviet border, as in the case of the Finnish Karelians, much of whose homeland was incorporated into the Soviet Union in World War II.

Second, in spite of the proliferation of ethnic Russians in all regions of the country, the other Soviet peoples are still usually concentrated in their ancestral homelands. Thus, ethnicity, in the Soviet context, has a territorial aspect that differentiates it in some degree from multi-ethnic societies that evolved through immigration. Furthermore, the Soviet Union is structured administratively as a federation of 15 nominally independent units (union republics), each of which is officially the homeland of a major national group. Smaller nationalities and some of the larger ethnic groups with homelands in the interior (where even nominal independence would be an obvious fiction) are recognized administratively by lower-level units of various types. All told, there are 53 ethnically defined political-administrative units in the Soviet Union, representing over half of all Soviet national groups.

Given this complex ethnic structure, it is imperative to investigate ethnicity with respect to Soviet history, contemporary reality, and the future of the "Union" itself. Unfortunately, in spite of the increasing number of relevant works appearing in the Soviet Union and in the West, and even though the best of them are insightful and factually informative, our understanding of Soviet society in general and of ethnicity in particular has been hampered by an approach to societal phenomena in that country that regards them as basically unique. This particularistic approach, it should be stressed, has generally been adhered to on both sides of the ideological divide.

Thus, Soviet scholars almost always adhere to the Marxist view that social dynamics—including ethnic group relations—are determined by the nature of the specific economic system, and they therefore maintain that societies based on a socialist economy will be inherently different from capitalist societies. Any cross-system similarities in social trends are dismissed by Soviet scholars as superficial and ephemeral.

In the West, on the other hand, comparative research in the social sciences has long been hampered by an unscientific tradition that holds that societal traits are unique to time and place and not amenable to broad generalizations because of cultural conditioning and human unpredictability. Moreover, as Robert Lewis has noted, Western scholars have attributed a uniqueness to Soviet society on the assumption that a "totalitarian" state is capable of decisively controlling basic social processes.[2] If a government could actually regulate, with even moderate success, such aspects of human behavior as migration, then a fundamental difference would indeed exist between totalitarian states and those in the West, where social trends are, in effect, the summation of myriad individual actions. A difference of that kind would then rule out the use of models derived from Western experience in explaining social change in the Soviet Union.

Partly as a consequence of this attitude we in the West have tended to impute to Soviet society a distinctiveness that is not usually warranted by the facts. It seems clear enough that, so far as ethnicity is concerned, today's Soviet Union has much more in common with other multi-ethnic societies than not. If we consider the ethnically related troubles in such Western states as Belgium, Canada, Spain, and the United States, it will come as no surprise that bilingualism, assimilation, ethnic intermarriage, affirmative action, regional autonomy, a shifting composition of the population along ethnic lines, and the geographical mixing of ethnic groups through migration are all contentious issues in the multi-ethnic Soviet Union as well.

Language is perhaps the most sensitive of these issues, especially the role and status of the official lingua franca, Russian, in relation to the various non-Russian tongues. The importance of this issue derives in part from the overtly ethno-symbolic quality of language, in part from the belief among scholars, both Western and Soviet, that the increasingly widespread use of Russian by non-Russians presages a loss of ethnic identity—or ethnic assimilation. And the most serious aspect of the issue concerns the use of Russian in education, whether as the medium of instruction or as the object of separate study.

Following the advent of Soviet rule, the network of indigenous language schools in the various national homelands was greatly expanded. Yet considerable variation exists today in the degree to which the non-Russian tongues are in fact an integral part of the school system. The use of non-Russian languages as the medium of instruction differs from group to group, with some nationalities granted much more extensive rights than others. These rights are tied to the ranking of the ethnic territories in the federal hierarchy. Students who are members of numerically larger ethnic groups can receive native-language instruction throughout secondary school and, in some cases, at the university as well (although the selection of courses available in the vernacular may be limited). Those from smaller nationalities may only be able to attend school in their own language in the primary grades, if that.

Another facet of this question is the choice available to parents. Schools in which Russian is the medium of instruction have been established in all of the non-Russian ethno-territories in addition to native-language schools, leaving parents of any nationality the choice of sending their children to either type of school. Until 1958, however, children were required to study Russian in the native-language schools and the local language in the Russian-language schools. Then the Soviet government promulgated a set of educational reforms, one of which made the study of languages other than the medium of instruction voluntary rather than mandatory. This led to some hostility and resistance among several of the largest non-Russian ethnic groups, apparently out of fear that non-Russian students in Russian-language schools would abandon non-Russian language courses. This move was also seen by some in the West as further evidence that the Soviet authorities were attempting to accelerate the process of ethnic homogenization or Russification.

If the Soviet government has been actively promoting the formal adoption of Russian as one's "native tongue" by non-Russians, it has not had much apparent success. The 1979 Soviet census revealed that only about 13 percent of the non-Russian population considered Russian their native tongue; the comparable figure was 10.8 percent in 1959 and 11.5 percent in 1970. At the same time, 49 percent of all non-Russians said that they had a fluent command of Russian as a second language, which represents a major increase, even since 1970, when the comparable figure was 37 percent. These and other linguistic data indicate a growing trend toward bilingualism among the non-Russian ethnic minorities. The number of Russians who speak another language remains quite small, however.

Brian Silver has suggested that whereas the influence of social change (urbanization, higher levels of education, and a greater frequency of inter-ethnic contact) has had the effect of promoting the use of Russian, retention of the non-Russian tongues has been perpetuated by the maintenance of the native-language schools and by extensive use of these languages in the media.[3] In short, allowing for differences among nationalities and especially between generations (today's young people tend to have a higher level of Russian fluency and to be less faithful to their native tongue), the ethnic minorities certainly are not yet disappearing linguistically.

Another way of judging the extent to which ethnic homogenization has taken place in the Soviet Union is to look at the frequency of intermarriage. Given the taboos generally associated with this subject, it is not surprising that among the non-Russian peoples of the Soviet Union there is a consistently high level of in-group marriage (endogamy). The major work on this subject, based on 1969 data from 14 of the large non-Russian nationalities, shows that in no case did the level of those marrying endogamously drop below 82 percent and that for nine of the 14 groups the percentage of endogamous marriages was over 92.[4] Even when demographic and sociocultural factors are taken into account, the impression remains that ethnic attachments are sufficiently strong to condition significantly the choice of a marriage partner—this in spite of the fact that the Soviet government views exogamy as "progressive."

Inasmuch as linguistic Russification and the incidence of exogamy have been relatively limited in scope, we may suppose that ethnic reidentification—or assimilation—has been similarly insignificant. While recognizing that it is extremely difficult to measure assimilation empirically, one study put the total number of non-Russians who from 1926 to 1970 assumed a Russian identiy at between 4 and 6 million or about 2 percent of the 1970 population.[5] The vast majority of those assimilated were Ukrainians and Belorussians, who are linguistically and culturally akin to the Russians. A few other groups—Karelians, Mordvinians, Germans, and Jews among them—accounted for almost all of the balance. Among most Soviet ethnic groups, therefore, assimilation is virtually unknown.

Sociologist Daniel Bell points to several key aspects of ethnicity that account for its salience and persistence in the contemporary world and are directly relevant to the Soviet situation.[6] The first of these is the politicization of ethnicity, wherein the proliferation of the power of the state forces people to rely on ethnic groups as a means of bringing pressure to bear on the system. The Soviet "revolution from above" made it obvious to all where the center of power was and established the state as the focus for any claims to be made by ethnic groups. As Glazer and Moynihan put it, the Soviet state is obviously "the direct arbiter of economic well-being."[7] The ethnic group turns out to be an ideal vehicle for exacting concessions from the state, as Bell noted, because it combines an interest-group function with an affective tie. Furthermore, the Soviet regime has done much to legitimate this approach, since it insists on labeling individuals ethnically and has acted (perhaps not always deliberately) to stimulate ethnic awareness in a variety of ways.

By far the most important sanctioning of ethnicity in the Soviet Union lies in the very political structure of the state. The creation of the Union of Soviet Socialist Republics as a federation of ethnic territories has been viewed as a clever solution to the problem of disintegration inherent in multi-ethnic countries, a problem of immediate concern in the early years of Soviet power.[8] Ethnic autonomy, as represented in the elaborate treaty arrangements binding the ethnic units to the Union, was plainly a tactical political concession, probably thought to be temporary. Yet by formalizing the ethnic configuration of the state, Lenin and his successors provided what turned out to be a lasting, legitimate focus of national aspirations. It could be argued, then, that what was viewed by some as a shrewd manuever and a fraud has instead proved to be a means whereby ethnic group interests, such as education and native-language rights, can be safeguarded and appropriate demands can be made on the state.

Moreover, because the ethno-territorial link was and is legally explicit, the regions have become the instruments for attaining the central goal of Soviet policy toward the nationalities: the approximate equalization of levels of socioeconomic development among them. The government has had some notable successes in this respect, in education and public health, for instance. But the following three interconnected factors have impeded further progress and are likely to continue to do so.

• As do most countries, the Soviet Union has its economic "problem regions." Owing to the geographically unequal distribution of natural resources, the exigencies of war and strategic considerations, and the pressing need to optimize scarce investment capital, some areas remain relatively backward.[9] Since ethnic groups are usually found mainly in their respective homelands, those groups inhabiting the backward regions will be relatively disadvantaged.

• A second reason for the failure to close the inter-ethnic development gap has been the proliferation of Russians throughout the Soviet Union. Unfavorable economic and social conditions, particularly in the rural areas of their own ethnic territory, provided the impetus for the out-migration of millions of Russians to other parts of the country, including the non-Russian lands, where their number rose from 6.2 million in 1926 to 23.9 million in 1979. The vast majority of these Russian migrants settled in urban areas and in many instances took the better jobs, thereby foreclosing opportunities for upward mobility by the local inhabitants. Once a Russian presence is established it takes on an inertial character, since a large Russian population in a non-Russian area provides the linguistic and cultural atmosphere attractive to other Russian migrants.

• The third and potentially most troublesome factor is the striking inter-ethnic variation in population growth (see table). Broadly speaking, the Baltic and Slavic peoples of the Soviet Union—the Estonians, Latvians, Lithuanians, Belorussians, Ukrainians, and, most notably, the Russians—are characterized by low rates of growth, whereas the ethnic groups of Central Asia (Uzbeks, Tadzhiks, Kirgiz, Turkmen, Kazakhs), like certain nationalities of the Caucasus region, are increasing at a phenomenal rate. Most of the peoples of the Volga-Urals area (for example, Udmurts, Tatars, and Bashkirs) and two of the largest Caucasian nationalities (Armenians and Georgians) are intermediate in population growth rates.

These different rates of growth are affecting the ethnic balance of the total Soviet population. A shift is clearly taking place toward the rapidly growing Central Asian and Caucasian nationalities and away from the slowly growing or even numerically decreasing European (Baltic and Slavic) peoples. However, because the latter still comprise such a large proportion of the total population, and because demographic trends typically take several generations to achieve real results, the much heralded change in the Soviet ethnic balance will be slow, and care should be taken not to exaggerate its pace. In 1959, the main European groups accounted for 78.5 percent of the Soviet population, whereas the major Central Asian nationalities amounted to 6.2 percent of the total. By 1979 the figures were 74.2 percent and 9.9 percent, respectively. Similarly, great and perhaps undeserved significance has been attached to the relative decline of the Russians over the same period, from 54.7 percent of the total Soviet population to 52.4 percent.

In sum, the long-term implications of any changes in the ethnic balance of the Soviet population do not warrant use of the term "crisis," which has been employed in the Western media. For one thing, the rapidity of change has been consistently overstated. Estimates that by the year 2000 one of every three Soviet citizens will be from one of the Muslim ethnic groups are highly improbable: something on the order of 20 percent seems more likely. The latest Soviet census (1979) revealed that a major deceleration in the rate of increase among the faster-growing nationalities is under way (see table), and fertility data—though sketchy—appear to confirm this. Still, the spatial variation in population growth means that virtually all new increments to the Soviet work force will be in Central Asia and the Caucasus.[10] And this in turn will complicate future economic decisions, as planners will be forced to choose between areas where labor is available and areas where other factors—natural resources, transportation, and return on investment—are more favorable.

Alternatively, it is possible that large-scale migration will take place from labor-surplus areas in Central Asia to labor-deficient regions such as Siberia and the western parts of the Soviet Union.[11] Yet if the interregional supply of and demand for labor were balanced through such migration, the social and political costs could outweigh the economic benefits. In other societies ethnic mixing has often led to heightened tensions and frequently to violence, and there is no reason to believe that the Soviet Union would be immune to such conflict.

Moreover, as the share of the population accounted for by the non-European ethnic groups continues to rise, the Soviet leadership will need to decide to what extent it should foster the further integration of these nationalities into the army, the Party, and the modern sectors of the economy. Affirmative-action schemes, which elsewhere have created discord, as individuals either seek advantage or attempt to maintain it through membership in an ethnic group, are bound further to divide Soviet society along ethnic lines. Not much is known about any such policies in force today. But in the 1960s, apparently, the Soviet government implemented some kind of an ethnic quota system to raise the percentage of previously disadvantaged nationalities in higher education. The quotas were not well received by "achiever groups" that had been proportionately overrepresented, and they contributed to the rise of the Jewish dissident movement and the resurgence of Russian nationalism.

After some 70 years of Soviet rule, the economic and social development fostered by the regime has for the most part strengthened the position of the ethnic minorities. In particular, modernization has produced educated, urbanized, and politically mobilized non-Russian elites.[12] In the future, these elites, working through the federal structure, may very well be able to pursue ethnic issues and to secure additional benefits for their regions. So long as such pressures are couched in acceptable terms and do not threaten the survival of the state itself, it would appear highly unlikely that the harsh measures employed during the Stalin era could now be invoked against them. Nor is it probable that a diversionary appeal to ideology or to the need to make sacrifices for the sake of future generations would succeed today.

In this regard the Soviet Union faces challenges similar—if not identical—to those that confront most multi-ethnic countries. This is not to say that issues such as bilingualism, regional autonomy, and socioeconomic equality are unimportant but rather that they are both critical *and* typical of such countries. Thus viewed, we can say that a major question in coming decades will concern the ability of the Soviet leadership to adapt to changing conditions and to satisfy ethnic group interests while maintaining the basic integrity of the system. As in Canada, Yugoslavia, Belgium, Nigeria, the United States, and a host of other multi-ethnic societies, the course of events in the Soviet Union will depend to a considerable degree on the ways in which ethnic-minority demands are dealt with. If such problems are handled in a sensitive and reasonable fashion, change will be evolutionary rather than revolutionary.

NOTES

1. Craig R. Whitney, "Soviet Georgians Take to Streets to Save Their Language," *New York Times* (April 15, 1978).

2. Robert A. Lewis, "The Universality of Demographic Processes in the USSR," in *Geographical Studies on the Soviet Union,* edited by George J. Demko and Roland J. Fuchs (Chicago: University of Chicago, Department of Geography, 1984), pp. 109–30.

3. Brian D. Silver, "Bilingualism and Maintenance of the Mother Tongue in Soviet Central Asia," *Slavic Review* 35, no. 3 (1976), pp. 406–23; see also Roman Szporluk, "West Ukraine and West Belorussia: Historical Tradition, Social Communication, and Linguistic Assimilation," *Soviet Studies* 31, no. 1 (1979), pp. 76–98.

4. L. V. Chuiko, *Braki i razvody* (Moscow: Statistika, 1975).

5. Robert A. Lewis, Richard H. Rowland, and Ralph S. Clem, *Nationality and Population Change in Russia and the* USSR (New York: Praeger, 1976), pp. 282–87.

6. Daniel Bell, "Ethnicity and Social Change," in *Ethnicity: Theory and Experience,* edited by Nathan Glazer and Daniel P. Moynihan (Cambridge, MA: Harvard University Press, 1975), pp. 141–74.

7. Nathan Glazer and Daniel P. Moynihan, "Introduction," in Glazer and Moynihan, pp. 1–26.

8. Richard Pipes, *The Formation of the Soviet Union* (New York: Atheneum, 1968).

9. See I. S. Koropeckyj and G. E. Schroeder, eds., *Economics of Soviet Regions* (New York: Pergamon, 1981).

10. Ralph S. Clem, "Regional Patterns of Population Change in the Soviet Union, 1959–1979," *Geographical Review* 70, no. 2 (1980), pp. 137–56.

11. Lewis, Rowland, and Clem, *Nationality and Population Change,* pp. 354–81.

12. See Ellen Jones and Fred W. Grupp, "Modernization and Ethnic Equalisation in the USSR," *Soviet Studies* 36, no. 2 (1984), pp. 159–84.

27

Religion

PAUL A. LUCEY*

The main factor affecting religion in the Soviet Union is the state's attitude. It has been characterized by a vigorous antitheistic orientation expressed primarily in antipathy to all religious institutions, initially because the latter were so heavily linked with the former tsarist regime. The Soviet state, implementing the policies of the Communist Party, which has been inspired in turn by the ideology of Marxism-Leninism, has varied its emphasis (or tactics) over the years between reeducating the masses in atheism and employing administrative measures (persecution) against religious bodies. But throughout the Soviet period Party and state have remained remarkably consistent in reiterating the basic objective of eliminating all vestiges of religion. At the same time, religion is the dominating factor in the lives of tens of millions of Soviet citizens. Its resilience in the face of varying forms and degrees of hostility and outright persecution has been remarkable.

Following their Revolution in 1917 the Bolsheviks moved to nationalize all property belonging to religious organizations, to end their philanthropic and educational activities, and to curtail their political influence. During the Civil War and in the early 1920s, churchmen declaring themselves opponents of the new regime or resisting the implementation of its program were dealt with summarily as counter-revolutionaries. When it was possible to influence the course of internal church affairs, either by playing favorites or by directly manipulating clergy sympathetic to Soviet power, the regime did not hesitate to do so.

Editor's Note: Chapter updated for this edition by Walter Sawatsky.

315

But as the political and military situation became more stable, open clashes between the state and the largest religious organization in the country, the Russian Orthodox Church, were less frequent. After his arrest in 1923 the Russian Patriarch, Tikhon, who had been elected by a church council in 1971, declared his personal loyalty to the Soviet government. This was followed in 1927 by the church's formal acceptance of subordination to the state in all "temporal" matters. Thus a kind of peace between the Orthodox Church and the Soviet state was achieved even while the state conducted anti-religious propaganda on a large scale. During the 1920s Soviet religious policy actually favored the small but rapidly growing Protestant "sectarians" who had been suppressed under the old regime. That Jewish religious life declined was due as much perhaps to the promotion of a distinctly secular Yiddish culture as to the zealous atheism of the Communist Party's "Jewish Section." At the same time, Soviet religious policy during this decade was tolerant of Islamic institutions. Islamic schools, courts, and clerical land holdings were still widespread in Central Asia as late as 1928.

The emergence of Stalin's dictatorship was accompanied by more drastically severe policies against all religions. The 1929 Law on Religious Associations prohibited virtually all religious activity other than worship on state-licensed premises and simplified the mechanism for dissolving unwanted religious associations. Nor was the assault on religion limited to such formal methods. Not only the churches as institutions but believers as individuals were subjected to intense persecution throughout the 1930s. By the outbreak of World War II, tens of thousands of clergy and probably several million believers had been arrested; all monasteries and seminaries and most places of worship had been forcibly closed; and centralized ecclesiastical administration had ceased.

The war brought a respite, however, as the regime sought to enlist in the defense effort any institution capable of inspiring traditional patriotism. Not long after the German attack in June 1941, Stalin allowed the few remaining Russian Orthodox bishops to begin rebuilding; and by the war's end, some 18,000 Orthodox parishes had been reconstituted, some seminaries and monasteries were reopened, and the patriarchal office, empty since Tikhon's death in 1925, was occupied by the newly elected Patriarch Sergei and then, following his death shortly thereafter, by Patriarch Aleksei.

The new policy did not affect all religions equally. While the Evangelical Christians, the Baptists, the Georgian Orthodox Church, and the Armenian Apostolic Church all enjoyed a renaissance, the

Eastern-rite Catholics of the Ukraine, the Ukrainian and Belorussian autocephalous Orthodox Churches, and the Jews did not. By 1946 all the autocephalous Orthodox Churches except Georgia's had been forcibly merged with the Russian Orthodox Church. The 4-million-strong Church of the Ukraine was abolished and its parishes, too, were absorbed.

The Jewish community, decimated by the Nazi occupation, was driven even closer to extinction by Stalin's anti-Semitic postwar policies. Islam enjoyed some of the benefits of the new policy—the reopening of many of its mosques and reduction of anti-Islamic propaganda—but was not allowed to resume its position of cultural and civil prominence in the Central Asian republics. Finally, religious communities (mostly Christian) in the newly annexed Baltic states were subjected to the kind of revolutionary terror that the other churches had experienced in the years after 1917.

This policy of limited and selective toleration of organized religion lasted only until the late 1950s. From 1959 to 1964 the Khrushchev regime conducted a virulent anti-religion campaign that brought about the closure of over half the remaining places of worship and of a number of seminaries and monasteries. The Moscow Patriarchate, the All-Union Council of Evangelical Christians and Baptists, and the leading bodies of the other religious communities were forced to adopt measures restricting the activities of parishes and congregations even further than required by the 1929 Law on Religious Associations. Church leaders who resisted these measures were arrested on trumped-up financial or other criminal charges.

Khrushchev's anti-religion policies were much moderated after his fall in 1964. Although anti-religion propaganda under Leonid Brezhnev (1964–82) remained an important feature of the "ideological training" conducted in schools, universities, factories, and the media, instances of arbitrary administrative action against religious groups were less common. Few of the losses sustained during the Krushchev persecution were made good, however. Indeed, there appears to have been a further net decline in the number of places of Orthodox worship since 1964, and known believers were still subject to discrimination in education and employment. On the positive side, a 1975 revision of the Law on Religious Associations virtually restored the right of legal entity to religious organizations, and in the late 1970s religious communities that operated seminaries or gave correspondence courses were allowed to increase their annual intake.

What is the situation of the major religious communities in the Soviet Union today? Certainly the largest and most important of such communities is the Orthodox Church.[1] With something like 50 million faithful in 73 dioceses in the Soviet Union, it still claims the allegiance of more than one-fourth of the Slavic population.[2] The Moscow Patriarchate, the administrative center of the church, has an annual budget on the order of 315 million rubles (of which an estimated 140 million rubles go to the Peace Fund). As the largest single member church of the World Council of Churches (since 1961), the Orthodox Church of the Soviet Union maintains a full program of international contacts and in 1982 opened a large new reception center in downtown Moscow to facilitate this activity. The church is the only noncommunist institution of its size to be officially recognized by the state.

Nevertheless, it would be a mistake to think that—apart from being offered, on occasion, a special platform to endorse Soviet foreign policy—the Orthodox Church enjoys anything like a privileged relationship with the Soviet regime. Orthodox believers are just as likely to suffer discrimination as are members of other religions. The right to worship, the most important religious freedom for Orthodox believers, is in practice denied to many millions of them owing to government restrictions on the number of open churches in the Soviet Union. There are about 6,500 "working" Russian Orthodox churches today, which is one church for every 7,700 worshipers. This compares unfavorably with the situation in Bulgaria, for instance (one church for every 1,600 Orthodox worshipers), or in Romania (one for every 1,110 worshipers), or even with the Baptists in the Soviet Union, who have approximately one church for every 600 believers.

Official figures suggest that in 1986 there were some 6,000 registered Orthodox priests in the Soviet Union (9,100 in Romania). This represents a decline since 1972 (6,200), when several bishops openly expressed alarm at the shortage of priests; and it is still necessary to assign monks and ostensibly retired priests to active duty in the parishes. But enrollment at the church's three seminaries—in Zagorsk (near Moscow), Leningrad, and Odessa—and two theological academies (in Zagorsk and Leningrad) has risen in recent years. Between 1,800 and 2,000 young men, including correspondence students, are currently being trained as priests.

Orthodox monasticism has been drastically curtailed in the last 70 or so years. There were 1,023 monasteries and convents functioning in 1917; today only six monasteries and 10 convents remain. These institutions had some 1,200 members at last count. Under-

ground monasticism is thought to be extensive, but there are, perforce, no reliable statistics.

The Moscow Patriarchate produces a monthly journal in English,
French, and German as well as in Russian; but probably only about
20,000 copies of each Russian issue are printed, and a large proportion of these are exported. The church does not have its own
printing presses, but, like other organizations, must arrange to have
its printing done on state-owned presses. Besides its journal, the
Patriarchate is permitted to publish an annual calendar, a theology
series, various service books, limited and infrequent editions of the
Bible, and publications for special events. It also has facilities for
producing candles, communion bread, holy pictures, and other religious items for personal use.

Prospects for the future of the Orthodox Church in the Soviet
Union are mixed. A policy of outward subservience to the government's domestic and foreign policies has secured for it the resources
necessary to sustain the level of activity to which it was reduced
by the Krushchev anti-religion campaign of the 1960s. But during
the Brezhnev years (1964–82) an implicit challenge to the church
leadership came from the religious wing of the dissident movement.
Human-rights monitoring groups documented numerous violations
of religious and other civil rights and called on the Moscow Patriarchate to defend believers in conflict with state authorities. The
Orthodox leadership has sought to avoid public involvement in
specific cases but, when pressed, has supported official charges
against individual believers. There is some evidence that church
leaders have privately sought more lenient sentences for several
convicted religious dissidents.

From comments in the Soviet press and from official and unofficial sources, it is increasingly evident that the young and the educated are finding in the Orthodox tradition a treasury of Russian
national culture and a personal, non-Marxist system of ethics. This
is one reason why the Church leadership is facing increased pressure to assume a more independent role in the social and political—
as well as in the spiritual—life of the country.

Protestantism has a long history in two of the Baltic republics,
Latvia and Estonia, where the Evangelical Lutheran Church remains loosely associated with Latvian and Estonian national identity. Lutheran seminaries in Riga and Tallinn train perhaps a dozen
pastors each year. Fewer than 200 registered pastors must serve
over 350 congregations with a combined membership of roughly
410,000. An additional 100,000 Soviet German Lutherans living in

Siberia and Central Asia receive periodic visits from the Latvian clergy.

Since the nineteenth century there have been active and expanding communities of Baptists, Evangelical Christians, and Pentecostals in the territory of the present-day Soviet Union. Although reliable statistics are hard to come by, it is probable that there are at least 550,000 baptized adult members of these denominations scattered throughout the Soviet Union, with the greatest concentration in the Ukraine. Taken together with children and unbaptized adherents, this represents approximately 3 million people in 5,000–8,000 congregations, many of which are not officially registered.[3]

The All-Union Council of Evangelical Christians and Baptists is the officially recognized umbrella organization of these denominations. The Council has existed since 1944, when Stalin imposed on Baptists and Evangelical Christians a unity they had been unable to achieve freely. The union's current baptized membership is perhaps 350,000, including some 50,000 Pentecostals and Mennonites.[4] From its headquarters in Moscow's Baptist church the All-Union Council publishes a journal, *Fraternal Messenger (Bratsky vestnik)*, and runs a theological correspondence course that some 350 students have completed since its inception in 1968. Current enrollment for the three-year course is just over 100. There have been negotiations with authorities about opening a small seminary, but there is no indication that this will be permitted.

Other evangelicals in the Soviet Union are organized under the Council of Churches of Evangelical Christians and Baptists, consisting of congregations that are not legally registered and have rejected the All-Union Council leadership because of its cooperation with the state. Originally a reform movement within the All-Union Council, the Council of Churches of Evangelical Christians and Baptists has no official status, and its leadership has periodically been decimated by arrests. It is thought to have a present baptized membership of close to 50,000 in perhaps 1,000 congregations. Moreover, the organization has the most impressive underground printing operation in the Soviet Union, having produced well over half a million pieces of religious literature since 1971. The Council of Churches is, after the emigration movement among Soviet Jews, the largest dissident movement in the Soviet Union. And if its renown abroad has not been as great as that of the Jewish emigration movement, it has forced Soviet authorities to make substantial concessions.

Two churches closely associated with nationality in their respective republics are the Georgian Orthodox and Armenian Apostolic—or Gregorian—Churches.

The Georgian Orthodox Church has its own patriarch and thus constitutes an independent sister church of the Russian Orthodox. The current Georgian Patriarch, Ilya II, has done much to restore his church's fortunes since he succeeded the corrupt and enfeebled David V in 1977. Most notable has been his effort to restore diocesan administration. Nine of 15 sees were vacant at the time of Ilya's election; now only three remain empty. The Georgian Patriarchate publishes a journal and calendar but has had great difficulties in disseminating other religious literature.

The Georgian Orthodox Church's most serious problem is the lack of registered churches and priests. Of some 2,000 churches and chapels functioning before the Revolution, there remain only about 40 "working" Georgian Orthodox churches. There are something over 100 registered priests, 40–50 nuns in four convents, and a smaller number of monks in the two monasteries (there were 27 in 1917) that were reopened in the late 1970s. The seminary in Mtskheta, the ancient Georgian capital, has an enrollment of about 25.

It is thought that something like two-thirds of the Georgian population—or roughly 3 million people—remain regular worshipers. And, as in other parts of the Soviet Union, a notable proportion of young people are showing a renewed interest.

The Armenian Apostolic Church is widely regarded as enjoying the greatest degree of freedom of any religious body in the Soviet Union. The Supreme Patriarch-Catholicos of All Armenians, Vazgen I, has authority over five dioceses in the Soviet Union, only three of which are in Armenia proper. The center of Armenian Christianity is the Patriarchal Cathedral at Echmiadzin, where four of six surviving monasteries and the theological seminary are also located. In 1982 seminary enrollment was reported to be 30 (down from 56 in 1978), so it appears that new priests are being trained at a rate sufficient to maintain the present total of 56 (down from 130).

There are some 40 working churches in Armenia (1,450 in 1917), and it seems most unlikely that this is enough, since at least 60 percent of the 3.5 million Armenians living in Armenia or neighboring Soviet republics remain practicing believers. Some 70 percent of newborn infants are baptized. This says much for the strength of Armenian nationalism, of which the church is a vital element. A revival of religious interest among young people has been gaining strength in recent years. Uniquely among religious communities in the Soviet Union, the Armenian Apostolic Church legally possesses its own printing facilities, as is evident in the well-stocked book stalls found in Armenian churches.

There are about 3 million Latin-rite Catholics in the Soviet Union, of whom the majority are in the Lithuanian republic. It is widely assumed that 75 percent of the Lithuanian population remains loyal to this church. Indeed, the Catholic faith and national identity are as closely related in Lithuania as they are in neighboring Poland. As have the Poles, Lithuanian Catholics have shown themselves to be remarkably resolute in resisting the anti-religion policies of the Communist government. But unlike Poland, Luthuania was fully incorporated into the Soviet Union at the end of World War II, and its Catholic Church has had to endure more brutal anti-religion policies than any employed in Poland.

The Lithuanian episcopate has been much weakened since the advent of Soviet rule. Though the Pope appointed two bishops in 1982, two of six dioceses are still run by administrators. Bishop Julijonas Steponavičius, who is believed to be a cardinal, has been in exile since Khrushchev's anti-religion campaign.

There are, to be sure, some 628 working Catholic churches in Lithuania, only 80 fewer than existed in 1940, when the country was annexed (more than 500 chapels and other nonparish churches were closed.) Yet something like 100 parishes are without priests. Today there are fewer than 700 Catholic priests in the country (1,450 in 1940) and nearly one-quarter of these are over 70 years old. All monastic orders were abolished in 1947, and the single surviving seminary, in Kaunas, had until quite recently produced only a handful of graduates each year. The state authorities have allowed the seminary to increase its enrollment since 1975, so that the current number may be between 70 and 100.[5]

The Lithuanian clergy and faithful have responded to anti-religion pressures with both public resistance and clandestine initiatives.[6] Since 1972 more than half the Catholic clergy and well over 200,000 laymen have signed petitions and appeals protesting Soviet policy against their church. A clandestine seminary seems to have been functioning since the early 1970s, and by 1979 some 19 of its graduates had been ordained. A Soviet source confirms the existence of clandestine convents that in 1976 housed some 1,500 nuns.

Perhaps the most beleaguered of the officially recognized religious communities in the Soviet Union are the Jews. According to the 1979 census, assimilation and emigration have reduced the Jewish population to 1,811,000, about 88 percent of whom live in the western regions. Soviet sources indicate that only between 1 and 3 percent practice their faith, although the figure is somewhat higher in the Baltic Republics. Jews living in the Caucasian Republics and in Central Asia are more religious; perhaps 20 percent are practicing.

In sum, there may be 60,000–100,000 observant Jews in the Soviet Union today, for whom the rabbi of Moscow's Arkhipov Street Synagogue and his assistant act as spokesmen. At the same time, there are between 50 and 60 open synagogues (as against some 6,000 in 1917) and an indeterminate number of smaller "prayer houses." Of the synagogues, approximately half are in Central Asia and the Caucasus.

The Soviet Union today has no more than a handful of trained rabbis. Certainly, most synagogues do not have one. The tiny, ill-equipped yeshiva (school) attached to Moscow's Choral Synagogue, with a current enrollment of five, cannot replace the rabbis who have retired or died during the past decade. Recently some half-dozen young Jews have been allowed to study at yeshivas in Budapest and New York. These programs are clearly insufficient to replenish the rabbinate in the Soviet Union.

Jewish religious literature has been virtually impossible to obtain for decades. The Moscow and Leningrad synagogues do publish calendars, but since the 1920s three editions of a prayer book and one edition of the Pentateuch comprise the sum total of Jewish religious literature printed in the Soviet Union.

Prospects for the survival of Jewish secular culture—of the Jewish "nationality," as it is officially described—are generally considered bleak. State-encouraged anti-Semitism will doubtless deter many from identifying with Judaism. But throughout the 1970s thousands of European Jews from precisely the most secularized strata of the population cultivated a sense of their Jewishness. And with the greatly reduced emigration of the 1980s, the Jewish cultural renaissance, stimulated by the emigration movement, may well develop a more religious direction.

The picture is somewhat different with respect to Islam. The largest and most important of its four "spiritual directorates" is that of Central Asia and Kazakhstan, with headquarters in Tashkent. Currently Mufti Shamsutdinkhan Babakhan is its president. The Spiritual Directorate of Muslims in Russia and Siberia, with headquarters in Ufa, is responsible for Islamic communities in the Tatar and Bashkir Autonomous Republics. Since 1980 its president has been Mufti Talgat Taziev. The Spiritual Directorate of the North Caucasus and Dagestan has headquarters in Makhach-Kala (Dagestan Autonomous Republic), with Mufti Mahmud Gekkiev as its president; and the Muslim Spiritual Directorate of Transcaucasia, centered in Baku, is responsible for the predominantly Shi'ite Muslims of Azerbaidzhan and the neighboring republics. Its president since 1980 has been Sheikh Hadji Ali Shukur Pasha, who is Shi'ite; the vice-president is, as a rule, a Sunni, in deference to the large Sunni minority in the Caucasus.

These spiritual directorates conform roughly to the old tsarist system for supervising Muslim affairs. The great majority of Soviet Muslims are of the Sunni rite, which does not favor centralized ecclesiastical administration. But as with the Baptists and Evangelical Christians, in the mid-1940s the Soviet government's interest in centrally organized religious life superseded any objections the believers might have had. And, again like the Evangelical Christians and Baptists, Islamic activity in the Soviet Union is bifurcated into the officially recognized and the clandestine.

The face of official Islam in the Soviet Union is in some respects a sad one. Of some 26,000 mosques in use at the time of the Revolution, only some 400–450 are believed to be functioning today. An army of some 45,000 mullahs has been reduced to fewer than 2,000. There are only two medressehs (seminaries), one in Tashkent and one in Bukhara, graduating no more than 15–20 students each year. Islamic religious literature is extremely scarce: only five small editions of the Koran since World War II. Yet, in spite of these deprivations, the officially recognized leadership of the Islamic community is perhaps the most abject in its support of Soviet propaganda regarding religious freedom.

Nevertheless, it has been plausibly argued that the Muslim leadership has gained rather more from its cooperation with the authorities than the authorities have gained from them. Muslims have won some significant concessions in recent years: the opening of some 30 new mosques since 1975, an edition of the Koran in 1977, and the opening in 1971 of a higher theological course at the Tashkent medresseh. The standard of theological education for the officially recognized mullahs has risen dramatically over the last 15 years, largely as a result of the new course. But it can also be argued that it has been in the Soviet regime's own interest to provide a small number of politically reliable Muslim clerics to make a favorable impression on Muslims from abroad.

Parallel to the official Islamic establishment, there appears to be a sizable unofficial Islam population.[7] Unregistered mullahs and religious activists belonging to Sufi brotherhoods (clandestine and highly disciplined religious orders) support themselves by religious ministrations to the faithful in areas where the services of registered mullahs are either unavailable or unwanted. The Sufi orders espouse an extremely conservative brand of Islam, considered to be fanatical and anti-Soviet by the authorities. Indeed, the most prominent of these orders have a history of resistance to Russian (and now Soviet) power. It is not known how many unregistered mullahs exist, but it is safe to assume that in many rural areas they are more active—and possibly more visible—than representatives of official Islam.

According to the 1979 census, as we saw in the preceding chapter, some 43 million people in the Soviet Union belong to traditionally Muslim ethnic groups—Uzbeks, Kazakhs, Tatars, Azeris, Tadzhiks, Turkmen, Bashkirs, and two or three dozen smaller nationalities. This represents an increase of more than 100 percent since 1959, bringing the proportion of ethnic Muslims in the Soviet population to 16.5 percent.

The extent to which these ethnic groups remain distinctly Muslim is of immediate concern to the Soviet authorities. Official statistics suggest that allegiance to Islam remains high in areas where the clandestine Sufi brotherhoods are active. Some 80 percent of the ethnic Muslims in these areas still perform or have performed Muslim rites of passage. One mufti told a British journalist in 1979 that, contrary to standard Soviet medical practices, more than 90 percent of newborn males in his republic were circumcised; he also said that the great majority of his compatriots were buried according to Muslim custom. The resistance of ethnic Muslims to intermarriage is even more striking.

For more than 60 years the state has encouraged in its Muslim territories a secular nationalism at the expense of Islam, so as to facilitate social and cultural integration into the Soviet Union. Obviously, widespread popular identification with Islam retards this process. Furthermore, the remarkable vitality of the clandestine and fundamentalist Sufi brotherhoods presents the possibility, however distant, of an Islamic revival that could have both anti-Soviet and anti-Russian overtones.

In conclusion, it is probable that not less than 30 percent of the Soviet population remain practicing believers. In the non-Russian republics, where religion and national or ethnic consciousness are closely related, the percentage is generally higher; and all of these religious communities report a significant increase in the interest shown by educated, urban young people over the past two decades.

The resilience of Islamic belief, coupled with the demographic dynamism of the ethnic Muslims, poses complex political and economic problems in the long run. Throughout the Soviet Union the Evangelical Christians and Baptists are active missionaries, and the various dissenters are determined to conduct their activities without regard to government restrictions.

The Orthodox Church, on the other hand, appears to be a sleeping giant. Nevertheless, this body, too, by its very presence in society, exercises a kind of influence. Since Khrushchev's fall its appeal to the young and the educated has steadily increased, and to the extent that the Orthodox Church becomes identified with Russian national feeling, this process can only accelerate. It is most unlikely, however, that the Soviet regime could ever accommodate itself to a Russian nationalism based on the faith that for 70 years it has sought to eradicate.

NOTES

1. See Jane Ellis, *The Russian Orthodox Church Today: A Contemporary History.* (Bloomington, IN; Indiana University Press, 1986); and Dimitry Pospielevsky, *The Russian Church Under the Soviet Regime, 1917–1982.* 2 vols. (Crestwood, NY: St. Vladimir's Seminary, 1984).

2. Figures are from William C. Fletcher, *Soviet Believers* (Lawrence, KA: Regents, 1981).

3. Walter Sawatsky, *Soviet Evangelicals since World War II* (Scottsdale, PA: Herald, 1981).

4. An additional 70,000 Pentecostals and 20,000 Mennonites form either autonomously registered or unregistered congregations.

5. There is also a much smaller seminary in Riga that trains priests for Latvia's 200,000 Catholics and for scattered Catholic parishes in Central Asia.

6. See Michael Bourdeaux, *Land of Crosses: The Struggle for Religious Freedom in Lithuania, 1938–78* (Chumleigh, Devon: Augustine, 1979).

7. Alexandre Bennigsen and S. Enders Wimbush, *Mystics and Commissars: Sufism in the USSR* (Berkeley, CA: University of California Press, 1986).

28

Women

MARY ELLEN FISCHER

A chicken is not a bird; a woman is not a human being.—Russian proverb.

The first class oppression coincides with that of the female sex by the male.—Engels, *The Woman Question.*

Women . . . should all know what the proletarian dictatorship will mean to them—complete equality of rights with men, both legal and in practice, in the family, the state, and in society.— Lenin, *The Emancipation of Women.*

We hate the bourgeois family, but . . . the main kernel of society . . . is the family.—Lunacharsky, circa 1926.[1]

A clearly stated goal of the Bolshevik Revolution was the elimination of the subordinate status of women in Russia. Marx and Engels had recognized and denounced the oppression of women in bourgeois society; Lenin promised that his revolution would establish a new society in which women would achieve equal status with men.

The 1917 Revolution brought profound changes in the political and economic organization of Russia and also in the ideological assumptions of that society, but the record of the revolutionaries in achieving their various goals is mixed. Not all of the promises have been fulfilled, and this is certainly true for what Engels termed "the woman question." The Revolution quickly brought legal equality to Russian women, but the struggle of these women to attain social and economic equality with their male comrades in both public and private life has been more prolonged and less successful. Indeed,

visible in the Soviet Union today are many of the differences between male and female patterns of political and economic participation that can be found in societies without such a strong ideological
commitment to the equality of women.

There can be no doubt that the situation of women has improved
since 1917. Their legal and socioeconomic status before the Revolution was miserable at all levels of society. In peasant families
the division of labor by sex did make the wife an important contributor to the economic well-being of the household. At the same
time, however, the separation of roles produced double standards
of behavior in which men were expected to drink, smoke, swear,
engage in extramarital sex, and use their fists freely against other
men and against their wives. None of these activities was permissible for women, who were expected to show "subordination, obedience, and a slavish devotion" and to forgive a beating since it
was "the nature of men" to be "hot-tempered." In Russian peasant
society, wife-beating demonstrated masculinity, whereas overt af-
fection was considered abnormal.[2]

In pre-Revolutionary Russia upper-class women in some ways
fared worse than did peasant women, since the greater economic
resources of the family meant that they could be completely seg-
regated from the outside world. In the seventeenth century the
seclusion of such women was a matter of family honor. The husband's horsewhip, used in the "training" of the wife, hung by custom at the head of the bed. Eighteenth-century reforms brought
some improvements, but nineteenth-century lithographs still depict
the public punishment of noblewomen by flogging.[3] The despotism
of the tsar over his subjects, based on divine right, was mirrored in
the husband's power over his wife and children. The 1836 Code of
Russian Laws stipulated that "the woman must obey her husband,
reside with him in love, respect, and unlimited obedience, and offer
him every pleasantness . . . as the ruler of the household." A Russian
woman did have certain property and inheritance rights denied to
her West European counterpart, but the fact remains that a woman
in tsarist Russia had few civil rights: without the express permission
of her father—and, after marriage, her husband—she could not work,
study, trade, or travel.

Nineteenth-century polemics between Russian conservatives who
wished to preserve the traditions of Russian society and reformers
hoping to bring about political and economic change reveal a contrast in the attitudes of these men toward the roles of women. Because the confinement of women to the home was considered by

many to be necessary to the preservation of indigenous Russian values, conservative politicians tended to advocate restrictions on women's access to education or to a wider role in society. In contrast, male reformers tended to advocate change in the status of women, particularly if they had themselves been influenced by Western concepts of social change and progress.

Until the late 1850s secondary education was available only to a tiny number of upper-class women, and that education focused on subjects such as music, needlework, or French, with the goal of providing a pleasant home environment for their future husbands. Limited access to higher and professional education was granted to women in the 1870s; but after Tsar Alexander II was assassinated in 1881 and a young woman was found to be one of the assassins, even that concession was rescinded. Conservatives were reinforced in their fears: women let out of the home endangered the political and moral fabric of society. Higher education was once more closed to women, and the employment of middle- or upper-class women remained limited to the private economy, usually in homes as teachers or governesses. Just as the moderate reform movement in Russia, frustrated by repeated failures and persecution, became a radical revolutionary movement, so the women's movement became radicalized. Many women, in fact, joined the wider movement for political revolution and the destruction of the tsarist regime.[4]

After 1890 Marxism became prominent in Russia as an ideology of revolution, and women revolutionaries were attracted to the writings of Marx and Engels for their analysis of sexual as well as class oppression. Engels in particular detailed the double oppression of women under capitalism: they were exploited as cheap labor in mills, mines, and factories, where they worked under terrible conditions, and were treated as possessions and instruments of production by their husbands. Under socialism, Engels promised, women would be liberated from both forms of bondage.

Lenin continued this emphasis on women's liberation, declaring that "we have to win over the millions of working women in town and country. . . . There can be no real mass movement without the women."[5] Lenin was a political pragmatist who did not scruple to make promises and to use whatever slogans and arguments were necessary to persuade different social groups to support him in his goals. The first need, he believed, was the political revolution to destroy the old regime; then would come, inevitably, the end of oppression based on class or sex.

In the three years following the Bolshevik seizure of power, many laws were passed to improve the status of women. They were granted full legal equality with men; mutual consent was required for marriage; and women were allowed the right to keep their own names and to obtain an abortion or a divorce on request. The Party also announced its intention of freeing women from household work by providing communal facilities for such traditional burdens as child care, laundry, and cooking. Women would be expected to do the work in these communal facilities—but it would be for wages, making it productive labor in the Marxist sense.

Finally, an organization was formed specifically for women: the *Zhenotdel* (Women's Department). Women were taught to read, to care for themselves, and to participate in the new socialist society; their rights were explained and their expectations raised. As early as 1923, however, a Party resolution condemned the *Zhenotdel* for "feminist deviationism," for turning people away from the class struggle. The next year the organization was criticized for excessive complaints about material conditions harmful to women. The most outspoken feminist within the Party leadership, Aleksandra Kollontai, was "banished" to diplomatic service in Norway.[6] By 1928 "feminism" had been declared to be anti-Marxist, an attempt to convert the class struggle to a sex struggle. Somehow in that first post-Revolutionary decade the two struggles had become separated.

Lenin had some blind spots, especially when it came to the oppression of Soviet women. For example, he usually ignored the basic conflict of interest between men and women Communists. He did not appear to realize that men would have to relinquish certain privileges for women to gain equality—or that men would probably be reluctant to give up these privileges. He did recognize that many loyal Bolshevik men did not accept women's equality and that some "educational" work was needed to "root out the old slaveowner" point of view even within the Party. One incident illustrates the difficulty: in 1918 the new Workers' Soviet (Council) of the town of Vladimir decreed that henceforth every woman over 18 would become the property of the state and be required to register at a central bureau of free love. In the interest of the state, men aged 19–50 could choose one registered woman a month, without her consent, and the children of these unions would become state property. The decree was quickly rescinded by the Bolshevik leadership, but less public forms of oppression continued. Particularly difficult was the situation of women in traditionally Moslem areas, where violence against *Zhenotdel* workers was not unusual.[7]

Another important factor in gradually reducing the drive for women's equality was the devastated economy. Marx had predicted that socialism would come first to a highly industrialized society, one that had achieved the means to abolish economic scarcity. There would be plenty for everyone, and inequalities—whether based on class or sex—would disappear. In fact, the Revolution took place in a semi-industrialized country badly weakened by World War I— and was followed by three years of civil war in which the Bolsheviks had to fight for survival before they could worry about their revolutionary goals. The socialist revolution occurred at a time of extreme economic scarcity—just the reverse of Marx's prediction— and the egalitarian goals of the revolutionaries began to evaporate. The economy in 1921 needed experts, technicians, and specialists. To gain their cooperation the state had to pay them higher wages than those paid to unskilled workers. Wage stratification brought with it social stratification—and a political and social system that was not egalitarian.

Later, the pressure of reconstruction would turn into the pressures of economic growth. The Bolsheviks, after all, were committed not only to equality but also to a program of industrial development. Indeed, Lenin had found it necessary almost immediately to restore both the hierarchy of command in the armed forces and one-person management in the factories, having concluded that just as councils of soldiers could not fight a war effectively, so councils of workers could not manage high rates of production. When women began to compete for the favored jobs, male factory workers objected to their employment in any but traditionally female capacities. So women were temporarily held back to prevent trouble and economic slowdown.

Then the post-Revolutionary legal changes affecting the family and family life were brought into question. The easy divorce laws, along with shifts in the living patterns and consciousness of men and women, were contributing to the breakup of many marriages. Easy abortion combined with economic difficulties had brought down the birthrate at a time when the Party wished to encourage population growth in order to replace the losses of war and famine. As revolutionaries, the Communists had condemned the bourgeois family as a reactionary institution; but as rulers, most had come to believe that the family was necessary for the stability of the new society. Commissar of Education A. V. Lunacharsky, in the mid-1920s, expressed the dilemma: "We hate the bourgeois family, but ... the main kernel of society ... is the family."

After 1928 the rapid development of heavy industry was given priority, as was a stable family and social system—to produce an efficient labor force. As a result, the laws affecting women and the family began to change again, culminating in a decree of 1936 making abortion illegal and divorce very difficult.[8] The gradual decline in revolutionary fervor throughout the 1920s saw the egalitarian goals of the old Bolsheviks lose out to the need for hierarchical social and economic organization in the army, the factory, and even the home.

Another set of factors contributed substantially to the Bolsheviks' failure to fulfill their promises to women. Lenin, like most of his male colleagues, never fully realized the extent of women's oppression *outside* the workplace. Therefore, he concentrated on institutional and economic reforms such as equality in law and in education. At home he assumed that women would be freed from housework and child care by "a reallocation of familial and societal functions . . . from the individual household to the social collective." [9] In other words, roles *within* the home would not change; men would not begin to share those responsibilities. Instead, the drudgery would be eased by communal kitchens, public dining rooms and laundries, crèches, kindergartens, and children's homes. Male privilege in the home was never confronted directly.

The provision of communal facilities to liberate women, however, turned out to be prohibitively expensive for the new revolutionary society. Even the new work laws limiting hours or providing maternity leave or child care were regarded as impractical and frequently were not implemented in the ruined economy. Here also the pressures arising from economic devastation turned into pressures for rapid development. Under Stalin, priority was given to development goals rather than to current consumption. This made the women's triple burden of job, home, and family still heavier, for it was home appliances and social services that remained among the most neglected and backward sectors of the Soviet economy.

As Marx might have predicted, economic scarcity has been crucial in the evolution of both Soviet society and the role of women in that society. Yet there is no doubt that the Soviet government has achieved tremendous gains for its population in living standards as well as in national power and that Soviet women have shared in these gains in two important ways. First, their legal equality with men has not been rescinded or questioned. Second, they have been mobilized into the labor force at rates unequaled by any other industrial society: Soviet women make up just over 51 percent of the labor force, and 85 percent of Soviet women are employed full time.[10] This has meant greater female participation not only in skilled and technical occupations and in the professions than is usual elsewhere but also in heavy, unskilled, physical labor for industry and agriculture. For the Soviet Union throughout its history has known not only shortages of labor, but also of *man*power—a demographic imbalance brought on by huge losses in both World Wars. Thus, there has been continuous pressure on women to work—as well as some room for them at the top. The ideological assumption that women would achieve liberation by employment outside the home has been reinforced by economic necessity.

Yet despite significant shifts in the status of Soviet women, their economic roles reflect patterns present in societies without such a strong ideological commitment to sexual equality. One such pattern is the concentration of women in economic sectors where they are assumed to have special skills or qualifications: the food and textile industries, for example, or education, or social services. Such sectoral segregation in the Soviet Union actually seems to be increasing, perhaps partly as a result of the improving demographic balance and the reappearance of males to fill their traditional occupations. In 1959, for example, only 33 percent of women were employed in "women's" sectors, but by 1970 the figure had climbed to 55 percent.[11]

Another pattern involves "professional takeover": as more women move into a particular profession or occupation, it becomes stereotyped as "women's work." Soviet medicine, in which 69 percent of doctors are women, is a dramatic example of this process. But the prestige, power, and financial rewards associated with such sectors usually are reduced as women enter them. The causal relationship is often unclear: Does a profession decline in desirability because women move in, or do men move out because it has become less rewarding or attractive for some other reason? Whatever the cause, Soviet women clearly are concentrated in sectors with lower prestige and financial reward.

A similar case is the pattern of salaries among categories of workers within a specific sector. The sector with the highest proportion of women—skilled non-manual workers—is at the middle range in educational level but at the bottom in income. Even skilled manual workers are better paid. The average Soviet woman earns about 65 percent as much as the average Soviet male. This is slightly higher than the comparable U.S. figure, but it is not equality.

Finally, in explaining the relatively low income of women in a system that guarantees equal pay for equal work, we must consider the vertical segregation within sectors of the Soviet economy. Women are clustered at the bottom. In agriculture, for example, where women make up over half the labor force, there is a clear division of labor: men operate the machines; women work with their hands. Men are

the directors, bookkeepers, tractor and combine drivers, and irri-
gators; women are the field-team leaders and members, the cattle
and poultry workers, the vegetable- and melon-growers, and the
non–specialized workers. Only during World War II did women
constitute as much as 14.2 percent of farm directors; by 1961 the
figure was back to the prewar proportion of less than 2 percent; by
1975, it was 1.5 percent. The situation in industry is comparable:
in 1975 women made up 65 percent of the age cohort of industrial
administrators; but only 9 percent of directors were female, and
these were concentrated in textiles or food processing.[12]

In the professions, the same pattern emerges. As responsibility,
status, and pay go up, the proportion of women goes down. One
Soviet source complained, for example, that "while men comprise
15 percent of all medical personnel, they are 50 percent of all chief
physicians and executives of medical institutions." In science and
scholarship, women have formed a rather stable share of the total
number of specialists, ranging from 36 percent in 1950 to 40 percent
in 1975. But they make up 50 percent of junior research associates,
24 percent of senior researchers, 22 percent of associate professors,
and only 10 percent of full professors. In 1977 there were 14 women
in the 749-member Academy of Sciences: three were full members;
11 were corresponding members.

The pattern of women's economic participation in the Soviet
Union thus resembles, in some respects, that found in other industrial societies: horizontal and vertical segregation with negative
impact on status, responsibility, and income. Political participation
is even more limited. As a rule, the proportion of women varies
inversely with the power of the office or legislative body. For example, women delegates make up between 44 and 48 percent of
the delegates to local soviets, and the proportion drops close to 30
percent in the Supreme Soviet. Among the delegates to the latter,
moreover, women are less likely to be Party members, hold less
important posts in their occupations, and show more rapid turnover
rates within the body. All these factors militate against their playing
an influential role. In addition, these legislative bodies are not seats
of power in the Soviet system, since the Party organs make policy
decisions and then use the soviets to ratify these policies and to
discuss methods of implementation (see chapter 4).

Real power lies in the Party, and here we find few women. Since
the early 1960s efforts to recruit women into the Communist Party
have intensified, and the female proportion of total membership is
now about 27 percent. (The figure was 8 percent in 1922.) But if
we examine age cohorts, we discover that 14.1 percent of all Soviet
males over 18 are members, as against 3.7 percent of all females

over 18. This discrepancy is not a function of educational lag, because the ratio remains the same for those who have completed higher education. As many as one-third of the first secretaries of primary Party organizations are women, but the proportion drops sharply in higher positions. For example, less than 4 percent of urban, district, or regional Party secretaries are female. Since 1918 the proportion of women in the Central Committee has never exceeded 4.2 percent. Even that low figure does not reflect the true situation in the Central Committee, since about a third of the women are there for honorary or titular reasons—the cosmonaut Tereshkova, for example. (Men are also there for such reasons, of course, but in much smaller proportion.)

At the top of the Party and state hierarchies women have been almost totally absent. The first female member of the Party leadership in the post–World War II era was Ekaterina Furtseva; she served on both the Secretariat and the all-powerful Politburo for four years under Khruschev and then remained Minister of Culture until her death in 1974. A Minister of Health in the 1950s was the only other woman in the Council of Ministers. In 1986 Aleksandra Biriukova was named to the Secretariat, with responsibility for consumer goods. This vertical segregation in the political system is matched by horizontal or occupational segregation. Women officials usually deal with health, culture, social security, light industry, and consumer services rather than with the armed forces, foreign or Party affairs, heavy industry, or internal security. Real political power remains firmly in the grip of men.[13]

Marx and Engels—and even Lenin—assumed that work outside the home in "productive" labor would liberate women from their subservient position in bourgeois society. Soviet women have not only the right but the duty to work side by side with men. Yet the issue of oppression in the home or of the possibility of shifting sex roles within the family has never been directly confronted by the Party leaders. And the triple burden—job, home, and family—has prevented women from competing effectively with their male colleagues for political or economic promotion. Their lower performance, in turn, has reinforced lower expectations of these women, expectations held by themselves as well as by the men supervising or competing with them. This has resulted in the patterns of political and economic participation so familiar to scholars studying women in other societies.

The prognosis for Soviet women is not clear. One important factor, however, contributes to pessimism: the demographic imbalance has largely been rectified, and whereas it is socially advantageous to have equal numbers of males and females in the younger and middle-aged cohorts, this could also mean that there will be less room for women at the top (or as students in educational institutions leading to prestigious occupations). In general, Soviet officials have not shown the commitment to the equality of women that would give women good jobs when they are competing with men. On the other hand, women's awareness of exploitation has been growing in recent years. In 1979 and 1980, members of a feminist dissident movement even managed to circulate two issues of an underground journal, *Women and Russia*, before they were arrested and expelled to the West in July 1980.[14] And if, as it seems, a major shift toward shared sex roles within the home has never been considered by most Soviet citizens, male or female, the Soviet media did begin to discuss the problem during the Brezhnev era.

There seem to be three major orientations among Soviet analysts regarding the proper policies to be adopted on "the woman question." One, with the smallest number of advocates, would encourage a better sharing of household work within the family. The second would emphasize the provision of communal facilities and consumer goods in gradually improving the lives of women. The third reflects another demographic problem facing Soviet society: the low birthrate, particularly among the Russian population. Analysts concerned with higher population growth stress the need to increase maternity leave (currently one year at 30–40 percent of salary) as well as subsidies—and perhaps even to offer women the option of quitting the labor force altogether to raise their children. This would reinforce sex role differentiation and intensify inequalities in the labor market, but it would give many women a choice not now available to them: staying home.

None of these three policy orientations would be clearly superior in fulfilling the Party's goal of increasing both the birthrate and economic production. The first might raise the quality of women's participation in the labor force, but it might reduce men's productivity without increasing the birthrate. The second might increase women's productivity but would be very expensive and might not bring more rapid population growth; the record in other industrial societies that have tried it does not promise a higher birthrate along with higher living standards. The third option would reduce the number of working women and would be ideologically unpalatable to a large proportion of Soviet women who have come to believe strongly in a career as a prerequisite to liberation. Yet it is the one most likely to increase the birthrate.

Brezhnev managed to postpone any major decision on this issue during his lifetime. The possibilities were widely discussed, how-

ever, and the new Soviet leadership will have to take a stand in the
near future. Although the outcome of the debate is unpredictable,
it is likely that Party choices in this area will affect the lives of more
Soviet citizens more profoundly than any other matter of internal
policy awaiting decision at the top. Meanwhile, the wide range of
opinion on the subject among Soviet citizens can be seen from the
following quotations culled from letters and articles in the Soviet
press:

> Free a woman from the kitchen and you give her the freedom of
> a silly hen. Who needs such a woman? Woman is supposed to
> adorn the hearth just as flowers adorn the meadow.

> Girls, for all your equality with us men, stay feminine, gentle,
> and weak (in the best, Marxist sense of this concept).

> The shop class teaches men's work. Girls have home economics,
> but men must be men.

> [Outside work] is the most important and primary condition for
> our liberation from the authority of men and is the guarantee of
> our independence, our sense of our own value and freedom.

> Under the new order of things, the kitchen will belong to anyone
> who wants to eat.

> I doubt that I will ever marry again. Why should I? Having a
> husband is like having another baby in the apartment.

NOTES

1. Jessica Smith, *Woman in Soviet Russia* (New York: Vanguard, 1928),
p. 4; Frederick Engels, *Origin of the Family*, excerpted in *The Woman
Question* (New York: International, 1951), p. 21; V. I. Lenin, *The Emancipation of Women* (New York: International, 1934), p. 113; and Lunacharsky, as quoted in Smith, p. 92.

2. See H. Kent Geiger, *The Family in Soviet Russia* (Cambridge, MA:
Harvard University Press, 1958); or David L. Ransel, ed., *The Family in
Imperial Russia: New Lines of Historical Research* (Urbana, IL: University
of Illinois Press, 1978).

3. Dorothy Atkinson, "Society and the Sexes in the Russian Past," in
Dorothy Atkinson, Alexander Dallin, and Gail Lapidus, eds., *Women in
Russia* (Stanford, CA: Stanford University Press, 1977), p. 17.

4. On the radicalization of the women's movement during the nineteenth century, see Richard Stites, *The Women's Liberation Movement in
Russia: Feminism, Nihilism, and Bolshevism, 1860–1930* (Princeton, NJ:

Princeton University Press, 1978); Vera Broido, *Apostles into Terrorists* (New York: Viking, 1977); and Barbara A. Engel, *Mothers and Daughters: Women of the Intelligentsia in Nineteenth Century Russia* (Cambridge: Cambridge University Press, 1983).

5. Lenin, *Emancipation of Women*, p. 110.

6. Barbara Evans Clements, *Bolshevik Feminist: The Life of Aleksandra Kollontai* (Bloomington, IN: Indiana University Press, 1979); and Beatrice Farnsworth, *Aleksandra Kollontai: Socialism, Feminism, and the Bolshevik Revolution* (Stanford, CA: Stanford University Press, 1980).

7. Gregory Massell, *The Surrogate Proletariat: Moslem Women and Revolutionary Strategies in Soviet Central Asia, 1919–1929* (Princeton, NJ: Princeton University Press, 1974).

8. In the post-Stalin period, abortion once again became the primary method of birth control in the Soviet Union; see Alastair McAuley, *Women's Work and Wages in the Soviet Union* (London: Allen & Unwin, 1981), pp. 203–5.

9. Gail Warshofsky Lapidus, *Women in Soviet Society: Equality, Development, and Social Change* (Berkeley, CA: University of California Press, 1978), p. 55.

10. Gail Warshofsky Lapidus, ed., *Women, Work, and Family in the Soviet Union* (Armonk, NY: M. E. Sharpe, 1982), p. x. This volume contains translations of current Soviet articles on these topics.

11. Lapidus, *Women in Society*, p. 174.

12. *Ibid.* pp. 178–83. See also McAuley, *Women's Work;* and Michael Paul Sacks, *Women's Work in Soviet Russia: Continuity in the Midst of Change* (New York: Praeger, 1976).

13. On women's participation in the political process, see Lapidus, *Women in Society*, chap. 6; and Genia Browning, "Soviet Politics: Where Are the Women?" in Barbara Holland, ed., *Soviet Sisterhood* (Bloomington, IN: Indiana University Press, 1985).

14. Tatyana Mamonova, ed., *Women and Russia: Feminist Writings From the Soviet Union* (Boston: Beacon, 1984).

29

Law

PETER B. MAGGS

Soviet law appears to have made major steps forward during the past 30 years.[1] In 1985, for the first time since Lenin, a law school graduate—Mikhail S. Gorbachev—was chosen as the top Soviet leader. The Soviet legal profession has achieved a high degree of professional training and competence. Soviet legislation has been systematized and recodified. Legal scholars have produced useful studies and reform proposals. Individuals now feel relatively secure against the recurrence of Stalinist terror. Serious attempts are being made to use the law to solve social and economic problems. Yet, Soviet law continues to be held in low regard both by foreigners and by Soviet citizens themselves. Partly, this low esteem is due to a natural delay in the perception of improvement. Largely, however, the problem is that the Soviet legal system continues to govern the people—but not their rulers.

The legal profession suffered greatly from the continual upheavals in the period from the Bolshevik Revolution to Stalin's death.[2] The pre-Revolutionary bar was proud of its independence and committed to democratic ideals. In the inevitable conflict with the authoritarian, antidemocratic Soviet state, lawyers were treated as expendable. The bar shrank as its members emigrated, went into other professions, disappeared in purges, and died in action in World War II. It gained members selected not for their educational background but for their loyalty to the Party. The result, by the end of Stalin's rule, was a bar that was small, timid, and, for the most part, poorly trained—but that still contained a nucleus of well-educated and capable lawyers and legal scholars. In the decades since Stalin, this nucleus has provided the leadership and education for the creation of a new, expanded, better-trained, but still largely timid bar. At present almost all judges, practicing lawyers, and government attorneys are graduates of law schools that have high admissions standards and provide excellent professional preparation. Many government attorneys have gone on to obtain either degrees in additional subjects or higher degrees in law. (Law is an undergraduate subject in the Soviet Union, as it is in Europe generally).

The technical quality of Soviet legislation has been greatly improved. Within 10 years of Stalin's death certain key areas of Soviet law, such as criminal law and procedure, had been recodified. However, the bulk of Soviet legislation was in scattered and often inaccessible publications (or it remained secret and unpublished). During the 1970s and early 1980s a major codification effort took place, following closely the approach used by Mikhail Speransky to codify Tsarist legislation between 1826 and 1832. A complete collection was made of all Soviet legislation in force. Legislation in the most important areas was rewritten to eliminate obsolete and contradictory provisions. An 11-volume *Code of Laws of the USSR* was published in loose-leaf form. This form was in recognition of the fact that continuing social and economic change makes the task of codification a permanent one. The new codification greatly increased the accessibility of Soviet legislation but did not affect the long-standing practice of keeping much important legislation secret. In the 11 volumes, one finds no useful information on such matters as defense contracts, KGB operations, quotas on employment of Jews, restrictions on emigration, or special stores for the Soviet elite. Although some of this secrecy may be related to perceived needs of national security, much is due to the fact that there are many aspects of Soviet legislation that the authorities are ashamed to have seen by either the Soviet public or foreign observers.

Soviet legal scholars deserve a great deal of credit for the successful creation of an educated bar and of a codified legal system. However, they must continue to operate under substantial censorship restraints, which are particularly severe in areas where law intersects with political questions but less stringent where questions of economic efficiency are involved. They are free to advocate such relatively innocuous reforms as merger of the present weak environmental protection organizations (see chapter 13) into a single, powerful environmental protection agency or the adoption of a comprehensive consumer-protection law. They are not free to discuss falsification of evidence against dissidents by the KGB or to propose constitutional changes that would affect the political system. Sometimes they evade the censor. For instance, in April 1986 the leading Soviet legal journal published an article by a Hungarian scholar concerning the reform of Hungarian election law that implemented contested elections with more than one candidate for most offices. The Soviet reader would undoubtedly see this article as a suggestion for reexamining the farce that passes for free elections under Soviet law.

The Soviet judicial system is a hierarchy extending from the lowest courts of general jurisdiction, called "people's courts," through city or provincial courts and the supreme courts of the 15 union republics, and up to the Supreme Court of the Soviet Union. Judges are selected for legal ability and political reliability; almost all are Party members. The Soviet Union follows the continental European practice of filling vacancies on higher courts by promoting judges from lower courts, in contrast to the English and American practice of appointing outstanding practicing lawyers to the higher courts. The result is that the judges of the higher courts have a "civil servant" mentality. About 4 or 5 million cases a year are handled by the judicial system.[3] The vast majority are decided fairly, with the notable exception of political cases, which will be discussed below. There is some corruption in the court system, but it is fought vigorously and, generally, successfully.[4]

Soviet citizens may be divided into three categories in terms of their contacts with the legal system. In the first instance, citizens have such contacts in their employment relationship, with respect to their housing, as consumers, as spouses and parents, and as subjects of minor administrative sanctions. Second, criminals (and, in very rare cases, law-abiding citizens who are mistakenly accused of crimes) are subject to the system of criminal law, criminal procedure, and punishments. Finally, a very small group of dissidents—mainly persons whose religious views put them at odds with the state—are subject to arbitrary repression disguised as legal proceedings.

Labor law regulates the employment relationship. To a large extent it is administered by what is called the "trade union" system in Soviet terminology but is in essence a government labor-relations agency that has branches at each employer organization. In recent years more and more labor-law questions have been transferred from the regular court system to these trade-union agencies. Almost all aspects of the employer-employee relationship are covered by legislation. Little change has been made in recent years in the basic rules of labor law. Under this law, ordinary employees enjoy considerable job security, but executives serve at the will of their superiors and Party authorities. Workers injured on the job have a right to workmen's compensation. The vast majority of labor cases in court involve suits by employers against employees who are alleged to have negligently or intentionally caused monetary damage to the employer.

There is a long-standing policy of setting the prices of urban housing far below those that would be set in a free market by supply and demand. The result is that the legal system has to bear much of the burden of the resulting conflict between the many who are willing and able to pay for urban housing and the few for whom it is available. A comprehensive resident-permit system has been in force since the 1930s, to control migration to major cities. Changes in the law and the use of computers for record-keeping have made the system more effective. Although the basic determinant of housing allocation is a citizen's status (with preference going to Party officials, top scientists, outstanding workers, etc.), there are also laws regulating housing allocation and ownership. The combination of low lawyers' fees and a high demand for housing leads to a great deal of litigation on housing-rights questions. A gradual shift toward ownership of cooperative apartments—rather than rental of state apartments—suggests that property rights are becoming relatively more important and status relatively less important in housing matters.

As consumers Soviet citizens benefit from various legal rights vis-à-vis both state agencies and other citizens. The government sets certain warranty standards for consumer goods. Because the cost of going to court is low, citizens can and do sue when expensive consumer goods prove defective and warranty obligations are broken. Although at one time cases of peasants suing other peasants over rights to cows were common in court, modernization of Soviet society means that automobile-accident, product-liability, and medical malpractice suits are becoming more frequent. Low legal fees and a perception that courts are fair in such nonpolitical cases lead to a great willingness to resort to litigation, with the result that there are about 3 million civil court cases brought each year.

Divorce cases are the largest single category of civil court cases, constituting about one-fourth of the civil case load. This is true even though reforms have removed from the courts cases of uncontested divorces in which no dependents are involved. Such divorces can be obtained merely by signing appropriate documents and paying a small fee at the civil registry office. The vast majority of divorce cases that get to court involve couples with dependents involved in conflicts over child custody and child support. Family property disputes, such as questions of inheritance, also commonly end in litigation.

Millions of Soviet citizens are subjected to administrative penalties each year for such minor matters as violations of traffic laws or fishing regulations. Such penalties are usually imposed on the spot by the appropriate enforcement officer, for example, traffic patrolman or game warden. The legislation concerning these "administrative offenses" has been codified, and the law has been clarified as to what constitutes offenses and who can impose penalties. In theory, a hearing before a judge may be obtained to contest the imposition of an administrative penalty, but, since the penalties are small and chances of success before the judge are poor, few citizens avail themselves of this option.

There are around three-quarters of a million criminal cases tried each year. A person accused of an ordinary crime faces a system weighted toward the prosecution, but he or she does have access to capable defense counsel.[5] However, the accused may be held incommunicado for months before being allowed legal assistance. Unlike the American system, where most cases are settled on plea bargains leading to guilty pleas, under the Soviet system a trial is held in all cases, even if the defendant admits guilt. The absence of guilty pleas, the better education of prosecutors, improved pretrial investigation, and a reluctance to bring weak cases (which might lower a prosecutor's conviction rate) have led to a situation in which well over 99 percent of those brought to trial are convicted. Members of the Communist Party are subject to internal Party discipline and are typically shielded by the Party from criminal prosecution unless their offenses are so serious as to bring expulsion from the Party. Criminal penalties remain harsh, in terms of both length of sentence and conditions in labor camps.

Although the ordinary Soviet citizen has no fear that he will be struck by the kind of arbitrary terror that was common under Stalin, he knows that taking any action perceived by the regime as politically threatening will lead to serious consequences. In addition, he knows that the safeguards and fairness that characterize ordinary Soviet civil and criminal cases will not stand in the way of a decision to deal with him as a political offender. Immediately after Stalin's death, the practice of sending large numbers of citizens to labor camps without a trial was abolished. Millions of innocent persons who had suffered from Stalinist terror were legally rehabilitated, as has been noted (chapter 3). A new system of using law for political control emerged. This system has undergone some evolution, with respect to both the kind of activities that are tolerated and the way in which sanctions are imposed. There are at least three major categories of activity that are likely to entail politically motivated legal sanctions: (1) saying or writing things perceived as politically threatening; (2) formation of any sort of group or the holding of any political meeting not approved of and controlled by the Party; and (3) applying to emigrate. I will discuss each in turn.

Restrictions on communication of ideas and information operate differently on the state-owned media versus private citizens. In the public media, again as we have seen (chapters 23 and 25), the most important method of control of speech is through the placing in positions of power of persons who know and will enforce Party policy. No book is published without being read by an editorial board that checks it for political acceptability. In particularly important cases, top Party leaders may intervene directly to enforce a particular policy. For many years a formal censorship agency has made a prepublication check of almost all publications, and it signifies its approval by assigning a censorship number that is included in the printed publication data. The details of legislation on the operation of this censorship are secret. Under Gorbachev, Party policy allowed somewhat more liberal reporting of news events and somewhat greater latitude to investigative reporting. And apparently the corresponding censorship guidelines have been revised.

Literature and social science were more free in the early 1960s than at any time since, and at this writing it is not clear whether censorship in these areas will ease significantly. In the public media, censorship is generally prior censorship. Sometimes, however, laxity by the censors or a change in policy results in a situation in which a person has published something that does not correspond to what is currently permitted to be said. In such a case the author may suffer the negative consequences described below—and despite the protections of the labor laws. Contrary to what seems to be a popular impression in the West, there is nothing illegal about an individual publishing his own uncensored writings, as long as the content of the writings contains nothing political or pornographic. Such publication is difficult, however, because the government has a monopoly on printing presses and copying machines, leaving individuals to use carbon paper or to copy audio or videotape cassettes. And if the content of such unofficial publication is politically unacceptable, the writer will suffer adverse consequences through the legal system—usually in an indirect way: loss of job, problems with residence permits, or prosecution on real or trumped-up charges for ordinary criminal offenses. But prosecution directly for a crime such as "anti-Soviet agitation and propaganda" is also possible.

Formation of any sort of unauthorized group for political purposes is almost certain to lead to severe sanctions. For example, some of the founders of a free trade union were placed in psychiatric hospitals, and others faced a variety of sanctions such as loss of jobs and residence permits. Most dissidents in labor camps are there for participating in religious organizations that refuse to bow to the state control that is required by the law (much of it unpublished) governing all officially permitted religious organizations. It has been rumored that officially recognized religious organizations will be given an improved legal status, the full right of "legal personality," involving the power to own property, make contracts, sue, and be sued. However, this improved status would not apply to the unauthorized religious groups discussed in chapter 27.

The mere filing of an application to emigrate typically results in a Soviet citizen's being fired from his job. Any provisions of labor law that might stand in the way are disregarded. Applicants for emigration must have the approval of their parents, who likewise will be persecuted if they approve. Some would-be emigrants are subject to further difficulties, such as prosecution for "parasitism" for not having a job, loss of apartments, or loss of residence permits. Despite the regularization in 1986 of the procedures for applying to emigrate, there is no judicial remedy for any of the difficulties connected with actually doing so.

A peculiar feature of Soviet law is the "campaign." A particular type of conduct is singled out for attack, and a variety of legal measures are brought to bear on it. Successes are announced, but eventually the campaign fades away, often without having made lasting changes in behavior. Often campaigns have seemed to depend on the personal prejudices of top Soviet leaders. More recently, campaigns have been undertaken after serious social science research has analyzed a problem in Soviet society and suggested some ways to correct it. There have been three major campaigns in recent years. One, under Yury Andropov (1982–84), was aimed at improving labor discipline. Penalties for absenteeism, appearing drunk on the job, and causing damage to the employer's property were increased. Workers were required to give longer notice to quit their job. Next, a well-publicized campaign launched in 1985 under Gorbachev aimed to reduce alcohol consumption by restricting planned production, restricting hours of sale, and raising prices. A third campaign, also launched under Gorbachev, was aimed at "nonlabor income." It included a stiffening of income-tax collections from persons privately employed, more serious penalties for improperly taking or using state property and for bribery, and a requirement that buyers of expensive items, such as houses and cars, file statements showing where they got the purchase money.

Indeed, Soviet law is of great importance in the operation of the Soviet economy. Although ultimate economic policy is set by the Politburo, and although Party organizations at many levels can intervene in economic decision making, it is the law that specifies the structure and operating rules of the economy, the powers of the various organizations that engage in economic activities, and the relations between these organizations and their employees. A little historical background may help in understanding current developments in legal regulation of economic activity, the last aspect of Soviet law that I will take up here.

In the early years of the Revolution, the new Bolshevik government tried to operate factories, stores, and railroads on direct orders from civil servants, without the use of such traditional legal institutions as corporations and contracts. The result was an economic disaster, which led to the New Economic Policy of the early 1920s. This policy had two components: (1) a limited retreat to private capitalism in agriculture, light industry, and retail trade; and (2) a complete reorganization of the government sector of the economy, which was put under the control of state-owned corporations operating on a profit-and-loss basis, making contracts, and having the capacity to sue and be sued. By the mid-1930s, however, the private capitalists had been eliminated—private farming, in particular, having been abolished by the notorious collectivization campaign. Yet, the system of operating the economy not through direct orders but indirectly through the operation of state-owned corporations prevailed. Stalin added to it the important element of central planning of all important aspects of economic activity, and since then the most basic features of the legal structure of the economy have remained unchanged. On the other hand, the details have changed constantly, as the leadership has searched for ways to fulfill the incompatible goals of economic efficiency and centralized power.

At present, economic operations are carried out by economic entities of various types and sizes. Each is a separate government-owned corporation, with its own balance sheet. Each is expected to cover its expenses from its income. Most economic activity is carried on by relatively large entities called "production associations," which typically are directly subordinate to industrial ministries. The State Planning Committee (*Gosplan*) formulates legally binding general plans that are then made more specific and transmitted to the individual production associations by the responsible ministries. These plans include a binding production plan and a plan for the supply of goods from other production associations and for the delivery of goods to other production associations. Although in some cases production associations may contract freely with one another, most contracts are required by plan, leaving only some details to be negotiated between the parties. Legal disputes can arise either when contracts are concluded or in the course of contract performance. In both instances, these disputes go to a special system of tribunals, called "Arbitrazh," for resolution. These tribunals handle only disputes between state agencies and deal with a total of about half a million such disputes a year. Their staff is highly knowledgeable about the legal regulations governing the economy.

Agriculture has been under a legal system different from that of industry and retail trade. Collective farms have had nominal independence, though they have long been subject to detailed "guidance" by local Party organizations. Recent changes in the law, involving the creation of a hierarchy of government "agro-industrial" management organizations, have brought the farms much closer to the legal position of industrial organizations. In a discussion on Soviet television, General Secretary Gorbachev, who has studied both law and agricultural economics, showed a clear understanding of the current issues in Soviet agricultural law and promised further changes.

A potentially major development has occurred in foreign-trade law. For decades, foreign trade has been monopolized by specialized foreign-trade organizations subordinate to the Ministry of Foreign Trade (chapter 18). Almost all sales and purchases have been channeled through these organizations, regardless of which Soviet organization was the producer or the end user. The result was a high degree of control of foreign-trade transactions, obtained at the expense of isolating producers from customers' needs and Soviet enterprises from easy relations with foreign sources of technology. A reform announced in 1986 would allow some 70 major organizations to conclude commercial arrangements directly with foreign trading partners, thus bringing the Soviet Union somewhat more into the mainstream of the world economy. At the same time, another reform somewhat expanded the decades-old practice of limited legal permissibility of individual enterprise in the domestic economy, adding some new categories and some ideological respectability to private operations in services such as auto or appliance repair, music or language instruction, and the making for private sale of shoes, clothing, or toys. The new law is part of the ongoing recodification of Soviet legislation referred to earlier in this chapter. It legalizes and taxes some types of private enterprise that were previously part of the underground economy but continues the prohibition on the use of hired labor in private business operations.

We might note that in both cases—in the regulation of both foreign trade and domestic private enterprise—Soviet law has been the instrument of potentially important change in the Soviet Union. The same can be said, as I have tried to indicate, with respect to other areas of Soviet life. However, the increasing flexibility and sophistication with which law is being used by the Party leadership to carry out its policies should not be taken to mean that the leadership will soon submit itself to any significant legal restraints.

NOTES

1. Two surveys of the Soviet legal system are William E. Butler, *Soviet Law* (London: Butterworths, 1983); and Olimpiad S. Ioffe and Peter B. Maggs, *Soviet Law in Theory and Practice* (New York: Oceana, 1983).

2. An excellent historical study is Eugene Huskey, *Russian Lawyers and the Soviet State: The Origins and Development of the Soviet Bar 1917–1939* (Princeton, NJ: Princeton University Press, 1986).

3. Despite the fact that most Soviet judicial statistics are secret, a Dutch scholar has been able to piece together a detailed statistical picture of the operation of the Soviet courts; see Ger P. van den Berg, *The Soviet System of Justice: Figures and Policy* (Dordrecht: Martinus Nijhoff, 1985).

4. See Konstantin Simis, USSR: *the Corrupt Society: The Secret World of Soviet Capitalism* (New York: Simon & Schuster, 1982), chap. 4.

5. Dina Kaminskaya, *Final Judgment: My Life as a Soviet Defense Attorney* (New York: Simon & Schuster, 1982).

30

A Troubled Society

DAVID E. POWELL

For most of the twentieth century Russian and Soviet society has experienced intense turmoil. World War I was an enormous cataclysm—and not only because millions of Russians were killed, wounded, or captured in this meaningless crusade. The conflict meant the forcible uprooting of millions of peasants; it produced destruction and devastation on a vast scale; and it led to peasant land seizures in the countryside and bread riots in the cities. Finally, it brought about the fall of the Russian monarchy and then of the Provisional Government that had replaced it.

The "Great October Socialist Revolution" of 1917, foreign military intervention, and the Civil War were followed by a famine that took more than 2 million lives and left the rest of the population exhausted and terrified. Although the New Economic Policy of the 1920s provided a brief respite, the population continued to experience other forms of pressure and disruption. The secret police, the Party, and the *Komsomol* (the Party's youth affiliate) carried out a campaign of terror against organized religion. More generally, the authorities initiated a wide-ranging program of undermining traditional loyalties and relationships. Church and state were separated, as were church and school; women were "liberated" to pursue their own educational, family, and career objectives; and children were encouraged to identify with the new "progressive" regime rather than remain in thrall to "backward" parental authority.

The late 1920s witnessed the beginning of what some have termed the *real* Russian revolution, the so-called "revolution from above" that Stalin imposed on the masses. His policies entailed collectivization of agriculture (the establishment of collective and state farms), rapid industrialization, and the introduction of Five-Year Plans with their all-but-impossible quotas and demands for "labor discipline."

Exceedingly high rates of investment, low wages, crowded housing, and an assembly-line speedup took a heavy toll on ordinary citizens, but the regime was unremitting and remorseless. In 1931, the head of the Institute for the Protection of Labor denounced as anti-Soviet the "fatigue theory" or "protective fatigue theory"—that is, the notion that the feeling of weariness is a "warning signal indicating that further exertion may have consequences harmful to the human organism." Anyone who argued otherwise was to be unmasked and declared a "class enemy"—not just scientifically incorrect but politically subversive. A 1932 law stipulated that persons who failed to appear for work without a valid reason could be dismissed, deprived of the right to use a ration card, and evicted from the apartment that had been allocated by the enterprise.

At the same time, the apparatus of terror was turned into an instrument designed to atomize society. Informers, spies, and incessant propaganda about "the class enemy" and the need to "intensify the class struggle" made it all but impossible for people to speak candidly, joke, or even relax. Officials called for eternal vigilance, and society had no choice but to accept their admonitions. The implications for relations within the family, between friends, and among fellow workers were devastating. The very authorities who sang the praises of collectivism were, of course, doing their best to destroy the ties that had linked society for centuries. For a time—but not forever—they were extraordinarily successful.

The constant fear of arbitrary arrest, incarceration, execution, or banishment to the camps did not end with the outbreak of World War II. The seizure and absorption of eastern Poland in 1939 and of the Baltic states in 1940 were accompanied by large-scale arrests and deportations. After the German invasion of the Soviet Union in 1941, Stalin ordered the forcible deportation of several million Volga Germans, Crimean Tatars, Chechen, Ingushi, Karachai, and other minority nationalities from their homelands inside the Soviet Union—the Volga Germans in 1941, the others in 1943 to 1944. Most were hauled off in boxcars and resettled in Kazakhstan, Central Asia, and Siberia. Thousands of these unfortunate individuals, regarded by Stalin as a potential fifth column ready to collaborate with the invader, perished on route to their new homes.

The war itself and its effects on Soviet society probably cannot be comprehended by an outsider. Some 20 million Soviet citizens died as a result of the German invasion, either in battle or from starvation or disease. Paradoxically, World War II wound up reinforcing powerful feelings of national pride and patriotism that the Soviet regime was desperately anxious to foster. Thus, even though Marx and Engels had taught that "workingmen of the world" had no country, Stalin encouraged his countrymen to see the conflict with Germany as "The Great Patriotic War" or "The Great War for the Motherland." Many of the controls that had been placed on the various churches were relaxed, and official propaganda likened the struggle against the Nazis to earlier battles to cast out other cruel invaders. There was an enormous upsurge of patriotic feeling, a willingness to sacrifice, and an identification of personal goals and feelings with those of the Soviet state. Society, in a sense, was reconstituted under the terrifying pressure of war.

The postwar years witnessed a return to many of the policies that had stifled Soviet society in the 1930s. The need to reconstruct the country's industrial base as quickly as possible meant housing that was as shabby as it was crowded and consumer goods that were limited in quantity and of poor quality.

Minimal attention was given to developing the agricultural sector and improving the people's diet. Long hours of hard work without commensurate rewards inevitably gave rise to low labor productivity, spoiled and defective goods, and to a labor force that made a mockery of the propaganda image of smiling men and women enthusiastically setting new production records. The situation in the countryside was, if anything, worse: an irrational system of incentives and rewards, along with a shocking lack of investment capital, kept the collective-farm system and the population that worked it backward and miserable.

Not until Stalin's death in 1953 could the authorities begin to improve their ties with society. They did so in ways that were both dramatic and subtle. Perhaps most important was the elimination of mass terror: Lavrenty Beria and other secret-police officials were arrested and shot as enemies of the people, and millions of ordinary men and women were released from labor camps. Promising "a return to Leninist norms of socialist legality," the Communist Party reasserted its control over all social and economic institutions and in large measure removed the arbitrariness that had prevailed under Stalin.

There was also a major effort to raise the standard of living, to reduce the differences between mental and physical labor, and to bring the quality of life in rural areas up to that of urban residents. These policies were implemented by improving the quantity and quality of health care, offering better educational opportunities and higher wages, and providing more consumer goods. A massive program of housing construction was undertaken, the minimum wage and old-age pensions were increased, and vastly greater attention was devoted to a variety of other social welfare programs. All of these measures, it would appear, were designed to demonstrate the regime's solicitude for the masses and, to use John F. Kennedy's famous phrase, "to get this country moving again." At a further remove, the new approach may well have involved an attempt to prove what the Communist Party leadership had long claimed: "The Party and the people are one!"

Although Lenin and especially Stalin brought about the deaths of millions of people, most of those who survived (and, even more so, their descendants) have witnessed genuine improvements in Soviet society. Before the Revolution, life expectancy among women in Russia was 33; today it is 74. Among men, the figure rose from 31 to a high of 66 in the mid-1960s. A similar development can be traced for infant mortality. According to official data, in 1913 more than one out of every four children (268.6 per 1,000 live births) died before the age of one year. By 1971, that figure had fallen to 22.9, an astonishing improvement in little more than half a century.

In the main, both the increase in life expectancy and the drop in infant mortality can be attributed to successful efforts in public health and sanitation. The authorities brought under control many of the life-threatening diseases that had affected infants and young children, and they did away with epidemics and certain debilitating illnesses. They trained more physicians and built more hospitals and clinics than did their counterparts anywhere else, and they introduced an elaborate program of prevention and early detection of disease. Despite continuing problems—rural-urban differences, technological backwardness, shortages of medicines and equipment, the generally low quality of medical care, and so on—the overall improvement in public health since the Revolution represents one of the truly extraordinary accomplishments of the Soviet regime.

Increasing degrees of freedom, prosperity, and modernity are, however, by no means incompatible with retrograde social developments. As the U.S. experience with environmental pollution, drug abuse, youth alienation, and vandalism suggests, less rigid social control in a time of expanding prosperity can give rise to various threats to the social order. Recent years in the Soviet Union have witnessed an increase in infant mortality, along with a drop in male life expectancy. Although the precise dimensions and timing of these shifts cannot be ascertained with total assurance—the statistical agencies in Moscow have refused to release certain data and have maintained a policy of strict secrecy with respect to other questions—it is clear that public-health standards have deteriorated in the past decade or two.

Before the partial embargo was placed on health-related information, official statistics acknowledged that male life expectancy had fallen from 66 to 64 by the end of the 1960s. No new data have been made public since then. The situation with respect to infant mortality is somewhat—but only somewhat—easier to discern. For a number of reasons (primarily increases in drinking and smoking, widespread ecological damage, and a drop in the quality and availability of basic foodstuffs), this figure began to rise after 1971. From its low of 22.9 in that year, it increased steadily, finally reaching 27.9 in 1974. A year later, the major statistical handbook (*Narodnoe khoziaistvo sssr*) ceased providing information on this subject.

After a decade of silence, the Central Statistical Administration (TsSU) suddenly and inexplicably released some of the missing data. While continuing to conceal some information (presumably out of embarrassment), the TsSU asserted that infant mortality had fallen to 27.3 in 1980 and to 25.3 in 1983. Since then, however, the figure has begun to move upward once again: in 1984, it rose to 25.9, and in 1985, it reached 26.0.[2] How to account for either the downward or the upward shift in these statistics remains a mystery; indeed, the changes may involve a certain amount of chicanery— new definitions, doctored data, or some other device known only to officials in Moscow and designed to conceal the true dimensions of an appalling human tragedy. (The current U.S. infant-mortality figure, it should be noted, is 10.6 per 1,000 live births; most West European countries have achieved even lower levels of infant mortality.)

Other demographic developments have more in common with the West. Thus, the Soviet population, like that of most other advanced industrial societies, has been growing older. The number of persons of pension age (55 and above for women, 60 and above for men) increases with each passing year. On the eve of World War II, approximately 9 percent of the population were eligible for retirement, but by 1959 the proportion had increased to 12 percent. The 1970 census revealed that the figure had risen to 15 percent, and even though the necessary data from the 1979 census were never published, Soviet experts put the figure at 15.5 percent today. One of every 15 individuals in 1959 was 60 or older; the proportion today is one of eight.[3]

The "graying" of the population has important implications for the country's manpower situation. Inasmuch as the process is expected to continue for the next several decades at least, prospects for continued economic development may well be severely threatened. While greater numbers of pensioners will place increased burdens on the planners' resources, lower birthrates will deprive the economy of badly needed workers for industry, construction, and agriculture. Young people are waiting longer before marrying, and married couples are deferring still further the decision to have a child. As a rule, those who do have children have fewer than their parents did, and this trend will probably continue. In fact, given the dramatic decline in marriage rates and the equally striking increase in divorce rates, it is clear that the population will continue to expand at a slow pace.

The rate of growth of the Soviet labor force has fallen even more sharply—and promises to continue to do so. According to two U.S. government specialists, the rate of expansion during the period 1970–90 will be only one-third of that which prevailed between 1950 and 1970. Central Intelligence Agency analysts predict that annual increments to the Soviet Union's working-age population will average less than 500,000 during the 1980s; the average figure for the 1976–80 Five-Year Plan period was 2,029,000 persons per year.[4]

As recently as 1950, more than one-fourth of the Soviet population was not involved in "social production" or full-time study; today, the figure is a mere 5 percent. In the past, additions to the work force could be secured by recruiting both women who were engaged in household work and rural dwellers who devoted their time to farming their private plots. But these reserves have essentially disappeared. Further, the relatively small 1960s generation who are entering the 1980s labor force will be unable to replace the much larger 1920s generation who are leaving it.

In an effort to cope with this situation, the authorities have moved in several directions. First, the educational system has been modified: the proportion of general-secondary-school graduates admitted to institutions of higher learning has declined and vocational training in the secondary schools has been expanded. Second, more resources have been channeled into preschool (or day-care) institutions, so that today 43.3 percent of all children under the age of seven years are enrolled in nurseries or kindergartens. Third, the regime has been increasing its use of child labor. According to one Soviet source, 10 million school children were responsible for production valued at 400 million rubles (approximately $560 million at the then official rate of exchange) in 1977 alone.[5]

Efforts have also been made to utilize older men and women in the work force. Planners have been recruiting retirees and encouraging workers who are approaching pension age to remain on the job. In 1965, only 12 percent of all pensioners living in the Russian Republic had jobs, but a decade later the percentage had doubled. In 1977, some 24 percent of all people of retirement age were employed in the public sector; today, the figure is 30 percent, which means that 7 million men and women eligible for pensions have decided to stay at work. When asked, most of these individuals mention financial need; but almost as many cite such motives as wanting to maintain ties with their fellow workers or to feel that they are doing something useful with their lives. Because wages have gone up far more rapidly than pensions, it is likely that this trend will continue.

Since Stalin's death, Soviet citizens have been permitted and even encouraged to seek employment opportunities that suit their needs. As a result, they have become increasingly sophisticated and demanding about where they are willing to work. Although there is nothing inherently harmful about men and women changing jobs— in a number of respects this is a healthy process for both the individual and the system—so many workers (approximately 22 percent) are doing so that labor turnover has become rather troublesome to Soviet planners.

When workers from factories or areas with a manpower surplus move to enterprises or localities suffering a labor shortage, the result is a gain for all. People attracted by higher wages or other inducements to new enterprises and construction projects, especially those in remote areas, can be put to especially good use. In addition, recent efforts to release superfluous workers from some enterprises have contributed to a more rational distribution of the labor force.

But there is widespread agreement that the level of job turnover in the Soviet Union today is not within acceptable limits. Soviet specialists have termed it "harmful" and say that it is "not justified by any objective need." They term it "a barrier to the progress of society," "a disease," and "a social evil which requires opposition on a joint and organized basis." The data they cite clearly indicate that the large numbers of workers quitting their jobs create economic problems for the enterprises they leave, for those they join, and for themselves and their families.

According to Soviet estimates, between 40 and 75 percent of those who change their place of work also change their occupation. Money initially spent for specialized training is therefore wasted, and new funds are required for retraining. Moreover, low morale and high labor turnover contribute to on-the-job injuries, introduce uncertainties into the housing market, cause a deterioration in "the psychological climate of work collectives," and lead to violations of "labor and social discipline." Sample surveys indicate that most violators of labor discipline have held a given job for only a brief time; they also suggest that some 75–80 percent of the workers who do not fulfill their production quotas have worked at their jobs for less than a year, and one study found that fully 60 percent of all defective goods produced at a particular enterprise were the work of individuals who had been employed there for less than a year.

In an effort to curb high rates of turnover, the authorities have tried to reward more conscientious workers and to punish "slackers" and "rolling stones." In the past decade, however, a number of Soviet sociologists and industrial psychologists have pointed out that the lack of industrial democracy—Soviet workers have virtually no influence over their wages, hours, or working conditions—has given rise to feelings of powerlessness. Such feelings in turn present a major barrier to job satisfaction and to raising productivity. The specialists argue that industrial morale will improve only if a more democratic "microclimate" is established at individual enterprises—if, that is, "everybody, regardless of his position, feels that he is significant and necessary." Some have urged that workers be permitted—even encouraged—to acquire a sense of ownership and have called for their participation in industrial planning and management. Such an approach would involve bringing ordinary workers into the decision-making process in individual shops and factories, thus encouraging personnel at all levels to help eliminate production bottlenecks and to participate in the setting of work norms and wage rates.

However laudable these proposals are—and whether or not they could help raise the level of job satisfaction and so increase labor productivity—it is highly unlikely that there will be anything more than cosmetic change in this sphere. Just as Marx observed a century ago that "no ruling class ever voluntarily gives up state power," the State Planning Committee (*Gosplan*), the Communist Party, and the managerial elite are hardly likely to give up their control over the labor force. Furthermore, the Yugoslav experience with workers' councils, as well as the more recent Polish experience with the independent trade union Solidarity, cannot help but reinforce the determination of Soviet officials to cling tenaciously to their power.

The post-Stalin relaxation of controls on population movement has resulted in large-scale voluntary shifts of people from the countryside to the cities and from one area of the country to another. According to official data, 65.6 percent of the population now live in urban areas—although the Soviet conception of "urban areas" and "urban-type settlements" entails a much less concentrated pattern of residence than other countries consider requisite for application of such terms. Still, a massive exodus from the villages has undeniably occurred, an exodus that until very recently showed no signs of slowing. Annually for the past 30 years or more some 1.5–2.0 million rural dwellers have migrated to the cities. The movement has not been spontaneous or unexpected; indeed, it has resulted primarily from official policy. Committed to a program of industrial development that required the skills of a large, urban labor force—and perhaps sharing the contempt of Marx and Engels for "the idiocy of rural life"—the government had actively encouraged peasants and their children to leave the countryside. Until a decade or so ago, the authorities welcomed urbanization, viewing it as a prerequisite for industrialization and economic development as well as a means of increasing social mobility and bringing "backward" citizens into the socioeconomic mainstream. Now, however, they are reassessing their unqualified endorsement of the process and are beginning to place restrictions on this movement.

Rural-to-urban migration is primarily a movement of teenagers and those in their twenties and early thirties. In the main, it is "the best and the brightest," the young people with energy, ambition, and skills who abandon the farm and make their way to the city. Machine operators (tractor drivers, truck drivers, and combine operators, among others) as well as members of the rural intelligentsia (schoolteachers, librarians, agronomists, or economists) are especially anxious to leave. Those who go to the countryside on obligatory assignments after finishing their education in the city generally leave as soon as their period of required service is up.

In a classic study of migrants and potential migrants, T. I. Zaslavskaia found that most respondents pointed to the quality of life in the city as the primary inducement to leave home.[6] In particular, they cited the diversity of the urban environment, better working conditions, more interesting and more remunerative jobs, more and better services, and better opportunities to continue their own education or that of their children. Zaslavskaia was bold enough to add that younger men and women not only found farm work uninteresting but also were frustrated because they were not "masters of the land." Yet, if the point is well taken, it is difficult to believe that the system of socialized agriculture will soon be abandoned. Collectivization was introduced for *political* rather than for economic reasons, and the same factors that mandate Party control over industry ensure that socialized agriculture will persist for the foreseeable future.

The Soviet authorities still view the rural exodus as "a historically legitimate, progressive process," one required by "the objective laws of social development." Yet officials and specialists alike are becoming increasingly uneasy with some of its consequences. There are four major areas of concern.

• Rural dwellers tend to move to the city from precisely those areas (Siberia and the Urals) that already suffer from manpower shortages, whereas villagers in areas of surplus manpower (Central Asia, Moldavia, and the Caucasus) have been the most reluctant to leave for the cities. Few individuals, whether peasants or urban residents, are anxious to move to the energy-producing areas of Siberia or to the Sino-Soviet border.

• People who reach the city tend to marry later and to have smaller families than those who remain in the village. There has also been a sharp decline in rural birthrates, largely because of the departure of men and women in their twenties and early thirties. In view of the labor shortage, official concern is clearly warranted.

• The enormous influx of rural folk into Soviet cities has led to or exacerbated a wide array of urban problems, ranging from crowded housing, crime, and delinquency to emotional disorders and marital instability. Statistics on crime and delinquency in the Soviet Union continue to be a state secret (as they have been since 1927), but increasingly frequent and pointed press coverage of such matters strongly suggests that antisocial behavior among the young is getting out of hand.

• Finally, uncontrolled rural out-migration has been found to be "in conflict with the needs of agricultural production." The most competent and promising youngsters abandon the land, leaving the farms to older, less skilled, and less productive workers. Soviet studies showing a decrease in the rural population generally have revealed an even sharper drop among those of working age. In fact, most research actually underestimates the disparity between young and old, since persons listed as "able-bodied workers" on some collective farms include women whose husbands work at nearby enterprises. These women remain on the farms to cultivate their private plots for family needs, contributing little to the collective's effort.

Until Mikhail Gorbachev came to power in 1985, alcohol consumption had been increasing at a dramatic rate throughout the Soviet Union and among virtually all population subgroups. Official sources acknowledge that between 1940 and 1980, when the country's population went up by some 36 percent, sales of alcoholic beverages increased almost eightfold. From 1970 to 1980, when the population grew by 9 percent, alcohol sales rose by 77 percent. Although some of these increases can be attributed to higher prices, it is clear that current levels of alcohol consumption are more than just a modern version of the traditional Russian "drinking problem." Indeed, according to the American economist Vladimir Treml, in the early 1980s the Soviet Union ranked first in the world in consumption of distilled spirits. Furthermore, Treml found that per-capita consumption of alcohol—including beer, wine, vodka, etc. (whether produced legally by state agencies or illicitly by ordinary citizens)—had been growing by 4.4 percent annually, that is, more rapidly than in all but a handful of the world's countries.[7]

An increase in consumption levels, even of this magnitude, does not necessarily imply a commensurate increase in alcohol abuse or alcoholism. Yet there has in fact been an enormous increase in problem drinking. A professor at the Academy of the Ministry of Internal Affairs reported in 1980 that 37 percent of the country's male workers abuse alcoholic beverages, and other Soviet analysts have expressed dismay at the rapid growth of alcohol-related crime, motor vehicle accidents, on-the-job injuries, birth defects, and similar misfortunes.

According to Boris M. Segal, a physician who carried out a large-scale study of the drinking habits of the Soviet population in the 1960s, the highest incidence of drinking and alcoholism occurred in the Russian Republic. There, 91 percent of the adult population were "drinkers" (that is, not abstainers), and 11 percent of the population over the age of 15 and 13 perent of those over 21 could be classified as alcoholics. The other two Slavic republics, Belorussia and the Ukraine, showed rates of alcoholism almost as high, and the three Baltic republics (Estonia, Latvia, and Lithuania) ranked fourth, fifth, and sixth. Throughout the country as a whole, Segal's data indicated, 44 percent of citizens 15 years of age or older drank, in contrast to 95 percent of those of Russian nationality. In regions of high wine consumption, primarily the Caucasus and Moldavia, there was a striking discrepancy between "the relatively high incidence of drinking and the relatively low incidence of alcoholism." The lowest figures for drinking and alcoholism were found among Jews and among Moslems residing in the Central Asian republics.[8]

Alcohol abuse is particularly widespread among poorly educated and relatively unskilled urban blue-collar workers, although other groups are by no means immune. But what seems to be especially troublesome to the authorities is the increased incidence of drinking and problem drinking among women and teenagers. Scientists, scholars, journalists, and public health law–enforcement officials have expressed genuine alarm at these changes, arguing that problem drinking poses a grave threat to society and to the economy.

In the Soviet Union today, alcoholism and associated diseases are the third leading cause of death; only cardiovascular diseases and cancer rank higher. In fact, given the close correlation between heavy drinking on the one hand and cardiovascular problems and cancer on the other, many specialists are inclined to place alcoholism first.

There is perhaps even more concern about the link between alcoholism and birth defects. The dramatic rise in alcoholism among women—which is far more rapid than that among men—has been accompanied by increasing numbers of miscarriages, premature births, and low-birth-weight and brain-damaged babies. Medical journals and the popular press note that among the offspring of female alcoholics there is a higher incidence of infant mortality, mental retardation, and a variety of serious physical defects.

Many other ills are associated with alcohol abuse in the Soviet Union. For example, approximately half of all divorces are attributed to drinking problems: in study after study, drunkenness is cited more than any other factor as a reason for the wife initiating divorce proceedings. Suicide, too, is often linked with alcohol. Soviet researchers have determined that more than half of all men and women who take their own lives are not sober when they do so, and one investigation found that almost half of those who committed or attempted suicide were alcoholics.[9]

The consumption of alcoholic beverages is also closely associated with crime and delinquency. Data from the 1920s indicate that 23–25 percent of persons convicted of crimes were drunk when they committed the act; today, approximately half (estimates range from 45 to 63 percent) of all crimes are committed by people who are intoxicated. Certain categories of criminal behavior are especially strongly correlated with drunkenness. Some 60 percent of all thefts and more than 80 percent of all robberies are attributed to intoxicated individuals. Figures for crimes against the person conform to this pattern: 74 percent of all premeditated murders, 76 percent of all rapes, and more than 90 percent of all acts of "hooliganism" (a highly elastic term that covers behavior ranging from disturbing the peace to assault and assault and battery) are the acts of people who were drunk at the time.[10]

It is unclear whether the Soviet authorities can prevent the situation from getting worse. They have raised the price of alcoholic beverages repeatedly; reduced the number of retail liquor outlets; introduced a wide array of criminal and civil penalties; disseminated anti-alcohol propaganda in the mass media, at schools, and at workplaces; and have tried in many other ways to curb people's desire to drink. The most recent of these efforts began on May 17, 1985, with the announcement that the Party Central Committee had adopted a resolution "On Measures to Eliminate Drunkenness and Alcoholism." Like most pronouncements issued on this subject in recent decades, the resolution focuses on four major concerns: (1) the need to expand programs of medical care for alcoholics; (2) the need for more vigorous law enforcement in order "to put a stop to violations of the regulations governing trade in alcoholic beverages and to eliminate home-brewing as well as speculation in alcohol;" (3) the need for more and better recreational facilities, along with a determined effort to organize and supervise the leisure-time activities of ordinary citizens; and (4) the need to improve anti-alcohol propaganda, especially among schoolchildren and other young people.

The new decree was critical of earlier attempts to control the population's drinking habits. It said that they invariably had degenerated into "short-term campaigns, without the requisite degree of organization and consistency," and promised that this time there would be *real* change. To date, the results of Gorbachev's assault on problem drinking are mixed. On the one hand, official data point to a sharp reduction in the production and sales of alcoholic beverages. Comparing the period June 1985–May 1986 with the same period a year earlier, one finds that the production of vodka and liqueurs declined by 33 percent, cognac by 44 percent, grape wine by 32 percent, and fruit and berry wines (which were found to contain excessive quantities of various contaminants and thus are scheduled to be phased out in the near future) by 68 percent. Similarly, Soviet sources contend that the number of fatal accidents attributable to on-the-job drinking has fallen by 20 percent; lost work-time caused by absenteeism (generally attributed to drunkenness or to a hangover caused by the previous evening's overindulgence) has dropped by 33 percent in industry and by 40 percent in construction; and the number of motor-vehicle accidents involving drivers who are intoxicated has declined by 15 percent. There are also claims of sharp reductions in the number of deaths from "accidents, poisonings, and injuries" as well as from diseases of the cardiovascular system. These developments, too, are said to be "attributable chiefly to the influence of [the new] measures to combat drunkenness and alcoholism."[11]

On the other hand, there is a good deal of evidence suggesting that officials and ordinary citizens alike are treating the May 1985 decree as just another "campaign." For example, *Pravda* pointed out (June 11, 1986) that "many" Party and government organizations, "content with their first partial results, have recently let up in their effort to eradicate drunkenness and . . . are exhibiting [an air] of smugness and complacency." Three months later, the Party Control Committee pointed to "serious shortcomings" in the anti-alcohol struggle. The hoarding of vodka and wine for purposes of speculation (for selling at a profit), as well as the sale of alcohol to persons under the age of 21, "have become widespread," the committee declared. It also noted "many instances" of the continuing sale of alcoholic beverages at stores and restaurants located next to industrial enterprises, schools, day-care centers, and various recreational facilities. In some parts of the country—generally those located far from Moscow or Leningrad—vodka and wine were being sold on days when they were supposed to be unavailable; indeed, the Ministry of Trade seemed at times to be all but indifferent to its legal obligations.

Even if it is too early to assess the overall effectiveness of the program (much less predict its likely future course), there are powerful reasons for remaining skeptical. Gorbachev and his colleagues are confronted with a country whose history has produced a distinctive "drinking culture," one that has made alcohol an integral part of most people's everyday life. Similarly, although some Soviet officials have recommended the introduction of a "dry law" (a complete prohibition of the production and sale of alcoholic beverages), the risks involved in such a policy might well outweigh the potential rewards. The existing problem of illicitly manufactured liquor presumably would grow worse; this, in turn, would lead to public-health and law-enforcement difficulties that the regime would prefer not to face. Besides, the sale of alcoholic beverages is highly remunerative, providing the state with its single largest source of revenue. The reduction in sales that has been achieved to date has already led to budgetary shortfalls, and unless the production of soft drinks, ice cream, jam, and other putative substitutes for liquor can be increased sharply, official income and expenditures will continue to diverge. Finally, the Gorbachev administration must be at least somewhat apprehensive about the political implications of its policies. For centuries, people have looked to alcohol as a way to help them escape their travails. What will happen if the regime is unable to raise living standards, increase the volume and quality of consumer goods, and make available high-quality foodstuffs while

Soviet citizens are denied their traditional outlet for pressures that they find too burdensome?

Turmoil has marked Russian and Soviet society since the beginning of the century. Before the Bolshevik coup, most of this turmoil consisted of anomalies—disruptive incidents and episodes that appeared against a backdrop of conservative institutions and processes. By contrast, since 1917 the Communist Party has deliberately sought to engineer a social and economic transformation—and to this end has consciously revolutionized the country.

As the years have gone by, however, and as the regime has consolidated itself, it has been increasingly inclined to pursue conservative rather than radical policies. The authorities reward hard work and obedience while punishing those who deviate from prescribed norms. Personal values and behaviors are also, in the main, highly conventional. Children go to school; are taught to be respectful toward their elders; and are enjoined to seek good grades, admission to an institution of higher learning, and a comfortable white-collar job. Adults tend to be highly family oriented and anxious to obtain a better apartment, a new car, a country *dacha*, or various other consumer goods that are in short supply.

Although the shortage of consumer goods has led to widespread corruption and a flourishing black market, it would seem that most people in the Soviet Union live out their lives either in a state of quiet desperation or in pursuit of their personal ambitions. And in this, it would seem, they behave much as do their counterparts in other parts of the world.

NOTES

1. *Narodnoe khoziaistvo SSSR v 1973 g.* (Moscow: Statistika, 1974) p. 43; Murray Feshbach and Stephen Rapawy, "Soviet Population and Manpower Trends and Policies," *The Soviet Economy in a New Perspective*. Report of the Joint Economic Committee, U.S. Congress. (Washington, DC: Government Printing Office, 1976); and Christopher Davis and Murray Feshbach, *Rising Infant Mortality in the USSR in the 1970s*. U.S. Bureau of the Census ser. P-95, no. 74. (Washington, DC: U.S. Government Printing Office, 1980).

2. *Ekonomicheskaia gazeta* 43 (1986), pp. 6–7.

3. Stephen Sternheimer, "The Graying of the Soviet Union: Labor and Welfare Issues for the Post-Brezhnev Era," *Problems of Communism* 31, no. 5 (1982).

4. Feshbach and Rapawy, "Soviet Population"; and USSR: *Some Implications of Demographic Trends for Economic Policies.* ER 7–10012. (January 1977), p. 3.

5. *Ekonomicheskaia gazeta* 20 (1978), p. 17.

6. T. I. Zaslavskaia, *Migratsiia sel'skogo naselniia* (Moscow: Mysl', 1970).

7. Vladimir G. Treml, *Alcohol in the USSR* (Durham, NC: Duke University Press, 1982).

8. Boris M. Segal, "Drinking Patterns and Alcoholism in Soviet and American Societies: A Multidisciplinary Comparison," in Samuel A. Corson, ed., *Psychiatry and Psychology in the USSR* (New York: Plenum, 1976), pp. 189–90.

9. *Molodoi kommunist* 9 (1975), p. 102; S. M. Livshits and V. A. Iavorskii, *Sotsial'nye i klinicheskie problemy alkogolizma* (Kiev: Mysl', 1975), p. 89 (cited in S. S. Iatsenko, *Ugolovno-pravovaia bor'ba s p'ianstvom i alkogolizmom* (Kiev: Mysl', 1977), p. 8.

10. The most comprehensive study of the relationship between alcohol and crime is Iu. M. Tkachevskii, *Pravovye mery bor'by s p'ianstvom* (Moscow: Nauka, 1974).

11. *Ekonomicheskaia gazeta* 43 (1986), pp. 6–7; and *Izvestiia* (October 12, 1986), p. 2.

Further Reading Suggestions

These suggestions are confined to books published in English in the last few years. Every title listed contains numerous further suggestions.

Two books somewhat similar to this one in coverage, but more detailed and specialized in their treatment, are Archie Brown and Michael Kaser, eds., *Soviet Policy for the 1980s* (Bloomington, IN: Indiana University Press, 1983); and Robert F. Byrnes, ed., *After Brezhnev: Sources of Soviet Conduct in the 1980s* (Bloomington, IN: Indiana University Press, 1983). More current—and much shorter—is Alexander Dallin and Condoleezza Rice, eds., *The Gorbachev Era* (Stanford, CA: Stanford Alumni Association, 1986).

A good general source of information is Archie Brown, John Fennell, Michael Kaser, and H. T. Willetts, eds., *The Cambridge Encyclopedia of Russia and the Soviet Union* (Cambridge and New York: Cambridge University Press, 1982).

HISTORY

Nicholas V. Riasanovsky, *A History of Russia*, 4th ed. (New York and Oxford: Oxford University Press, 1984) remains the best single-volume textbook of the whole of Russian history, including the Soviet period (to 1983). An excellent introduction to the period just before the Revolution is Hans Rogger, *Russia in the Age of Modernisation and Revolution, 1881–1917* (London and New York: Longman, 1983). Marc Raeff, *Understanding Imperial Russia: State and Society in the Old Regime,* translated (from French) by Arthur Goldhammer (New York: Columbia University Press, 1984) is a stimulating discussion of pre-Revolutionary Russia by another leading historian.

Textbooks covering Soviet history (with some pre-Revolutionary background) include Martin McCauley, *The Soviet Union since 1917* (London and New York: Longman, 1981); Woodford McClellan, *Russia: A History of the Soviet Period* (Englewood Cliffs, NJ: Prentice-Hall, 1986); and Geoffrey Hosking, *The First Socialist Society: A History of the Soviet Union from Within* (Cambridge, MA: Harvard University Press, 1985; London: Fontana Press/Collins, 1985). Basil Dmytryshyn, *USSR: A Concise History*, 4th edition (New York: Macmillan, 1984) contains a substantial appendix of translated documents.

A provocative set of essays on the career of American "Sovietology" among other topics is Stephen F. Cohen, *Rethinking the Soviet Experience: Politics and History since 1917* (New York and Oxford: Oxford University Press, 1985). An altogether different sort of book is by the émigré Soviet historians Mikhail Heller and Aleksandr Nekrich, *Utopia in Power: The History of the Soviet Union from 1917 to the Present*, translated from the original Russian by Phyllis B. Carlos (New York: Summit Books, 1986): a massive history, as its title indicates, of the Soviet Union, the book focuses on both repression and the internal resistance to repression, aiming in this way to "keep hope alive."

POLITICS

Merle Fainsod, *How Russia Is Ruled* (Cambridge, MA: Harvard University Press, 1963) has been revised by Jerry F. Hough and published under the title *How the Soviet Union Is Governed* (Harvard, 1979). The change in title as well as Hough's extensive revisions of the text indicate how much perceptions of Soviet politics have changed since Fainsod's classic first appeared (1953), the "totalitarian" model of the 1950s now giving way to a less monolithic, more complex one. John N. Hazard, *The Soviet System of Government*, 5th ed., rev. (Chicago: University of Chicago Press, 1980), legal-administrative in approach, remains a basic work; and Darrell P. Hammer, *The USSR: The Politics of Oligarchy*, 2d ed., rev. (Boulder, CO: Westview, 1986) offers a good introduction to the dynamics of the contemporary Soviet political system. A more interpretive analysis is Seweryn Bialer, *The Soviet Paradox: External Expansion, Internal Decline* (New York: Knopf, 1986).

On foreign policy, Adam B. Ulam, *Expansion and Coexistence: The History of Soviet Foreign Policy, 1917–1973* (New York: Praeger, 1974) is a standard work, to be supplemented by his *Dangerous Relations: The Soviet Union in World Politics, 1970–1982* (New York and Oxford: Oxford University Press, 1983). More recent and specialized studies include Curtis Keeble, ed., *The Soviet State: The Domestic Roots of Soviet Foreign Policy* (Boulder, CO: Westview, 1985); G. W. Gong, A. E. Stent, and R. V. Strode, *Areas of Challenge for Soviet Foreign Policy in the 1980s* (Bloomington, IN: Indiana University Press, 1984); Rajan Menon, *Soviet Power and the Third World* (New Haven, CT: Yale University Press, 1986); Raymond L. Garthoff, *Detente and Confrontation: American-Soviet Relations from Nixon to Reagan* (Washington, DC: Brookings Institution, 1985); and Arnold L. Horelick, ed., *U.S.-Soviet Relations: The Next Phase* (Ithaca, NY, and London: Cornell University Press, 1986).

On the arms race in particular, see David Holloway, *The Soviet Union and the Arms Race*, 2d ed. (New Haven, CT: Yale University Press, 1984); Coit D. Blacker, *Reluctant Warriors: The United States, the Soviet Union and Arms Control* (New York: W. H. Freeman, 1987); and, more generally, Coit D. Blacker and Gloria Duffy, eds., *International Arms Control: Issues and Agreements*, 2d cd. (Stanford, CA: Stanford University Press, 1984).

THE ARMED FORCES

The main introductory work has been Harriet Fast Scott and William F. Scott, *The Armed Forces of the USSR*, 3d ed. (Boulder, CO: Westview, 1986); but Ellen Jones, *Red Army and Society: A Sociology of the Soviet Military* (London and Winchester, MA: Allen & Unwin, 1985) is in many respects more comprehensive and detailed. David R. Jones, ed., *The Soviet Armed Forces Review Annual*, now in its tenth volume (Gulf Breeze, FL: Academic International, 1986), is an important work of reference.

Three further studies are John Erickson, Lynn Hansen, and William Schneider, *Soviet Ground Forces: An Operational Assessment* (Boulder, CO; Westview, 1986; London: Croom Helm, 1986); Kenneth R. Whiting, *Soviet Air Power* (Boulder, CO: Westview, 1986); and Bruce W. Watson and Susan M. Watson, *The Soviet Navy: Strengths and Liabilities* (Boulder, CO: Westview, 1986).

For studies of the relationships between Soviet military power and Soviet foreign policy, see Stephen S. Kaplan et al, *Diplomacy of Power: Soviet Armed Forces as a Political Instrument* (Washington, DC: Brookings Institution, 1981); and Michael MccGwire, *Military Objectives in Soviet Foreign Policy* (Washington, DC:

Brookings Institution, 1987); and, for a systematic examination of Soviet military strength as compared with that of the West, Tom Gervasi, *The Myth of Soviet Military Supremacy* (New York: Harper & Row, 1986).

THE PHYSICAL CONTEXT

Leslie Symons et al., *The Soviet Union: A Systematic Geography* (London: Hodder & Stoughton, 1983 and 1985; Totowa, NJ: Barnes & Noble, 1983) is a compact, well-illustrated introduction to the subject, whereas two other works—Paul E. Lydolph, *Geography of the USSR: Topical Analysis* (Elkhart, WI: Misty Valley, 1979); and John C. Dewdney, *A Geography of the Soviet Union*, 3d ed. (Oxford and New York: Pergamon, 1979)—offer considerably more detail.

See also Robert G. Jensen, Theodore Shabad, and Arthur W. Wright, *Soviet Natural Resources in the World Economy* (Chicago: University of Chicago Press, 1983); and, for a guide to the literature on Soviet planning, Paul M. White, *Soviet Urban and Regional Planning* (New York: St. Martin's, 1980). William C. Brumfield, *Gold in Azure: One Thousand Years of Russian Architecture* (Boston: David R. Godine, 1983) ranges over the whole history of Russian and Soviet architecture and is splendidly illustrated with the author's own photographs.

THE ECONOMY

A good brief introduction is Franklyn D. Holzman, *The Soviet Economy Past, Present and Future*. Headline Ser. no. 260. (New York: Foreign Policy Association, 1982). Longer, but still intended for the lay reader, are James R. Millar, *The ABCs of Soviet Socialism* (Urbana and Chicago: University of Illinois Press, 1981); and, more topical, Marshall I. Goldman, *Gorbachev's Challenge: Economic Reform in the Age of High Technology* (New York: Norton, 1987). Abram Bergson and Herbert S. Levine, eds., *The Soviet Economy: Toward the Year 2000* (London and Winchester, MA: Allen & Unwin, 1983) contains specialized studies by 15 experts.

Raymond Hutchings, *Soviet Economic Development*, 2d ed. (New York: New York University Press, 1982) is a useful textbook, as is Paul R. Gregory and Robert C. Stuart, *Soviet Economic Structure and Performance*, 2d ed. (New York: Harper & Row, 1981), which has an extensive bibliography. Alec Nove, *An Economic History of the* USSR, rev. ed. (London and New York: Penguin, 1982) is the standard work in its field, but see also the same author's *The Soviet Economic System,* 3d ed. (London and Winchester, MA: Allen & Unwin, 1986).

On foreign trade, Bruce Parrott, ed., *Trade, Technology, and Soviet-American Relations* (Bloomington, IN: Indiana University Press, 1985) is a collection of highly readable essays, whereas H. Stephen Gardner, *Soviet Foreign Trade: The Decision Process* (Boston, The Hague, and London: Kluwer-Nijhoff, 1983) is fairly technical. See also Vladimir Sobell, *The Red Market: Industrial Cooperation and Specialization* (Aldershot, England: Glower, 1984) on Soviet intrabloc trade; and Elizabeth Kridl Valkenier, *The Soviet Union and the Third World* (New York: Praeger, 1983) for Soviet trade with developing countries.

SCIENCE AND TECHNOLOGY

Bruce Parrott, *Politics and Technology in the Soviet Union* (Cambridge, MA: MIT, 1983) studies Soviet "technological strategy" since the late 1920s in both its theoretical and its organizational aspects, and Robert W. Campbell, *Soviet Energy Technologies: Planning, Policy, Research and Development* (Bloomington, IN: Indiana University Press, 1980) deals thoroughly with that subject. Ronald Amann et al., *Technical Progress and Soviet Economic Development* (Oxford and New York: Blackwell, 1986) ranges widely, including chapters on Soviet computing technology and biotechnology.

For a more theoretically oriented work, see Loren R. Graham, *Science and Philosophy in the Soviet Union* (New York: Knopf, 1972). Peter Kneen, *Soviet Scientists and the State* (Albany: State University of New York Press, 1984) deals with the political as well as the more academic context of Soviet science; and for a variety of approaches and themes, see also Linda L. Lubrano and Susan Grosse Solomon, eds., *The Social Context of Soviet Science* (Boulder, CO: Westview, 1980). On education, Mervyn Matthews, *Education in the Soviet Union: Policies and Institutions since Stalin* (London and Winchester, MA: Allen & Unwin, 1982) takes the story up to the educational reforms initiated in 1983.

CULTURE

Two outstanding books on recent Soviet literature are Geoffrey Hosking, *Beyond Socialist Realism: Soviet Fiction since Ivan Den-*

isovich (New York: Holmes & Meier, 1980) and Katerina Clark, *The Soviet Novel: History as Ritual* (Chicago: University of Chicago Press, 1981). For more background, see Edward J. Brown, *Russian Literature since the Revolution* (Cambridge, MA: Harvard University Press, 1982); Vera Dunham, *In Stalin's Time: Middle Class Values in Soviet Fiction* (Cambridge and New York: Cambridge University Press, 1976); and Richard Freeborn, *The Russian Revolutionary Novel: Turgenev to Pasternak* (Cambridge University Press, 1985).

Harold B. Segel, *Twentieth-Century Russian Drama from Gorky to the Present* (New York: Columbia University Press, 1979) is a good history of the theater; for the texts of three translated plays (by Mayakovsky, Babel, and Schwartz), see Michael Glenny, ed., *The Golden Age of Soviet Theatre* (London and New York: Penguin, 1981). Numerous other Soviet literary works have been translated into English: Clarence Brown, ed., *The Portable Twentieth-Century Russian Reader* (London and New York: Penguin, 1985) provides a good sample. An intriguing look at Soviet reading habits is Klaus Mehnert, *The Russians and Their Favorite Books* (Stanford, CA: Hoover Institution, 1983).

Boris Schwarz, *Music and Musical Life in Soviet Russia* (Bloomington, IN: Indiana University Press, 1983) is the authoritative work in this field. On the history of the cinema, Jay Leyda, *Kino: A History of the Russian and Soviet Film*, 3d ed. (Princeton, NJ: Princeton University Press, 1983) is the best overall study; but see also Mira Liehm and Antonin J. Liehm, *The Most Important Art: Soviet and East European Film after 1945* (Berkeley, CA: University of California Press, 1980).

S. Frederick Starr, *Red and Hot: the Fate of Jazz in the Soviet Union* (New York and Oxford: Oxford University Press, 1983) is a pioneering work, as is Gerald S. Smith, *Songs to Seven Strings: Russian Guitar Poetry and Soviet "Mass Song"* (Bloomington, IN: Indiana University Press, 1984). For other aspects of Soviet culture, see James Riordan, *Sport in Soviet Society* (Cambridge and New York: Cambridge University Press, 1980); and Ellen Propper Michiewicz, *Media and the Russian Public* (New York: Praeger, 1981).

SOCIETY

On national or ethnic questions, see John B. Dunlop, *The Faces of Contemporary Russian Nationalism* (Princeton, NJ: Princeton University Press, 1983); Jeremy R. Azrael, ed., *Soviet Nationality Pol-*

icies and Practices (Chicago: University of Chicago Press, 1978); Rasma Karklins, *Ethnic Relations in the* USSR: *The Perspective from Below* (London and Winchester, MA: Allen & Unwin, 1985); Michael Rywkin, *Moscow's Muslim Challenge: Soviet Central Asia* (Armonk, NY: M. E. Sharpe, 1982); and Shirin Akiner, *Islamic Peoples of the Soviet Union* (London and Boston: Kegan Paul, 1983). See also Ludmilla Alexeyeva, *Soviet Dissent: Contemporary Movements for National, Religious, and Human Rights* (Middletown, CT: Wesleyan University Press, 1985).

On religion, the best general treatment is Trevor Beeson, *Discretion and Valor: Religious Conditions in Russia and Eastern Europe,* rev. ed. (Philadelphia: Fortress Press, 1982); but see also Pedro Ramet, ed., *Religion and Nationalism in Soviet and East European Politics* (Durham, NC: Duke University Press, 1984) and, for the major Christian denomination, Jane Ellis, *The Russian Orthodox Church Today: A Contemporary History* (Bloomington, IN: Indiana University Press, 1986).

A good overall introduction is Basile Kerblay, *Modern Soviet Society,* translated (from French) by Rupert Swyer (New York: Pantheon, 1983). Henry W. Morton and Robert C. Stuart, eds., *The Contemporary Soviet City* (Armonk, NY: M. E. Sharpe, 1984) deals with major aspects of that subject. Among recent firsthand depictions of Soviet life by Western journalists, see David K. Shipler, *Russia: Broken Idols, Solemn Dreams* (New York: Times, 1983) or, more comprehensive if anecdotal in approach, Michael Binyon, *Life in Russia* (London: Hamish Hamilton, 1983; New York: Pantheon, 1983).

For further titles on various aspects of Soviet society today, see the notes appended to the individual chapters.

A Note for Travelers

Traveling both to and within the Soviet Union has become relatively easy for American and other Western tourists. Given the distances involved, the differing customs, the language barrier and, above all, the Soviet way of organizing things, it is better to go with a group—at least for the first time. It is also much cheaper.

Group tours are arranged by travel companies (American Express, Lindblad, Finnair, and others), by various private organizations (college alumni associations; friends of art museums; church, fraternal and professional societies), and by such agencies as the Travel Department of the Chicago Council on Foreign Relations (104 S. Michigan Avenue, 60603) or the Citizen Exchange Council in New York (18 East 41st Street, 10017). Or they can be arranged directly with Intourist, the Soviet bureau responsible for foreign tourism in the Soviet Union (its office in the United States is at 630 Fifth Avenue, New York 10020). Any reputable travel agent can also provide information. And students should be aware of the special opportunities for longer stays and language study available to them (contact the study-abroad or Russian—or Slavic—Department of your own school or of the nearest large university).

Meanwhile, travelers with firm arrangements or even would-be travelers might want to consult various of the practical guidebooks available at any good-sized bookstore, the most comprehensive of which is Victor and Jennifer Louis, *The Complete Guide to the Soviet Union* (New York: St. Martin's Press), which is periodically updated. Almost as comprehensive in its coverage of the Soviet Union but with much more background information and practical advice is *Fodor's Soviet Union* (New York: Fodor's Travel Guides), a new edition of which is issued annually. For Moscow and Leningrad, the best overall guidebook by far is the *Blue Guide: Moscow and Leningrad*, edited by Evan and Margaret Mawdsley (London: Ernest Benn, Ltd.; Chicago: Rand McNally & Co.) and first published in 1980.

Authors

HARLEY D. BALZER teaches Russian and Soviet history at Georgetown University.

MARK R. BEISSINGER is Assistant Professor of Political Science at the University of Wisconsin, Madison.

WILLIAM C. BRUMFIELD teaches Russian art and architectural history as well as Russian language and literature at Tulane University in New Orleans.

JOHN E. CARLSON is the pen name of a longtime student of the Soviet Union.

IAN CHRISTIE, of the British Film Institute, London, has a special interest in Soviet film.

RALPH S. CLEM is Professor of International Relations at Florida International University, Miami.

STEPHEN F. COHEN is Professor of Politics and Director of the Russian Studies Program at Princeton University.

JAMES CRACRAFT, currently a Research Fellow at the Russian Research Center, Harvard University, is Professor of History at the University of Illinois at Chicago.

ALEXANDER DALLIN is Professor of History and Political Science at Stanford University.

MARY ELLEN FISCHER is Professor of Government at Skidmore College, Saratoga Springs, New York.

MARSHALL I. GOLDMAN is Professor of Economics at Wellesley College and Associate Director of the Russian Research Center, Harvard University.

LOREN R. GRAHAM is Professor of the History of Science at the Massachusetts Institute of Technology.

CHAUNCY D. HARRIS is Samuel N. Harper Distinguished Service Professor of Geography Emeritus at the University of Chicago.

DAVID HOLLOWAY is Professor of Political Science at Stanford University.

GEOFFREY HOSKING is Professor of Russian History at the School of Slavonic and East European Studies, University of London.

D. GALE JOHNSON is Eliakim Hastings Moore Distinguished Service Professor of Economics at the University of Chicago.

DAVID R. JONES is Director of the Russian Micro-Project at Dalhousie University, Nova Scotia.

JOHN M. KRAMER is Professor of Political Science at Mary Washington College, Fredericksburg, Virginia.

VLADIMIR Z. KRESIN, trained as a physicist in Moscow, is now a staff scientist in the Materials and Molecular Research Division, Lawrence Berkeley Laboratory, University of California.

PAUL A. LUCEY, currently practicing law in Milwaukee, Wisconsin, was formerly on the staff of Keston College, England, a research institute devoted to the study of religion in the Soviet Union and Eastern Europe.

PETER B. MAGGS is Professor of Law at the University of Illinois, Urbana-Champaign.

ELLEN MICKIEWICZ is Professor of Political Science at Emory University in Atlanta, Georgia.

JAMES R. MILLAR is Professor of Economics and Director of International Programs and Studies at the University of Illinois, Urbana-Champaign.

EUGENIA V. OSGOOD is a Research Analyst in Soviet Affairs at the Library of Congress.

PERRY L. PATTERSON is Assistant Professor of Economics at Wake Forest University, Winston-Salem, North Carolina.

DAVID E. POWELL is Senior Research Fellow, Russian Research Center, Harvard University.

JOSHUA RUBENSTEIN is Northeast Regional Director, Amnesty International, U.S.A.

MIKHAIL TSYPKIN, a graduate of Moscow State University, held a reserve commission in the Soviet Army before coming to the United States in 1977, where he is now on the staff of the Heritage Foundation, Washington, D.C.

NINA TUMARKIN is Professor of History at Wellesley College.

IRWIN WEIL is Professor of Russian at Northwestern University.

Index

Abortion, 330, 331, 332

Academy of Sciences, 62, 80, 120, 225–32, 234–43, 246, 263

Afghanistan, Soviet invasion of: and the armed forces, 98, 100, 112; domestic repercussions of, 61, 183, 189, 298; international dimensions of, 10, 55, 68, 218

Agriculture, 198–209; climatic effects on, 139 (fig. 2), 144, 146–48, 200–3; and the consumer, 191–92, 194–95; grain imports, 181, 182, 194, 198, 199, 206–7, 212; U.S. and Soviet, compared, 201–6

Air Defense Forces, 98–99

Air Forces, 99–100

Aitmatov, Chingiz, 270, 272, 279

Alcoholism, 275, 345, 358–63

Andropov, Yury V., 39, 42, 84–85, 91, 132, 209, 345

Architecture, 164–71

Armed Forces, 87–125 ; conscription for, 89–90, 105–13; discipline in, 98, 102, 107–111; ethnic diversity in, 108, 109, 112; leadership of, 91–95; political control of, 90–92, 94, 95, 107, 108; reserves, 90, 102–3, 112–13; strategy, 94–95, 114–25, 128–29; training, 109–10, 111–12; U.S. and Soviet, compared, 102, 103, 122

Armenians, 67–68, 69, 316, 321–22

Arms control, 59, 73, 87–88, 120–21, 126–34, 184

Army. *See* Ground Forces

Art, 268–69

Brezhnev, Leonid I.: "Brezhnev doctrine," 87; economic policy of, 178–81, 191, 199–200, 206; neo-Stalinism under, 27–31, 64; nuclear strategy of, 130–31; and the political system, 38–39, 42, 50, 91

Censorship, 32, 272–83, 344

Central Committee of the Communist Party, 13, 15, 35, 165, 211, 276, 294, 335; role of in the political system, 37–51

Chekhov, Anton, 264–65

Chernenko, Konstantin U., 91

Chernobyl, nuclear accident at, 55, 160, 229, 243, 298–99

Chronicle of Current Events, A, 65, 70, 71

Chukovskaia, Lydiia, 28, 239, 263

Chukovsky, Kornei, 262–63

Cinema, 259, 284–91, 295

Climate, 143–46; effect on agriculture, 139 (fig. 2), 144, 146–48, 200–3

Committee for State Security. *See* KGB

Communist Party of the Soviet Union (CPSU): and culture, 276, 291; and the economy, 151, 169, 191, 211, 351–52, 356, 362, 363; and Lenin cult, 13–20; and mass media, 294; and political system, 35, 37–51, 341; and religion, 315; and society,

Communist Party (*continued*)
351–52, 356, 362, 363; and Stalin,
24–30; and women, 331, 334–35
Council of Ministers, 37, 38, 154, 165,
167, 211, 295, 335
Crime, 343–45, 358
Crimean Tatars, 70–71, 112, 350
Cuban Missile Crisis, 127, 181

Daniel, Yuli, 28, 64
Defense Council, 49, 62, 91–92, 95, 96
Demographic trends, 103, 141 (fig. 6),
151–53, 228, 275, 309–13, 333, 352–
58
Dissent, 27–29, 64–76, 84–85, 230,
334–45
Divorce, 330, 332, 342

Economy, 175–219, 346–347; and the
consumer, 180–81, 191–97, 342;
growth rate of, 179, 180, 183, 187,
189; militarys' role in, 181–82;
prospects of, 183–90, 196–97, 206–
9; women's role in, 332–34
Education, 245–56; higher, 240–41,
247–48, 251–54; language in, 307–
9; recent reforms, 245, 249, 254–56;
scientific, 222, 247, 252–54;
secondary, 106, 246–49; specialized
secondary, 249–51
Energy, 140 (fig. 5), 148–50, 160, 229–
30
Environment, 154–62, 275, 281;
international cooperation in
protecting, 160–61; legislation on,
158–59, 340. *See also* Chernobyl;
Pollution
Estonians, 69, 71
Ethnicity, 151–53, 301, 303–13;
architecture and, 164; armed forces
and, 108–9, 112; and culture, 269–
70, 281; and dissent, 69–72; and
economy, 187

Foreign policy; making of, 53–63, of
Stalin, 54, 60, 115–16; and World
War II, 10, 126
Foreign trade, 175, 210–19, 347

Geography, 135, 137–53, 306
Georgians, 69, 303, 316, 321

Germans in the Soviet Union, 67, 350
Glavlit, 276–77, 294
Gorbachev, Mikhail S.: and agriculture,
208, 347; anti-alcohol campaign of,
345, 358–63; and arms control, 132–
33; and culture, 280–81, 285; and
education, 254, 256; and foreign
affairs, 55–56, 60, 62; and military,
91, 124; and policy of *glasnost*, 162,
272, 280–81, 294, 297–98, 344; and
political system, 39, 43, 50, 51, 82,
339, 344, 345
Gorky Institute of World Literature,
263–64, 265
Ground Forces, 96–98

Health, 229–30, 352–53, 360
Helsinki Watch Group, 65–66, 68, 70,
71, 72
Housing, 135, 165–71, 193, 342
Human rights. *See* Dissent; Religion

Ideology, role of, 17, 58, 59, 119–21,
239, 278, 284, 315, 329
Infant mortality, 230, 352
Islam, 323–25, 326

Jews: discrimination against, 66–67,
75, 241, 317, 322–23, 340; and
dissent, 66–67, 230; emigration of,
66, 75, 216, 241, 345; religious life
of, 316, 322–23

KGB (also *Cheka*, NKVD): organization
and operations of, 24, 36, 42, 44,
77–86, 89, 92, 96, 107, 340;
suppression of dissent by, 64, 67–74
Khrushchev, Nikita S.: and de-
Stalinization, 24–27, 28, 64, 284–
85; economic policy of, 177–81,
192, 198–99; and Lenin cult, 14,
17–18; literature under, 274–75;
and nuclear strategy, 116–17, 121,
127; and political system, 37–38,
49–50; religion under, 317; science
policy of, 224
Komsomol (Communist Youth League),
94, 349

Landau, Lev Davidovich, 236–37
Language question, 307–9
Laws, 301, 339–48

Lenin, Vladimir Ilyich: cult of, 13–20; ideology of, 17, 58, 59, 119–21, 239, 278, 284, 315, 329; on women, 327, 329–30, 332
Ligachev, Yegor, 44, 282
Literature, 259, 262–64, 269–70, 272–83
Lithuanians, 69, 71, 322
Liubimov, Yury, 264–66

Marxism-Leninism. See Ideology
Mass media, 293–300, 336–37, 344
Military: and political system, 44–45, 48, 49, 62; strategy in nuclear age, 114–25, 127–34; training in public schools, 106. See also Armed Forces
Music, 266–68

Navy, 100–102
Nekrich, Aleksandr, 11, 28, 76
Newspapers, 295, 297–98
Nomenklatura system, 45, 48, 276, 294
Nuclear Weapons, 116–25, 127–34

Ogarkov, Marshal N. V., 45, 90, 93, 94, 95, 122
Okudzhava, Bulat, 265, 282
Orlov, Yury, 65–66, 68, 75
Orthodox Church, Russian, 316–19, 326

Pasternak, Boris, 281, 282
Pipes, Richard, 5–8
Politburo of the Central Committee of the Communist Party, 15, 85, 92, 211, 294; role of in the political system, 35, 37–51, 61–62
Political elite, 35, 37–51
Political system, 35–51, 53–63, 142 (fig. 7), 310
Pollution, 154–60
Protestantism, 319–20
Psychiatry, abuse of, 65, 68, 74, 84–85, 345

Radio, 293–94, 295–96
Rasputin, Valentin, 272, 278, 279, 290
Religion, 69, 72, 301, 315–26
Revolution, Bolshevik (1917), historical significance of, 14, 42, 53, 126, 210, 293, 315, 327, 331, 339, 349
Ruble, dollar value of, xii

Sakharov, Andrei, 28, 68, 73, 75, 224, 239, 298
Samizdat, 28, 29, 32, 75
Science, 221–56; and the economy, 228–32; in education, 222, 245–56; international exchange in, 230, 242; policy and organization of, 225–30; practice of, 235–41; publishing of, 242. See also Academy of Sciences; State Committee on Science and Technology
Sinyavsky, Andrei, 28, 64
Society, 275, 301–2, 306–7, 349–63
Solzhenitsyn, Aleksandr, 4, 8, 9, 24, 27, 28, 33, 74, 273, 277
Stalin, Joseph V., 21–33; and the cinema, 284, 289; cult of, 17, 26–27; economic policy of, 178–79, 191–92, 198, 212, 332, 349–50; education policy of, 245–46; foreign policy of, 54, 60, 115–16; literature under, 273, 274; and political system, 37, 38, 51, 339–40, 350–51; religion under, 316; science policy of, 226
Stalinism, 22, 26, 30
State Committee on Science and Technology, 80, 211, 225–28, 231
Strategic Rocket Forces, 95–96, 117–24, 128

Tchaikovsky Conservatory, 266, 267
Technology. See Science and Technology
Television, 291, 293–94, 295, 296–97, 298, 300
Theater, 264–66, 270
Tourism, 373–74
Transliteration, system of, xii
Trifonov, Yury, 265, 272, 273, 279

Ukrainians, 66, 69–70, 316–17
Urbanization, 141 (fig. 6), 356–58

Vegetation, 140 (fig. 4), 146–47
"Village prose," 273–74
Voznesensky, Andrei, 281, 282
Vysotsky, Vladimir, 265

Women, 301, 327–37; in the economy, 332–34; in political system, 334–35; pre-Revolutionary status of,

Women (*continued*)
328–29; prospects of, 335–37; and the Revolution, 327, 329–32
World War II (Great Patriotic War): and Crimean Tatars, 70, 71; destruction during, 135, 165, 193, 198, 213; significance of in Soviet history, 22, 178, 350–51; Soviet foreign policy and, 10, 126; and Soviet military, 105, 106, 115; and Stalin cult, 22, 26, 28, 31
Writers' Union, 276–77, 281–82

Yevtushenko, Yevgeny, 9, 25, 33, 281